H. E. Dennehy

The Church of the First Three Centuries

A Work Founded on the Sacred Scripture and Early Patristic Writings

H. E. Dennehy

The Church of the First Three Centuries
A Work Founded on the Sacred Scripture and Early Patristic Writings

ISBN/EAN: 9783337259228

Printed in Europe, USA, Canada, Australia, Japan

Cover: Foto ©ninafisch / pixelio.de

More available books at **www.hansebooks.com**

THE CHURCH

OF THE

FIRST THREE CENTURIES.

A WORK FOUNDED ON THE

Sacred Scripture and early Patristic Writings,

AND BUILT OF MATERIALS WHICH ARE PRESENTED TO THE READER UNWROUGHT,
AS THEY CAME FROM THE LIPS OF INSPIRED MEN AND CHRISTIANS
SOUND IN PRACTICE AND ORTHODOX IN FAITH.

BY

THE REVEREND H. E. DENNEHY.

Sæpe igitur modo magno studio et summa attentione perquirens a quamplurimis sanctitate et doctrina præstantibus viris, quonam modo possim certa quadam et quasi generali ac regulari via Catholicæ fidei veritatem ab hereticæ pravitatis falsitate discernere,—hujusmodi semper responsum ab omnibus fere retuli; quod sive ego, sive quis alius, vellet exsurgentium hæreticorum fraudes deprehendere laqueaque vitare, et in fide sana sanus atque integer permanere, duplici modo munire fidem suam, Domino adjuvante, debent; primum, scilicet, Divinæ legis auctoritate, tum deinde Ecclesiæ Catholicæ traditione.—*Vinc. Lerin. common. No.* 11.

LONDON:

Catholic Bookselling & Publishing Company, Limited,

CHARLES DOLMAN, MANAGER,

61, NEW BOND STREET, & 21, PATERNOSTER ROW;
DUBLIN: J. MULLANY, 1, PARLIAMENT STREET.

1861.

S.S.O.

[*The Right of Translation is reserved*].

PREFACE.

The objects of this work on the early Christian Church may be plainly stated. In these comparatively free countries, united under the British crown, religious associations, with various names, have been and are daily being formed, for the propagation of the Gospel, and the distribution of the Bible at home and in foreign parts. It is assumed, by Protestants of all denominations, associated for such purposes, that the Catholic Church is afraid of the Bible, because "this sacred volume exhibits primitive Christianity in its true colours." Here, in Ireland, it is amusing to listen to the silly attacks, made by the orators of these associations, upon Catholicism, through the instrumentality of affected praises of the "Word of God." We are told by them, at one time, that a Bible has been dropped in Andalusia, and that in consequence southern Spain is in a ferment of religious exultation: at another time, the story goes, that Bibles have been planted in Florence, and are bearing fruit through Central Italy,— this fruit being the expulsion of Catholicity from the minds of the Tuscans and Romagnols. Alas! that we should be so indocile as still to believe that the Bible is the second great argument for the Catholic, while, in the hands of the Protestant, it is a tacit recognition of the apostasy of his

Church from the doctrine of the Redeemer and His Apostles!

The first object of this work, is to exhibit, in the interest of Catholicity, the discipline, rites, usages, and belief, as detailed in the Sacred Scripture, of the primitive followers of Christ.

It was difficult to resist the temptation of passing from the Church of the Scriptures to that of the early Fathers, as it was but natural to hold, that no better interpreters of the sense of the New Testament could be found than these learned and holy men, who touched upon the time when the Apostles wrote and spoke. And, surely, if the patristic pages, reproducing Scriptural images, showed at the same time, a complete picture of what we believe and practise, the argument in favour of Catholicity was irresistible. Therefore, the second and third parts of this work are composed of delineations borrowed from the early Christian writers, of the faith and worship of the Church, after the Apostles had been removed from the scene of this world.

In such a work as this, it was desirable to avoid mere assertion as much as possible. Hence it was deemed advisable to introduce into the text the words of the inspired writers and fathers, which embody or illustrate the various subjects discussed. All these passages have been carefully verified, and all the references will be found strictly correct. The texts of Sacred Scripture are quoted from the English version by the divines of Douay and Rheims. The words of the Holy Fathers are original, sometimes, I fear, uncouth because strictly literal translations of passages, taken, for the most part, from the editions of their works published in the "Complete Course of Patrology," by the Abbé Migne.

A peculiar system has been followed in the preparation of these pages. All the events recorded are given on the authority of contemporary writers exclusively. Much additional information might have been gathered from writers of a subsequent period: for example, St. Augustin might have told us a great deal about the African Church of the third century. We have listened to the testimonies of such witnesses only as recount what passed under their own eyes.

To those who have read the dissertations of Tillemont, Orsi, or Natalis Alexander, this volume must appear little more than a summary of the events of early Christian times. So learned are our great ecclesiastical historians, and so searching and minute are their investigations of the early periods of Christian history, that one to whom they were once familiar, as old and dear friends, cannot but feel somewhat embarrassed in presuming to transmit to the public so small a portion of their light as is reflected in these pages.

QUEENSTOWN, MAY 5, 1861.

CONTENTS.

Part the First.

THE CONFLICTS, VICTORIES, DIFFUSION, AND ORGANIZATION
OF CHRISTIANITY DURING THE APOSTOLIC OR
PRIMITIVE PERIOD.

ANNO 33—110.

Introduction.—The world without.................................*Page* xiii

Division the First.—The Romans:
   § 1. Classes of the Roman population 3
   § 2. Paganism 7

Division the Second.—The Greeks:
   § 1. Manners and morals 10
   § 2. Philosophy 13

Division the Third.—The Jewish element of opposition 20

Division the Fourth.—Conflict of Christianity with Jews, Greeks, and Romans:
   § 1. Prospect of success 24
   § 2. Divine co-operation by grace............................. 30
   § 3. By miracles 33
   § 4. By fulfilment of prophecy 42

Division the Fifth.—Victory of Christianity and its organization:
   § 1. Its diffusion 47

§ 2. Its material position ....*Page* 53
§ 3. Jurisdiction of priests.................................... 55
§ 4. Jurisdiction of bishops 63
§ 5. The head of the Church 69

Division the Sixth.—The clergy and the rites they administered :
§ 1. Who were the επισκοποι, πρεσβυτεροι, and διακονοι ?... 75
§ 2. Baptism.. 89
§ 3. Imposition of hands...................................... 91
§ 4. The Eucharist 95
§ 5. Penance.. 101
§ 6. Extreme unction... 107
§ 7. Holy orders 108
§ 8. Matrimony a sacrament.................................... 108

Division the Seventh.—The great rite of sacrifice :
§ 1. Hypothetical... 117
§ 2. Authoritative 122

Division the Eighth.—The suffering Church 131

Division the Ninth.—The Church triumphant :
§ 1. Veneration of saints...................................... 138
§ 2. Prayers to them 145
§ 3. Their relics 148
§ 4. Relative worship, the cross, &c........................... 150

Part the Second.

PERPETUATION OF THE FAITH AND PRACTICE DELIVERED TO
THE FIRST SAINTS.

ANNO 110—216.

Division the First.—Identity of Christian faith 165

Division the Second.—What the Church believed on the subject 169

CONTENTS.   xi

Division the Third.—How the Church acted in reference to the
    deposit of faith..*Page* 176

Division the Fourth.—Infallibility of the Church in these ages:
    § 1. The Old Testament 190
    § 2. The New Testament 198

Part the Third.

HOW THE EARLY PATRISTIC WRITINGS REPRODUCE THE
SCRIPTURAL PICTURE OF THE CHURCH OF GOD.

ANNO 200—300.

Introduction.—Controversy... 207

Division the First.—Polemical writings:
    § 1. The Jews again 211
    § 2. Detailed conflict with Paganism 218
    § 3. Conflict with philosophic theories...................... 226

Division the Second.—The second victory:
    § 1. Progress of the Church 235
    § 2. Characteristics of the Church 237

Division the Third.—The clergy of the third century:
    § 1. Priests and bishops... 242
    § 2. Difference between the two first orders of the hier-
        archy 248
    § 3. Episcopal succession 253
    § 4. Episcopal election 255
    § 5. Jurisdiction of bishops 264
    § 6. Jurisdiction of priests.. 267
    § 7. The Roman pontiff the head and governor of the
        Church 270

CONTENTS.

Division the Fourth.—Prayer and sacrifice:
- § 1. Oblations and prayers for the dead .... *Page* 280
- § 2. Sacrifice.. 283

Division the Fifth.—Sacred rites:
- § 1. Baptism... 290
- § 2. Confirmation 295
- § 3. Eucharist 305
- § 4. Penance 317
- § 5. Extreme unction 327
- § 6. Holy orders 329
- § 7. Matrimony 332

Division the Sixth.—The martyrs:
- § 1. Respect rendered to their bodies 335
- § 2. Anniversaries of their martyrdom 340
- § 3. Prayers to the Martyrs 343

Division the Seventh.—Veneration of the cross 348

Conclusion 351

APPENDICES 367

INTRODUCTION.

A VAST extent of the known world, and unquestionably the most civilized part of it, was comprised in the Roman empire at the time of the first propagation of Christianity. The old civilized empires of the East had passed away, or had become merged in each other, and their civilization removing from one to the other, and always advancing towards the West, had finally been absorbed by Roman society, where it was reproduced in the buildings and amusements, the tastes and vices, of imperial pagan Rome. In the eyes of other nations, the empire was not alone awful in consequence of its power, but it was revered for its military skill, for its learning and its progress in the arts, refined and mechanical. It was but natural to suppose, that if this great civilized empire were brought under the yoke of the Redeemer, a noble example would be given, and a most formidable obstacle to the conversion of the other nations of the earth would be removed; and hence in reason, we were to expect to find the Church, in the very beginning of her career, endeavouring to penetrate Roman society, and to effect a secure lodgment in the very heart of the empire.

In forming an estimate of the obstacles to be encountered in this attempt, we must keep before us the fact, that the different nations composing the empire were allowed, after their incorporation, to retain their national usages and superstitions; and it is an historical fact, that the majority of them adhered with tenacity all through to their ancient traditions and prejudices. For instance, a Greek was a sceptic and a debater, though circumstances made him a Roman citizen; an Egyptian did not give up the divinities of his country from the fact of his having been incorporated in a Roman cohort.

There were numberless races in that vast community, which extended from Britain to central Asia, and from the shores of the Baltic to the confines of the Great Desert. They were different in language, in education, in intelligence. Their superstitions were different. Their degenerate tastes were not the same. Their vices assumed different forms, and found different channels wherein to escape. Christianity had to meet with them all, to contend with them, to overcome them successively. This was not the work of a century or two centuries, nor would the struggle well commence with some of them until many years had passed away. But from the very beginning, Christianity was confronted with three forms of society within the empire, which it will be necessary to examine, if we would estimate with tolerable accuracy the amount of opposition that the apostolic church encountered. These were Jewish society, Grecian society, and society distinctively Roman. The Church was from Jerusalem. It went forth through the country of the Jews, passed through the territory of the Greeks, entered the capital city of the Romans; all three united in one vast empire, though retaining individually their national characteristics, and consequently presenting phases of opposition to Christianity peculiar to each, and in many particulars differing from each other.

It is absolutely certain that while the Apostles were still living, the torch of faith was carried even beyond the limits of the Roman empire; and it is more than probable that before the end of the first century, its light was shining upon some favoured groups dwelling by the shores of the Indian Sea. While faith glanced upon other lands, it rose upon the empire and became fixed over it. While Christianity commenced the struggle with the countries of the extreme East, it followed up victory after victory in the Roman empire. While the history of the fortunes and misfortunes of Christianity and faith in the very remote countries during this early period is involved in the deepest obscurity, the narrative of their proceedings in Rome can be studied in the documents of the age. The obstacles which Ethiopia and Parthia presented cannot be accurately ascertained in the dim traditions and feeble narratives of the state of these societies which we find in contemporary writers. The amount of opposition that Rome put forth can be determined with the greatest accuracy.

In treating, then, of the first conflict of Christianity with the world without, every consideration compels us to confine our view to the subject as connected with the Roman empire; and as within the Roman empire there were three distinct societies, external to the Church and antagonistic to her; as, moreover, it was with these three societies that the Church first contended, we will make them a subject of study here, not in all its details, but in as far as they were anti-Christian, or raised up a standard of belief and morals in opposition to that of the Gospel.

# Part the First.

THE CONFLICTS, VICTORIES, DIFFUSION,
AND ORGANIZATION OF CHRISTIANITY DURING THE
APOSTOLIC OR PRIMITIVE PERIOD.

ANNO 33—110.

Part the First.

DIVISION I.

THE ROMANS.

§ 1. *Classes of the Roman Population.*—In the parts of the empire distinctively Roman, we discover three great classes, to one or other of which every individual of the population might be referred, namely, the Patricians, the Plebeians, and the Slaves. Like the rich of ancient nations generally, the Roman patricians were men of pleasure and softness, and as the noble and powerful ones of an organized empire, they were attached to their government and their hereditary institutions. They were intoxicated with the glories of Rome—"the city,"—the centre of all that was magnificent, and they were enamoured of that national policy, which rendered Rome so powerful, and which consolidated and perpetuated its greatness. Then they were attached to the government of the Empire, from the protection it afforded themselves. They dwelt at home in peace. Abroad they were feared for their power, or revered for their wealth. Their days passed away amidst the amusements and dissipation of the city in winter; and in summer they retired to their magnificent villas in the country, where they read Sophocles or Homer along their "shady walks of vines," or through "gardens full of figs and mulberries." Their tables were the most sumptuous that the world ever saw. When the gratification of the palate was in question, no expense was made any account of, and no extravagance was regarded as excessive. Their houses were models of splendour and luxury: mosaics, frescoes, statues, vases, furniture of gold and silver, everything that wealth could procure, or the most fastidious whim desire, were brought together to adorn the dwelling and gratify the taste of the princely Roman noble.

Alas! how different was all this from the privation and self-abnegation which the Gospel was about to recommend; and how difficult a task to induce the Roman patrician to come forth from his gorgeous palace to worship at the crib of Bethlehem!

The plebeians were a very different class from the patricians, and they might be supposed to offer fewer obstacles to the admission of evangelical teaching, inasmuch as they were more trained to dependence and obedience, and less attached to the fascinating objects of sense. Yet, the lower orders of the Roman population were not altogether free from the sensual predilections of the rich. They frequently hung about the palaces of the great, under the name and in the character of "clients," where they feasted their eyes on forbidden pleasures, and tutored their hearts into luxurious and enervating desires. Then they had their own unholy amusements, in which they indulged freely and without restraint. The amphitheatre was their paradise. They laughed, shouted, and became intoxicated at the feats of gladiators and the fierce combats of wild beasts. Human life lost all its inviolability in their eyes, as they saw human beings daily sacrificed in sport, and feelings of humanity must have been almost stifled within their breasts, as they heard their dying groans without emotion. On the whole, however, there was this circumstance in favour of the conversion of the plebeian: he was in many cases a poor man, with a poor house and a poor family; and a poor man with few domestic joys is often sighing for repose and happiness. Might not the glory of the next life, held out by the Christian teacher, be a great attraction to him whom this world slighted and neglected?

The slaves were another element of population in the "Roman" parts of the empire. They were a very numerous class, and might naturally be supposed to be objects of primary interest to those men, who, like their divine Lord and Master, had come "to preach peace to the poor and deliverance to them that were shut up." The slaves were strangers imported to Rome from divers remote countries. They were mere machines in the hands of their owners; yet many of them were not devoid of considerable intelligence, and there were not a few who were distinguished for tastes the most refined, and considerable acquired knowledge and skill in various arts and accomplishments. They had one property in common, they were bondmen. It ought to be easy for a bondman to become a Christian. He would only have to pass from bondage to bondage; from a material to a spiritual subjection—from submission to the will of man to submission to the law of God. Besides, the slave is presumed to be free from pride, which is a great bar to the admission of Gospel truth, and from the circumstance of his position, he ought to be well prepared "to bring every intellect captive to the obedience of faith."

Such were the principal classes of the Roman population at the time of the first emperors: and such were the facilities and repugnances they presented as such to the progress of the Gospel and the establishment of the Christian Church. It would be, however, false to suppose that the apostles had no other difficulties to encounter here, but the prejudices of castes, or the views of the individuals that composed them. There was combination in the Roman world. All the orders of society were closely bound into one thick phalanx of opposition to any foe that came from without. Their connecting link was nationality. Their watch-word was Rome and civilization. Who could teach them— mighty Romans!—the descendants of princes, heroes, and gods? What could they learn from "barbarous" nations, they who were the legitimate inheritors of all that had been discovered, and the acknowledged possessors of the civilization of their age? They were perfect in the arts. The

Grecian models were scarcely more exquisite than the pictures and statues they could produce. They were perfect in literature. Virgil was scarcely less admired than Homer, and Livy might stand side by side with Herodotus, Thucydides, or Xenophon. In practical science they excelled the Greeks, and had gone beyond the Assyrians and Egyptians in the most flourishing periods of their respective monarchies. Every man in the community felt that he was a Roman, and though he might be, in fact, a clown, he was by tradition a superior being. Pride was the chain which bound the Roman classes together—a subtle pride of country, a pride of civilization. If the Roman abandoned this pride, and consented to receive instruction, and above all, fundamental religious instruction from a foreign nation, he would disgrace his illustrious ancestry, and give up the predominance of his race. The difficulties in the way of his conversion were exaggerated by the fact, that Christianity came from Judea, which he regarded as an insignificant, if not a contemptible country, —weak, divided, and involved in the common haze of barbarism, which hung over kindred states. He had in former times consented to receive instruction, and borrow inspiration from the Greeks on his onward journey to civilization. He was now thoroughly civilized, and he believed most firmly that every future development of intellect must originate with himself. Even in modern times, religion and intellectual progress are often placed in the same category by profane men; and it appears to have been a capital error of the ancient Roman to regard the Christian religion as a system of philosophy, based upon uncertain premises, and consequently difficult to believe; prescribing an austere morality, and consequently impossible to practise: and he was disposed to hate it for many reasons, but primarily because it professed to teach him, and by consequence supposed him to be in a state of darkness and ignorance; and, secondly, because the adoption of it (and it pressed hard for a hearing and a trial), would be a sign of subjection and an acknowledgment of victory; the victory of weakness over power, of ignorance over knowledge, of barbarism over civilization, of an obscure province over a powerful and well-organized empire.

§ 2. *Paganism.*—In the early days of the republic, when the hardy Roman had not yet come in contact with civilization, but lived at home on the ancient soil of Latium or Etruria, his religion was as simple as his divinities were few. He worshipped the " Penates " and " Lares," and propitiated " genii," and such imaginary spirits of the air. Old Saturn was his god of time ; and Janus, with his double face, looked down on peace and war. As the Roman state extended its dominion, the number of its deities increased; for it was not unusual to assume as objects of worship the "gods" of the conquered nations. After the fall of Greece, and the adoption of Grecian ideas, the system of Roman theology may be regarded as almost complete.

The Romans were very superstitious. They feared ; and they worshipped a god of terrors. They hoped ; and they worshipped a goddess of flowers and fruits—a god of seasons, and a goddess of flocks and herds. With them there were deities that presided over the sources of rivers. They sacrificed to fountains, and deified the passions and affections of the soul. In their gardens, on the Capitol, in their houses, everywhere, there were deities,—everywhere they propitiated, they sacrificed everywhere. Paganism was in the city, in the country, on the sea.

Alas! how different was this multiform and material idea of the Divinity from that "Trinity in Unity," that "unity in essence," and that "equality in majesty," which Christianity was about to unfold to them !

But there were other considerations against the Roman form of paganism, besides that arising from its pantheism. It proposed no moral rule to its professors ; and, from the vices that it recognized and even lauded in its divinities, it became a rock of scandal, and patronized, so to speak, the grossest immoralities. In the written sacred traditions of most barbarous nations, there is a code of social and moral duties more or less defined. In the Roman superstition, as there was no authorized sacred volume, there may be said to have been no principle of right, morality, or justice. All was external, barren, dead, as the victims that were offered, and cold as the altars of immolation. Philosophy taught, but it was not the exponent of the principles of paganism. It entered into a higher sphere; it would be free: and if it sometimes succumbed to the notions of the day, it was through fear of public opinion, or through deference to interested priests. Roman paganism was not only barren and bare of the leaves of moral instruction, and only occupied with vows and sacrifices, but it was putrid to the core, and it corrupted all that came within its influence. Its deities were the embodiment of sensuality. What Roman was there who had not heard of the immoralities of Jove,—or the dissipation of Bacchus,—or the revenge of Juno,—or the bloody feats of Minerva? And what man, hearing such things, did not become less the child of reason, and more the slave of wild and uncontrollable passion? Human nature, fallen from its original innocence, is weak and frail enough, independent of external excitement; it became wonderfully depraved in the Roman world, where sensuality was a part of its religious worship of God.

Paganism, thus gross in principle and practice, was the religion of the Roman empire, and this fact consolidated and strengthened its position. It was constantly brought before the people in its priests, its augurs, its sacrifices. When an undertaking of public importance was about to be entered upon, victims were slain, and omens, which often decided the fate of kings and nations, were taken from their entrails. When a general was about to enter on a warlike expedition, he sacrificed and propitiated the gods; and on his triumphant return home, as he wound along the "Via Sacra," and up the side of the Capitoline hill, he stopped at the temple of "Fortuna Virilis," to hang up his laurels, and to offer his thanksgiving for the victory obtained. The glories of Rome were associated with vows and the official acts of priests; and, even in the details of individual life, such as adoptions, wills, private speculations of moment, the influence of paganism was felt, and the presence of the "Pontifex" solicited. Paganism was associated likewise with the recreations and amusements of the people. The state-holidays, with their games, shows, and dissipation, were its festival days. It was a god that sent them gladiators and wild beasts, or, at least, it was in honour of a god that they were immolated. Then the domestic hearth was rendered doubly dear to the Roman, from the fact that he had always regarded it as the sanctuary of the gods.

It must, therefore, be admitted that the people of Roman descent were interested in the preservation of their old religious traditions. It is clear that the absurdity of paganism, in many particulars, was recognized by the thinking members of the community; but old institutions must be preserved, and ancestral ideas must be respected; and, above all, there must be some influence from the next world to co-operate with the terrors of the law in rendering the masses good subjects. Now the present system, paganism, was sufficient for this purpose. It was earthly and material in its ends, while it was indulgent and severe in its sanctions; and as it attached the people to the civil government, by conjointly with it legalizing their contracts; as it attached them to their families by witnessing their domestic joys; it answered all the purposes for which the Romans wanted a religion, and to reject it for an untried system would be exposing their national institutions to the danger of being subverted, but to abandon it for a system like Christianity would be to give up the ideas upon which many of their institutions rested, and their race had conquered and prospered.

So in the Roman parts of that great empire which ruled the destinies of the world, when the foundations of the Christian Church were laid, there were many principles maintained, and many influences at work, which were directly opposed to the maxims and precepts of the Gospel. Let us see, if the manners of the Greek population were less infected with the leaven of sin and error.

DIVISION II.

THE GREEKS.

§ 1. *Manners and Morals.*—Adown the promontory of ancient Greece, there were cities renowned in olden story, and still renowned for literature and the arts; where men of mind were congregated, Greeks in poetry and philosophy as well as in name. And on the opposite shores of the Mediterranean, and through the provinces of Asia Minor, there were towns and cities, rich and idle, where the tones of the lute and lyre were ever heard; where a light-hearted, gay population passed the eve in feasting, dancing, and amusement. Pleasures, mental and physical; indulgence, refined and beastly; appear to have been the distinguishing characteristics of Grecian manners at the time of the first propagation of Christianity.

Who had not heard of Athens, that city of the sciences? Old "literati," dwelling in distant lands, dreamed of Athens and its classic groves, and the rich reading ones of Rome voyaged over land and sea to visit the City of the Muse, and to drink inspiration at its source. On they came, annually hastening to Athens, from which, as a centre, they made the tour of the other cities of Greece.

It is an ordinary observation that the morals of cities are not much improved by a confluence of strangers,—a consequence of the fact that the morals of idlers, loungers, and seekers of pleasure are not apt to be the purest in the community. The cities of Greece were generally full of strangers, dissipated men from Rome, who came in search of intellectual enjoyment, and profligates from the East, who came to while away their hours in the midst of the amusements which these cities developed. There was but little energy in the Greek character at this time. War had become, so far as the Greeks were concerned, a matter of history, and the spirit of enterprise had almost died out. They lived in a fine climate, where nature was very bountiful, and having enough of the necessaries, and even the luxuries of life, without much labour, they sank into indolence and inactivity, and yielded themselves ready captives to pleasure. Sensuality broke out among them in a revolting form. It was fanned by the foreign influence in the cities. It spread from mind to mind, involving in a common conflagration the learned and the uneducated classes.

Corinth was at this time an exception in one particular among the indolent cities of Greece. It was a commercial place, full of traders and foreign merchants. Its position on the isthmus of Peloponnesus attracted to it a considerable trade, for it was on the high road of all the ships that traded between Italy and Africa. One would have thought that the energy of character required for the maritime pursuits of its inhabitants, would have rendered Corinth a moral "oasis" in the wild desert of Greek impiety. Corinth might naturally be supposed to have embraced the stern virtues of paganism, while Athens was given up to softness and idleness. But if busy, bustling Corinth was steeped in immorality, what must not have been the depravity of the inactive cities of the Peloponnesus? Yet there is a fact related of Corinthian vice by Strabo, which has scarcely a parallel in history; it is as follows:—"There was at Corinth a temple of Venus, to which were attached more than a thousand prostitutes — slaves, who had been presented to the goddess, to whom the whole city was dedicated. It was a common practice to vow such offerings as these. These women of Venus were employed on important occasions to implore the succour of the goddess. They were honoured by public monuments, and in the verses of the most illustrious poets."[1] Our ideas of indecency can scarcely descend below this picture, prostitutes propitiating the divinity in the name of the community at large,

[1] Strabo lib. viii. p. 378, D. Athen. lib. xiii. p. 573, C.

their praises sung, their "virtues" honoured, and their names transmitted to posterity!

Greece was steeped in sensuality, and its tendencies in consequence were not in the direction of a system whose fundamental doctrine is unspotted purity of life. Nevertheless, it cannot be denied, there were evidences of inclinations appearing in some parts of Greece, which, considered naturally, gave some grounds for the hope, that Christianity would get a hearing at least in the towns of Lesser Asia, and in the classic cities of the Peloponnesus. For Greece *theoretically* proclaimed its admiration of chastity, while it was *practically* given up to the indulgence of every vile passion. Corinth, it is true, worshipped impure Venus, but then Ephesus, not less a Greek city, was ardently devoted to the service of the chaste Diana, as we learn from the 18th chapter of the "Acts of the Apostles;" so much so, that the possibility of having her privileges intruded upon, was sufficient to cause a popular tumult, and "to throw the whole city into confusion."[1] Then there was the insatiable desire of novel theories, excited among the Greeks, by the philosophic spirit there so prevalent, which could not but be in favour of the diffusion of Christian truth. We are told on the best authority, that, "all the Athenians and strangers that were there, employed themselves in nothing else but either in telling or in hearing something new."[2] And notwithstanding all their inquiries after truth, their disputations, and philosophic discussions, the feeling of the multitude was, that there were some religious truths beyond their reach, and some fundamental principles which history had not touched, and of which the wise men said nothing. That this was the impression is sufficiently evinced by the fact related in the Sacred Scripture, that there was at Athens, an altar "on which was written, To the Unknown God."[3] Might not Christianity be the undiscovered mine of truth for which they sought? And might not the true God announced by the Apostle, be the being whom they

[1] Acts xviii. 24—35.   [2] Acts xvii. 21.   [3] Acts xvii. 23.

adored, though his attributes had been hitherto wrapped in mystery?

A minute examination of the state of public morals and sentiment in Grecian society, at the period immediately preceding the first preaching of the Gospel, reveals two phases of character, one of which was opposed to Christianity, while the other might be almost said to be in its favour. The first was the moral depravity of the people. The second was the desire of novelty in religious and intellectual teaching, with the conviction that much truth was yet to be discovered. The first was a practical,—the second was a speculative element. The first was the carnal man,—the second was the intellectual man. Unfortunately in this world, immoral practice is stronger than moral theory; and in the creature, unsubdued, without grace or moral culture, the finest principles give way before the workings of passion. So it was in the Greek quarter of the Roman empire; a pure morality was beautiful in theory; a sublime theology was wanted; but the Gospel was too austere for men whose lives were tainted with every hue of vice,—sunk down to the bottom of an abyss, from which they contemplated the "Divine" as patron of the orgies of the debauched.

§ 2. *Philosophy.*—The philosophic spirit which pervaded civilized European society at the time of which we write, was another great bar to the diffusion of Christian truth. Five hundred years before the Christian era, the Greeks were far advanced in civilization, and that matured development of mind had taken place, in which systematical philosophy originated. Time passed on, and philosophy, arising out of the tenets of Pythagoras and Thales, diffused itself through the towns of Greece, and became localized in the Greek colonies of southern Italy, and principles originally simple, gave birth to many sects. On went the Grecian empire, domineering over the countries of Asia, and with it, Grecian philosophy, seizing on the minds of the vanquished. A philosophy had arisen in the East. The similarity of ends and objects became a source of mutual attraction for the systems, and the eclectic scheme of Alexandria was the result of this amalgamation. Thus as time progressed, philosophy went on modifying itself, assuming every variety of form, combining, dissolving, falling off into numberless minute divisions. But the Romans,—rude conquerors! were rolling on the tide of victory and empire towards the East. They swept over the classic cities of Greece and Asia Minor, and made a conquest of these entire countries from sea to sea. So Grecian liberty fell, but Grecian philosophy survived. Roman power domineered over the empire of Philip and Alexander, but Grecian refinement and wisdom penetrated the ranks of the conquerors, and carried back the standard of victory to the very capital of Augustus. Thus it was that philosophy[1] was very widely spread in the early days of Christianity, through Grecian, through Roman society, through the west of Asia and the north of Africa. Musonius, the Cynic, taught in Babylon; Favorinus, the Platonist, in Arles of Gaul; Athenodorus, the Stoic, in Tarsus of Cilicia. All the sects of ancient wisdom were reproduced in the schools of Greece, or by the wandering philosophers who traversed every part of the Roman empire,—the Pythagorean, the Epicurean, the Peripatetic. Athens arose again as a leader in the intellectual movement, and professors of the principal philosophies were established there by Adrian and Antoninus. Philosophy was, in truth, everywhere; but how far were the tenets of its professors opposed to the doctrines of Christianity!

The conclusions of philosophy, if fairly deduced, cannot be opposed to the revealed word of God. To philosophize, in the proper acceptation of the word, is to argue *rationally*, and reason, like revelation, is a gift from the Source of Truth. Moreover, if we take a cursory view of philosophy in its three great branches,—Logic, Metaphysics, and Ethics, we must perceive, that so far from coming into collision with revelation, it is capable of demonstrating

[1] *Enfield*, "History of Philosophy," ii. p. 31, *et seq*. Dublin, 1742.

many truths from rational principles which have come to us by the Sacred Scriptures. Thus in metaphysical science, the existence of the Necessary Being is shown from the existence of beings contingent—the existence of a Creator from the disposition of this well-ordered world. The metaphysician tells us that the soul, which is a simple substance and has no parts, cannot perish in the only way we are acquainted with, namely, by the dissolution of parts : so he leaves us to infer that the soul is immortal. In like manner, from the providence of God, as regards the good and bad in this world, we argue logically the existence of a plan of rewards and punishments in the next life, on a basis established by metaphysics; namely, that God is by nature infinitely perfect, and by consequence infinitely just. Then in ethical science, philosophy brings to light many truths, identical with the "dicta" of the inspired writers: for example, temperance, chastity, justice, charity, and other moral virtues, are, in their primary principles, discovered by reason, and recognized as obligatory, and the violation of them is known to be a crime. Sound and legitimate philosophy being but another means of coming to the knowledge of many truths, which God has given to man through His prophets and apostles, it is evident that the Grecian systems, if they had been faithful to their duty, would have prepared the minds of the learned ones of the empire for the reception of the Apostolic preaching. Unfortunately, however, there were countless errors in them; errors in theory, errors in practice, errors in principle, errors in detail, vital errors, which grew over the whole field, and absorbed all the sap and nutriment that was there, and corrupted by their pestiferous contact the few sound maxims that had been planted there by reason, guided from on high.

To form an idea, however imperfect, of the philosophic errors of Greece, it would be necessary to pass before us the materials of innumerable systems. Such an undertaking would be endless. We must, therefore, limit ourselves here to a few illustrations of this subject; and for them we are indebted to the "Biographical History of

Philosophy," by G. H. Lewes, a work in which the tenets of the leading schools are closely and critically investigated. "The Pythagoreans," says the writer referred to, quoting the authority of Aristotle, "did not separate numbers from things. They held number to be the principle and material of things, no less than their essence and power."[1] (*Arist. Met.* 1, 5.) "The soul is a monad (a number one) which is self-moved."[2] (*Arist. de Animâ*, 1, 2.) Of course the soul, inasmuch as it was a number, was One, *i.e.*, perfect. But all perfection, in as far as it is moved, must pass into imperfection, whence it strives to regain its state of perfection. Imperfection he (Pythagoras) called a departure from unity: *two*, therefore, was accursed. The soul in man is in a state of comparative imperfection: it has three elements, Reason (νοῦς); Intelligence (φρήν), and Desire (θυμός); the two last, man has in common with brutes; the first is his distinguishing characteristic." These principles appear to be a harmless description of nonsense; but behold the sad results and conclusions to which they lead! "The one soul may have two aspects: intelligence and desire, as in brutes; or it may have three aspects, as in man. But each of these aspects may predominate, and the man will then become eminently rational, or able, or sensual; he will be a philospher, a man of the world, or a beast."[3] . . . "This soul, which can look before and after, can shrink and shrivel itself into an incapacity of contemplating aught but the present moment. Of what depths of degeneracy is it capable! What a beast it may become! And if something lower than itself, why not something higher? And, if something higher and lower, may there not be a law accurately determining its elevation and descent? Each soul has its peculiar evil tastes, bringing it to the likeness of something beneath itself; why may it not be under the necessity of abiding in the condition of that thing to which it had adapted and

---

[1] "A Biographical History of Philosophy," by G. H. Lewes. Series I. Ancient Philosophy, vol. i. p. 65. London: Charles Knight, 1845.

[2] *Id.* p. 68.   [3] *Id.* pp. 69, 70.

reduced itself?" The soul, then, according to the Pythagorean doctrine, may be perpetually changing its dwelling from the form of man to the form of a beast, and from the form of one beast to another; and this not by accident, but in virtue of a fixed and unchangeable natural predetermination. What is this but the doctrine of the transmigration of souls — so eminently anti-Christian and so directly opposed to the words of revelation, "It is appointed unto man to die once, and after death the judgment."

Plato's theory of the soul and ideas is not less repugnant to revelation. According to him:[1]—Ideas are not the images of things, but things are the images of ideas. Ideas are the "substantial forms," the "intelligible essences" of things. Whence these ideas, of which things are representations? Plato answers—from the previous state of the soul. The soul is and ever was immortal. It looked into the region of real existences in the course of certain revolutions to which it was subjected in times past. It saw there "existence itself colourless, figureless, intangible." It retains the ideas of what it then saw. Thus it is, that sensible objects participate in ideas and receive their name from them; "for it is in consequence of their participation in ideas anteriorly existing in the soul, that all objects of the same genus receive the same name as the idea they represent." The doctrine of an increated soul, which is the foundation of these Platonic dreams, is subversive of the first principles of revelation; and it is a plain denial of the truth of the 27th verse of the 1st chapter of the book of Genesis: "And God *created* man to his own image: to the image of God he *created* him: male and female he *created* them."

But here is another philosopher, the gentle, the amiable Socrates: surely he will be a safer guide than those we have hitherto cited? What of his teaching? No doubt he demonstrated the existence of a beneficent Providence in words of earnest truth and beauty almost inspired; but

[1] Biog. Hist. Phil. vol. ii. art. "Plato," c. iv., v.

listen to him speaking on an ethical subject. "Vice," he says, "of every kind is ignorance, and involuntary because ignorant. If a man is cowardly, it is because he does not rightly appreciate the importance of life and death. He thinks death an evil, and flees it. If he were wise, he would know that death is a good thing, or, at the worst, an indifferent one, and, therefore, would not shun it. If a man is intemperate, it is because he is unable to estimate the relative value of present pleasure and future pain. Ignorance misleads him. It is the nature of man to seek good and shun evil; he would never seek evil, knowing it to be such; if he seeks it, he mistakes it for good; if he is intemperate, it is because he is unwise."[1] The obvious consequence of such positions as these is the eminently unchristian and fatally immoral doctrine, that there are no sins of passion; that the wise man, while acting with a knowledge of all the bearings of his act, cannot transgress against the moral law; and it would follow from them that the Apostle was wrong when he said, "I find another law in my members, warring against the law of my mind, and leading me captive to the law of sin, that is in my members."

The Sceptics[2] who, on the one hand, denied that a true knowledge of things can be had through the senses, and on the other, refused to admit that reason is the "criterion" of truth, subverted the principles on which the Christian revelation is authoritatively declared to be demonstrated—"Faith from hearing, hearing from the word of God."

The Epicureans,[3] who defined happiness to consist in pleasure, and who affirmed that philosophy is that power by which reason conducts men to happiness, were in obvious collision with that divine teaching which enjoined its disciples "to mortify their members upon the earth," and "to crucify the flesh with its vices and concupiscences."

When we say that philosophy occupied the minds of the

[1] Biog. Hist. Phil. vol. i. 223.   [2] *Id.* vol. ii. art. "Sceptics," 131.
[3] *Id.* art. "Epicureans," 139.

learned among the Greeks and Romans at the time Christianity first sought to propagate itself, we mean to say that such principles as these were still in vogue. Men were seeking for truth, and grasping at happiness; but whim and passion predominated in their movements, and the few sound principles they had discovered were warped and whirled down into the abyss of sensuality and selfishness. The philosophers had all gone astray in their own conceits—Peripatetics, Stoics, Cynics—all were out at sea, without a helm to guide them to the port. The old systems had fallen down from very old age; new ones had been constructed from their materials. Pythagoras had gone off the stage long since, and Parmenides, and Empedocles, and Antisthenes, and Socrates, and Plato, and the primitive founders of sects; but Musonius, Favorinus, Athenodorus, and a thousand others perpetuated their views, modified, and under other names. Error and Truth! the aggressor and the assailed. Error and Truth irreconcilable; moral Error, leading, under the name of wisdom, to crime; intellectual Error, under the same name and standard, leading its votaries to a denial of evident principles. Truth, come down from heaven, necessarily came into collision with Error, intellectual and moral, and consequently with philosophy as it then existed; for her mission was to seek the lost sheep, and to bring back profligate children who had been wandering on the hills, far away from the house of God.

Greece, with its profligacy and its unsound philosophical theories, was fully as unprepared as Rome to receive the "good tidings" that the Apostles were commissioned to announce. Both were infected alike with the blighting effects of pagan training; but surely there was one nation better disposed towards the Gospel, from its long familiarity with true and holy things, where it was natural to expect that every facility would be given to the spread of doctrines which are only a further development of the revered principles of an ancient revelation of which it had been the depository and the guardian. This nation was Judea.

DIVISION III.

THE JEWISH ELEMENT OF OPPOSITION.

Of the Messiah it had been predicted in the Sacred Scripture that the Lord " shall give the nations in his sight, and he shall rule over kings: he shall give them as the dust to his sword, as stubble driven by the wind, to his bow;"[1] and in reference to his reign upon earth it had been said: "I will open rivers in the high hills, and fountains in the midst of the plains: I will turn the desert into pools of waters, and the impassable lands into streams of waters. I will plant in the wilderness the cedar, and the thorn, and the myrtle, and the olive-tree: I will set in the desert the fir-tree, the elm, and the box-tree together."[2] And of the prosperous change that should follow his coming, the prophet Jeremias[3] had written: "There shall be again in this place, that is desolate without man, and without beast, and in all the cities thereof, an habitation of shepherds causing their flocks to lie down. And in the cities on the mountains, and in the cities of the plains, and in the cities that are towards the south: and in the land of Benjamin and round about Jerusalem, and in the cities of Juda shall the flocks pass again under the hand of him that numbereth them, saith the Lord. Behold the days come, saith the Lord, and I will perform the good word that I have spoken to the house of Israel, and to the house of Juda. In those days, and at that time I will make the bud of justice to spring forth unto David, and he shall do judgment and justice upon the earth. In those days shall Juda be saved, and Jerusalem shall dwell securely: and this is the name that they shall call him, the Lord, the

---

[1] Isaias, xli. 2. [2] *Id.* v. 18, 19. [3] Jeremias, xxxiii. 12, *et seq.*

just one." One seer hath proclaimed the perpetuity of his kingdom : "And I have gathered them together unto their own land, and I have not left any of them there. And I will hide my face *no more* from them."[4] "Whose kingdom," said Daniel, "shall be an everlasting kingdom, and all kings shall serve him and obey him."

The Jews were only too happy to interpret these and similar predictions in a strictly literal sense. From the days of Moses they had been invariably a repining and dissatisfied race. They had become tired of their prophets, their judges, and their kings in turn. They had been put in possession of a land "flowing with milk and honey," and it was not fertile enough for them. They had a temple, which all the world respected, and they turned it into a "house of 'traffic." They longed to return to Zion, when they were in the Babylonish captivity; and when they were conducted back to their own country, their first act was to rebel against their leaders. They complained of being obliged to serve in war. They complained of taxes. They complained of everything. Through the deep cloud of despondency that hung over them, there was but one ray of hope shining, and this was from the Messias that was to come to deliver their race from bondage, and to elevate it above the surrounding nations. There was but little spirituality among the Jews, though they were the most spiritually favoured nation on the face of the earth. Their ideas were earthly and carnal. Their tastes were sensual. Their conceptions of even the most sublime truths were not unmixed with grossness. They expected a deliverer, but they aspired to be delivered from their temporal evils only. They desired to be redeemed; but they wanted a redeemer according to their own hearts. They looked forward to the Messias, and they discovered in him a great temporal sovereign mighty in peace and unconquerable in war. It was scarcely to be expected that the Redeemer, born in poverty, nurtured in privations, would be consonant to the tastes of the Jews. They would

---

[1] Ezekiel, xxxix. 28 *et seq.*

discover grounds of insurmountable objection to him in the declaration so clearly and frequently put forth, that his "kingdom is not of this world." They would be, in all probability, lashed into fury against him, his doctrine, and the religion he founded, by the absolute termination that he appeared to put to their long-cherished hopes of temporal preponderance and ascendancy: for he had declared that their "habitation should become desolate;" he had insinuated that the Gentiles should come to lay it waste; he had gone so far as to say that of their renowned temple not "a stone should remain upon a stone."

Apart from the consideration of the lowly appearance of the Saviour, and the unearthly nature of his conquests and reign, a feeling of insecurity with regard to its exclusive possession of spiritual things, came upon a selfish race, and filled its soul with jealousy and spite. The grace and favours of heaven were now about to be communicated to the Gentiles. It would have been some consolation to the Pharisees, in their disappointment as to the character of the Messias, if they were allowed to continue to be regarded as the models of true believers and the teachers of morals. And the Scribes, if they were to be continued in their office as expounders of the law, might have made up their minds to interpret the prophetic writings in a sense less favourable to the pretensions of their race. But, if Christianity was true, there was an end to all exclusiveness. The monopoly of the Scribes and Pharisees, as well as of the people at large, was destroyed, and the descendants "of Abraham, Isaac, and Jacob," were to stand side by side in the sanctuary with the profane and impious. Now were the words of Osee to be fulfilled in the vocation of extern nations: "I will call that which was not my people, my people; and that which was not beloved, beloved; and her that had not obtained mercy, one that hath obtained mercy."[1] The appellation of "children of God" was to be communicated to aliens, in verifi-

---

[1] Osee, ii. 24.

cation of another saying of the same prophet. "And it shall be, in the place where it was said unto them, you are not my people: there they shall be called the sons of the living God."[1] And, worst of all, the strangers were to be preferred to the old domestics of the house of the Lord, for the words of Isaias, when he announces the adoption of the Gentiles and the reprobation of the Jews,[2] were declared to be applicable to present times. "I was found by them that did not seek me: I appeared openly to them that asked not after me."[3] But to Israel he saith, "All the day long have I spread my hands to a people that believeth not, and contradicteth me."[4]

A large amount of spirituality, and a total absence of selfishness, were the dispositions necessary for the Jewish people as a preparation for the reception of Christ and his heavenly doctrine. If they had such dispositions in the era of the successors of Augustus Cæsar, they must have undergone a great revolution of sentiment and feeling within a few years, and must have realized a state of national morals, for which we are little prepared by their previous annals and history.

Such were, at the time of the Apostles, the elements of opposition to the Gospel in the Roman, Grecian, and Jewish societies—elements restless and chafing, repelling each other, but united in a common repugnance to all that is just and true; and it was among these that the Church was now to enter for the first time, and with them to combat for the mastery over the heart and intelligence of man. They may be summed up in a few words:—philosophy, pantheism, passion, prejudice, and pride. Philosophy occupied a place in the minds of the educated Greeks and Romans of the day, offering as it did, a thousand solutions for the moral problems that are most interesting to man, and chained in a particular manner to Grecian society as a principle and centre of the olden glories of the Peloponnesus. The poetry and literature of the age were tinged

[1] Osee i. 10.   [2] Romans x. 20, 21.   [3] Isaias lxv. 1.   [4] Isaias lxv. 2.

and affected by the partiality of each writer for some philosophic system. Rome was full of philosophers. Judaism, with its prejudices and antipathies, was not confined to Judea, for the Jewish race had been scattered long before through the nations of Asia and Eastern Europe; and they dwelt there at the time of which we write with their synagogues, their peculiar institutions and traditions; and the further they were removed from home, the more strongly they appeared to be confirmed in their utter hatred of all that is not "the law." Then there was Roman society, the most antagonistic of all to the "good tidings" that were about to be made to the world. A universal corruption of morals prevailed there, and the light which God had enkindled in man, appeared to have gone out there in utter darkness, so deluded were the men, worshipping their idea of the Divinity, and including in their conception of God attributes of crime, lust, and weakness. In a word, crime and power were on the side of the "kingdom of this darkness;" but how striking was the contrast presented by the invading army of the "children of light."

DIVISION IV.

CONFLICT OF CHRISTIANITY WITH JEWS, GREEKS, AND ROMANS.

§ 1. *Prospects of Success.*—The Apostles, as one of themselves declares somewhere, were in a certain sense "the last of men," and certainly in the circumstances of their mission and opponents, the designation can scarcely be said to be exaggerated. They were the last men in the world that, in the human view, would appear to be fit instruments for the subjugation of error, as it then existed, or the propagation of Christian truth. It is but little to say of them that they were Jews, of an obscure and despised nation; they were, with a few exceptions, of the humblest class of Jewish society, and they were devoid of learning and human knowledge. They were, as St. Paul [1] says, "the foolish things of the world," and "the weak things of the world, and "the things that are contemptible," and the "things that are not." This was not all; they were the heralds of a new philosophy, which to sensual human nature was revolting in its principles, while in practice it was destructive of the cherished idol, self-love. The Christian religion, which it was their mission to diffuse, was the embodiment of poverty, mortification, patience, humility, denial, disengagement from this world. Its speculative sublime science of the incarnation of the Son of God, might perhaps be listened to with patience by such as were accustomed to the theories of Plato; but the deification of the austere moral virtues in the person of Christ on the cross, was a practical lesson, for which no one was prepared, and from which philosophy in its most unearthly forms recoiled. And yet this one lesson was the epitome of all they had to say, and it was the first stone in the edifice they had to build:—" We preach Christ crucified, unto the Jews indeed a stumbling-block, and unto the Gentiles foolishness: But unto them that are called, both Jews and Greeks, Christ the power of God and the wisdom of God."[2] It was this preaching of "Christ crucified," that constituted the real difficulty, in a human sense, to the propagation of Gospel truth; the chances of success were diminished by the circumstances of the nation, the position, the outward appearance of the men who preached, and obstacles apparently insurmountable must meet them at every step in the prejudice of the Jews, and the philosophy and profligacy of the Gentiles.

Let us carefully examine the method of enforcing truth, pursued by the Apostles, and the means they adopted for propagating Christianity and attracting converts to the

[1] 1 Cor. i. 27 *et seq.* [2] 1 Cor. i. 23, 24.

faith. In the beginning of the seventh century Asia saw a new creed, announced at the point of the sword, and pushed upon reluctant kingdoms, by war, pillage, confiscation, and death. The mild genius of Christianity was not such. The extermination of the wicked nations of Palestine, to make way for God's chosen people, had been a command under the law of terror; under the law of love, the tone was altered, and peace and mercy, were to be the announcements of the divine messengers. "How beautiful are the feet of them that preach the gospel of peace, of them that bring glad tidings of good things!"[1] said a prophet,[2] looking forward to the coming of the Apostles. In our own days, money, food, clothes, and such inducements were held out in certain impoverished countries, as motives for a change of faith. To become a Protestant in Ireland, in the year 1846, was to become plump, well-dressed, and a picture of material comfort. Such a mode of propagating religious opinions was in the circumstances manifestly opposed to the law of God. "Everything," says St. Paul, "which is not according to faith," that is, according to conviction or conscience, "is sin." The immediate result of such a system, was to make men profess and practise a religion that was contrary to their convictions; the ultimate effect of it, was a confirmed habit of the lowest moral depravity and dissimulation. It may be a question, whether the purchase of consciences to Christianity by the Apostles, whose conviction was unwavering, and principles manifestly true, would have been contrary to any maxim of revealed morality. Probably not: if such a change were merely external, if the judgment of the converts was suspended until such time as truth should be demonstrated, if it amounted merely to a promise on the part of the disciple to examine the proffered principles, with an engagement on the part of the teacher to demonstrate their truth. Even with this limitation, the traffic in religious convictions would lead to the saddest results. Certain it is, that Divine Providence did not make use of it as a means for the

---

[1] Quoted by St. Paul—Romans x. 15.   [2] Isaias lii. 7.

diffusion of Christianity. The apostles were poor men; they had nothing to offer, nothing to give but faith and grace. They laboured for their daily sustenance, "working with their own hands." What St. Paul says of himself, was literally true of them all; their days were spent in "hunger and thirst, in fastings often, in cold and nakedness."[1] The purchase of the right to educate and bring up children in the doctrines of the Reformation, was another means by which Protestantism was attempted to be propagated in modern times. Such a practice involved the deprivation of a privilege actually acquired by baptism; and as it operated in secret, while the infant mind was yet shrouded, and the faculties of unawakened reason were still inactive and unperceiving, it was equivalent to a robbery of the most serious and grievous character. Error might be taken away by such means without moral guilt; truth could not. Children might be bought to a religious system, demonstrated and true, unwavering, fixed, guaranteed by God, derived from his revelation, with actual merit to the purchasers; but to an uncertain system, unfixed principles, a system originating with men of unproved mission and suspected motives, children could not be so aggregated without much hypocritical affectation and fearful moral responsibility. The apostles bought no consciences. They did not surreptitiously possess themselves of the young, the sleeping, the unsuspecting. They proposed truth openly, and spoke it out in the broad day. Their aim was to make truth heard, and preach the "word of God" to nations waking and vigilant. "Faith," said one of them, "comes by hearing, and hearing by the word of Christ,"[2] and "their (the Apostles') sound hath gone forth into all the earth, and their words unto the ends of the whole world."[3]

Neither by violent means, nor by the gentle inducement of a bribe to the grown and thinking, nor by the surreptitious purchase of the young, did the Apostles endeavour to propagate the doctrines of the Redeemer among the

---

[1] 2 Cor. xi. 27. [2] Rom. x. 17. [3] Rom. x. 18.

erring nations of the universe. Faith was to come from preaching and hearing the "word of God;" and it was the effort of their lives and the end of their mission, to propose the grounds of faith in Christ *to all,* for they were "debtors in this particular to Greeks and barbarians, to the wise and the unwise." Philosophers had professed to teach truth, and to point out the way to a "happy life." By induction, often raised upon doubtful and uncertain premises, they had somehow brought out the particular tenets of their respective sects, and they evolved their favourite theories in the most pompous and intricate language, all the time enveloping them in mysticism and obscurity. In fact, as it is said in the revealed word, they had "gone astray in their own conceits," and "professing themselves to be wise, they became fools." From the very outset, the Apostles adopted a different and a much simpler method of teaching. When they argued, they as a matter of course adhered to the principles of sound logic; but their entire manner of address was distinguished by a total absence of affectation, and a clear straightforwardness that was perfectly intelligible. They could not act otherwise, for "Christ sent them .... to preach the gospel, not in wisdom of speech, lest the cross of Christ should be made void."[1] And by the contrast of their manner with that of the philosophers, and its different and larger results, they were "to destroy the wisdom of the wise, and to reject the prudence of the prudent;"[2] for as St. Paul says, "seeing that in the wisdom of God, the world by wisdom knew not God, it pleased God, by the foolishness of our preaching, to save them that believe."[3]

We must sum up the difficulties that beset the apostolic preaching. They were sent to announce Christ, his crucifixion and Divinity, "not in the persuasive words of human wisdom," but simply and plainly. The end of this preaching was to lead all nations to believe in him. Would this end have been attained by human agency alone, or have we any reason in history or experience for

[1] 1 Cor. i. 17.   [2] 1 Cor. i. 19.   [3] 1 Cor. i. 21.

thinking, that it could be attained without *special* assistance from on high? The truth is, we meet with no parallel case in the entire history of the world. If it be said that Mahommedanism was propagated to an immense extent through Asia, Africa, and Europe, from the seventh to the fourteenth century, the answer is ready: Mahommedanism is a religion of pleasure and sensual indulgence. There can be no conceivable difficulty in driving a man into a bed of roses at the point of the sword. Protestantism, was propagated extensively through Europe in the sixteenth century, without other propelling influence, than the energy and talents of the Reformers? No doubt it was; but to the sensualists of those days Protestantism presented itself as the Catholic religion shorn of everything that is difficult in belief and practice; while to men of austere lives and scanty religious knowledge it appeared in the guise of a reformation. Then Protestantism kept many of its principles in abeyance at first, in order not to provoke opposition; it made a special aim to acquire the prestige of learning and superior genius and information; it compromised, retracted, pleased every one; it forced itself on some nations by fire and the sword, where there was no chance of success by conciliation and gentleness. In a word, it appeared to act upon the maxim that the "end justifies the means," and it left no means, however questionable, untried, and no expedient unresorted to in order to disseminate its doctrines, and to extend its flock. But in the history of the world, there is no case similar to that of the Apostles. Poor, as they were, and looked down upon, they offered but one inducement, namely, the happiness of the next life, to attract men to the difficult doctrines and practices of Christianity. But the same inducement was held out by philosophy and paganism; and, in addition, they offered pleasant days in this world, or they did not prohibit the unfettered freedom of the mind or the licentious indulgence of the body.

The position of Christianity, at its first propagation, was unique. The circumstances of the Apostles were equally so; they were despised men. Their doctrine was, to a

Jewish or Pagan community, more despicable than themselves. The world was guided by principles antagonistic to Christian morality. If they had been left to their own efforts alone, if failure or success depended upon what they could do as mere human beings, it is philosophically clear from our knowledge of agency and result, of cause and effect, that they would never have succeeded in bringing the proud nations of the universe captive under the sceptre of Christ. But the assistance of God was promised them, and Divine co-operation was enlisted on their side: and it is to this point, namely, the influence of the Divine action in the propagation of Christianity, that we must now direct our attention, if we would fully understand the nature of the conflict and the victory.

§ 2. *Divine co-operation by grace.*—Somewhere in one of his epistles St. Paul attributes all the success of his ministry, as well as of the other labourers in the vineyard of the Lord, to the influence of the Holy Spirit. "I have planted (the Gospel seed), Apollo watered, but God gave the increase."[1] And though, at first sight, the apparent exaggeration of the sentiment would appear to be traceable to the humility of the Apostle, if we calmly examine it by the combined light of other passages of revelation, we will find that it contains nothing but strict and unquestionable truth. It is a fact, that without the Divine assistance and co-operation, the labours of the Apostles must have been without any solid fruit; it is equally incontrovertible, that it was the power of the Divinity exercised in favour of their ministry, that enabled them to bring forth so many children to the Gospel. God co-operated with his Apostles in the "building up of the body of Christ" in two ways principally, that is to say, by *external* operation and *internal* action; or in other words, by grace on the one hand, and by prophecy and miracles on the other. He gave them the power to work many and wonderful miracles as a confirmation of the truth of their

[1] 1 Cor. iii. 6.

doctrine. He also enlightened the minds of their hearers to see the truth, and he attracted them to it by sweet and secret impulses; and it is to such causes as these, and not to any natural qualifications or efforts of the Apostles, that we are to attribute the triumphs of Christian morality and the diffusion of Christian faith during the first century of our era.

Faith is not merely an external profession of the doctrine of Christ, and an outward aggregation to the community of his followers. Faith is even something more than such a profession, associated with an inward belief in the truth of such doctrine, natural and uninfused. How vain it is for conflicting parties of modern religionists to endeavour to diffuse faith through the medium of their wild theories. How unwise the conceits of the ministers of the reformation, who imagine that they constitute the soul in faith by exciting its natural affections towards the Redeemer! Divine and saving faith is not a fancy of the imagination, or a feeling of affection, or an opinion, or even a *conviction* merely. If faith were any of these things, the Apostle could not say of it, that "it is not of him that willeth, or of him that runneth, but of God that showeth mercy."[1] He could not again and again point so clearly to the gratuitous nature of faith, nor insist so strongly on the operativeness of Divine vocation. "For whom he foreknew, he also predestinated to be made conformable to the image of his Son: that he might be the first-born among many brethren. And whom he predestinated; *them he also called.*"[2] No! faith is undoubtedly a gift of God. A wanderer may come into the fold of Quakerism, attracted by the external propriety of that sect; or, by the startling eloquence of a camp-preacher, or the puritanical arguments of a follower of Knox, he may be added to the congregation of the Methodists or Presbyterians. But does he thereby become a believer? No! unless he has been attracted by the grace of God first, and faith has been subsequently infused. He has a conviction, I may perhaps

[1] Rom. ix. 16.   [2] Rom. viii. 29, 30.

admit, that he is believing in God salutarily. It has been demonstrated to him that Christ is among the sellers of plaided stuffs in Edinburgh, or the serious manufacturers of Manchester, and he believes it, and becomes a follower of John Wesley or John Knox. But is his state of mind that of the man who has Divine or Christian faith? If it be, there is much faith upon the earth; for everyone has, or persuades himself he has, or feels a conviction of his own orthodoxy. Faith, then, is a gift of God, superadded to the conviction arising from the rational consideration of the motives of credibility of the Christian religion; and hence, in modern times, no one can have salutary faith in a false human system, no matter what his convictions may be: hence too, in the Apostolic age, we attribute the principal glory in the triumphs of the Church, not to man, but to God.

We suppose the disciples of the Apostles, and the first converts to the Christian faith, to have been genuine believers. They came to Christ, not by outward aggregation to his Church only, but really and in fact, so as to believe in him *salutarily;* and coming to him in this way they were attracted by the grace of the Father. The necessity of this attraction or vocation to the faith had been affirmed by Christ in the clearest terms. "No man can come to me, except the Father, who hath sent me, draw him."[1] And again, "Every one that hath heard of the Father and hath learned, cometh to me."[2] And lest we should have any doubt that Christ, in the words *coming to him*, meant *believing in him*, the evangelist added a commentary to the passage that removed all ambiguity from it. "For Jesus knew from the beginning who they were that did not believe, and who he was that would betray him. And he said: therefore did I say to you, that no man can come to me unless it be given him by my Father."[3]

The Christian religion would never have been propagated through the entangled mazes of sin and error which met

---

[1] Gospel of St. John, vi. 44.　　[2] vi. 45.　　[3] v. 65, 66.

it at every step, unless God had co-operated substantially with its preachers by an action on the minds of their auditors; and to this co-operation the Redeemer pledged himself in the words that he addressed to his Apostles when bidding them a final farewell. "Going therefore, teach ye all nations . . . and behold *I am with you all days even to the consummation of the world.*"[1]

§ 3. *By Miracles.*—The second means by which God co-operated with His apostles in the propagation of the Christian religion, was by producing miraculous effects at their command in proof of the truth of their doctrine. It is not necessary for me to enter into the difficult controversy as to the nature and properties of a miracle. There is no assignable reason why God, who framed the laws of nature, might not suspend their operation in particular cases, and produce effects superior to them or contrary to them; and it will be enough for me to say, that the miracles of which the Sacred Scripture speaks, were such effects, produced at the bidding of the Apostles as an evidence of their mission from on high, and as a seal to the truth of their teaching. I likewise decline discussing here the question whether an effect, which in the circumstances of the parties before whom it is produced, *may* and *probably will be regarded as miraculous*, should be regarded as a voucher for the truth and morality of those at whose command it begins to exist. It is easy to conceive, that an effect may appear miraculous because unusual; thus an eclipse of the sun would be a sort of miracle in the eyes of a savage witnessing it for the first time: an effect too, such as a galvanic shock, the result of scientific discovery, will appear miraculous to the simple peasant whose life has been spent in the fields. If an eclipse calculated to the hour, were adduced by a wandering impostor as a proof of his favour with the Ruler of the universe; or, if galvanic or electrical effects were exhibited to a crowd of savages as an evidence of the truth of the "revelations" of Joe

[1] Gospel of St. Matthew, xxviii. 19, 20.

Smith, it is for Divines to decide upon the means of escaping hallucination, and detecting error, within the reach of the parties addressed. That such means would exist, there can be no question, for God cannot allow His creatures to be necessarily precipitated into imposture and immorality. They would possibly consist in the detectable fallacy of the apparent prodigies, or the innate perception of the broad principles of morality, latent in the mind of the savage even, or in the faults of the doctrine and the faults of the miracle combined. We can afford to pass lightly over such difficulties as these, because the miracles of which we are about to speak, those of the Apostles, were genuine, in which there was no deception.

The miracles wrought by the Apostles in proof of their mission and doctrine were not, it is needless to say, in any way traceable to human agency, or attributable to their knowledge or cunning as men. Such works as the raising Tabitha to life; the healing of Eneas, who had been "eight years ill of the palsy;" the cure of the man who had been "lame from his mother's womb;" the successive judgments upon Ananias and Saphira; the deliverance of Peter from prison; the healing of the cripple by Paul, bore upon the very face of them the impress of Divine power. And it was impossible for the men of those days, if they would act reasonably, to resist the probative force of such effects as these, which they must certainly judge to be contrary to the ordinary and well-known effects of the laws of nature.

There is in man a tendency to be attracted by outward phenomena: this is a property of his nature which anticipates reflection; and in correspondence with this almost material attribute, there are secret springs of intelligence in man's soul, which, when phenomena present themselves are ever ready with the question,—Whence are these phenomena, and wherefore have they come? Here was precisely the question that rose up before the minds of the Jews and Pagans in looking upon the miracles of the Apostles. Whence are these phenomena? Of heaven or hell? Of God or of the spirit of evil? And in seeking a clue to escape from this labyrinth of perplexity, they must have argued with themselves as follows: "These are supernatural effects certainly,—an instantaneous cure of an inveterate disease,—a calling back the spirit to the lifeless clay. They are contrary to the operation of ordinary and well-known natural laws, according to which the rooted maladies of the human frame are not expelled but by slow degrees, and regular counteracting remedies; and the spirit once fled never returns. They are wonderful phenomena; whence have they come? They are so striking of their own nature; they are so transcendent; they appear to outstrip the limits of the operation of every created power; they would seem to be attributable to God alone. But are they from God or the enemy of God?" The Jews, in their insane, blind prejudice, endeavoured to say, "from Beelzebub, the prince of devils;" but the words faltered on their lips, for a voice within them said, "the raising of the dead to life cannot be the work of any created power." Peter raised Tabitha publicly; Christ raised himself from the tomb, and the Apostles gave demonstrative proof of his resurrection. But why are these stupendous things wrought or witnessed by the Apostles? In favour of a doctrine. What doctrine? The Divinity of Christ, and his mission to redeem the world and instruct all nations. The Messias had been promised; his life and death foretold; about this time He was expected; and here are stupendous miracles, wrought to prove that this Jesus of Nazareth, in whose life the ancient prophecies have been obviously, to ourselves, in many particulars, and, it is said, in every circumstance fulfilled, is the Messias, so long waited for. But what of His moral teaching? Wonderfully pure and heavenward. What of his life? Pure and holy beyond all suspicion. What of the lives of his Apostles? Wonderfully mortified and disinterested. But they are ignorant men? No, strange to say, these men, who are well known to have been poor fishermen, living by the sea of Genesareth, are thoroughly versed in the Scriptures, and speak languages fluently which they had no opportunity of learning. Everything,—the supernaturality of the miracles,—the sublimity of the doctrine,—the life of Christ,—the lives of His apostles, coalesce into one grand demonstration of the truth of Christianity. Can we resist the force of it? Yes! Jew; yes! Pagan, you can. God does not take away your liberty. You are still free to blind yourselves by false reasoning, and if you will, to act against the convictions of your rational souls.

After the express declaration of the Word of God, there is nothing that convinces us so clearly of the necessity of Divine grace, to enable one to embrace and adhere to the true faith, as the delusions to which sensible and far-seeing men have allowed themselves to be subjected in the matter of religious conviction. A man believes that this is the true faith, and that this Church is the legitimate interpreter of revelation; but his passions tell him that its morality is too severe, and his self-love suggests to him that it cannot be embraced without many sacrifices, and his prejudices endeavour to persuade him that he cannot be wrong in his present religious associations, where so many good and learned men have lived and died; and the ultimate result will be, that he will search for and discover some reasons, false, no doubt, but plausible, to justify him in remaining in his errors.

It must be candidly admitted, that the pagans of the Roman world, who saw the demonstrations of Christianity, but for various reasons were unwilling to become Christians, found a specious pretext for remaining as they were in certain events that were occurring under their eyes. The events to which I refer, are the miracles that were said to be wrought in favour of infidelity. If we are to believe Philostratus,[1] a certain Apollonius was endowed with miraculous powers. He was by birth a Cappadocian. He had studied rhetoric in Tarsus of Cilicia. At the age of sixteen he was a philosopher, and a rigid observer of the precepts of Pythagoras. He was silent, reserved, mortified, and disinterested. He professed to seek for truth rather

[1] Phil. Vita Apol. lib. i. cap. 3, 4.

than to teach it. Thus he conciliated the esteem of many, and became the best representative of the severe type of Paganism. His thirst for knowledge led him to far distant lands. He visited the Magi of the Persians, and conversed with the Brahmins of India; and after protracted travels in foreign countries, he returned to a more congenial sphere, to communicate a new system of belief and morals, which was the result of his great experience, and his long and learned researches. It was after his return home, that he commenced to work miracles, in proof of his commission to teach. He averted a plague from the city of Ephesus;[1] he expelled a demon from the body of a youth at Athens;[2] he raised a young woman from the sleep of death at Rome;[3] and as these and many similar prodigies were wrought professedly in favour of infidelity, it is easy to perceive that they must have raised a barrier against the advance of Christian truth. On the same side as Apollonius was Simon, another great wonder-worker in those days. He had been a magician, and had attracted great attention in the East, and had already many followers, when he encountered Philip the deacon, in Samaria.[4] Struck with awe at the stupendous miracles he beheld, St. Philip operating upon "the lame, the palsied, and the possessed," he became a Christian, but shortly afterwards abandoned the faith again, and became the parent of a system of Paganism, of which the Platonic philosophy was the foundation.[5] He now resumed his magic wand, and, if we are to believe contemporary writers, he confirmed his tenets by strange and extraordinary prodigies. These were not singular cases, for it was a popular belief at the time of which we write, that the divinities spoke out in the temples, and that cures were commonly effected before the altars of Æsculapius. Was there anything in these apparently wondrous works to shake the edifice of demonstration erected for Christianity by the

---

[1] Phil. Vita Apol. lib. iii. *in fine*.   [2] *Id*. cap. 3, 4.
[3] *Id*. cap. 10.   [4] Acts of the Apostles, viii. 13.
[5] Orig. in Cels. i. p. 272, 115 ed. 1630.

great Apostolic miracles, or the miracles of Christ? Or could the Pagan in contemplating them hesitate reasonably, or stop in his onward march towards the Church? Let us look closely into this case, as between Christianity demonstrated by miracles, and Paganism upheld by such men as Simon Magus, Apollonius, or the priests of the heathen deities.

We will not venture to deny, that events of an almost miraculous nature might take place at the command of a philosopher or pagan priest, in proof of the divine origin of the whole system of paganism. Paganism is the delusive theology of the spirits of darkness: there is no reason why, with divine non-resistance, they would not maintain it to the utmost limits of their power. That the devils would, if not prevented, uphold Paganism by the production of a sort of miraculous effects in favour of it, appears to be a fact beyond dispute; for, being spirits of a higher creation, invisible, and endowed with great natural strength, they can move earthly bodies of great magnitude, suspend them in the air, transfer them from place to place, collect and join together their dissolved and scattered fragments. We are free, then, to admit, that many of the prodigies wrought by such men as Apollonius, Simon Magus, and others, were miracles, in a certain sense, produced by the "prince of darkness," and of their nature calculated to delude the beholders of them, or to lead them into error, and to confirm them therein. We cannot allow that Satan ever operated a miracle of the first order, such as raising the dead to life. Such an exercise of a power truly divine has never been vouchsafed him. Such a fact, no doubt, is recorded of Apollonius; but it is clear even from the recital of his panegyrist, Philostratus, that in the patient operated upon by him, life was not certainly extinct.[1] But with this limitation we allow that miraculous operation is within the capacity of the evil spirit; consequently we freely admit that Simon Magus may have been raised into the air, so as to fly a considerable distance, as an early writer records,[2] and that the devil for

---

[1] Phil. in Vita Apol. cap. 10.   [2] Justin apud Cyril.

his own ends may have entered into a human body, to be expelled from it by Apollonius, with a view to the deception of the multitude who witnessed the event. Allowing, then, that miracles, improperly so called, were used to be performed within the domains of Paganism, the question we have to consider is,—What was their probative force as compared to the great miracles of Christ and his apostles?

The circumstances in this case involved a triple contest —of miracles, of preachers, and of doctrines. With regard to the preachers first: This was not a dispute between two men, each claiming a divine mission, and professing to teach a system of morals, which he affirmed to have received from on high. But there was on the side of Christianity a large number of men, the twelve apostles, the seventy-two disciples, closely banded together, working in unison, agreeing in everything, and each separately performing stupendous miracles in different places, for the same object, namely, to prove the Divinity of Christ. On the side of Paganism there were several prodigy-workers, too; but their efforts were fitful and desultory, and their objects varying and undefined. Apollonius did not profess to support the fantasies of Simon, and the magician knew him not. The priests of Æsculapius did not want to prove anything more than that their divinity was still a good physician; nor did the priests of Apollo aim at anything beyond evincing the fortune-telling powers of that god. A miracle of any description ought not to be taken as proving more than the truth of the particular doctrine in favour of which it is wrought; consequently the Pagan miracle-workers of those times, labouring for peculiar and different objects, did not in any sense demonstrate Paganism as a whole.

But must it not be said, that the miracles wrought in Paganism, so far coalesced as to evince in some general way, the presence of the divinity there? No! for Paganism was the mother of all impiety and immorality. The Divinity could not countenance or favour systems fraught with ruin and degradation to the immortal souls of his creatures. The miracles were, so far as could be seen, real and genuine. The doctrines they tended to enforce were, for the most part, gross, degrading, and repugnant to the principles of natural reason. The probativeness of the miracles was tested by the nature of the doctrines; and the professed systems were to be rejected as a whole, because the miracles wrought in favour of them had no probative force. And then, if those vile Pagan teachings were put side by side with the sublime truths of Christianity, they appeared doubly disgusting and revolting. The coarse, rude, and sensual lives of the Pagan deities, and the austere and heavenly life of our Lord Jesus Christ—the doctrines of revenge, avarice and lewdness, and the sublime precepts of charity, chastity, disengagement from sensible things—the demonstrations of the amours of Venus and the rashness of Jove, and the proofs of the patience and sufferings of the Saviour—the shades, and the punishment of fire that shall never be extinguished—the Elysian fields, and the glories of the empyrean heavens. Whatever might be the force of the Pagan prodigies absolutely, they had relatively no efficacy when the doctrines they promoted were put in contrast with the Gospel; and unenlightened Pagans even, on the tablet of whose minds some general precepts of the moral law[1] are written in plain and legible characters, could not but be fully sensible of the utter worthlessness of the labours of the Æsculapian priests, the oracle-givers, Apollonius, Simon, and the others, seeing that the drift of all they did was the maintenance of imposture and deceit.

Finally there was the contrast of the miracles themselves. The pagan prodigies were strikingly insignificant, if compared to what Peter and Philip, John and Stephen, Paul and James, had wrought, and the other Apostles, whose exploits are imperfectly told; but, above all, " the crucified," whose works they proclaimed and attested. There were not among them any of what we may designate first-class miracles, such as raising the dead to life. There was nothing effected by Pagan priests which could be

[1] Romans, chap. i.

regarded as a set-off against the raising of Lazarus, the raising of the daughter of Jairus, the restoration of Tabitha to life, the resurrection of Christ witnessed by the facts of his death and subsequent apparitions. There were cures, it was said, in the temples, sudden and preternatural; but assuredly none of them bore comparison to the healing of the lame man at the "beautiful gate" of the Temple of Jerusalem, or the opening of the eyes of him who had been blind from his mother's womb, or the reanimation of those limbs that had been affected with palsy and other blighting diseases. By pomp and parade, and after much and often very suspicious manipulation or preamble, Apollonius contrived to effect something marvellous. The very handkerchiefs which had touched Paul's body, and the shadow of Peter, produced the most wonderful changes in the objects that they touched or fell upon. Oracles issued forth from Pagan shrines—what was their testimony to that of the voice that spoke in numberless strange tongues through the mouths of the Apostles and their disciples?

On a fair and comprehensive examination of the demonstration by miraculous effects, of Paganism as compared to Christianity, the conclusion arrived at must be as follows: The former was sustained by the general fact that some prodigies of a secondary order were wrought within its territory for private and peculiar ends. The latter was upheld by numberless real miracles, coalescing, mutually sustaining, establishing one fact, its revelation, its divine origin. By the number and vast superiority of the Christian miracles the Pagan prodigies were dwarfed, annihilated. Christianity was a consistent and sublime code of belief and morals. Paganism a disjointed mass of foolish histories, absurd to reason and repugnant to natural law. Such being the case, Christianity having been demonstrated by miracles, the Pagan, if he would be rational, had no alternative but to embrace it, and he should not hesitate at beholding the operations of Apollonius and others; and the Jew, who, from the history of his race, was made familiar with the use and object of miracles, was still less excusable if, with the wondrous works that were daily occurring before his eyes, he continued to adhere to the Synagogue.

§ 4. *By fulfilment of prophecy.*—When prophecy was superadded to the miracles of the New Testament, the demonstration of Christianity became irresistible, that is, in the supposition that minds were unprejudiced and honest. The Jews were manifestly neither unprejudiced nor honest in their mode of receiving or considering the Christian religion; and the Gentile, prepossessed in favour of loose morals and unconstrained liberty of thought and judgment, was with difficulty open to conviction, however conclusive the argument of virtue and purity against passion, vice, and crime. Thus, as we may suppose, the fulfilment of prophecy was questioned by the Jews, while the Gentiles professed to ignore both the Redeemer and those who foretold his coming and the establishment of his kingdom on earth. How vain were the pretences of both! The Saviour did not come as a stranger. The whole world had been expecting him. Holy men had looked forward to him, through the mist of centuries; and had described him in his power, his weakness, in his triumphs, his sufferings; and they had told when he was to be born, and how he was to die. "A star shall rise out of Jacob,"[1] said one prophet, preparing the Gentiles for the heavenly messenger that was to conduct them into his presence. "And thou, Bethlehem Ephrata, art a little one among the thousands of Juda: out of thee shall he come forth unto me that is to be the Ruler in Israel."[2] Even the precise date of his coming had been specified[3] and the week of his demise.[4] His rejection by his own people had been lamented ages before,[5] and his reception by the people that had hitherto "sat in darkness and shadow of death."[6] And now the time was come of which it had been written, "And I will pour out upon the house of David, and upon the inhabitants of Jerusalem, the spirit of grace

---

[1] Balaam, Numbers xxiv. 17.   [2] Micheas v. 2.   [3] Daniel ix. 25.
[4] Daniel v. 26.   [5] Isaias lxv. 2.   [6] Isaias ix. 2.

and of prayer, and they shall look upon me whom they have pierced."[1]

Vain were the pretences of Jews and Greeks when they sought to reject the demonstration of prophecy! Outside the people of God prophecy was almost unknown as an argument of the truth of a religious system. Such an argument then, because it was novel, ought to have been attractive and striking in the eyes of the Gentiles. The Jews had been familiar with prophecy from the time of their incorporation as God's elect; and to their joy sometimes, and sometimes to their bitter sorrow, they knew that what had been authoritatively foretold would come to pass. For Jews as for Gentiles prophecy should now become a study—in its nature, its probativeness—for to hold their own against Christianity they could not rationally suppress or smother the exciting sentiments of curiosity or fear which arose in them from the declaration often repeated by the Apostles: Christianity is the fulfilment of all that has been foreshadowed from the beginning. They were, therefore, naturally led to the consideration of the question, What is prophecy? Prophecy is a foretelling something as about to come to pass which cannot be known *naturally*, either in itself, or its cause, or in anything existing. The fulfilment of prophecy is the actual coming to pass of the event foretold. The argument of prophecy is the proof of something by the agreement of the event with its prediction. What time does prophecy come into force as an argument? When it is uttered, or when it is fulfilled? Not when it is uttered, for its truth has not yet been proved. Not when it is fulfilled, independently of the object for which it has been uttered and the time. It becomes a convincing argument in the following conjuncture: "I have come to announce to you a truth from on high," says the prophet; "will you hear me?" "No! we don't believe in you." "Then," continues the prophet, "you will believe my words when the following unlikely event comes to pass: the house of Achab shall be

[1] Zacharias xii. 10.

blotted out, and the dogs shall lap up the blood of the last of his descendants in the field of Jesrahel." "We suspend our judgment then until your prediction be verified; and if the event foretold by you happen as you say, we will believe that you are a heavenly-taught man." It could not be otherwise: the fulfilment of prophecy involves a miracle in the intellectual order of the very first class, the perpetration of which could be given to the friends of God only, and for the furtherance of the cause of morality and truth.

It would be idle to argue against prophecy in the following way: "The event you foretold may be naturally foreseen, therefore it proves nothing more than that you are a good connecter of cause and effect." It would be equally futile to say, "You have fulfilled fradulently what you predicted, in order to complete the proof you proposed." Prophecy is a *supernatural* prevision of something about to happen: its supernaturality is *manifest, evident;* this is its nature, the nature of prophecy. It would not be such if its object could be naturally foreseen or fraudulently accomplished.

It remained, then, for the Greeks and Jews to see if the evident supernaturality of prophecy fulfilled could be adduced by the preachers of Christianity in favour of Christ, his mission, his doctrine; for they must yield to such a demonstration, if it could be given, unless they chose to impugn the truth and justice of God, or to withdraw themselves from the guidance of reason. There was no need of much investigation. Hundreds of years had elapsed between ancient prophecies and the events which the Apostles sought to connect with them; ages through which no human vision could by natural possibility trace the birth of minute and complicated occurrences. After the lapse of centuries a great event should happen, unless the prophets had conspired to deceive. They could not conspire; they had no object in so conspiring. They were men of different dispositions, living at different times. They had even proved the truth of the great prophecy in which they all agreed by minor prophecies, which their own generation had seen fulfilled. Then they were unimpeachable as prophets, unimpeachable in their prediction of a great event, the coming of a King to rule and of a Messias to save. Then he should come; and if the prophets spoke truth, as they did, the time of his coming was arrived. Evident consequence of the seventy weeks of years of the prophet Daniel, determining the date of his death! This was not all—a variety of minor events were to shroud and surround his coming. These, too, should fall out, for the veracity of the prophets was equally pledged to them. Both should come to pass, the great event and its attendant circumstances, with this difference, that the latter were to be a proof of the former, as if the ancient prophets said: "When Elias comes watch for the coming of the Messias; when a star appears in the East, know that his coming is nigh; receive not any claimant to the dignity of Messias, unless he be born in Bethlehem, born of a virgin. Are the Gentiles summoned to his presence? Is he wounded and bruised for the iniquities of men? Do they dig his hands and feet and number all his bones?"

We need not point out the verification of these items, in the coming, birth and sufferings of Christ, as affirmed and proved by the Apostles. It is enough to say, that they affirmed them, proved them, and had hundreds of witnesses to attest their truth. They were accomplished to the letter and in every particular. Above all, the most painful part was fulfilled, that is, the dereliction and death of Christ in an ocean of grief and suffering. All that now happened accorded most perfectly with all that had been formerly predicted. Sublime and unquestionable miracle, or rather series of miracles, proving the identity of Christ with the promised Messias!

There was no resisting the argument of prophecy, as wielded by the Apostles, unless faith and reason were trampled under foot. And it was growing apace in magnitude and importance as new events were daily occurring, the prototypes of which were traceable in Isaias, Jeremias, and Daniel. And then it was not an insulated argument, but it was a miracle in the intellectual order, coalescing with numerous miracles in the physical order wrought by

Christ, and attested by living witnesses, or operated by the Apostles under the eyes of those who wished to see. So Jews and Greeks were defied, the former on religious, the latter on rational grounds to keep their traditions, if they could, against the fulfilment of promises and pledges, as old almost as the world itself. And they were drawn forth from their security and inertness, drawn forth by curiosity, perhaps, to examine first, then to doubt, to be perplexed between their attachment to what was old, and the manifest truth of what was new; finally to yield, unless the paramount ruler of the spirit in their case, was prepossession, passion, and blind ungovernable prejudice.

There is a pretty city, rising on terraces above the water, at a point where the bold and dark sublimity of mountains meets the undulating plains and smiling meadows that skirt the shores of Lake Leman. It was here, that on the 27th of June, 1787, Gibbon finished his great work on "the Decline and Fall of the Roman Empire." This remarkable production reflects in its pages the characteristics of the place where it was written. Its style and arrangement are fresh and beautiful, like the meadows beneath the town. Its ideas very often, and its tone are bold and precipitate, like the mountains that tower in the background. Among the daring assertions of Gibbon there are two that deserve a passing notice from us at this stage of our history. The first is, that the propagation of Christianity in the primitive ages was slow, and its conversions from Paganism and Judaism insignificant. The second is (and it is the consequence of the first) that the progress of Christian principles was the result of *natural* causes. The latter assertion we have already met with a negative. We have seen the difficulties that the Apostles encountered among Jews and Greeks, difficulties of such magnitude, and of such a nature, as could never be overcome by the *natural* powers that they could bring to the undertaking. And so we inferred "à priori," that *supernatural* aid was essential to them, if they would succeed in establishing the

Church on a large scale. The Sacred Scripture has enlightened us as to the nature of this supernatural aid; and we have discovered it to consist of grace, miracles, and the fulfilment of prophecy. Thus we have disposed of one of the rash assertions of Gibbon: in the next division of our work we shall have occasion to refer to the other.

DIVISION V.

VICTORY OF CHRISTIANITY AND ITS ORGANIZATION.

§ 1. *Its Diffusion.*—Christianity, entering into a strange world, that was full of barrenness and noxious weeds, conversing among nations, whose minds were averted from God who made them, combated successfully with the obstacles that were opposed to its progress, and diffused itself beyond the limits of civilization and the Roman empire. Its first mission was in the province of Judea. In the persons of St. Peter and St. John it laboured for some time in the conversion of the Jews. It passed the limits of that province; crossed the sea to the island of Crete; laboured there, converted many; to the opposite shore of Asia Minor, a great part of which it traversed, carrying faith and grace from city to city. It bent its course westward, and entered Greece from the north-east; conversed in the cities, where Sappho sung and Socrates uttered parables; on by Melita and Puteoli, until it arrived in the capital, Rome.

These were the successes of Christianity in one direction, and under the guidance of three Apostles.

The other apostolic missionaries turned their eyes in different directions, some to the east, others to the north and south. One of them preached in Scythia, whence he passed into Epirus and the adjacent countries. Another traversed the sands of Arabia. Ethiopia, and Persia, Armenia and Parthia were theatres of apostolic labour, —were fertilized by the blood of apostolic men. The bones of St. Thomas found a resting-place in Judea.

Thus, if we cast our eyes over the map of the world we see vast regions to the south and east of Judea. Through many of these had Christianity penetrated even before the end of the apostolic age; to the west and north—in them it had become naturalized. Doubtless, there was much difference between the positions occupied by the Christian congregations in the various countries which the Gospel had penetrated. In some places they were few and wide apart. In others they were numerous, and in some districts continuous. In Asia Minor, for example, and in Greece, many of the provinces were covered with Christian colonies. There is no reason for supposing that Persia or Arabia were similarly blessed. But the faith was growing apace, and the glad tidings of salvation were travelling in every direction, propelled by the breath of the Divinity.

Everything leads us to believe that the propagation of Christianity was very rapid, and that the number who embraced the faith was very considerable, even before the end of the first century of the Christian era. We have many passages in the sacred writings which bear directly upon this subject; and the documents of profane history which remain to us, throw some light upon it in their casual allusion to the "hated" and "much dreaded" sect.

The first conversions among the Jews are detailed in the "Acts of the Apostles." In reference to them, we have such passages as the following :—" They, therefore, that received the word were baptized; and there were added in that day about *three thousand souls.*"[1] " But *many of them* who had heard the word believed, and the number of men was made *five thousand.*"[2] " And the word of the Lord increased, and the number of disciples *was multiplied in Jerusalem exceedingly.*"[3] But the Scripture narration does not limit itself to enumerating the accessions to

[1] Acts of the Apostles ii. 41.   [2] iv. 4.   [3] vi. 7.

Christianity in Jerusalem and among the Jews: it has many passing allusions to the magnitude of the successes in other quarters. Thus—" And they (Paul and Barnabas) *taught a great multitude*, so that at Antioch the disciples were first named Christians."[1] " And the word of the Lord *increased and multiplied*."[2] " And *a very great multitude* [in Iconium] both of the Jews and Greeks, did believe."[3] " And when they had preached the Gospel in that city [Derbe,] *and taught many.*"[4] " And the churches were confirmed in faith, and *increased in number daily.*"[5] " And some of them [in Thessalonica] believed, and were associated to Paul and Silas, and of those that served God, and of the Gentiles *a great multitude*."[6] " And *many of them* [at Berea] believed."[7] So numerous, indeed, were the defections from the ranks of Paganism, that the subject was made a cause of special thanksgiving on the part of the apostles, and it was a source of the most bitter acrimony among the enemies of God and His Church. Thus, when St. Paul went up to Jerusalem and narrated the successes of his ministry to the assembled "ancients," St. Luke says that, " They hearing it, glorified God, and said to him—Thou seest, brother, how *many thousands* there are among the Jews that have believed."[8] And when Demetrius, the silversmith, at Ephesus, endeavoured to excite the ire of his countrymen against the apostles and their doctrine, he appealed to the great wound inflicted by them upon Paganism as an established fact. " And you see and hear, that this Paul, by persuasion hath drawn *a great multitude*, not only of Ephesus, but almost of all Asia."[9]

Gibbon, as I said before, endeavours to reduce the number of Christians to a mere handful scattered over Judea, Asia Minor, and Greece. It is needless to remark that he cannot be a believer in revelation who ventures to question a fact so clearly affirmed in the sacred writings, and so frequently and forcibly insisted upon. The converts were very numerous, according to St. Paul and St. Luke—" a

---

[1] Acts of the Apostles xi. 26.   [2] xii. 24.   [3] xiv. 1.   [4] xiv. 20.
[5] xvi. 5.   [6] xvii. 4.   [7] xvii. 12.   [8] xxi. 18.   [9] xix. 26.

great multitude,"—"three thousand,"—"five thousand,"
—"many thousands." They were computed by "thousands," not only in Jerusalem, but in the cities of Asia Minor. The Pagans were cut to the heart at their ever-increasing numbers. So far the inspired Scriptures: and in addition, as if to take every excuse out of the mouth of the unbeliever, we are enabled to trace in the other writings of the period, Pagan as well as Christian, evidences of the same, clear, strong, and incontestable. Pliny, the younger, writing from Bythinia to Trajan, not later than the end of the first century, on the persecutions to which Christians were exposed within his province, has the following passage, containing the groundwork of his appeal:—" The thing has appeared to me worthy of consideration, principally on account of *the number of* the accused. For the lives *of many* are endangered, of *every age*, and of *both sexes*. This superstition has infested, *not only the cities*, but *the villages and the country parts;* and it appears that we have the power to arrest its progress, and remove its effects. However this be, certain it is, that the people begin again to frequent the temples, which *were almost altogether deserted*, to celebrate the solemn sacrifices, *after a long interruption;* and everywhere we see victims *instead of a total lack of purchasers*. Whence we may easily judge of *the great number* that will amend their ways, if room be given for repentance."[1] Ignatius, the martyr, writing about the same time to the church of Ephesus, commences in terms of congratulation on the number of its faithful members. "I have received your *great multitude* in the person of Onesimus, your bishop, a man of inexpressible charity."[2] Bardasanus, in his treatise on destiny, written half a century later, after speaking of the customs and manners of various classes, cries out in admiration—" But what shall I say of the Christians *so numerous*, and spread through so many nations, &c."[3] It is unnecessary to enter

---

[1] Plin. lib. 18, ep. 97.
[2] Ignat. ep. ad Ephes. No. 1, p. 12, tom. 2. ed. Cot.
[3] Euseb. præp. Evang. lib. vi. c. 8.

further into this subject here, as the history of the three
first centuries must in many ways indirectly chronicle the
progress and victories of the Church; and the number of
distinct congregations of Christians in the several provinces
of the empire, to which we shall afterwards have to refer,
the number of priests—four, and five, and six in a city,[1]
besides the bishop, and the magnitude of the persecutions
raised by the Roman emperors, are facts which prove
that the Christian community must have grown to
mighty proportions at a very early period, while the
long lists of those who suffered for the faith is an
evidence of the magnitude of the body to which they in
common belonged.

At the time of the first diffusion of Christianity, all
nations, with a solitary exception, and the various classes
of society comprising them, were sunk in moral degradation. Within the Roman empire, the degrees of refinement and civilization differed very widely; stolid ignorance
was often the characteristic of the artisan or peasant,
while the "dicta" of abstruse philosophy were circulated
at the banquets of the higher orders even from the lips of
matrons and ladies; yet all were involved in the same
maze of speculative ignorance of the immutable principles
of virtue, and of practical forgetfulness of their duties as
immortal beings. Or, as St. Paul briefly expresses it,
"All had sinned and needed the grace of God." All were
in darkness, poets and philosophers, learned and unlearned,
Greeks and Romans, freedmen and slaves. It must be
interesting to inquire in what order they approached the
light, whether the teachers of the people came first, or the
higher classes, who might be supposed to influence the
vulgar by their example; or, whether the untaught multitude approximated in the first instance to Christianity and
drew on the learned in their train.

From the Acts of the Apostles and the epistles of St.
Paul, we are able to satisfy, to some extent, our curiosity
on this subject; for they furnish us occasionally with in-

---

[1] See Epistles of St. Ignatius.

formation as to the rank or employment of individuals whose conversion they relate. Thus, in the 15th chapter of the Acts, we are incidentally informed that " some of the sect of the Pharisees "[1] embraced the faith ; and St. Paul, in his epistle to the Romans, gives us to understand, that " Erastus, the treasurer of the city"[2] from which he wrote (Corinth), was one of the brethren ; Zenas, to whom St. Paul refers in his epistle to Titus, [3] was a " lawyer ;" and Luke was a " physician."[4] Caius, the host of St. Paul, and Cloe,[5] and several others, in whose mansions the faithful assembled to hear the instructions of the apostles, and to join in public worship, belonged to the upper class of society. Philemon, to whom St. Paul directed a short epistle, was a rich man, as we must infer from his extensive charities, and his hospitality to " the saints."[6] Pudens, who is mentioned in the last chapter of the second epistle to Timothy,[7] was a senator of Rome ; and from the epistle of St. Paul to the Philippians, [8] we learn, that some of the members of " Cæsar's household " had embraced the faith. Among the converts at Athens, was Dionysius,[9] the areopagite, that is to say, a member of the supreme council of the nation. In Cæsarea, Cornelius, [10] the centurion, that is, an officer of the Roman army, became a Christian. There was another class, that in these primitive times, came in large numbers into the Church, whose conversion ought to be a subject of considerable interest at the present day, from circumstances that have recently occurred in a neighbouring and sister country. The class to which I refer, is that of ladies of rank : a movement towards orthodoxy has within the last few years made good progress among the titled dames of Britain ; and it is at the least remarkable that a movement, similar in many respects, took place among the Grecian ladies in the first century of the Christian era. Among several passages illustrating this subject, which occur in the "Acts of the Apostles,"

[1] Acts xv. 5.   [2] Romans xvi. 23.   [3] Epistle to Titus iii. 13.
[4] Romans xvi. 23.   [5] 1 Cor. i. 11.   [6] Philem. i. 5, 7.
[7] 2 Tim. iv. 21.   [8] Philip iv. 22.   [9] Acts xvii. 34.   [10] x. 1.

we select two plain ones from the seventeenth chapter. In Berea St. Luke tells us, "Many of them, indeed, believed, and of *honourable women* that were Gentiles, and of men *not a few*."[1] In Thessalonica "Some of them believed, and were associated to Paul and Silas, and of those that served God, and of the Gentiles, a great multitude, and of *noble women not a few*."[2]

There came out of the Babylon of Roman corruption a varied and motley crew, noble ladies and rich proprietors, treasurers and tax-gatherers, officers of the army, physicians, lawyers, senators, counsellors of kings. Still, with the evidences before us of the conversion of numbers of the higher and educated classes, and of all the professions, it must be admitted—the fact is beyond all dispute—that Christianity in the first century faithfully fulfilled the mission of "preaching peace to the poor." The vast majority of the conversions to Christianity were among the poor and humble classes. It was the laborious peasant and the unlettered maiden, and the toiling artisan, that swelled the ranks of the Christian congregations. It was not yet fashionable to be a Christian, and they who disregarded "the fashion of the world," knowing that it "passeth away," carried off the prize of eternal life. This is affirmed by St. Paul, in his first epistle to the Corinthians, where he says, "For, see your vocation, brethren, that *there are not many wise according to the flesh, not many mighty, not many noble*. But *the foolish things of the world hath God chosen*, that he may confound the wise, and *the weak things of the world*, that he may confound the strong. And *the base things of the world*, and *the things that are contemptible*, hath God chosen, and *the things that are not*, that he might bring to naught the things that are. That no flesh should glory in his sight."[3]

§ 2. *Its Material Position*.[4]—The first Christian congregations were in towns. There is not a passage in the

[1] Acts xvii. 12.
[2] Acts xvii. 4.
[3] 1 Cor. 26—29.
[4] See Appendix

whole narrative of St. Luke which could lead us to suppose that the apostles preached through the country parts of the nations they evangelized. Indeed, it would appear to have been their policy to preach in the largest and most thronged cities,—places from which the faith, if once embraced, should be visible to surrounding and dependent districts. In the Roman world, society circulated between the towns. Men hurried along the great public "ways" that traversed the empire from city to city. Husbandmen and men of letters, philosophers and merchants, all classes were attracted to the towns, the centres of life and enterprise. The apostles mingled with the crowd. They, too, hurried along to meet the multitude, to speak to it, to convince it, to draw it to Christ, to gather from it the favoured elements of a Christian congregation. During their long and arduous journeys, they doubtless took every opportunity of announcing the truths of religion to individuals whom they met; but, as it was with them a paramount object to consolidate as they built, they naturally preferred to raise the edifice of Christianity in populous places, whence the action of governing heads would be more sensibly felt, and where the mutual support of many numbers would be secured.

Though Christianity was in the first instance established in the cities and towns of the Roman empire, it appears to have found its way into the country parts adjacent at a very early period. If the apostles confined in a great measure their labours to the towns, the ecclesiastics, whom they placed over the town congregations, would seem to have carried the faith into the surrounding districts long before the end of the first century of the Christian era. It is of the nature of all truth to be diffusive; it was the nature of gospel truth to be diffused, God having pledged himself to its propagation. Was it the "coloni," the farmers of Rome and Greece, that came to the towns to sell the produce of their lands, and there heard of Christianity and embraced it? Or was it the zealous Christian pastors located in the towns, who undertook occasional journeys to the country to converse with the tillers of the soil ? We cannot say by which cause the conversion of the rural districts was occasioned; probably both causes together operated in bringing about that event. But certain it is, that Christianity was soon diffused through the hamlets of the Roman empire, and embraced by the rural population. Of this we have evidence in the celebrated letter of Pliny the younger, governor of Bythinia, to Trajan, written in the beginning of the second century. " This superstition," he says, speaking of Christianity, " has infected not only the cities, but *the villages and the country;* and I think we can arrest its career."[1] And some years later, St. Justin, in his first Apology, inscribed to Antoninus Pius and Lucius Verus, has a passage, which leads us to conclude, that the churches established in the cities and towns had a portion of their congregation scattered through the neighbouring country districts. "And on the day of the sun, as it is called, all, whether living in the town or country, come together to the same place; and the commentaries of the apostles, and the writings of the prophets, are read."[2]

§ 3. *Jurisdiction of Priests.*[3]—From considering the material position of Christianity in the Roman world, we are naturally led to the interesting question of church government in these early ages; and we cannot but feel anxious to ascertain whether the pastor, who presided over the congregation, composed of the Christians of the town and its annexed country district, was a bishop or a priest —did he belong to the first or the second order of the clergy? Some writers[4] have imagined that they dis-

---

[1] Plinii, lib. 18, epis. 97.
[2] St. Justin, Apol. i. No. 67, p. 83, ed. Wirceburg, 1777.
[3] In this and the following section there are views maintained which may appear novel, perhaps even irreconcilable with the interpretations of approved commentators : I put them forward with some degree of timidity. Still, as there seem to be grounds for them in the sacred text, I thought it well to submit them to the judgment of learned and orthodox divines. As a matter of course they are subject to the approval of the church.
[4] L'instituz. divin. de' Parochi. e loro diretto al governo generale della Chiesa. Florentii, 1783.

cover in the passage above cited from the first Apology of St. Justin an allusion to the parochial system; and they believe that it illustrates a state of things in which the town, and a circumscribed district of the adjacent country, were united under the jurisdiction of a priest, resident in the town. Others, on the contrary, are of opinion that St. Justin exhibits here a picture of a small diocese, with its bishop resident in its centre.

On this question the immediate government of the first Christian churches, founded by the apostles,—a question involved in considerable obscurity,—we may be able to come to some definite conclusion when we have glanced at certain facts bearing upon it, which are mentioned in the Sacred Scriptures, and in the writings of St. Ignatius the martyr.

1. St. Ignatius, in his epistle to the churches of Asia, distinguishes very clearly the three orders of the hierarchy, the bishop, the priests, and the deacons. He is the first ecclesiastical writer that uses the words ἐπίσκοπος and πρεσβύτερος in contradistinction to each other. In his farewell epistle to the churches of Asia he sends his salutations and adieus to the ἐπίσκοπος (singular), and the πρεσβύτεροι (plural), and διάκονοι of the churches to which he wrote. From Ignatius, therefore, we have the fact, that at the beginning of the second century the churches of Trullis, Ephesus, Magnasia, and Phyladelphia had each a hierarchy governing it, composed of a bishop, priests, and deacons.

2. From the Acts of the Apostles, we learn that the same church of Ephesus and the church of Jerusalem had several πρεσβύτεροι or ἐπίσκοποι each, while the apostles were yet living. I designedly use the particle *or*, for it is to be distinctly borne in mind, that the words ἐπίσκοπος and πρεσβύτερος are used indiscriminately in the writings of the New Testament to designate the *same* order of the hierarchy, whether such order be of priest or bishop. The use of the former to designate the bishop *exclusively*, and of the latter to designate the priest *exclusively*, does not occur in the writings of the age, before the time of Ignatius the martyr.

3. We know from the Apocalypse that Ephesus was an episcopal city; and the writer of the Acts gives us to understand that the church of Jerusalem was presided over by St. James the Less.

4. By comparing the 14th chapter of the Acts of the Apostles with the 2nd and 3rd chapters of the Apocalypse, we are forced to the conclusion that there were some towns in Asia Minor that were immediately governed by priests. For, from the Apocalypse, we infer that there were only seven episcopal sees in Asia Minor at the end of the first century, viz., Ephesus, Smyrna, Pergamus, Thyatira, Sardis, Phyladelphia, and Laodicea; and from the chapter of the Acts referred to it is quite clear that Lystra and Iconium had each of them at least, one πρεσβύτερος, ordained by St. Paul or Barnabas.

Here are a few of the most remarkable facts bearing on the government of particular churches that present themselves in the documents of the period. They will throw some light on the question of the rank and order of the clergy who governed the primitive churches of Asia and Greece, if we narrowly examine the meaning of them, and compare the inferences they give rise to.

A class of writers, alluded to above, led in a great measure by the use of the word ἐπίσκοπος in the apostolic writings, have advocated the theory, that each of the towns in which Christian congregations were first formed, had a bishop appointed there by the apostles, and a deacon or two, and that the ordination of priests, though of divine institution, and in theory coeval with the apostles, was practically a dead letter until the close of the apostolic period. Every primitive church was in this view an episcopal church, and every bishop had his deacon.

The foundation of this system is subverted by the fact, to which allusion was made in No. 2, namely, that the word πρεσβύτερος is as often applied to the clergy of the primitive church higher than the order of deacon as the word ἐπίσκοπος; besides, the word ἐπίσκοπος is frequently used in the Sacred Scriptures to designate the priest, as, for example, in the 20th chapter of the Acts of the Apostles, where St. Paul characterizes by this epithet the entire body of the clergy of Ephesus; and in the Epistles to Timothy and Titus, where the same apostle distinguishes but two orders of the clergy, the διακόνους and the ἐπισκόπους. And there is absolute demonstration against this theory in the fact referred to in No. 4, namely, that some of the towns of Asia Minor, which were not episcopal towns, had πρεσβυτέρους ordained for them, who were the local governors of their respective flocks.

If, then, the primitive churches founded by the apostles were not *all* episcopal churches, are we necessitated to fall into the second opinion put forth at the beginning of this section, and to hold that they were parishes, or something similar, governed by the clergy of the second order? After a full and candid examination of this question, I believe we must come to the conclusion that the first ordinations by the apostles were of priests, with quasi-parochial jurisdiction. Before assigning the grounds of this conclusion, it will be well to meet a difficulty which arises out of the statements made in Nos. 1 and 3. From these statements, it appears, on the authority of the Apocalypse, that Ephesus was an episcopal city; and, on the authority of St. Ignatius the martyr, that there were some episcopal towns and cities in Asia Minor, at the time that he wrote his Epistles. How, then, can it be held consistently with these facts, that the primitive churches founded by the apostles were not immediately governed by bishops, but by priests? The answer to this difficulty is obvious: it may be comprised in a few words. St. John wrote the Apocalypse at the close of the first century; St. Ignatius wrote his Epistles at the beginning of the second century. The first Christian churches, of whose foundation record is preserved in the sacred Scriptures,[1] were formed at a far earlier period.

We return to the main question. In the first place, I think, we may assume that the same system of parochial or episcopal churches was established by the apostles in

---

[1] Acts of the Apostles xiv. 22.—Epistle to Titus i. 5.

countries similarly circumstanced. In Asia Minor, for example, Greece and Crete, where the churches were numerous, and where they bore much the same relation to each other in point of distance, there would appear to be no reason for establishing episcopal churches exclusively in one country, parochial churches in another, and episcopal with parochial in a third. Whatever the system was, —being introduced by the same apostles, and for the regulation of the church of God, which was to be essentially one and uniform,—it must have been similar in all parts of the Roman empire, where the faith was equally diffused.

This being presupposed, we ask ourselves, what was the system of church government first established by the apostles? Again we answer, the quasi-parochial system. We proceed to assign the grounds of this opinion. The πρεσβύτεροι, ordained by St. Paul and Barnabas, to whom allusion is made in the 22nd verse of the 14th chapter of the Acts of the Apostles, and the πρεσβύτεροι ordained by Titus for the churches of Crete, appear to have been all of the same rank; and none of them appear to have been bishops. We must suppose them to have belonged to the same order of the hierarchy, because they are simply designated by the same name, and there is no distinction made between them. If the commission of St. Paul to Titus involved the appointment of bishops over some churches of Crete, and of priests over others, we would reasonably expect to find the apostle directing his attention to this twofold duty, when he reminds him of the end of his mission to this island. His words would be, in all probability, "I left you at Crete to appoint a certain number of bishops in the principal cities, and to subject to their authority priests, ordained by you, in the lesser towns and villages," instead of being as they are. "For this cause, I left thee in Crete, that thou shouldst set in order the things that are wanting, and shouldst ordain 'πρεσβυτέρους' in every city, as I also appointed thee."[1]

[1] Epistle to Titus i. 3.

In the same sense, we must understand the words of St. Luke, in the 14th chapter of the Acts,—"And when they had ordained to them 'πρεσβυτέρους' in every city, and had prayed with fasting, they commended them to the Lord, in whom they believed."[1] The Evangelist does not say *priests and bishops*, or priests of the first and second order; but, without any qualification, he says,—" When they had ordained to them ' πρεσβυτέρους.' " The clergy, therefore, ordained by the apostles through the cities of Asia Minor, and those whom Titus ordained for the towns of Crete, were obviously priests *or* bishops, but probably not priests *and* bishops.

I have said that none of them appear to have been bishops. I think this assertion is borne out by various circumstances. In the first place, there was no necessity for erecting episcopal sees, while the apostles were still living. They were themselves the bishops of the church. They went about from place to place performing episcopal functions, correcting abuses, eradicating errors, ordaining the clergy. The churches of Troas and Iconium did not require a bishop resident immediately in their neighbourhood; they were sufficiently directed by the apostles and their companions, who visited them from time to time.

Then it would have been very difficult, after the first propagation of Christianity, to determine the limits of episcopal jurisdiction. The faith was speading in every direction, and ramifying through countries strange to the apostles, and in a great measure unexplored. The churches were increasing in number day after day. If bishops were in the first instance appointed in churches at certain distances from each other, it is clear that there could be no rule for determining the extent of their jurisdiction, and that numberless disputes must arise as to the ownership of the new churches, which were every day being erected; so that confusion and chaos should have been the result of the immediate erection of episcopal sees.

Apart from these considerations, there are two impor-

[1] Acts xiv. 22.

tant facts that must not be lost sight of, viz.: first, the character of the men whom the apostles should select; and, secondly, the great authority and dignity of the episcopal office. There was no choice, but among the recent converts from Paganism or Judaism. There was evidently a difficulty in raising them at once to the highest rank among the clergy. They might be priests in submission; they ought not to be bishops in authority. There was still greater difficulty in placing them in a position of such independence and authority at a distance from the centre of government. Might they not rebel? Might they not divide the church? Might they not dissolve the union, before the joints were well knit together? The appointment of bishops immediately upon the first diffusion of Christianity would have resulted in raising up rivals to the apostles, and endangering the unity of the church.

Such considerations as these lead us naturally to the conclusion, that the first ordinations in the primitive church were of priests and deacons, and the truth of this view is confirmed and illustrated by a passage in the first epistle of St. Clement of Rome. The epistle is inscribed, "The church of God which is in Rome, to the church of God which is in Corinth, &c.," and the principal object for which it is written is manifestly to put an end to certain dissensions which had arisen between the faithful and their priests. From the body of the epistle it appears that the Christians of Corinth had rejected certain priests from the sacred ministry, and deprived them of their position in the church. "We see," says St. Clement, "that you have banished some of them [the priests] who lived piously, and who acquitted themselves in the ministry, not only without reproach, but even with honour."[1] Obviously there is question of priests only, not of bishops. The church of Corinth had but one bishop, whereas the clergy referred to by St. Clement must have been numerous in the church of Corinth. They had rejected

---

[1] Ep. Clem. i. No. 45, ed. Cot.

some of their priests; and the drift of the epistle of St. Clement is to convince them that "it will be no trifling sin to deprive of the episcopacy those who worthily offer the sacred gifts."[1]

What argument does he adduce in favour of this conclusion? He shows that the priesthood is of apostolic ordination; and in establishing this fact, he uses words which distinctly signify that the primitive appointments by the apostles were limited to deacons and priests. "Thus preaching in the countries and the cities, they established the 'primitiæ' of the flocks, after having approved them by the Holy Spirit for the 'ἐπισκόπους' and deacons of those who received the faith."[2] He then goes on to affirm that the priests of the church are the properly-constituted successors of the "ἐπίσκοποι," established by the apostles in their first missions. "Our apostles, enlightened by the Holy Spirit, have well known the contentions which must arise for the name of the episcopacy. . . . . Wherefore have they established the aforesaid, and have ordained that after their deaths other approved men should succeed to their ministry."[3] So it appears that the whole argument rests on the appointment of priests by the apostles in their primitive missions. They appointed, he says, priests and deacons: not a word about their appointing bishops. It cannot be argued that St. Clement, from the nature of his argument, had no need of referring to the bishops, if they were appointed; for, it may be answered, that he had less need of referring to the deacons. They appointed, he says, priests and deacons, and no more; and these priests appointed by them are the direct predecessors of the priests of the Church at the present day. St. Clement does not directly touch the question as to whether the apostles subsequently appointed bishops. He insinuates that they did, in the words "other distinguished men," which he employs in a subsequent part of the passage last adduced; but he clearly agrees with me in the thesis I

[1] Ep. Clem. i. No. 45, ed. Cot.   [2] No. 44, *ibid.*   [3] *Ibid.*

have been endeavouring to establish, viz., that the "πρεσ-βύτεροι" and "ἐπίσκοποι," of whom mention is made in the 1st chapter of St. Paul's epistle to Titus, and in the 14th chapter of the Acts, were not bishops, but priests,—the primitive governors of the churches first established, and the possessors of extensive and probably of parochial powers.

There are reasons for believing that the priests of the primitive church were not curates holding a temporary jurisdiction at the will of the bishop. From examining the mode of their ordination and the position they occupied, we must incline to the opinion that their authority resembled that of parish priests. In the first place, they were ordained by the apostles or by their immediate representatives, by Paul or Barnabas, or Timothy or Titus. Then there is not a word said of their dependence upon the bishop; they were placed over towns, with their adjacent country districts at a distance from the apostle who ordained them. If they had been simple curates, we might expect to hear of a general ordination of them in some town or city, and of their subsequent location at the will of the ordinary; but no, the instructions of St. Paul are, "to ordain priests in every city, as I also appointed thee."[1] The tenor of the words would lead us to think that they were fixed and immovable, and permanently attached to the congregations over which they were placed. There was another class of priests in the episcopal towns towards the end of the first century, who appear to have been dependent entirely upon the bishops; but for the priests of the remote towns and villages, there is no evidence to prove that they were bishops—vicars, or curates.

§. 4. *Jurisdiction of Bishops.*—We will take it for granted, that the primitive churches founded by the apostles were presided over immediately by priests. They were, in all probability, a series of quasi-parishes spread over the countries where the three continents meet each

---

[1] Epistle to Titus i. 3.

with its town or city in the centre, to which the Christians resident in the adjacent country flocked to partake of the sacraments, and to be present at public worship on the first day of the week.

We want to ask a most important question touching these parishes or quasi-parishes—that is, what was their position in the universal church? They were not a series of independent ecclesiastical governments, such as in the civil order were the free towns or the petty principalities of Germany before the French revolution. We want to know what was their dependence upon each other, or upon a governing power outside themselves? What were the bonds which bound them into one community, and rendered them dependent members of that mystic body to which St. Paul so often refers, of which the Saviour himself is the head?

If we glance over the Acts of the Apostles, especially those chapters in which allusion is made to the journeys of St. Paul, or if we read attentively the epistles of the apostle of the Gentiles, we cannot fail to be struck by the extraordinary care bestowed upon the early converts, and the laborious assiduity with which all their spiritual wants were supplied. When converts were made, and a church assembled in a town, it was not abandoned to the care of the "presbyter" placed over it, so as to be withdrawn from apostolic inspection. The apostles visited it again and again; it was the object of their fostering care. They kept near them, and took about with them on their journeys a number of young men selected from the different congregations, whom they sent about from city to city, or despatched with messages from church to church. Such were Sosthenes, Luke, Apollo, and many others.

They did not lose sight of the Christian congregation. They governed it from a distance sometimes, and anon they inspected it personally, and its presbyter and faithful were dependent upon them alike, and obliged to receive their commands and be subject to their authority.

The primary bond of union in the Christian Church was the plenitude of jurisdiction resident in its founders. The source of the union of its parts was the foundation on which it was built—" Built upon the foundation of the apostles." There were, however, within the wide circle of apostolic influence and authority, other combining influences, links and chains which bound together certain numbers of parochial churches, and made them radiate about particular centres of authority before they fell into the common revolution. There were steps in ecclesiastical government. The apostles were the heads of the Church. There were under them those whom we now properly designate by the name "Bishops." Between them and the parochial churches which they founded, there were soon to be seen, though not at the beginning, men few in number at first but possessed of extraordinary powers, to whom, with certain reservations, the plenitude of apostolic authority was communicated.

How soon, or at what precise period the apostles ordained the first bishops of the Church,—those who were to govern conjointly with them, and to transmit their authority to succeeding ages, we cannot with accuracy determine. Timothy and Titus were certainly bishops—the former in Asia Minor, the latter in the island of Crete, about the year sixty-six of the Christian era. This much is apparent from the epistles directed to them by St. Paul.

They were at first the companions of the apostle. They were not ordained bishops until they had travelled some years with the apostle, and laboured much, and until they were well acquainted with the position of Christianity and the circumstances of the Christian congregations.

There is frequent mention of them both in the epistles of St. Paul. Their missions and occupations are referred to, but there is not a single passage which could lead us to think that they were bishops,—placed over certain districts and churches, before the middle of the first century. The erection of their episcopal sees, was not coeval with the appointment of the first presbyters of the churches of Asia; and yet Titus and Timothy appear to have been the first bishops of Crete and Asia Minor, outside the apostolic college. Timothy, for example, was not known to St. Paul until the period of his second journey through the churches of Asia;[1] whereas, he with Barnabas had ordained priests in every church, at the time of their first preaching there.[2]

I remarked before, that in a church essentially one and uniform, it is not too much to suppose that the system of ecclesiastical polity established by the apostles was the same in all parts of the world. The mode of ecclesiastical dependence and government was not different in Africa, in Syria, and in Eastern Europe. We may then assume without danger of error, that the erection of sees, and transmission of the episcopacy in Asia Minor, are a fair illustration of the same events in the different countries in which Christianity was first diffused.

Now what was the system in Asia Minor? From the 14th of the Acts of the Apostles, we have the fact that parishes, or at least churches, presided over by priests, were constituted in Asia Minor, by Paul and Barnabas, about the year of the Christian era 43. The first bishop appointed to govern these churches, outside the college of the apostles, was Timothy, the beloved disciple of St. Paul. If there was a bishop in Asia Minor before Timothy's ordination, it is probable we would have some record of the fact in the writings of the New Testament.

Timothy was bishop in Ephesus, the capital of Lesser Asia, about the year 65. He was stationed in Ephesus. His jurisdiction appears to have extended over all the churches of the country. His powers with respect to the ordination of priests and the promotion of the clergy generally, were very extensive; and we have no mention of a second bishop, contemporary with him, outside the apostolic body enjoying or dividing with him the jurisdiction of the Asiatic churches.

Lesser Asia was originally one bishopric. There were seven bishoprics in Asia Minor, when St. John wrote the Apocalypse; that is to say, sometime after the year 90. The seven angels of the churches referred to in the

---

[1] Acts xvi. 1.   [2] Acts xiv. 22.

2nd and 3rd chapters of that inspired book, were no others than the seven bishops of the cities associated with their names. From the style and tenor in which they are addressed, they are evidently the superiors and governors of their respective churches. They are responsible for the existence of scandals. It is for them to eradicate heresies. They are the pastors of their respective flocks; and yet it is quite clear from the Sacred Scriptures that they were not the only clergy of the superior orders in the cities that they governed. Ephesus, for instance, had several επισκοποι or πρεσβυτεροι as we learn from the Acts of the Apostles. It had a body of presbyters, but one "Angel;" several clergy, who were appointed by the Holy Ghost to govern the flock, but one only who was the responsible representative of the entire church.

Smyrna, too, had its body of clergy, but only one angel, presiding over priests and people. But could this angel of the church of Ephesus or Smyrna have been a simple priest, but enjoying parochial jurisdiction? No! For St. Ignatius designates him by an entirely different name from the others. He was, properly, the επισκοπος, the others were simply πρεσβυτεροι. If he was not a bishop, it would follow that there was no bishop in Asia Minor; for certainly the admonitions in the Apocalypse are addressed to the heads of the churches of Asia Minor. If they were not bishops, there were no bishops there; which in the hypothesis of ordination, in which we consider the question, no one will venture to affirm. The seven churches of Asia Minor mentioned in the Apocalypse, were therefore episcopal churches.

As the churches increased in extent and number, it became absolutely necessary to multiply the episcopal authority numerically. There were seven centres of unity in the year 93, on which depended the parish churches surrounding them respectively. If it be asked who remodelled the ecclesiastical face of the country, we answer the authority which erected the see of Ephesus,—apostolic authority; for St. John was still living,—"the light of the churches of the east." As time goes on, we find the episcopal churches of Asia still increasing in number. Magnesia and Trullis were not episcopal sees when St. John wrote the Apocalypse; yet we find them both sending their priests and bishops to meet St. Ignatius at Smyrna, about the beginning of the second century. Who erected them into episcopal sees,—for the last of the apostles had now retired from the scene? The church which the apostles had founded; and which was now advanced to mature years,—the governing body of the church, to which in his twelve disciples, the Redeemer had given the commission "to bind and loose" with the assurance that "he would be with them all days to the end of the world."

The congregations of Christians were from the middle to the end of the first century, as St. Paul beautifully expresses it in his Epistle to the Ephesians, "Growing up in the head, which is Christ." They were all united in the oneness of their invisible ruler, from whom was derived the power of the episcopacy, by which, as the joints in the human body, they "were compacted and joined together;" for the body and spirit of the church should be one, even as there is "one Lord, one faith, one baptism, one God."[1] And therefore "he gave some apostles . . . some pastors and doctors for the work of the ministry, for the building up of the body of Christ." So far the system of ecclesiastical government in all parts of the church was parochial and episcopal. The presbyters governed the laity; and the bishops governed the laity and the priests. The greater churches governed the lesser; and the country churches radiated from the greater, as from the centres of their life and being, from which their pastors were directed, by which their faith was preserved, to which their respectful obedience was tendered. The system of episcopal government, even as we have it now, was complete and operating; and dioceses, in fact, were fully constituted, though, in name, they did not begin to exist until many years after.

[1] Ephes. iv.

§ 5. *The Head of the Church.*—The characteristic of the Church of God, which is most prominently put forward in the inspired books of the Sacred Scripture, is its unity. It is at one time "a kingdom,"[1] in the language of prophecy. Then it is "a sheep-fold."[2] Now it is "a marriage feast."[3] It is compared successively to "a mountain,"[4] "a fishing-net,"[5] "a tree."[6] Every earthly object to which the Church is likened is such as to give us an idea of oneness, the most complete,—of union, the most inseparable. We in no passage in the Sacred Scripture find the Church represented by objects whose elements are discordant and jar with each other; but everything in it is harmony and all its parts are so "compacted and joined together" that they form one undivided and indivisible whole. In a word, "the body and spirit"[7] of the Church are one with a unity similar to the unity of God.

The Church, as the word εκκλησια by which it is designated in the Sacred Scripture implies, is an assemblage of men, called together for certain definite objects. It is verily and in fact a society; and as it is a society essentially one, it is necessary that its members be well knit together, and consequently there must be some external bonds drawn round the elements of ecclesiastical society, and binding them together into one solid and compact mass. The individuals composing the Church would not form one community if there was no governing head placed over them. Therefore they were united under the jurisdiction of priests. The parishes thus formed would not constitute one society if there was no governing principle to bring them together. Therefore, by the divine ordination, they grouped themselves under the authority of bishops. We want to discover if the principle of union stopped here, and if the scriptural unity of the Church might be sufficiently realized though there was no higher

---

[1] Matt. xiii. 47. [2] John x. [3] Matt. xxii. 2.
[4] Isaias ii. 2. [5] Matt. xiii. 47. [6] Matt. xiii. 47.
[7] Ephes. iv. 45.

ecclesiastical authority to which dioceses should be subject and which bishops should obey.

Certain it is that, in the first century of the Christian era, there was in the Church a power distinct in jurisdiction from the merely episcopal, and above it, to which priests and bishops, and parishes and dioceses were subjected by the ordination of Christ himself.

A glance at the Sacred Scriptures suffices to establish the fact that some very peculiar prerogatives were conferred upon St. Peter, which raised him to a singular eminence in the Church. The texts which occur in reference to his dignity are many; and the force of them is irrefragable; they are unquestionably some of the clearest in their language, and the most unmistakable in their meaning, which we find in the sacred writings. 1st. The Church was built upon him. "And I say to thee," the words of Christ, "that thou art Peter (a rock), and upon this rock I will build my Church."[1] 2nd. He was made the gate-keeper of the kingdom of heaven. "And I will give to thee the keys of the kingdom of heaven."[2]

3rd. To him singularly was granted the power of binding and loosing which was granted to the apostolic body conjointly.[3] "Whatsoever thou shalt bind upon earth it shall be bound also in heaven; and whatsoever thou shalt loose on earth it shall be loosed also in heaven."[4]

4th. He was commissioned to feed the lambs and sheep of the flock of Christ. "When, therefore, they had dined, Jesus said to Simon Peter, Simon, son of John, lovest thou me more than these? He said to him, Yea, Lord, thou knowest that I love thee. He saith to him, Feed my lambs. He saith to him again, Simon, son of John, lovest thou me? He saith to him, Yea, Lord, thou knowest that I love thee. He saith to him, Feed my lambs. He said to him the third time, Simon, son of John, lovest thou me? Peter was grieved, because he had said to him the third time, Lovest thou me? And he said

---

[1] Matt. xvi. 18.   [2] Matt. v. 19.   [3] Matt. xviii. 18.
[4] Matt. xvi. 19.

to him, Lord, thou knowest all things; thou knowest that I love thee. He said to him, Feed my sheep."[1]

5th. Finally he was ordered to confirm his brethren in faith. "Simon, Simon, behold Satan hath desired to have you, that he may sift you as wheat. But I have prayed for thee that thy faith fail not; and thou being once converted confirm thy brethren."[2]

What is the meaning of all these passages of the Sacred Scripture? Could they be interpreted as conferring upon St. Peter a primacy of honour and a precedence of rank, but not a primacy of authority? It is unquestionable that they confer a right to feed the whole flock—"lambs and sheep"—and an unlimited power "to bind and loose," and an authority "to confirm the brethren in faith;" but may the meaning of these expressions simply be—to be first on the list of bishops, and to take precedence at the meetings of the Church? A spiritual pastor, to feed a spiritual flock, must feed them with spiritual food. St. Peter is constituted a spiritual pastor. The food he is appointed to distribute must be instruction in faith and morality. St. Peter was to instruct the flock by the appointment of Christ; and, therefore, his primacy was an active one—a primacy of jurisdiction and authority. But this is not all, the Church was built upon him; he was the rock consolidating the edifice of the Church to such a degree that the opposing power of the kingdom of darkness cannot overthrow it—"The gates of hell cannot prevail against it."[3] How does he support the Church? The Church is a spiritual kingdom; he binds it together by spiritual bonds. He legislates for it; he appoints its governors; he eradicates abuses from it; he unites its parts together; he strengthens it against the enemy without; he preserves it uniform in discipline and unchangeable in faith. Is this the meaning of the Church being built upon Peter? Else why did Christ tell him "to confirm his brethren in faith," or why did he say to him these words so full of active significance—legislate—"Whatsoever thou shalt bind upon

---

[1] John xxi. 15. [2] Luke xxi. 31, 32. [3] Matt. xvii. 18.

earth, it shall be bound also in heaven." St. Peter, beyond all doubt, was first in rank among the apostles. His name occurs frequently in the Sacred Scriptures associated with the names of others of the apostles; and the name of St. Peter is always mentioned first. Peter is the first that opens his mouth to preach to the people after the descent of the Holy Ghost. He is the first that speaks in the council of Jerusalem. He is the first to receive the Gentiles into the Church. He is first in everything. But this is not enough. He was the pastor of the flock—the support of the edifice—the law-giver of the Church—the defender of the faith. Therefore he was the primate of the kingdom of God upon earth—in authority—in jurisdiction—in government.

But a question naturally arises in reference to this conclusion, and an obvious difficulty against the existence of the primacy is discovered in the often repeated assertion that there is no evidence of the exercise of primatial authority in the documents of the primitive Church.

If Peter was primate in authority, where are the records of the exercise of his power?

It must be candidly admitted that there is no *positive* proof in the writings of the New Testament that the power of "binding and loosing" was exercised by St. Peter in the first century in detail after the same manner in which the Roman pontiff exercises it at the present day. The existence of the primatial authority is *positively* demonstrated. The exercise of it can only be inferred. To be sure, we have Peter presiding at the meetings of the apostles. We see him opening the gates of the church to the Gentiles. We find St. Paul going up to Jerusalem to compare his doctrine with Peter's. These are facts which have their own strong significance in pointing out Peter as the actual ruler of the Church. They do not prove that all bishops were appointed by him, or that he enacted general laws, which were binding on *all* the people of God.

But while we allow that the exercise of the primacy in all its details is not *positively* demonstrated, for the first century from contemporary documents, we can affirm with absolute certainty, that there is no positive proof that the primacy at this time was a power, and not a fact. The Scripture is silent about the exercise of it in all its details. What then? Is the silence of the Scripture a positive demonstration? Assuredly not. A positive demonstration is a pile of evidence, assertion, and inference; *præmissæ* and conclusion, the foundation of which is something existing, or supposed to exist, obvious and tangible. And there is no statement in the sacred writings which can be laid down as a foundation upon which a positive argument against the exercise of the primacy in the first century can be firmly, or even safely built. But perhaps the silence of the Sacred Scriptures on the subject is equivalent to a negative demonstration; or, in other words, if the primacy was exercised it must of necessity be mentioned in the sacred writings. In the history of the Acts of the Apostles there is not much about the life or preaching of Peter. The narrative of St. Luke, which is the sole contemporary authority on this subject, is principally taken up with the voyages and labours of Paul. When Peter is mentioned in the first chapter of the Acts, his name is associated with pre-eminence in the Apostolic College—active, as when he speaks first in the meetings of the Church, or honorary and inactive, as when his name is first upon the list of apostles. But when the life of Paul is detailed, or the history of James, where was the necessity for referring to the authority of Peter? Peter might be ruling the Church, and governing all its bishops, and exercising a certain amount of authority over the other apostles, and yet the silence of the Scripture on the subject is perfectly intelligible, as the scope of its writers was manifestly confined within certain limits, and the object of their delineation was a partial, and not a general view of the Church.

There were besides in the primitive Church peculiar circumstances, which, if they did not prevent the exercise of the primacy of Peter altogether, may be reasonably supposed to have rendered the exercise of it in all its details unnecessary. I might almost say impossible. The apostles were not as the bishops of the Church in subsequent times. They were men specially raised up, and enlightened in their capacity of bishops, after a manner extraordinary and supernatural. They could not err in writing. They could not err in believing. They could not err in making laws for the government of the Church. They possessed individually, that which Catholics claim for the whole Church and for its head. They were all and each of them infallible. Peter was the governor of them all; but each of them from the special light and grace that he received from above was irresponsible for the exercise of his ministry, as a founder and governor of the Church. And Peter knew this well. Why, therefore, need he interfere with their appointments of "bishops," or why should we expect to find him recasting their institutions or remodelling their laws? Each of the apostles was in principle subjected to Peter, but in fact, we may suppose him to have been independent in the exercise of his apostolic powers. Did the jurisdiction of bishops, then, come through the apostles, without any reference to the primatial power? Not necessarily, as far as the Scripture is concerned, because the primacy of Peter might have been the fountain of all jurisdiction communicating its effects tacitly, and not overtly, or by express agreement, conferring the plenitude of episcopal authority on all the appointments made by the apostles, without a reference to them individually.

We may suppose, therefore, and our supposition has firm foundation in the Sacred Scripture, that the primacy conferred on St. Peter was given with a view to succeeding ages principally. It was so extensive, and the sphere of its operation was so varied, and its functions were so defined that it was not given as a mere power to be dormant in its original possessor, and then to expire for ever; but as its activi'y as from circumstances restricted in the apostolic age, it was born for times succeeding, to outlive the first century, and to be developed by time, and to grow, in fact, and practice gradually but surely into the mighty proportions assigned it by the lips of wisdom undeceiving and infallible.

DIVISION VI.

THE CLERGY AND THE RITES THEY ADMINISTERED.

Who were the επισκοποι, πρεσβυτεροι, *and* διακονοι?

Protestant Version. (Oxf. 1839.)   *Catholic Version.* (Dublin, 1840.)

"And when they had ordained them *elders* in every church ... they commended them to the Lord."—Acts xiv. 23.

"And when they had ordained to them *priests* in every church .. they commended them to the Lord."—Acts xiv. 22.

"They determined that Paul and Barnabas ... should go up to Jerusalem, unto the apostles and *elders*."—Acts xv. 2.

"They determined that Paul and Barnabas ... should go up to the apostles and *priests* to Jerusalem."—Acts xv. 2.

"Let the *elders* that rule well be counted worthy of double honour."—1 Tim. v. 17.

"Let the *priests* that rule well be esteemed worthy of double honour."—1 Tim. v. 17.

"Against an *elder* receive not an accusation, but before two or three witnesses."—1 Tim. v. 19.

"Against a *priest* receive not an accusation but under two or three witnesses."—1 Tim. v. 19.

"For this cause I left thee in Crete—that thou shouldst ordain *elders* in every city."—Tit. i. 5.

"For this cause I left thee in Crete that thou shouldst .. ordain *priests* in every city."—Tit. i. 5.

"Is any man sick among you? Let him bring in the *elders* of the church."—James v. 14.

"Is any man sick among you? Let him bring in the *priests* of the church."—James v. 14.

"Take heed therefore unto yourselves and to all the flock, over which the Holy Ghost hath made you *overseers*."—Acts xx. 28.

"Take heed to yourselves and to the whole flock wherein the Holy Ghost hath placed you *bishops*."—Acts xx. 28.

"Paul and Timotheus ... to all the saints, with the *bishops* and deacons."—Philippians i. 1.

"Paul and Timothy to all the saints, ... with the bishops and deacons."—Philippians i. 1.

"A bishop then must be blameless."—1 Tim. iii. 2.

"It behoveth therefore a bishop to be blameless."—1 Tim. iii. 2.

Protestant version. (Oxf. 1839.)	Catholic version. (Dublin, 1840.)
"For a bishop must be blameless."—Tit. i. 7.	"For a bishop must be without crime."—Tit. i. 7.
"Paul and Timotheus .... to all the saints ... with the bishops and *deacons*."—Philip. i. 1.	"Paul and Timothy ... to all the saints ... with the bishops and *deacons*."—Philip. i. 1.
"Likewise must the *deacons* be grave."—1 Tim. iii. 8.	"Deacons in like manner be chaste."—1 Tim. iii. 8.
"Let the deacons be the husbands of one wife."—1 Tim. iii. 12.	"Let deacons be the husbands of one wife."—1 Tim. iii. 12.

I give here, in parallel columns, the English Catholic and Protestant translations of the words, *episcopus, presbyter*, and *diaconus*, in all the passages in which they occur in the Sacred Scriptures of the New Testament. From an examination of these texts, it appears that the compilers of the authorized version do not approve of the translation "priest" for πρεσβυτερος, whereas they have no objection to render the words επισκοπος and διακονος "bishops" and "deacons"; whilst the Catholic translators are so far consistent that they depart from the literal meaning in the three cases equally. The word επισκοπος does not *literally* mean a bishop, but an overseer, and the translation the Protestants give it in Acts xx. is in consequence *literally* correct. The word διακονος means literally a minister or distributor. The Scriptural meaning of a word is, however, often different from its literal meaning; and thus it is that, according to the Protestants, two of the words in question, and, according to the Catholics, all three appear in the Scriptures in an English dress in which they would be quite a mystery to those who used them formerly, as parts of their vernacular language. This controversy will have little to say to the question we are now about to discuss, namely, "Who were the clergy of the primitive Church, and what were their functions?" and in reference to it I deem it expedient to make but one or two remarks. 1st. The German word Priester, and the old French word *prêtre*, and the English word *priest*, are all evidently modifications of the word πρεσβυτερος, and they are all used to designate one who offers sacrifice. It would appear, therefore, that the Catholic translators of the Sacred Scriptures into English had a very general usage in their favour when they gave the word "priest" as a proper translation for the word πρεσβυτερος, as it occurs in the New Testament. 2nd. The word πρεσβυτερος occurs eighteen times in the Scriptures of the Old Testament. In all these places it is translated by the Catholic divines of Douay, "ancients," with the exception of the Book of Daniel, where it is invariably translated "elder." If it were similarly translated in the New Testament, it might appear that the πρεσβυτεροι of the primitive Church were the same as the πρεσβυτεροι of the Jews. Now, the πρεσβυτεροι of the Jews are always distinguished from the ιερες, or sacrificing ministers; and they were simply the presidents of the synagogues in the towns of Judea, or the members of the great council of the Sanhedrim at Jerusalem. The πρεσβυτεροι of the primitive Church were not such. Their ordination and functions invested them with quite a different character. It was, then, to say the least of it, reasonable to give the word πρεσβυτερος a different translation in the New Testament from that which it had in the Old; but whether it was properly rendered, "a priest" or a "sacrificing minister," will appear in the sequel of what we are about to say.

Who, then, were the πρεσβυτεροι, επισκοποι, and διακονοι, that are so often mentioned in the Acts of the Apostles, and the writings of St. Paul, and what were their functions? The πρεσβυτεροι, επισκοποι, and διακονοι, in question, were ordained ministers of the primitive Church. In stating that they were ordained ministers, I mean that they received an external rite which conferred upon them an internal grace for the due performance of their functions; or, in other words, that they received the

sacrament of holy orders by which they were consecrated
to the service of religion and the Church. This I believe
to be the first characteristic of the πρεσβυτεροι, επισκοποι, and διακονοι; and I further believe that the
solid grounds of this conviction must be clearly evinced
from an accurate examination of various texts regarding
them which are found in the New Testament. I take here
a sacrament to mean an external rite which confers an
internal grace. In reality, it means more, because an
external rite conferring grace would not be a sacrament,
according to the orthodox view, unless it were instituted
by Christ, destined to be permanent, and producing grace
by virtue of its due performances, as distinguished from
the dispositions of the recipient.

I purposely limit the meaning of the word *sacrament* to
the two characteristics first mentioned, because if they
are shown to have belonged to the ordinations of the
primitive church, the three latter will follow as an easy
consequence. The rite of ordination by which the
επισκοποι, πρεσβυτεροι, and διακονοι were constituted such,
was an *external* rite. Here are numerous examples. St.
Paul, after instructing Timothy as to the qualities of the
men to be ordained, adds—"*Impose not hands* lightly
upon any man, neither be partaker of other men's sins."[1]
The men who are alluded to are designated επισκοποι by
St. Paul, in the second verse of the third chapter of the
same epistle. The ordination of St. Paul and Barnabas
who were επισκοποι and πρεσβυτεροι, is thus announced in
the Acts of the Apostles. "Then they fasting and
praying, and *imposing hands* upon them, sent them away."[2]
Then we have the ordination of the διακονοι in the sixth
chapter of the Acts of the Apostles. "These they
set before the apostles; and they praying *imposed hands*
upon them."[3] Timothy, an επισκοπος, is reminded of his
ordination by St. Paul. "Neglect not the grace that is
in thee, which was given thee by prophecy with *imposition
of the hands* of the priesthood."[4] And again, the same to

[1] 1 Tim. v. 22.   [2] Acts xiii. 8.   [3] Acts vi. 6.   [4] 1 Tim. iv. 14.

the same: "For which cause I admonish thee, that thou stir up the grace of God which is in thee by the *imposition of my hands*."[1] The concurrent testimony of these passages shows us beyond all doubt that "imposition of hands," an eminently external and visible economy, was a principal part of the rite by which the επισκοποι, πρεσβυτεροι, and διακονοι of the primitive Church were ordained. But this external rite conferred an internal permanent grace. This is quite evident from the two last texts quoted. "Neglect not *the grace that is in thee*, which was given thee by prophecy with imposition of the hands of the priesthood."[2] What is the meaning of this passage? Timothy's ordination arose from prophetic warnings touching him vouchsafed to St. Paul. This is evident from another passage in the same epistle, which is as follows:— "This precept I commend to thee, O son Timothy, according to *the prophecies going before on* thee that thou war in them a good warfare."[3] Timothy was ordained by imposition of hands, and the result of this external rite in his case, was a grace which continued in his soul permanently. What was this grace? Clearly it was something invisible, because it was "in Timothy," that is to say, in his soul. But what was this grace in itself? The Greek texts designate it χαρισμα (a gift, donum). But what was this gift? It was no other than that which our Lord conferred upon the twelve apostles at their ordination, when he said, breathing upon them, "Receive ye the Holy Ghost."[4] Timothy then received the Holy Ghost by his ordination. So did all πρεσβυτεροι and επισκοποι similiarly ordained. To receive the Holy Ghost in scriptural language, means to receive sanctifying or sacramental grace which are specially attributed to Him. Therefore the επισκοποι and πρεσβυτεροι of the primitive Church received the internal gift of sacramental and sanctifying grace through the external ceremony by which they are ordained. Lest we should have any doubt that the χαρισμα here referred to

[1] 2 Tim. i. 6.
[2] 1 Tim. iv. 14.
[3] 1 Tim. i. 18.
[4] John xx. 22.

means sanctifying grace, St. Paul uses a word in relation to it, in his Second Epistle, which must satisfy any reasonable mind. "For which cause I admonish thee, that thou *stir up* the grace of God which is in thee by the imposition of my hands."¹ The grace or gift is such that it may be *stirred up*. The Greek word so translated is αναξω- πυρειν, which means "to blow up embers slumbering and buried in ashes." Such a word can be properly applied to sanctifying or sacramental grace, which is a habit permanently residing in the soul—there sleeping, as it were, when not applied to use—there covered as it were and hidden, because not sensibly affecting the soul with a consciousness of its presence. As it is most natural and appropriate to apply this word to sanctifying and sacramental grace, as it is understood by Catholic divines, and most inappropriate to apply it to any other "donum" to which St. Paul could possibly refer, we are constrained to conclude that the χαρισμα of which there is question means the internal grace of the episcopacy or priesthood, which is grace supernatural, sanctifying and sacramental. The πρεσβυτεροι and επισκοποι were unquestionably ordained ministers of the Church. They were not seculars or laics; but they had the grace of their ordination perpetually abiding in their souls, which distinguished them from others, not externally or before the world, but internally and before God; and invisibly to men they were stamped with a sacred character which fitted them for the functions of their state. Let us take a clergyman so ordained, and examine him in respect to his tenure of office, and the source of his ecclesiastical authority. Once ordained could he minister where he pleased? He was ordained a presbyter at Antioch. Could he preach and minister in Jerusalem or Cesarea according to his fancy? Was his character, as governor of a Christian flock, completed in the act by which he was ordained? Could he lead an inert and stay-at-home life, if he was so disposed? Or if taste and inclination so dictated was it competent

---

¹ 2 Tim. i. 6.

to him to become an ecclesiastical traveller, disposing of his wares along by the banks of the Jordan, or up towards the source of the Nile? He preached in Antioch after his ordination, with the approval and authority of Paul or Timothy, who ordained him. Could he, without their authority, and against their positive orders, baptize in Berea, or perform some other ecclesiastical function in Syria, Pisidia or Greece? In other words, besides ordination, was authority or jurisdiction necessary for him, in order that he could validly, or at least licitly, perform his functions as a Christian teacher or administrator, or governor of a Christian flock. The question is an important one. It involves such details as the following:—Did a given Christian flock appoint him to be their minister? Or did he appoint himself, or was he appointed to his position by ecclesiastical authority residing in the apostles and their successors? He is orthodox in faith. He is blameless in morals; but he is obstinate and dogged in disposition. Peter wishes to remove him from Bethlehem to Pella, or Paul desires to transfer him from Thessalonica to Athens. He won't go. He loves Athens, or the flock at Bethlehem loves him. He will minister where he is of his own authority, or that of his flock who choose him, and he will hold his authority, independent of Paul or Peter, Titus or Timothy. Does he, by the fact of so doing, lose all authority to minister in the Church, and is his flock bound to withdraw its allegiance from him? To answer these questions, fraught with interest and importance, it will be necessary to trace to its very source the spiritual authority that existed in the primitive Church. The authority of our Lord Jesus Christ first, then the apostles, then their successors or the επισκοποι and πρεσβυτεροι they appointed. The Redeemer tells us in the gospel that He was sent by his eternal Father. Again and again He refers to His *commission* to announce salvation to the world. He did not come of himself, but as the envoy of one whom He declares to be "greater than Himself," the first Person of the Most Holy Trinity. "I was not *sent* but to the lost sheep of the house of

G

Israel."[1] "And last of all He *sent* to them His Son."[2] "I am not alone, but I and the Father that *sent* me."[3] "And the Father that *sent me* giveth testimony of me."[4] "But He that *sent* me is true."[5] "For I came not of myself but he *sent* me."[6] Being sent forth from the bosom of His eternal Father to unfold the new law and lay the foundation of Christianity, He *sent* forth His Apostles to announce the Gospel to the world. He *sent* them; they were his commissioned officers. "These twelve (the Apostles) Jesus *sent*, saying: go ye not into the way of the Gentiles."[7] "Behold I *send* you as sheep in the midst of wolves."[8] And lecturing these same twelve on the humility with which they should behave towards each other, he says, as recorded in the gospel of St. John, "For I have given you an example, that as I have done to you, so you do also, Amen, Amen. I say to you: The servant is not greater than his master: neither is the apostle greater than He that *sent* him."[9] And finally in one of His last and most solemn interviews with the twelve after His resurrection, He identifies the mission He gives them with the mission He had received from His Father. "Peace be to you. As the Father hath *sent* me, I also *send* you?"[10] The Apostles were thus practically initiated to the necessity of a designation and commission from a higher spiritual power for any and every ordained person entering upon the ministry of the gospel. Hear St. Paul upon the subject. "How shall they (the Jews) call on Him in whom they have not believed? Or how shall they believe Him, of whom they have not heard? And how shall they hear without a preacher? And how shall they preach unless they be *sent?*"[11] The doctrine of the apostle is general; it applies to all; it admits of no exception. Without a commission from superior authority no preacher is to be listened to. No wonder that St.

---

[1] Matt. xv. 24. [2] Matt. xxi. 37. [3] John viii. 16.
[4] John viii. 18. [5] John viii. 26. [6] John viii. 42.
[7] Matt. x. 5. [8] Matt. x. 16. [9] John xiii. 15, 16.
[10] John xx. 22. [11] Romans x. 14, 15.

Paul so taught, for in his own case, inspired lips had declared that a " mission," or a being sent by ecclesiastical authority, was being sent by the Holy Ghost Himself. "And as they were ministering to the Lord, and fasting, the Holy Ghost said to them : Separate to me Saul (Paul) and Barnabas for the work whereunto I have taken them. Then they, fasting and praying, and imposing their hands upon them, *sent* them away. So they being *sent* by the Holy Ghost went to Seleucia."¹ These passages are quite sufficient to convince any reasonable mind that the authority to govern and tend the Christian flock in the early times originated in Heaven, and was transferred through the founder and rulers of the Church. The suffrages of a Christian village did not render a πρεσβυτερος or επισκοπος, a legitimate minister; nor dare he, on his own authority, assume any ecclesiastical function. It was the authority of his superiors that gave him a place to occupy, and a church to tend, and without the exercise of this authority his position was an anomaly and his ministrations unlawful or null.

The limits of ecclesiastical jurisdiction I will not yet undertake to define. Its moveability or immoveability, I do not now propose to discuss. A judge would be a legitimate expounder of the law, if the legislature appointed him to administer justice for a time, and within a very limited territory. During the period of his commission his acts would be valid within the limits of his jurisdiction; but if a lawyer, without any authority from the state, mounted the bench and put on the ermine, and imposed fines, and inflicted penalties, he would render himself an object, not of respect but of contempt; and instead of the obedience of the multitude he would earn its derision. So to be an επισκοπος in the early Church, it was necessary to have a definite appointment and a distinct commission from superior ecclesiastical authority; though for what we yet see, the latter might be terminable and restricted; but to assume the episcopacy by private

---

¹ Acts xiii. 2, 3, 4.

authority, or without any authority, was unlawful; and to take it away unduly amounted to a veritable act of injustice.

This is the sole point that I intend to establish by the united force of the Scripture texts I have given. It is further and strongly confirmed by a passage which occurs in the 1st Epistle of St. Clement, written about the beginning of the second century.

"The Apostles have preached the gospel to us on the part of Jesus Christ, and Jesus Christ has preached on the part of God. God *sent* Jesus Christ, and Jesus Christ *sent* the Apostles. . . . . So preaching in the country and cities did they establish the first fruits, or first converts (primitiæ), among them, as bishops and deacons of those who believed. . . . . Our Apostles, enlightened by our Lord Jesus Christ, have well known that there would be a contest for the name of the episcopacy. Wherefore they established the aforesaid, and they have given orders that, after their death, other approved men should succeed to their ministry. These, therefore, who have been established by them, or afterwards by other distinguished men, with the consent of all the Church, and who have tended the flock of Jesus Christ, humbly, peaceably, and without reproach, to whom all have rendered good testimony for a long time. These we believe it not just to repel from the ministry." [1]

It is evident, then, that the ἐπισκοποι and πρεσβυτεροι of the primitive Church were invested with a sacred character by the sacrament of orders which they received, and that they were endowed with authority to preach the gospel and administer spiritual things, by receiving a "mission" from the Apostles or their immediate successors. Without ordination they would have been simply laymen. Without jurisdiction their spiritual action, even though they were ordained, would have been invalid in some instances, and in all cases illicit and criminal. This however gives us but a very partial view of

[1] 1 Ep. Clem. Rom. No. 44, p. 112, F. ed. Cot.

their character; and we have yet to ask—What were their employments and functions, and what were the fruits accruing to the churches in which they ministered, from those radical powers implanted in them by the right reception of the sacrament of holy orders, and matured by a legitimate mission from the divinely-constituted authorities of the Church of God upon earth?

What were the duties, powers, and functions of the πρεσβυτεροι, επισκοποι, and διακονοι?

This will be an appropriate place to consider, as far as rational conjecture founded upon the Sacred Scriptures will allow us, why it was that these names were given by the Apostles to the ordained ministers, or clergy of the Church; for a name denoting a species or class is frequently derived from the employment common to its members.

In the first place, I must state my belief that no stress is to be laid upon the words πρεσβυτερος and επισκοπος, as distinguishing different orders of the hierarchy in the writings of the New Testament. The grounds of this belief are easily discernible. St. Paul, in his Epistle to Titus, designates the same men by both names in the following passage:—"For this cause I left thee in Crete, that thou shouldst set in order the things that are wanting, and shouldst ordain priests (πρεσβυτερους) in every city, as I also appointed thee. . . . . . For a bishop (επισκοπος) must be without crime."[1] The same occurs in St. Luke's narration of Paul's parting interview with the clergy of the Church of Ephesus. "And sending from Miletus, he called the ancients (πρεσβυτερους, Greek text) of the Church. And when they were come to him, and were together, he said to them. . . . . Take heed to yourselves, and to the whole flock, wherein the Holy Ghost hath placed you bishops (επισκοπους) to rule the Church of God."[2] Further it is observable that St. Peter employs both titles in reference even to the apostleship. "For (said he, speaking of the apostacy and fall of Judas)

---

[1] Ep. to Titus i. 5—7.   [2] Acts xx. 17, 18.

it is written in the Book of Psalms, let their habitation become desolate, and let there be none to dwell therein, and his bishopric (ἐπισκοπὴν αὐτοῦ) let another take."[1] And speaking in the first person in one of his epistles he designates himself a priest. "The ancients, therefore, that are among you, I beseech, who am myself an ancient (συμπρεσβύτερος)."[2]

Though both appellations were used indiscriminately by the writers of the New Testament to designate the same men, there is yet no doubt that they were used for a different purpose, and they pointed to different qualities. The duty of the clergyman as an ἐπίσκοπος was, as St. Paul says, "To rule the Church of God, which he had purchased with his own blood."[3] As a πρεσβύτερος he was a senior of the Church, not precisely in years, but in wisdom and vocation to the faith, for, as St. Paul says in another place, "Not a neophyte: lest being puffed up with pride, he fall into the judgment of the devil."[4]

Not without some alarm perhaps, it will be observed that, in endeavouring to discover the powers and occupations of the primitive clergy, I attach but little importance to the interpretation of their names. Yet so it is. Call them elders if you wish, or ancients, inspectors or overseers, priests or bishops, you do not bend the scale of controversy to one side or the other. In my opinion they were ancients, inspectors, overseers, elders, bishops, and priests, all together, if they belonged to the first order of the clergy. If they belonged to the second order of the hierarchy, they were elders, ancients, and priests.[5]

The clergy of both orders were sacrificing priests; but I would not conclude as much from the fact that they were denominated presbyters. The word presbyter was most

[1] Acts i. 20. [2] 1 Peter v. 1.
[3] Acts xx. 28. [4] 1 Tim. iii. 6.

[5] Still I freely admit that there is a very distinct meaning given to the word ἐπίσκοπος in the tradition of the Church from the beginning of the second century, when it began to be applied to the episcopal office exclusively.

appropriately used to designate them for many reasons: *first*, because they were the elders in the faith of the Christian congregation to which they belonged; *secondly*, because they were the most advanced in wisdom; *thirdly*, because they were the presidents at the religious meetings of the congregations to which they were attached. The use of the words πρεσβυς, πρεσβυειν, to designate a man advanced in years and wisdom, is common in the classical authors. So much so, that the latter word, which literally means *to act the old man*, is employed by Xenophon[1] to designate the function or office of a counsellor or ambassador. Then the word πρεσβυτερος is frequently used in the Old Testament as an appellation of the venerable men who presided over the synagogues in the cities of Judea. It was such uses of the word as these, and its proper application in all these senses to the clergy of the Church they had founded, that justified the Apostles in denominating πρεσβυτερους those whom they ordained and sent. It would be folly to suppose that the Apostles, on entering into a town or city, and converting a few or many of the Jews or Greeks, immediately assumed some of these converts to a share in the "ministry of the Word." The newly baptized had neither knowledge or prudence enough; they were not sufficiently tested and approved to be raised to so high a dignity. The consequence was that a church was in a state of probation for a while; it heard again and again the preaching, admonitions, and instructions of the Apostles; it attended to the explanations of the Scriptures: in a word, it grew in knowledge and wisdom, and became confirmed in faith and piety, before it had a clergy placed over it, selected from its own members. Then when a given church was sufficiently advanced, its clergy were selected, not from the young, or thoughtless, or giddy, but from the elders of the congregation—from those who had been longest converted—who had heard for the longest time the instruction of the Apostles, and who had become confirmed in virtue and

---

[1] Xen. Anab. lib. ii. p. 74, Glavani, 1817.

knowledge. If these qualities could be found in the somewhat advanced in years, and in many cases undoubtedly they could, they gave a prior claim to the dignity of the priesthood; for, in a society which was full of wickedness, where all the passions had freely raged and swelled, among men whose days had been spent in immorality and general sensuality, it was a matter of much importance to select, as the "models of the flock," "the teachers," the guides, the rulers of the congregation, men in whom the heat and passions of youth were naturally beginning to subside. For many reasons, then, they were designated presbyters. They were elders perhaps in years; they were elders in wisdom; elders in rank, position, and authority; elders in piety, and elders in the faith. If they were sacrificing priests, some one asks, Why were they not rather designated $\iota\epsilon\rho\epsilon\iota\varsigma$? It is for the Apostles to answer this question; for us it is sufficient to say that they were in their age, their position, and their character, congruities which rendered the name $\pi\rho\epsilon\sigma$-$\beta\upsilon\tau\epsilon\rho\sigma\varsigma$ peculiarly applicable to them.

From all that has been said, it is clear that the duties and offices of the clergy of the primitive Church cannot be adequately determined from their names. No doubt the Apostles would not have called them by the name $\pi\rho\epsilon\sigma\beta\upsilon\tau\epsilon\rho\sigma\varsigma$, a name quite familiar to the Jews, unless, like the presbyters of the Jewish cities, they were appointed to certain spiritual functions, such as to preside at the meetings of the Church, to take a leading part in its religious deliberations. Unquestionably, too, the appellation $\epsilon\pi\iota\sigma\kappa\sigma\pi\sigma\varsigma$ could not be given them, unless a close inspection of the faith and morals of the flock was in their case a duty or a right; yet giving to these, their scriptural titles, all the significance that they may be reasonably supposed to have, who does not see that the knowledge of them thereby acquired is partial, confused, and unsatisfactory? Failing, then, to discover a perfect image of all that they did, and a clear reflection of their lives and duties in this source, we must open a new well of scriptural knowledge, where by minute and careful examination we may hope to find the picture that we look for strongly and clearly traced.

A convert from Paganism entering the primitive Church saw about as much of the functions and prerogatives[1] of the επισκοποι, διακονοι, and πρεσβυτεροι, as the foregoing remarks have unveiled to our view; but, as time went on, and his acquaintance with the Christian doctrine increased, and spiritual requirements founded upon it, and its corresponding advance in fervour began to exist, he experienced at the hands of these "leaders of the flock" a series of ministrations which completed his knowledge of their sacred character. He had perhaps been taught from the very beginning of his conversion to account of them as the "ministers of Christ," and the "dispensers of the mysteries of God;" and he learned the force and meaning of these words by attendance at public worship and the gradual and successive reception of the sacraments which were administered by them to him.

Let us follow him into the Apostolic Church.

§ 2. *Baptism.*—He was converted from Paganism by the Cross. No human inducement influenced his change of mind, for in becoming a Christian he was to pass from all that was free and sensual in belief and practice to hard and difficult ways. The faith of the Redeemer had been preached to him plainly: its truth was demonstrated by reason, history, Scripture. It was confirmed by the fulfilment of prophecy and by miracles past and occurring. He was attracted by the grace of the Most High. Finally, he consented to become a Christian, following the light of that eternal spark that God had implanted in his soul. Thus he came to the Apostles, and when under the influence of strong and newly-awakened religious feelings, he said to them, in words of tremulous earnestness,— "What shall we do, men and brethren?"[2] They answered,

---

[1] See Appendix.   [2] Acts ii. 37.

—" Do penance, and be baptized, every one of you, in the name of the Lord Jesus, for the remission of your sins."[1] For the Apostolic Church believed that the administration of baptism was of *precept*, and that its reception was *necessary for salvation*. Christ had given the precept. "Going, therefore, teach all nations: baptizing them in the name of the Father, and of the Son, and of the Holy Ghost."[2] These were his last words to his Apostles. Christ had laid down the doctrine of the indispensable necessity of baptism for all. "Amen, amen, I say to you —(His words)—unless a man be born again of water and the Holy Ghost, he cannot enter into the Kingdom of God. That which is born of the flesh is flesh: and that which is born of the spirit is spirit."[3] To enter into the kingdom of heaven according to this teaching is to be spiritualized—that is to say—to be purified, justified, sanctified, glorified. Else why does the Redeemer add the words at once explanatory and demonstrative, "That which is born of the flesh is flesh; and that which is born of the spirit is spirit"? Consequently, "the Kingdom of God" in this passage does not mean the external body of believers in Christ's doctrine upon earth—a signification which the words sometimes have in the writings of the New Testament, but the assemblage of the glorified in heaven, or the assemblage of the sanctified on earth. No one can be admitted to sanctity and glory unless through baptism. It was therefore rightly inferred that baptism is absolutely necessary unto salvation. And this conclusion accorded most perfectly with the doctrine of the Redeemer in another passage, when having commanded the Apostles to administer baptism to their converts, he added, "He that believeth and is baptized shall be saved."[4] The Pagan convert then entering the Christian Church, was baptized, that is to say, he was washed with water. Like the eunuch, mentioned in the 8th chapter of the Acts of the Apostles, he "went down into the water," or,

[1] Acts ii. 38. [2] Matt. xxviii. 19.
[3] John iii. 5, 6. [4] Mark xvi. 16.

like the Gentile converts, referred to in the 10th chapter, water was brought and applied to him. An external ceremony was gone through in his regard, which consisted in a mundatory[1] application of water, and the invocation[c] of the three persons of the Godhead, and the result of this ceremony was an internal "cleansing"[3] of the soul, "the remission of his sins,"[4] and a "new and spiritual birth"[5] of grace and sanctity.

It was one of the functions of the επισκοποι, πρεσβυτεροι, and διακονοι to administer the sacrament of baptism. The Apostles, who, as I stated before, were both επισκοποι and πρεσβυτεροι, were commanded to baptize, and this command they fulfilled in person, as we learn from various passages in the Acts of the Apostles. The administration of baptism by διακονοι is illustrated in the history of Philip, the διακονος, related at length by St. Luke.

§ 3.—*Imposition of hands.*—How soon after baptism a second rite was administered to the Pagan convert it would be difficult to state with accuracy; but certain it is, that all who were made members of the Church by baptism were subsequently submitted to another sacred process, which the apostolic writings designate the "imposition of hands." The doctrine of the "imposition of hands" was an elementary truth of the Christian faith. It was impressed upon the convert as a fundamental principle at the beginning of his conversion. It formed a part of his catechism.

St. Paul classes it with the "doctrine of baptism . . . . of the resurrection of the dead and of eternal judgment." "Wherefore," he says, "leaving the word of the beginning of Christ, let us go on to things more perfect, not laying again the foundation of penance from dead works, and of faith towards God, of the doctrine of baptism, and

---

[1] Heb. x. 22.   [2] Matt. xxviii. 19.   [3] Ephes. v. 26.
[4] Acts ii. 17.   [5] John iii. 5, 6.

imposition of hands, and of the resurrection of the dead, and of eternal judgment."[1] The theory of it was a portion of the Christian alphabet in the apostolic times; the practical reception of it was of imperative and indispensable necessity. So 'much so indeed, that we find the apostles, Peter and John, undertaking a journey from Jerusalem to Samaria for no other purpose but to administer it to the newly baptized. "Now when the Apostles who were in Jerusalem, had heard that Samaria had received the word of God; they sent unto them Peter and John. Who when they were come, prayed for them, that they might receive the Holy Ghost. For he was not yet come upon any of them: but they were only baptized in the name of the Lord Jesus. Then *they laid their hands upon them*, and they received the Holy Ghost."[2] Hands were imposed upon the convert from Paganism or Judaism, that he might through this ceremony "receive the Holy Ghost." As it is a favourite theory of Protestant controversialists that the descent of the Holy Ghost upon the early Christian *laity*, meant nothing more than the collation of miraculous gifts, such as tongues, prophecy, &c.; and as they are in the habit of affirming that this "dwelling with the faithful" in scriptural language implies neither more nor less than the presence of the *external* operations of his power; it will be well to gather here and represent to ourselves together the various passages of the New Testament illustrative of this subject. If I mistake not, they will prove to us very clearly that when the Holy Spirit is there said to come upon a person, or to abide with a person, the meaning is that he takes up his abode by charity in his heart—that the dwelling of the Holy Ghost in the soul is different from the dwelling there of his outward gifts—that he dwells there as an operative principle, the source of power and virtue.

"And he (John the Baptist) shall drink no wine nor strong drink; and *he shall be filled with the Holy Ghost*, even from his mother's womb."[3] Again, "And behold

---

[1] Heb. vi. 1, 2, 3.   [2] Acts viii. 14—17.   [3] Luke i. 15.

there was a man in Jerusalem named Simon, and this man was just and devout, waiting for the consolation of Israel: and the *Holy Ghost was in him.*"[1] From the tenor, expression, and bearing of these passages it is obvious that the Holy Ghost abides with the just, so as to increase his holiness and to perfect his charity. Again, we have examples of the Holy Ghost dwelling in the soul as the source of sanctity and fortitude. "Receive ye the Holy Ghost: whose sins you shall forgive, they are forgiven them."[2] "But you shall receive the power of the Holy Ghost coming upon you, and you shall be witnesses to me in Jerusalem and in all Judea and Samariah, and even to the uttermost parts of the earth."[3] Then the dwelling of the Holy Ghost in the soul is something distinct from the habits of supernatural virtue. "Wherefore, brethren, look ye out among you seven men of good reputation, full of the Holy Ghost and wisdom, whom we may appoint over this business."[4] "And they chose Stephen, a man full of faith and of the Holy Ghost."[5] In such passages as these it is observable that the Holy Ghost, abiding with the Christian, is as internal, as intimate to him, as much in his soul, as the virtues that he possesses, or the good qualities that adorn him. Other passages or rather all the passages on the subject that can be culled from the Sacred Scriptures, only tend to strengthen the conviction that the dwelling of the Holy Ghost with the Christian soul is something different from the dwelling of his gifts, whether internal, as of faith or charity, or external, as of miracles or prophecy. "For he (Barnabas) was a good man and full of the Holy Ghost and of faith."[6] "Because the charity of God is poured forth in our hearts by the Holy Ghost who is given to us."[7] "And the manifestation of the Spirit is given to every man unto profit. To one, indeed, by the Spirit, is given the word of wisdom: and to another, the word of knowledge, according to the

---

[1] Luke ii. 25.   [2] John xx. 22, 23.   [3] Acts i. 8.
[4] Acts vi. 3.   [5] Acts vi. 5.   [6] Acts xi. 24.
[7] Romans v. 5.

same Spirit: to another faith in the same Spirit: to another the grace of healing in one Spirit. . . . . But all these things, one and the same Spirit worketh, dividing to every one according as he will."[1] This last passage especially is of great importance when contrasted with the text from the 8th chapter of the Acts, on which Catholic divines rely so much as proving the existence of the sacrament of confirmation in these primitive times. According to the latter text the Samaritans "received the Holy Ghost," whose presence was made manifest by miraculous gifts; according to the text just quoted, these miraculous gifts "of wisdom," "of knowledge," "of healing," "of faith," are not the dwelling of the Holy Spirit, but the effects of his dwelling in the Christian's soul. When, therefore, the Samaritans are said to have received the Holy Ghost, and his external gifts, there is no reason for believing that the former was received by attribution only and the latter in effect, but, on the contrary, that both were received—the former as the operating principle, the latter as the work of his power dwelling in the midst of the soul. To receive the Holy Ghost is, then, to receive the Holy Ghost and nothing else, just as to receive faith is to receive faith. To receive the Holy Ghost, as the words imply, is to receive the spirit of sanctification—to be sanctified. By the imposition of hands the Holy Ghost was received in the primitive Church, that is to say, sanctity was received. Gifts of prophecy were received, too? Yes! but sanctity all the time. Gifts of prophecy, miraculous gifts, were received with the Holy Ghost in two cases, as we learn from the Sacred Scriptures,—by the Samaritans, as recorded in the 8th chapter of the Acts of the Apostles, and by the Ephesians, as recorded in the 9th chapter of the same book. If they were received on other occasions when hands were imposed, we know not; but of this we are certain, that hands were imposed upon all, and that the principal effect, that is, the presence of the Holy Spirit in the soul, remained permanently.

[1] 1 Cor. xii. 7.

"Now," says St. Paul, "he that confirmeth us with you in Christ, and that hath anointed us, is God: Who hath also sealed us, and *given the pledge of the Spirit in our hearts.*"[1] "Or know you not, that your members are the temples of the Holy Ghost, who *is in you*, whom you have from God?"[2] "And in this we know *that he abideth in us, by the Spirit which he hath given us.*"[3] "And grieve not the Holy Spirit of God: *whereby you are sealed unto the day of redemption.*"[4]

Here then is a second rite administered in the primitive Church, visible in itself, consisting in the "imposition of hands," invisible in its primary effect; that is the collation of the Holy Spirit in the soul of the recipient. It was not competent to the διακονοι to administer it, otherwise Philip might have conferred it himself upon the Samaritans without bringing the Apostles from Jerusalem; nor to the clergy of the second order, as far as we can discover in the Acts of the Apostles, but to Paul in person, or Peter, or John, who were at the same time πρεσβυτεροι and επισκοποι. "And it came to pass while Apollo was at Corinth, that Paul, having passed through the upper coasts, came to Ephesus, and found certain disciples: and he said to them: Have you received the Holy Ghost since you believed? But they said to him: We have not so much as heard if there be a Holy Ghost. And he said: In what then were you baptized? Who said: In John's baptism. Then Paul said, John baptized the people with the baptism of penance, saying: That they should believe in him who was to come after him, that is to say, Jesus. Having heard these things they were baptized in the name of the Lord Jesus. And when Paul had imposed his hands on them, the Holy Ghost came upon them."[5]

§ 4. *The Eucharist.*—In the lapse of time, not at once, but at the expiration of a reasonable period after his aggre-

---

[1] 2 Cor. i. 21, 22.   [2] 1 Cor. vi. 19.   [3] 1 Ep. of St. John iii. 24.
[4] Ephes. iv. 30.   [5] Acts xix. 1—6.

gation to the faithful, our convert was admitted to the Eucharist. The Eucharist was most holy. The reception of it ought to be preceded by decency, and accompanied by solemnity. All frivolity and disorder ought to be banished from the church in which it was administered. A clean conscience and a pure mind were alone worthy of it; and so imperatively necessary was holiness in the receiver, that to eat or drink the Eucharist unworthily was in the first place to be guilty of treason against the King of Kings; secondly, to be punished by visible judgments in this life, and finally, to fall under the sentence of eternal reprobation. All this is affirmed by St. Paul in his First Epistle to the Church of Corinth.

He reproves them for their dissensions and irreverence in the church. "I hear that when you come together in the church, there are schisms among you. . . . When you come together into one place, it is not now to eat the Lord's Supper. For every one taketh before his own supper to eat. And one indeed is hungry, and another is drunk. What! have you not houses to eat and to drink in? Or despise you the church of God, and put them to shame that have not? What shall I say of you? Do I praise you? In this I praise you not!"[1] He points to the doctrine of the Redeemer at the institution of the Eucharist as a conclusive argument in favour of respect and reverence in the church. "For I have received of the Lord, that which also I delivered to you, that the Lord Jesus, the same night in which he was betrayed, took bread: and giving thanks, broke and said: Take ye and eat: this is my body, which shall be delivered for you: this do for the commemoration of me. In like manner also the chalice, after he had supped, saying, this chalice is the new testament in my blood: this do ye, as often as you shall drink, for the commemoration of me. For as often as you shall eat this bread, and drink the chalice, you shall show the death of the Lord, until he come."[2] He is not satisfied with the grounds of respect and reverence to

---

[1] 1 Cor. xi. 18—22.   [2] 1 Cor. xi. 23—26.

the Church deducible from the fact, that in it the rite is administered by which the passion and death of the Redeemer are commemorated; but he manifestly argues as follows,—they who so dishonour the Church receive the Eucharist unworthily; they who receive the Eucharist unworthily are guilty of treason against the body and blood of the Lord, and in eating it partake of their own damnation. " Therefore whosoever shall eat this bread and drink the chalice of the Lord unworthily, shall be guilty of the body and blood of the Lord. But let a man prove himself, and so let him eat of the bread and drink of the chalice; for he that eateth and drinketh unworthily eateth and drinketh judgment to himself, not discerning the body of the Lord." [1] And as a farther consequence of his conduct the unworthy receiver is sometimes subjected to temporal calamities and visible punishments. "Therefore there are many infirm and weak among you, and many sleep." [2] This is the doctrine of St. Paul on the Eucharist. Does it demonstrate conclusively the nature of that Sacrament?

The points that may be adduced in favour of a spiritual or figurative presence of the Redeemer in the Eucharist, are the following:—1st. The mystery is, according to St. Paul, "*a commemoration*," which shows the death of the Lord until he come. 2nd. It is denominated bread, even after its consecration. "For as often as you shall eat this *bread.*" In favour of the real presence of Christ in the Eucharist there are these:—1st. It is, according to St. Paul, the identical body which was delivered up to the executioners and the painful death of the cross ("this is my body *which shall be delivered for you*"). 2nd. It is a testamentary gift in the blood of Christ ("This chalice is the *New Testament in my blood*"). 3rd. The profanation of the Eucharist is the crime of treason which in ordinary language means not a violation of a picture, or statue, or representation of royalty, but of the *person* of the king ("Whosoever shall eat this bread or drink this chalice unworthily, shall be *guilty of the body and blood of the*

---

[1] 1 Cor. xi. 27—29.   [2] 1 Cor. xi. 30.

Lord"). 4th. And is punished with temporal chastisements in this life and an unfavourable judgment in the next ("For he that eateth and drinketh unworthily, *eateth and drinketh judgment to himself*, not discerning the body of the Lord. Therefore *there are many infirm and weak among you, and many sleep"*). If we compare these points, we can have little doubt that the doctrine of the real presence is involved in the teaching of St. Paul. We can scarcely conceive how an insult to a mere type of the passion could be denominated treason against the body and blood of the Lord; and it is difficult to understand why the profanation of bread and wine should be punished so rigorously in the present life and for ever. Then why denominate the sacred elements "the body of Christ" and "the New Testament in his blood," if they are not so, but figures of them. On the other hand, in the supposition of the real presence, the Eucharistic mysteries most strikingly commemorate the Passion. And even the words "unless you eat this bread," used in reference to the body of Christ, offer no great difficulty, as the appearance of bread still remaining, the substance may be fairly designated by that, whose taste, and form, and colour it retains. But it is desirable while on this great subject of the real presence, to grasp at once and represent to ourselves conjointly all the passages in the New Testament which touch upon this mystery, rather than to contract our view of it by dwelling upon the arguments for and against it, founded on insulated texts.

Here is the plain and broad picture of the subject:—

The blessed Eucharist is foretold, promised, and the necessity of receiving it is insisted upon long before its institution. "*The bread that I will give you is my flesh*" (the words are of the Redeemer) for the life of the world. The Jews, therefore, strove among themselves, saying, how can this man give us his flesh to eat? Then Jesus said to them: Amen, amen, I say unto you: *except you eat the flesh of the Son of Man, and drink his blood*, you shall not have life in you. He that *eateth my flesh and drinketh my blood* hath everlasting life; and I will raise him up on the last day. For *my flesh is meat indeed;* and my blood is drink indeed. He that *eateth my flesh and drinketh my blood* abideth in me and I in him. As the living Father hath sent me, and I live by the Father, so he *that eateth me,* the same also shall live by me."[1]

The words of promise are clear and strong in favour of the real presence. I hasten to the words of fulfilment. "And whilst they were at supper (St. Matthew) Jesus took bread, and blessed, and broke, and gave to his disciples, and said, take ye and eat: *this is my body.* And taking the chalice, he gave thanks, and gave to them, saying: drink ye all of this. For *this is my blood of the New Testament which shall be shed for many unto the remission of sins.*"[2] "And whilst they were eating (St. Mark) Jesus took bread: and blessing, broke and gave to them, and said: take ye: *this is my body.* And having taken the chalice, giving thanks, he gave it to them. And they all drank of it. And he said to them: *this is my blood of the New Testament which shall be shed for many.*"[3] "And taking bread (St. Luke) he gave thanks, and broke and gave to them, saying, *this is my body, which is given for you.* Do this for a commemoration of me. In like manner the chalice also, after he had supped, saying: this is the chalice, the New Testament *in my blood which shall be shed for you.*"[4] The words of institution are plainly confirmatory of the only rational interpretation of the words of promise. It only remains to consider the language of the Apostle referring to the celebration of the Eucharist as a confirmed practice in the Church. "The chalice of benediction which we bless is it not the *communion of the blood of Christ?* And the bread which we break is it not the *partaking of the body of the Lord?*"[5] To these may be added the words of St. Paul, before adduced, which occur in the 11th chapter of the First Epistle to the Corinthians.

There need be no argument on these texts, outside the

[1] John vi. 52—58.   [2] Matt. xxvi. 26—28.
[3] Mark xiv. 22—24.   [4] Luke xxii. 19, 20.
[5] 1 Cor. x. 16.

meaning of the words. With great reverence we may put the question—Did our Redeemer, and Paul, and Mark, and John, and Luke, and Matthew, fall into the error of using language inapt and inadequate to convey a simple and plain doctrine? Was there, I repeat with profound respect, a conspiracy to deceive? Was there an inability to employ suitable language? Plainly enough these difficulties rise up before us in the supposition of a *spiritual* presence only in the Eucharist. What is said to be the body of Christ is not so; what is said to be the chalice of his blood is simple wine blessed. Oh! but what our Lord says, as quoted by John, he explains, as quoted by Matthew? No! but repeats it; or Paul explains? No! or the Evangelists throw out some hint to show us that plain words are not to be taken in a plain sense? No! The argument, then, that I would form—if one must be built on the passages recited—is cumulative, its strength is gathered from the number of its component parts, and from the accuracy with which they fit into each other. There is no discrepancy between them, either in the mode of thought they reveal or the form of expression. It is in every case "the body and blood of Christ" that is there, that is to be received, that is to be venerated. The body and blood of Christ are then really present in the Eucharist, under the appearance of bread and wine.

Here again in the Eucharist we discover some ingredients of a sacrament of the new law, that is, divine institution—a visible cause or function—a spiritual and invisible effect. The words of Christ and of the consecrating minister—"This is my body"—"this is the chalice of my blood"—are something external and sensible: equally sensible are the species or appearances of bread and wine, which remain after the change of substance; but the effect of these words, namely, the presence of the body and blood of the Redeemer is invisible, and the precious deposit received into the soul, when the Holy Communion is given, is not perceived by the senses. The ministers of the sacrament of the blessed Eucharist were—1st. The Apostles; they were commanded[1] to do as Christ hath done at the institution of this holy mystery. 2nd. As St. Paul in the 11th chapter of his First Epistle to the Corinthians speaks of the Eucharist as a rite administered among them, no doubt by their clergy, we rightly infer that the ministers of the sacrament were the επισκοποι and πρεσϐυτεροι generally.

§ 5. *Penance.*—Woe to the convert if, after being enlightened by baptism, confirmed in grace and sanctity by the descent of the Holy Ghost upon him, and admitted to the holy Eucharist, he abandoned the faith or fell into grievous sin. Salvation was difficult in either case. In the former it was scarcely attainable. "For," said St. Paul, "it is impossible for those who were once illuminated, have tasted also the heavenly gift, and were made partakers of the Holy Ghost; have, moreover, tasted also the good word of God, and the powers of the world to come, and are fallen away, to be renewed again to penance."[2] Nevertheless, hopeless almost as the case of the wilful prevaricator was, the Apostles had received great powers for the remission of actual sin. 1st. An unlimited commission to bind and loose their subjects, was given them by the Redeemer. "Amen, I say to you whatsoever you shall bind upon earth, shall be bound also in heaven; and whatsoever you shall loose upon earth, shall be loosed also in heaven."[3] 2nd. A specific charge with reference to the remission or retention of sin was delegated to them, as one of the last behests of the Redeemer's love. "Receive ye the Holy Ghost. Whose sins you shall forgive, they are forgiven them; and whose sins you shall retain, they are retained."[4]

Let us leisurely turn over the items of these two texts, in order that we may catch their spirit, and imbibe their sense. Binding and loosing are about as extensive terms as forgiving and retaining. If we may bind or loose in a physical, or civil, or moral sense, we may forgive or retain

[1] Luke xxii. 19, 20.
[2] Heb. vi. 4—6.
[3] Matt. xviii. 18.
[4] John xx. 22, 23.

the sense of an injury—a debt—a duty—an obligation imposed by the law of the country in which we live. Binding and loosing may be said of the sinner with as much propriety as forgiving and retaining may be said of sin. To forgive sin, to retain sin—to bind the sinner, to loose the sinner—one is as good English, Latin, Greek, French, or Spanish, as the other. As sin is conveniently likened to trammels, fetters, or a chain, that holds the sinner captive, the expression to loose sin is not forced or grating. Now what does our Redeemer say? "Whatsoever thou shalt loose upon earth, shall be loosed also in heaven."[1] Under the generic term *whatsoever* sin *may* be comprised, nay more, *it is* comprised, because the term is generic; it *ought to be* comprised, because the mission of the Apostles was for the eradication of sin and the establishment of justice; because *it is* sin by excellence that binds the sinner before God and the citizens of heaven. The Apostles, therefore, by virtue of the extensive powers conferred upon them by the Redeemer, when he said—"Whatsoever thou shalt loose, &c.," would appear to have received the authority to remit sin by a judicial sentence—to remit it verily and intrinsically before heaven, and not before this world. Oh, some one says, there is question here of binding and loosing "in foro externo" only. No! but of loosing in heaven by virtue of a sentence of forgiveness pronounced on earth. Well then! there is question of loosing sin, if you will, but by the administration of the sacrament of baptism? If the common-sense interpretation of the text admits of this meaning, I shall not object, but the commission to baptize, and the effects of baptism, are elsewhere explained by the Redeemer, and the words *bind*, *loose*, cannot be easily applied to a sacrament which operates in regard to sin like a bath or lotion which cleanses away its stains.

The text from the 20th chapter of the Gospel according to St. John is somewhat more explicit. "Whose sins you shall forgive, they are forgiven them; and whose sins you

[1] Matt. xviii. 18.

shall retain, they are retained."[1] Let us remove as far as possible all ambiguity that may attach to these words. Protestants have objected to the proof of the judicial power of remission deducible from these words, on the principle that they prove not the *physical* efficacy of the rite of absolution. It is enough to say that Catholic doctrine does not decide whether the sacraments operate physically or morally. Such an objection, then, falls to the ground. Other opponents say that the reference here is to the remission of sin, which occurs in the administration of baptism, and to the retention which takes place when that sacrament is withheld. It cannot be; there is no such discretionary process directed to the conscience of the sinner previous to baptism, as could afford foundation for the judgment as to aptness or unworthiness in that case implied by the text. A new and extraordinary power is here given. With a view to its exercise, the Holy Ghost is given again; or rather the foundation and operation principle of it is the Holy Spirit for this purpose abiding in the soul. What is this power? The power of forgiving or retaining sin. Forgiving or retaining sin—How? By forgiving or retaining it; not by baptism, or any other means, but by a special form, that form—I forgive—I retain. This is the meaning. "Whose sins you forgive, they are forgiven; whose sins you shall retain, they are retained." First comes the cause, that is, the apostolic forgiveness or retention or sin; then the effect, that is, the *de facto* retention or forgiveness. The forgiveness in the visible world first; then the forgiveness in the invisible world. The forgiveness on earth first; then the forgiveness in heaven. And mind it is *the forgiveness* of sin, not the cleansing of sin, or the washing away its stains. Nay more, it is the forgiveness or the *non-forgiveness*—the forgiving or refusing to forgive. It is the soul of the sinner so completely in the hands of the Judge, as to hang upon his sentence for life and death.

Let us ponder more fully the meaning of the words.

---

[1] John xx. 22, 23.

Sin may be external, visible, or internal and invisible. The sinner's conscience may be burdened with internal sins, such as hatred; or with external sins, such as theft, blasphemy, or with both. Whatever state his conscience be in, the Apostles here receive the power to forgive him, or the privilege to retain his sins. Of course this power must be judiciously exercised, for in its results it must accord with the fiat of Eternal Justice, in other words, because the judgment of man (the Apostles) must agree with the judgment of God. Can it be said that the power given to the Apostles does not contemplate the case where the sinner may present himself burdened with internal sins only? No, the text makes no distinction. The word "sins" is altogether generic, and there is no reason why it should not be taken in the widest possible signification. The Apostles, beyond all controversy, are given here the wonderful authority to forgive and retain sins of any kind and species, in such a way that their pronouncement upon them must be ratified in heaven, and consequently their investigation of the state of the sinner's conscience and dispositions must be most searching and judicious. Now what is requisite with a view to a *judicious* exercise of the rite of forgiveness? What externation of the sinner's disposition is necessary, in order that the sentence pronounced upon earth may be worthy to be ratified in heaven? 1st. Let us suppose that a sinner presents himself for pardon, whose life is not marked by any public or scandalous crime. Are his general acknowledgment of sin and his overt protestation of sorrow sufficient? No, for a deep state of mental depravity is reconcilable with such acts. The wish for pardon may inspire them, it may be their sole influencing cause; and any one can see that a wish for pardon may co-exist with a wilful pursuit of criminal objects and a guilty attachment to unlawful pleasures. If all that were required in this case, as a foundation of the apostolic judgment, was the desire of forgiveness, manifested by the general signs aforesaid, the ratification in heaven of the sentence pronounced upon earth would not be the universal rule, but perhaps the exception, or at most the casual result. Something more is necessary, then, in the case of internal sins, than a general acknowledgment of guilt, or a protestation of sorrow and amendment.

Let external sins be added—what will be sufficient? 2nd, Let the supposition be that the sinner, who presents himself for pardon, is internally and externally a sinner— his mind defiled by criminal views and desires, and his conduct or conversation scandalous, how must he make himself known in order that his aptness or inaptness for forgiveness may be judiciously determined, and his forgiveness or non-forgiveness infallibly pronounced? Will an external change of life be sufficient? No! for it can only evidence his repentance for external sins; and consistently with it his internal sinful habits may still be fondly cherished. In the third supposition that may be made—when the criminality of the sinner is limited to external sin, such a change of life may be a rational proof of amendment, and a solid foundation for a judicious sentence; but when internal sins exist protestation of sorrow is no proof of sorrow, confession of guilt is no proof of amendment, and outward reformation is no convincing argument of the cleansing and purification of the interior man; therefore, I think, it comes to this, the Apostles are to judge the sinner—to acquit him, and condemn him, according to his dispositions. They must be acquainted with his dispositions in order to acquit him or condemn him judiciously. But a general acquaintance with his dispositions, such as they might derive from his acknowledgment of guilt or protestation of sorrow, or external change of life would not be sufficient, because his sentence must not be simply judicious, but just, efficacious, and almost infallible with regard to his external and internal sins. "Whose sins you shall forgive, *they are forgiven them*, and whose sins you shall retain, *they are retained.*" No! a perfect knowledge of the state of his conscience, a scrutation, an examination of all that he does, says, and thinks—a many-sided picture of his whole moral being must be placed before them before they can pronounce the unerring decree, therefore I conclude that the words of

Christ, "Whose sins you shall, &c.," which confer a privilege on the apostolic judge, impose an obligation on the culprit; on the judge the authority to pronounce a just sentence, on the culprit the duty to manifest unfeignedly the state of his conscience. It is not, as in a court of criminal justice, where the prisoner is accused specifically of the charges against him; in the court of conscience the sinner must accuse himself specifically. He must accuse himself sincerely, and, therefore, as a matter of moral obligation, he must accuse himself fully; for all his sins are to be forgiven or retained together. He must manifest, and he must be conscientiously bound to manifest, the whole state of his interior in respect to sin and repentance for it, otherwise the apostolic judges must act upon insufficient evidence, and their sentence must be in many cases materially unjust and effectively futile, instead of being always, as it is said to be, efficacious in the remission or retention of sin, and in accordance with the infallible judgments of the Divinity.

Confession of sins by the penitent appears to be the necessary result of the judicial power of forgiveness, as it was conferred upon the Apostles by the Redeemer; confession not general but particular, not partial but integral, not public, but from the nature of the case private in many of its details. To this confession it may be that there is reference in the last chapter of the Epistle of St. James—" Confess therefore your sins one to another: and pray for one another that you may be saved."[1]

We have discovered another Sacrament. There is an outward rite or ceremony in it, consisting of the self-accusation of the penitent, and the absolution pronounced by the priest, and an internal effect, namely, the purification of the conscience of the penitent and the forgiveness of his sins. The ministers of this Sacrament were the disciples referred to in the twentieth chapter of St. John,

[1] James vi. 16.

viz., the twelve apostles—the πρεσβυτεροι and επισκοποι of the Church.

§ 6. *Extreme Unction.*—The last rite in which the dying Christian, be he convert or otherwise, participated in the apostolic times, was a ceremony, external like those to which we have referred, consisting of prayer and anointing with oil. Its effect was invisible, viz., the remission of sin, if sin existed in the soul of the dying Christian. The ministers of this rite were the πρεσβυτεροι of the Church. All these affirmations are put forward by St. James, in a passage that is so clear as to require neither argument nor elucidation. I will content myself with citing the words of the Apostles—" Is any one sick among you? Let him bring in the priests (πρεσβυτερους) of the Church, and let them pray over him, anointing him with oil in the name of the Lord. And the prayer of faith shall save the sick man : and if he be in sins, they shall be forgiven him." [1] I will only add that it is little less than absurd to argue that St. James advises here a sanitary ordinance for the restoration of the health of the body, for he attributes to it the remission of sin. It is equally unfounded to suppose that the Apostle is introducing a religious rite of his own devising : for unless the divine power interposed, human authority could never attach the effects here enumerated to an external ceremony.

If it be objected that the remission of sin is attributed in this text to the " prayer of faith " and not to the sacramental rite, an easy answer is found in the text itself. 1st. The " prayer of faith " is evidently the Sacramental prayer said over the sick man by the " priests." "And they shall pray over him." 2nd. It is the temporal cure of the sick man that is attributed to the prayer of faith." And the " prayer of faith shall *save* the sick man," while the remission of sin is the result of the entire economy, "And if he be in sins, they shall be forgiven him."

[1] James v. 14, 15.

§ 7.—*Holy Orders.*—The Sacrament of Holy Orders consisted in an external ceremony—" the imposition of hands," the invisible effect of which was a grace or gift, permanently abiding in the soul. As it has been already shown to be a Sacrament, at considerable length, it will be sufficient here to indicate its ministers. They were first the Apostles. Barnabas was ordained by them: Paul ordained Timothy: Paul and Barnabas ordained priests in the churches of Asia Minor. Secondly, they were the bishops. Titus, certainly a bishop, received authority from St. Paul to ordain priests in the churches of Crete; and Timothy, as is evident from the epistles addressed to him, ordained επισκοποι and πρεσβυτεροι in the churches subject to him.

§ 8. *Matrimony.*—It is difficult to suppose that the Redeemer, or the Apostles as his delegates, made no regulation affecting the rite of marriage. We can scarcely bring ourselves to believe, even with the silence of the Scripture on the subject, that this solemn act, on which the temporal always, and frequently the eternal, happiness of man depends, was left to the disposal of Rabbinical doctors, or Roman lawyers, or customs diverse and changeable. The civil law, no doubt, or general or local usage, might invest the marriage contract with just and reasonable conditions. The validity of marriage, even among Christians, might have been made to depend on the observance of legal forms. Yet, as the contract is so different from others in its general bearings, and so much superior to them in the obligations it imposes and the effects it produces, we might reasonably expect that Christianity would throw more solemnity about it than the barter of a wheat-field or the purchase of an estate. This conviction is strengthened by various circumstances. 1st. Sacramental rites had been instituted for the critical periods of human life,—baptism for admission among the faithful,—confirmation for the commencement of the Christian's campaign with the powers of darkness,—orders for his admission to the ministry,—extreme unction for his departure from this world. Marriage is a critical step, which transfers those who contract it into an entirely different state of existence from that in which they had hitherto been.

They become transferred civilly, physically, spiritually. As members of society they assume new relations—as Christians new duties. It might not be just to say that sacramental grace was necessary for them in this important change; but analogy would lead us to believe that it was expedient, and we would not be going beyond the bounds of legitimate inference if we looked for the elevation of the marriage contract to the grace and dignity of a sacrament in the economy of the Founder of the Christian Church. 2nd. Another circumstance concurs to strengthen this conclusion. Marriage, under the Christian law, was declared by the Redeemer to be strictly and in all cases indissoluble, "quoad vinculum." Once married, married for ever—bound during the life of both parties to misery or bliss. "Therefore, now they are not two, *but one flesh. What, therefore, God hath joined together, let no man put asunder.*" .... "Whosoever shall put away his wife and *marry another committeth adultery against her. And if the wife shall put away her husband and be married to another she committeth adultery*"[1] (St. Mark). "*Everyone that putteth away his wife* and *marrieth another committeth adultery; and he that marrieth her that is put away from her husband committeth adultery*"[2] (St. Luke). "And I say unto you, that whosoever *shall put away his wife, except it be for fornication, and marry another, committeth adultery; and he that shall marry her that is put away committeth adultery*"[3] (St. Matthew). "But to them that are married, not I, but the Lord commandeth that the wife depart not from her husband. And if *she depart that she remain unmarried or be reconciled to her husband. And let not the husband put away the wife.*"[4] "A woman is *bound by the law as long as her*

---

[1] Mark x. 8, 9, 11, 12.
[2] Luke xvi. 18.
[3] Matt. xix. 9.
[4] 1 Cor. viii. 10, 11.

husband liveth; but if her husband die she is at liberty."[1] The ever-pressing yoke is hard to be borne; the interminable obligation is hard to be fulfilled. What numberless cases must occur where, in the supposition of the indissolubility of the bond of marriage, a great conflict must take place between duty and inclination—between the law of God and the dictate of human passion. Divine providence might provide the special help of sacramental grace to enable the Christian to overcome in this trying warfare, or he might leave him to avail himself of the ordinary helps derivable from general spiritual sources; but, undoubtedly, a special sacramental grace—permanent to maintain the married Christian in the fulfilment of a permanent duty—is more in accordance with the tender solicitude of the Redeemer for his flock, and the liberal enonomy of the gospel dispensation by which he proportions his helps to the difficulty of the obligations he imposes. 3rd. The Apostle of the Gentiles, in affirming the lawfulness of a second marriage, in case of the husband's death, makes a limitation, which may have some significance as bearing upon this point. "Let her marry to whom she will, *only* in the *Lord.*"[1] The exceptive clause may simply mean, *only among the disciples of the Lord,* thereby implying a prohibition from contracting marriage with an infidel, or its meaning may be *according to the rules and ceremonies which the Lord hath prescribed* for the regulation of such contracts. Which soever signification we give the words, and most probably both meanings conjoined would express the sense of the Apostle, it must follow from them that the marriage contract was an object of the effective care of the Redeemer; and, if such were the case, there can be no difficulty in supposing it to be endowed by him with a sacramental efficacy when made between members of his Church. 4th. But the strongest reasons in favour of the point we examine, are found in the 5th chapter of St. Paul's Epistle to the Ephesians. The Apostle there compares the marriage union

---

[1] 1 Cor. vii. 39.

to the union of Christ with his Church, which is strictly a union of grace. "Because the husband is the head of the wife, as Christ is the head of the Church."[1] The wife is to be subject to her husband, as the Church is subject to Christ. "Therefore, as the Church is subject to Christ, so also let the wives to their husband, in all things."[2] Clearly the utter subjection of the Church to Christ, arises from his vivifying and conserving operation in her by grace. Moreover, the husband is to love his wife unto death, after the sublime model of the love of Christ for his Church. "Husbands, love your wives, as Christ also loved the Church, and delivered himself up for it; that he might sanctify it, cleansing it by the laver of water in the Word of Life."[3] He is to love her with firmness, earnestness, and beneficence. The question here is, Can the comparison of the Apostle be realized, if marriage in the early Christian Church was a civil contract, and not a grace-giving sacrament? Well! it is clear enough that if Christian marriage was a sacrament, there would be no difficulty in understanding the exhortation of the Apostle. In this case, perfect and docile obedience might be reasonably required of the wife, enlightened and assisted by sacramental grace, and chastened and undying love from the husband. But the case is otherwise; marriage is a simple contract; the chapter is involved in difficulties. 1st. Why should the Apostle compare a union—social, civil, and important, no doubt, but carnal and worldly—to that union which ranks second among the external relations assumed by the Divinity? It will be said, because of the foundation afforded by the undying nature of both. No! it is not under the respect of permanence or durability that the Apostle compares them. Quite clear. Then it will be said that the Apostle, wishing to give an instruction to married people on the subjection and authority respectively incumbent on them as man and wife, draws his conclusions from a comparison instituted with the

[1] Ephes. v. 23.   [2] Ephes. v. 24.
[3] Ephes. v. 25.

highest example of both. This is nearer the truth; but yet the real difficulty remains—Why profane so sacred a mystery as the spiritual union of the Church with its mystic spouse, by likening it to a carnal social union, devoid of grace and sanctity. 2nd. The exhortation of the Apostle is liable to rejoinder and exception. The Church is subject to Christ truly; but it is rendered so by grace. Christ loves the Church, but by grace the Church is rendered always beautiful in his eyes. It is different, however, with the wife and husband. Their union is not cemented by grace. The adornment and attractions of the one are fading, changing. The love of the other is natural, inconstant. Give us the help of sacramental grace, the married may say, and we will strive to imitate the love and duty of the Great Model. But, weak as we are, and united by natural ties only, we must despair of realizing, under any conceivable respect, a picture of such high perfection.

3rd. If the reasoning of the Apostle from the 25th to the 30th verse be closely looked into, it will be found to be as follows:—Husbands are to love their wives as Christ loved the Church. Christ loved the Church by cleansing, sanctifying, and purifying it. Husbands, then, if they are to love their wives after the example of Christ, literally are to sanctify them by this love, or, if figuratively only, are to cherish and adorn them. Is the imitation to be figurative or literal? Clearly it is to be *figurative* from the tenor of verses 28 and 29. "So also ought men to love their wives as their own bodies. He that loveth his wife loveth himself. For no man ever hated his own flesh, but nourished and cherished it, as also Christ the Church."[1] And partially, I contend, *literally* also, for the Apostle adds, as the fundamental reason, why the duty of imitation is imposed upon husbands. "Because we are members of his body, of his flesh, and of his bones."[2] Therefore are husbands to love their wives, because they are members of the mystic body of Christ.

---

[1] Ephes. v. 28, 29.   [2] Ephes. v. 30.

As members of the mystic body of Christ, they are bound to imitate their head—not figuratively, but literally—not in natural, but supernatural duties. Christ sanctifies the Church. The husband and wife, with a view to imitate him as members of his mystic body, must sanctify each other by their chaste love. But how can this be? In no other conceivable way but by the marriage contract infusing grace, which permanently abides between the married parties, and is made to operate by the recurring and faithful discharge of the conjugal duties on the part of both.

Thus it would appear that there are at least some grounds in the sacred Scripture for pronouncing Christian marriage a sacrament. And to any one who impartially considers the question, it must appear most reasonable that it should be so constituted under the Christian law. For there was the world—Pagan—Grecian—Roman—Oriental—even Jewish—countenancing various abuses. Polygamy, divorce, the slavery of the wife, unnatural degrees of proximity by blood and other ties, were the fashion of the day. Christianity was to resist them all. The Christian marriage was to be in bright contrast to all of them. A special grace appeared necessary for carrying out the designs of God.

In the supposition that the Christian marriage is a sacrament, it consists of an external sign—the contract—and an invisible effect—the grace it infuses.

Thus it appears that there are some grounds, to speak moderately, in the sacred Scripture, for the Catholic doctrine of " Seven Sacraments." There is a strong insinuation of the elevation of the marriage contract to a sacramental rite; and there is obvious proof of the existence, in the primitive Church, of six other ceremonies, external, visible, grace giving.

A sacrament, according to Catholic theology, has five essential qualities :—1st, Outward significance of its effect, that is, grace. 2nd, Divine institution. 3rd, The virtue, or power, of producing the invisible effect it signifies.

4th, Which effect it produces "vi operationis," in virtue of its right ministration, as distinguished from the acts of the receiver. 5th, Permanence. I believe there can be little difficulty in showing from the Scriptures, that all these qualities belonged to six ceremonies of the. Apostolic Church; that is, baptism, imposition of hands, the act by which bread and wine were changed into the body and blood of the Lord, the judicial act by which sins were remitted, the imposition of hands by which Christians were raised to the dignity of the priesthood, the final act by which the dying were anointed and prayed over. Here are the grounds that establish one in this conviction.

These ceremonies have been shown to be outward, obvious to the senses, visible, palpable, or audible. Furthermore, they have been shown to produce grace, which is an impalpable and invisible effect. Now, compare in each case the effect with the ceremony that produced it, and you discover the significance of the sacramental rite. Take them in succession: 1st, *Baptism*—The outward ceremony is a washing with water; the invisible effect is the abolition of original sin; the significance is cleansing the soul from its defilements. 2nd, *Imposition of hands*—The outward ceremony is the imposition of hands with prayer; the invisible effect is the infusion of the grace of the Holy Spirit; the significance is strengthening and enlightening the soul. 3rd, *The consecration of the Eucharist*—The outward ceremony consists of words pronounced over bread and wine; the invisible effect is the real presence of the body and blood of the Lord; the significance is nourishing and feeding the soul. 4th, *Remission of sins*—The outward ceremony is the pronouncing of pardon with the judicial hearing of the case; the invisible effect is the remission of sin. The significance is obvious. 5th, *Ordination of Priests*—The outward ceremony is the imposition of hands; the invisible effect is the grace of the priesthood; the significance is the endowing with power and aptitude for priestly functions. 6th, *Anointing of the sick*—The external ceremony consists of prayer and anointing with oil; the invisible effect is the remission of sin and the cure of bodily distempers; the significance is healing the body and the spirit. Therefore, the first quality of a sacrament, that is, outward significance of its invisible effect, was common to six rites in use in the primitive Church.

2. The six sacred ceremonies of which we have been speaking were instituted by the Redeemer mediately or immediately. This we would be justified in inferring from the fact that they produced grace in the souls of those who received them worthily. Besides the institution of four of them, namely, baptism, the Eucharist, penance, and orders, is either detailed, or strongly insinuated, in the gospels of the four Evangelists. That these sacred rites were to be permanent, would follow from their peculiar importance, I should rather say, vital necessity, coupled with the fact that the Church, of whose outward worship they formed a distinguished part, was to last to the end of time. They produced their invisible effects in virtue of their due administration. Baptism for example; the Redeemer says of it, "Unless a man be born again of water and the Holy Spirit," &c. Water is here made the instrument by which sanctification and justification are produced in the souls of the newly baptized. Confirmation: to the terms "imposition of hands" is attributed the infusion of the grace of the Holy Ghost, instantaneously, infallibly, "vi ritûs." "They laid their hands upon them, and the Holy Ghost came upon them," &c. The Eucharist: here we have no need of illustration; for, if God was given in this sacrament, grace was given *instrumentaliter*. Holy Orders: of this sacrament St. Paul says, "the grace that is in you *by* the imposition of the hands of the priesthood." Extreme Unction: St. James attributes the effect of this sacrament to the anointing and prayer as to their physical or moral cause. Penance: where the Redeemer says, " whose sins you forgive they are forgiven," he necessitates the conclusion that the judicial sentence of the priest is the immediate efficient cause of the expulsion of the sinner's guilt.

So it appears the Catholic idea of the nature of a sacrament accords with certain symbolic rites of the primitive

Church. The coincidence is striking, even as regards Scripture illustrations: it becomes complete when the omissions of the sacred volume are supplied, and its obscurities removed by the more abundant materials which tradition furnishes.

Under the shade of the classic hill of "the modern Athens" perhaps, or hard by old Holyrood, slumbering in the smoke and dust of ages, or freshly looking out upon "the monument" and the pleasant grounds surrounding it, somewhere assuredly in the city of the Catholic Mary Stuart, the general assembly of the Church of Scotland sits in solemn state once a year, canny and astute, to hear ecclesiastical appeals, and, if required, to decide weighty questions, touching morals, discipline, and faith. There are presbyters among its members, lay and ecclesiastical, who fancy they represent the πρεσβυτεροι and επισκοποι of the primitive Church, and reproduce their office and functions. John Knox was the institutor of the Presbyterian system, and we are told on good authority that he took his ideas of Church government from the system established in Geneva. Singular enough that the "low lands" of a small and rugged kingdom at the western side of Europe, should pass by the great and mighty nations of the Continent, to learn Church government from the low lands of a country small and rugged like itself. Better had it been, and from what we have seen, more nearer truth, if these wise reformers sought for a model in the cantons bordering upon the "Waldstatler see," or hunted it up among the looming valleys of "Schwyz." However this be, the Presbyterian system is established—a system of laymen and lay parsons without ordination, with few ecclesiastical functions, without sacrifice, sacramental action, or authority, save John Calvin's behest to John Knox, written, or by word of mouth.

The presbyters of the primitive Church were ordained ministers, ordained by ecclesiastical superiors, by Paul, Peter, Titus, Timothy, who were bishops in the true sense. If not all, certainly many of those presbyters were επισκοποι, charged with the direction of the faithful and the government of the Church. Επισκοποι or πρεσβυτεροι as they were, they appointed not themselves to the care of souls, but they were "sent" by ecclesiastical authority, their mission or commission coming down to them from the Redeemer through the Apostles "sent" by him, or through the bishops sent by them in turn. So constituted in the Church, they had a strict right to be regarded as the "ministers of Christ," the denomination St. Paul fixes upon them. It was their office and duty to baptize; if they were of the higher order, to confirm by the imposition of hands, to consecrate the Eucharist, to absolve from sin, to anoint the dying with oil, to perpetuate the ministry by ordination if bishops, to look to the marriage contract, to offer sacrifice, and thus they realized in practice the second characteristic given them by the Apostle in the passage just referred to, "dispensers of the mysteries of God."

It is easy to find the office and functions of these early priests and bishops in the one great church that is everywhere; and no one who has an honest perception of the writings of the New Testament will look for them among the Vaudois or the Moravian brethren, or the Latter-Day Saints, or religious communities that rise and fall by "the great lakes," or live and die in "Merry England."

DIVISION VII.

THE GREAT RITE OF SACRIFICE.

§ 1. *Hypothetical.*—In the supposition that Christ our Lord changed bread and wine into his body and blood, when, according to the Evangelist at His Last Supper He "took bread, and blessed, and brake, and gave to His disciples, and said, Take ye and eat: this is My body. And taking the chalice, He gave thanks, and gave to them, saying, Drink ye all of this; for this is my blood of the new testament, which shall be shed for many unto the remission of sins;"[1] and in the additional supposition that he commanded all the priests and bishops of his church, then existing, to effect a similar conversion of substance by the use of similar words, when he added, "do this for a commemoration of me"[2]—would it follow that the Eucharistic rite of the Christian Church is properly and strictly speaking a sacrifice?

Let us examine the result of these two suppositions. It may be thus simply evolved—Every Christian priest or bishop, by the consecrating words which he uses, brings Christ in His humanity and divinity from heaven, and constitutes Him, soul and body, in the very place — neither greater nor smaller—that had been occupied by the substance of bread and of wine. The one act of the priest, or rather the one sentence that he pronounces, has a double effect; it constitutes the presence of Christ upon the altar, and it constitutes His body and blood, and soul and divinity, where the bread and wine existed up to that moment: consequently, by this act or form of words, duly performed and pronounced, Christ is, morally speaking, immolated and slain upon the altar. For, constituted under the forms of bread and wine, he cannot naturally speak or breathe, or see or feel, or exist: *naturally*, I say, because for a due performance of such functions, a human body requires extension in a place commensurate with its own size. Christ is slain then morally, because, in reference to the natural order, his life is taken away. But this is not all; he is likewise morally slain, because living and active himself, he is placed under the form of a material dead and inactive—bread and wine. Undoubtedly then, in the supposition of the real presence caused by the words of consecration, there is an immolation of the body and blood of Christ, if not precisely physical and actual, at least moral, and by implication in the strongest sense of the words.

---

[1] Matt. xxvi. 26, 27, 28. [2] Luke xxii. 19.

The question is, Is such an immolating rite necessarily a sacrifice?

It would be incorrect to say that any rite, no matter how solemn or public, is of its own nature a sacrifice, independent of the divine appointment, or of the scope and design of man in performing it. An ox might have been slain in the old times of priests and altars, in the presence of a whole town or nation, kneeling and bareheaded, and its flesh might have been burnt upon an altar there erected; and yet it would be no sacrifice if God did not ordain or sanction it, and if man only offered it in sport. An Edomite, on the high hills of his country, or an Ismaelite, on his sandy plain, might have offered a lamb or buck-goat, his people looking on, and approving, in jesting imitation of what he had seen in Jerusalem: and no one would say that he had offered a sacrifice. A rite, then, of its nature may be such that it may be fit material for a sacrifice : there may be an aptitude in it to be constituted a sacrifice : it will not, however, be a sacrifice unless God and man have made it so.[1]

The question originally raised, therefore, will necessarily depend upon two issues :—1st Whether in the immolation of Christ upon the altar there is sufficient matter for a true sacrifice. 2nd Whether, if there be, there are circumstances involved in this immolation which should determine us to believe that it was ordained as a true sacrifice? We will take up both these points in succession.

1st. Is there sufficient matter for a sacrifice in the Eucharistic immolation of Christ? To answer this question, it will be well to examine what are the recognized scriptural sacrifices as to matter and rite. First as to matter, they are animate and inanimate; rational and irrational: Jephte's daughter was matter for sacrifice, so was the person of our Lord Jesus Christ. Oxen, doves, goats, rams, lambs, were matters for sacrifice in the times of the Jewish law. Flour, cakes, and oil are represented as

---

[1] This is the more common, though not the universal opinion of divines.

matter for sacrifice in the following passages of the Book of Leviticus:—"This is the oblation of Aaron and his sons. . . . They shall offer the tenth-part of an ephi of flour for a perpetual sacrifice (In sacraficio sempiterno—Vulg)."[1] "But when thou offerest a sacrifice baked in the oven of fire . . . thou shalt divide it in little pieces and pour oil upon it."[2] "They shall offer the tenth part of an ephi of flour for a perpetual sacrifice, half in the morning, and half of it in the evening. It shall be tempered with oil, and fried in the frying-pan."[3] If such are as to their matter the sacrifices presented to us in the Sacred Scripture, the body and blood of Christ, animate and living, though under an inanimate form in the Eucharist, is sufficient matter for a sacrifice,—as animate and living it resembles the sacrifice of the Cross,—as inanimate in appearance it resembles the sacrifices of oil, of flour, and bread.

Secondly as to rite. In the old law there were many sacrifices, which implied or involved physical immolation and taking away life: there was one—the holocaust—which not content with this, required the total destruction by fire of the victim thus slain. The sacrifices of inanimate objects, on the contrary, required but a very partial destruction, and appear to have consisted principally in the moral change of use and destination of the "oblata" which followed their oblation, and arose from it.

This is evinced by many passages in the Book of Leviticus, amongst others by the following, which has been partially quoted before:—"But when thou offerest a sacrifice, baked in the oven of fire, thou shalt divide it into little pieces, and pour oil upon it. And if the sacrifice be from the gridiron in like manner the flour shall be tempered with oil. And when thou offerest it to the Lord, thou shalt deliver it to the hands of the priest. And when he hath offered it, he shall take a memorial out of the sacrifice and burn it upon the altar for a sweet savour to the Lord."[4]

[1] Levit. vi. 20.
[2] Levit. vi. 21, 22.
[3] Levit. ii. 3, 4.
[4] Levit. ii. 4, 6, 7, 8, 9.

It would appear from the words, "He shall take a memorial out of the sacrifice," that the rite of sacrifice was the oblation made by the priest, and that the immolation of the "oblata" was the moral change which took place in them in being withdrawn from secular purposes, and consecrated to the service of God. This view of the rite of sacrifices is further confirmed by other passages in the Book of Leviticus. The emissary goat was truly sacrificed, and so were the loaves of proposition, and in either case there was no physical destruction.

The emissary goat was sacrificed. " He shall make two buck-goats to stand before the Lord in the door of the tabernacle of the testimony. And casting lots upon them both. . . . that whose lot fell to be offered to the Lord, he shall offer (evidently in sacrifice) for sin. . . . After he hath cleansed the sanctuary, and the tabernacle and the altar, then let him offer the living goat."[1] As both the goats are said to be "offered" by the priest, it is but fair to infer that both were offered in sacrifice, as the first most certainly was. Now, if the second goat, here referred to, was offered in sacrifice, the rite of such sacrifice was entirely a moral immolation, as the only change that took place in the victim was a change of value, appreciation and security. It was not killed, but by being offered it was separated from its fellows, and withdrawn from the use of man to be driven away to the desert, far from human habitations, and exposed to be devoured by wild beasts.

The loaves of proposition were also offered in sacrifice. "Thou shalt take also fine flour, and shalt bake twelve loaves thereof . . . and thou shalt set them six and six one against another, upon the most clean table before the Lord. And they shall be Aaron's and his sons', that they may eat them in the holy place, because it is most holy of the sacrifice of the Lord by a perpetual rite."[2]

Here again the rite of sacrifice was a moral, not a physical immolation, consisting entirely in the change

---

[1] Levit. xvi. 7, 8, 9, 10.   [2] Levit. xxiv. 5, 6, 9.

arising from the consecration of those loaves to religious purposes.

These examples will suffice for our purpose. From them it is apparent that for genuine sacrifice a bloody rite is not required, for inanimate objects were offered in sacrifice by divine appointment; it is further evident that, in the sacrifices of animate and inanimate things, physical destruction or change was not always required, but moral immolation was in some cases sufficient. In the supposition of the real presence there is, therefore, amply sufficient for a true sacrifice in the rite of immolation to which the body and blood of Christ are subjected.

If, as to matter and rite, there is sufficient for a genuine sacrifice in the conversion of the substance of bread and wine into the body and blood of Christ, the further question recurs—Are there circumstances connected with this conversion which should determine us to believe that it has been instituted as a sacrifice for the Christian Church? I believe we will discover that there are. In the supposition of the real presence, the Eucharistic rite must become the great centre of Christian worship. It could not be otherwise. All other public acts of religion must sink into comparative insignificance beside this which involves the presence of a God. Now, if it be true that the people of God were never without a sacrifice divinely appointed from the beginning of the world, is any one prepared to say that the Christian Church has a heavenly-constituted rite, resembling a sacrifice in every particular, but no sacrifice? Could we bring ourselves to say this, with the important fact before us, that the coming of Christ upon earth was for the purpose of sacrificing himself? He became man to furnish us with a victim worthy of the majesty of God. Does he not remain among men for a similar purpose?

§ 2. *Authoritative.*—Whatever may be said as to the meaning of the word presbyter ($\pi\rho\epsilon\sigma\theta\nu\tau\epsilon\rho\circ\varsigma$) as employed in the sacred Scriptures of the Old and New Testament, there is evidence to show, that they who were designated by this name were sacrificing priests in the strict and literal sense of the word. Sacrifice was offered in the early Church by the Apostles; and it is undeniable that any rights which the Apostles received with respect to sacrifice or sacrament were communicated to the επισκοποι and πρεσβυτεροι.

In reality sacrifice was offered in the primitive Church, because the primitive Church had a veritable altar distinct from the altar of the cross. The ideas of an altar and a sacrifice are correlative, inseparable. A figurative altar argues a figurative sacrifice. A spiritual altar and a spiritual sacrifice co-exist. A real altar in the Pagan, or Jewish, or Christian sense, is, and must always be, an argument as to the existence of a real sacrifice. An altar is an altar, for no other reason but because it is intended for a sacrifice.

The apostolic Church had its altar. This St. Paul affirms in two distinct passages of his Epistles. 1st. In the 13th chapter of his Epistle to the Hebrews, where he says plainly, "We have an altar, whereof they have no power to eat who serve the tabernacle."[1] It is worth while to observe the context of this passage. The two subsequent verses appear to identify the altar referred to by St. Paul with the altar of the cross. The two preceding verses appear to indicate a different altar from the altar of the cross. "We have an altar whereof they have no power to eat who serve the tabernacle." Here are two distinct assertions. 1st. That the primitive Church had an altar. 2nd. That the Jews could not eat of it. And then the Apostle subjoins as a reason, or in illustration of what he had said, "For the bodies of those beasts, whose blood is brought into the holies, are burned without the camp. Wherefore Jesus also, that he might sanctify the people by his own blood, suffered without the gate."[c] Are these verses to be taken as a proof or illustration of the first or second assertion, to which verse the tenth is equivalent, or are they to be undersood as a proof and illustration of both? If we take them to be an illustra-

---

[1] Heb. xiii. 10.   [2] Heb. xiii. 11, 12.

tion of the first assertion—" We have an altar "—the drift of the argument might be, we have an altar, just as you, the Hebrews, have an altar, for Jesus suffered "outside the gate" to sanctify us by the oblation of his blood, just as your victims were consumed without the camp, when their blood was offered in expiation within: and in this sense the altar of the cross would appear to be identified with the altar to which St. Paul refers. Or, in this interpretation of the passage, the sense would possibly be—" We have an altar" within the city of Jerusalem on which the blood of Christ is offered; and we ought to have such an altar, because the burning of the animals outside the camp—the type and figure of the oblation of Christ—argued the existence of the altar within. In the latter sense there would be a manifest allusion to the Eucharistic sacrifice.

However, viewing the whole context impartially, it would appear to me that the object of the Apostle in the 11th and 12th verses is to prove that the Jews, while they continue to serve the tabernacle, cannot eat of the Christian altar. They could not expect such a privilege as Jews. While they continue to serve the tabernacle, they are under the tabernaclar law as regards sacrifices. They cannot eat of the victims (the victims are consumed without); they can only partake of the fruit of their oblation. This is their law! while they " serve the Tabernacle," they must abide by it. "We have an altar:" as Jews, they cannot eat of it, it is contrary to the provisions of the Jewish law of sacrifices.

This is the meaning of the whole passage, and this is the bearing of verses the 11th and 12th upon verse the 10th. The manifest object of St. Paul in this place is to warn the converted Hebrews against adhering to the Jewish rites. He expresses this object plainly in verse the 9th, when he says—" Be not led away with various and strange doctrines." The doctrines to which he refers are, as he says in the same verse, the Jewish doctrine of sanctification—by the distinction of meats—" the establishing of the heart with meats." The connection is—be not led away by such doctrines, for by submitting yourself to their influence you serve the tabernacle. "We have an altar, whereof they have no power to eat who serve the tabernacle." You serve the tabernacle. You cannot eat of the Christian altar. Therefore, if you suffer yourself to be led away by these strange doctrines, you exclude yourself from the Christian altar, because (the reason suggested above) becoming Jews in principle, you adhere to the doctrine that the bodies of the victims offered cannot be eaten, but must be consumed by fire without the camp. Now the practical question is, Must the altar referred to by St. Paul be a different altar from the altar of the cross in this, the obvious sense of the passage? I believe it must; and from the very nature of the argument. The argument is "a pari"—You cannot eat of the victims offered on the Jewish altar. Therefore you cannot eat of the victim offered on the Christian altar. The conclusion is legitimate, if we admit that the victim offered on the Christian altar might be eaten, not figuratively but *really*; and in this case, of course, the existence of the Eucharistic sacrifice is clearly proved. The conclusion is legitimate, because the parity is complete. On the other hand, if it be affirmed that there is question of eating Christ *figuratively*, and that the Apostle refers to the sacrifice of the cross alone, there is no argument in his words, and there is no sense in the passage. In this hypothesis his argument would be—You cannot participate in the fruits of the sacrifice of the cross, because serving the tabernacle you admit the principle that the bodies of sacrificed victims cannot be eaten at all. Where is the conclusiveness in this argument? Clearly there is none. But, on the contrary, there is a ground afforded to the Hebrew on which he can powerfully retort upon the Apostle. Admitted, he can say, that I cannot eat the victim of the Jewish sacrifice, but I can partake of the fruit of it. Therefore "a pari," I can partake of the fruit of the Christian sacrifice, as this fruit is a spiritual and not a material eating of Christ, the victim offered.

There is really no subtilty in this interpretation, when we

consider that the passage was inspired by God. It might be going too far to urge St. Paul thus closely as to the meaning and consequences of his words if he were a fallible man. But the passage was written by St. Paul under the influence of the Spirit of God. Every word of it was weighed in the scales of the sanctuary. Every bearing of it was seen. Every conclusion it might give rise to legitimately was considered. The passage, with its argument, was the work of God.

The passage logically considered clearly proves the existence of an altar in the primitive Church, from which the body of Christ was eaten; and the existence of such an altar proves, beyond all dispute, the existence of a sacrifice in the primitive Church different from the sacrifice of the cross.

The other passage, in which St. Paul refers to the Christian altar, is found in the 10th chapter of the First Epistle to the Corinthians. It is even clearer in its bearing and signification than that which we have been considering.

The object of the Apostle in this passage, as in that which occurs in his Epistle to the Hebrews, is exhortation; and to any one who reflects ever so little on the 19th and 20th verses, the object of the exhortation must appear to be to warn the Corinthians against partaking of meats which had been offered in sacrifice to idols. In another place, the apostle had given his converts permission to eat of meats indiscriminately which were offered in the markets for sale. Some of these meats might have been offered to idols, it is true; but they were not bound to make inquiries on this point; but they might eat "whatever is sold in the shambles, asking no question for conscience sake."[1]

If they did not know whether the meat had been offered to idols or not, or if there would be no scandal given by eating of it, as would be the case when it was publicly sold them in the market, they need not disquiet their con-

---

[1] 1 Cor. x. 25.

sciences; but it would be quite another thing if this meat were offered them at a pagan temple, or in such circumstances that it might be proximately connected with pagan worship. In this latter case they should not eat of it, for by doing so, they would associate themselves in the worship of idols.

Here is the thesis of the Apostle. How does he prove it? *First*, by a reference to the Jewish sacrifices. *Secondly*, by a reference to a Christian sacrifice—and this sacrifice no other than the oblation of the body and blood of Christ in "the bread and the chalice." He first draws his argument from what was generally understood of those who partook of the meats which were offered in sacrifice under the old law. They eat of the victim. By doing so, they participated in the sacrifice; they associated themselves in the worship of Him to whom this sacrifice was offered, that is, God. "Behold Israel according to the flesh: are not they that eat of the sacrifices, partakers of the altar?"[1] The argument is—such was the case with the Jews. Such will be the consequence in your case, if in the circumstances referred to you eat of the meat offered to idols. By eating of the sacrificed meat, the Jews worshipped God. By eating of the sacrificed meat, you will worship idols, or rather devils; because as an idol is nothing (pretending as it does to be a likeness of God whom it does not represent), the real deity of the pagan sacrifice is the devil. "But the things which the heathens sacrifice, they sacrifice to devils and not to God."[2] Such is the argument, clear and concise. Then follows the exhortation. "You cannot drink of the chalice of the Lord and the chalice of devils. You cannot be partakers of the table of the Lord, and of the table of devils."[3] What chalice of the Lord? Evidently, the chalice referred to in verse the nineteenth. "The chalice of benediction, which we bless, is it not the communion of the blood of Christ?"[4] What table of the Lord? Clearly the table on which the bread referred to in the

---

[1] 1 Cor. x. 18.   [2] 1 Cor. x. 20.
[3] 1 Cor. x. 21.   [4] 1 Cor. x. 16.

same verse was placed and offered. "And the bread which we break, is it not the partaking of the body of the Lord?"[1] It is unquestionable, that in this twenty-first verse, the Apostle refers to the Eucharistic bread and the Eucharistic chalice; and he refers to the former in the words, "table of the Lord," and designates the latter by the words "chalice of the Lord," in the same verse in which he refers to and designates the meat and drink offered to idols, as "the chalice of devils," and "the table of devils."

The chalice of devils is the chalice of devils, because its contents have been sacrificed to devils. The table of devils is denominated so, because meat has been sacrificed upon it to devils. Therefore the Eucharistic chalice is "the chalice of the Lord," because its contents have been sacrificed to the Lord, and the Eucharistic table is "the table of the Lord," because the Eucharistic bread has been sacrificed upon it.

The Apostle supposes in the 16th verse that Christians were in the habit of partaking of the Eucharist. "The chalice of benediction which *we bless*, is it not the communion of the blood of Christ? And the bread which *we break*, is it not the partaking of the body of the Lord?" He fears that these same Christians are about to get into a habit of partaking of meat and drink offered to idols. He argues them out of the idea, by proclaiming that the two participations are inconsistent and irreconcilable. Why are they inconsistent and irreconcilable? Because one of them associates the participators with the worship of devils, and the other associates the participators with the worship of God; and the worship of God and the devil are inconsistent and irreconcilable. But why, again, does the partaking of the pagan meat and drink, associate its participators with the worship of idols? Because it has been sacrificed to devils, and the eating it in the circumstances is a moral participation in the sacrifice. Therefore, it must be said, if the argument be complete and conclusive, that the partaking of the Eucharist according to this passage

[1] 1 Cor. x. 16.

makes Christians worshippers *of God*, because the Eucharistic food and drink have been truly offered in sacrifice.

The Apostle speaks here of a Jewish altar, a pagan *table* (by which he means a pagan altar), and a Christian table; of a Jewish sacrifice, a pagan sacrifice, and he contrasts them with the Eucharist; of a partaking of the victims offered by the Jews, a partaking of the meat and drink offered by Pagans, and of a partaking of the body and blood of the Lord. He speaks of one, the Jewish, passed; of another, the Christian, occurring; of the third, the Pagan, as likely to occur. He contrasts them all. He argues upon them, evidently "a pari." There must be some element of similarity running through them as the ground of comparison, and the foundation of argument. And this can be no other than that contained in the proposition, that the three equally involved the rite of sacrifice in the strict and literal sense of the word.

But let us look to the prophetic writings. They throw some light on this subject. "Christ is a priest for ever according to the order or rite of Melchisedech." So says St. Paul. To be a priest for ever according to a certain rite, is evidently to offer sacrifice for ever according to that rite. Now, what was the rite of Melchisedech? The Book of Genesis tells us, "But Melchisedech, the king of Salem, bringing forth bread and wine, for he was the priest of the most high God, blessed him "[1] (Abraham). Is there anything in this inspired sentence which determines the rite of sacrifice which Melchisedech employed? I believe there is. Observe, he did not bring forth bread and wine because he was a king, but because he was a priest. Then he retained with him bread and wine, inasmuch as he was a priest. He had it in store, not inasmuch as he was a man, or a king, but a priest. The priest Melchisedech was distinguished from the man Melchisedech, and from the king Melchisedech, by the privilege of offering sacrifice. Retaining bread and wine then, inasmuch as he was a

---

[1] Genesis xiv. 18, 19.

priest, was retaining it inasmuch as he was a man ordained to offer sacrifice. It is, therefore, natural to conclude that bread and wine were the matter of Melchisedech's sacrifice, and his rite was the rite of immolating bread and wine physically or morally. If, then, as St. Paul says, "Christ be a priest for ever according to the rite of Melchisedech," it requires no further process of reasoning to prove that the blessed Eucharist, in which he as principal priest immolates so as to place himself under the appearances of bread and wine, is truly and properly a sacrifice according to the strict meaning of the term.

After rebuking the Jewish priesthood because they offered "polluted bread upon His altar," and because they immolated animals, "blind, and lame, and sickly," the Spirit of God, by the mouth of the prophet Malachy, proceeds to reject the sacrifices of the Jews and to foretell a sacrifice among the Gentiles in the following terms:—
"I have no pleasure in you, saith the Lord of Hosts: and I will not receive a gift of your hand. For, from the rising of the sun even to the going down, my name is great among the Gentiles, and in every place there is sacrifice, and there is offered to my name a clean oblation: for my name is great among the Gentiles, saith the Lord of Hosts."[1] The prediction is this:—After the rejection of the Jews and the call of the Gentiles, sacrifice shall be offered from the rising to the setting of the sun. This universal sacrifice, different from the Jewish sacrifices, which were contaminated by the physical imperfections of the victims, shall be unspotted and undefilable—"a clean oblation." This interpretation of the passage goes on the assumption that the Vulgate reading is correct. The literal interpretation of the Hebrew word that is translated, "a clean oblation," is an "oblation of clean white flour." In either case the prediction of the prophet Malachy can receive no literal verification unless the blessed Eucharist be regarded as a sacrifice.

Then it is evident that there is not only sufficient mat-

---

[1] Malachias i. 10, 11.

ter for a true sacrifice in the blessed Eucharist, but that the circumstances of the case are such that no rational man can doubt of the fact of its being instituted and ordained as such.

DIVISION VIII.

THE SUFFERING CHURCH.

WE should not expect to find in the Sacred Scriptures of the New Testament a minute description of purgatory. It is remarkable that neither heaven nor hell are there described, except under general terms, which present but a partial idea of the joy or sorrow of these places of eternal abode. The inspired writers appear to have thought it sufficient to tell their disciples and the Church, that heaven is a place of eternal happiness, and hell a prison of everlasting fire. The Apostle will not even attempt to lift the veil that conceals the glories of that third heaven to which he "had been wrapped," and which he knew so well, but contents himself with telling the Corinthians that "neither eye hath seen, nor hath ear heard, neither hath it entered into the heart of man what things God hath prepared for those who love him."

Religionists of a certain training complain that there is not a vivid and detailed picture of purgatory in the Gospels or Epistles. Some rejoice at the fact, and bring an argument against the doctrine from the silence of the Sacred Scriptures. In the event that the Scripture was totally silent on the existence of a place of temporal punishment in the next life, the argument would not be admissible as a *negative one*; but if the allusions to a middle state in the next life are almost as frequent and as clear as those to heaven and hell, it appears unreasonable, partial, and bigoted, to object to receive the universally taught doctrine of purgatory.

We will make a supposition. Suppose there are texts in the New Testament which are of doubtful significance as regards the existence of purgatory. More than this: suppose that all the texts in the New Testament which appear to favour that doctrine are of such a nature that they can be explained in another sense, though they do not necessarily require such an explanation. In a word, suppose that they are as much for it as against it, would it be lawful to say in this case, purgatory existeth not? Would it be reasonable? Would it be common sense? Yet so argue most of those who are outside the Catholic Church. Purgatory is not painted for us in fixed and vivid colours in the Gospels and Epistles. Therefore, it existeth not. And, mind you, they so argue with tremendous odds against them, as will appear from the second part of this work. In the face of facts, which put it beyond all question that prayers for the dead were offered systematically in the third century, the reformers explain away the force of all the texts in the Sacred Scripture which in their obvious and literal signification convey to every rational mind the idea of a middle state beyond the grave. They appear to have made up their minds previous to all examination of the question that they will not, under any circumstances, admit the existence of purgatory; and from this gratuitous and dangerous resolve they are hurried to the fatal conclusion that all antiquity is wrong on this point—that the believers of the second and third century were wrong in the interpretation of texts that were obviously in favour of their practice of praying for the dead —that the texts themselves do not mean what they appear to mean;—whereas it should have been the contrary; and men of just and impartial minds should determine the interpretation of scriptural passages of doubtful meaning by the belief and practice of that portion of the Church which almost touched the time when divine wisdom spoke on earth.

All this is said in the supposition that the scriptural

passages commonly cited in favour of the existence of purgatory, are of very doubtful significance. Such, however, is not the fact—these passages are clear and intelligible; and if some one or two of them appear a little ambiguous and dark, the concentrated light of the whole of them dispels the gloom, for they lean upon and sustain each other.

If according to the Sacred Scriptures there be in the other life a prison where souls are detained *for some time*, not always; if there be sins that *are remitted in the next life;* if there be a possibility of *going to heaven through sufferings and fire;* if there be souls under the earth who *bow the knee in reverential awe* at the mention of the name of the Redeemer; if all these suppositions be verified in the words of the Redeemer and his inspired Apostles; if, in addition, friends of God in more ancient times distributed alms and had sacrifices offered for the dead; it will be reasonable to admit the existence of a middle state in the next world different from heaven, because on the way to heaven—different from hell, because transitory and terminable. If Silas argued so, what reply could be given him? If Timothy so taught from the "chair" of Ephesus, how could the "gainsayers" dispute the strength and conclusiveness of his words? Yet there would be found some to do so then as now. Profane men would be found to say, "The Scripture is not fairly quoted." Well, then, here is the Scripture as it fell from inspired, and more than inspired lips. Here are the texts which exhibit the different items of the broad affirmation that has been put forth. "Be at agreement with thy adversary" (the words are of the Redeemer) "betimes, whilst thou art in the way with him: lest thy adversary deliver thee to the judge, and the judge deliver thee to the officer and thou be cast into prison. Amen I say to thee, *thou shall not go out from thence until thou repay the last farthing.*"[1] As it is said "thou shalt not go out from thence until thou repay the last farthing," the natural inference is—the last

---

[1] Matt. v. 25, 26.

farthing being paid thou shalt go out from thence. The last farthing, then, shall or may be paid; and, as the sentence is conditional, liberation from prison will follow as a consequence. An objection is made against the probativeness of this text from another passage of the Sacred Scripture, which appears to be parallel. The passage is, "The Lord said to my Lord: sit thou at my right hand, until I make thy enemies thy footstool."[1] The Redeemer, it is argued, will never cease to sit at the right hand of God. St. Paul affirms it. All revelation tells us so. Therefore the particle "until" in scriptural use is not necessarily terminative. When, consequently, in the words of the Redeemer, it is announced that souls shall not go out of prison until, &c., it does not follow that they shall go out when the event predicted shall take place.

Granted for the moment; but it is quite clear in both cases that the absolute event on which the principal affirmative is made contingent, must come to pass in due time; in other words, the enemies of the Redeemer shall be all brought to his feet at the last day, and the last farthing due to the divine justice shall be paid by the sinners whom the Redeemer contemplates. Now, if the last farthing be paid to God's justice in the next life, it can only be in purgatory. And if the debt be cancelled, the prisoners must be released.

"And whosoever shall speak a word against the Son of Man it shall be forgiven him; but he that shall speak against the Holy Ghost it *shall not be forgiven him*, neither in this world nor in *the world to come*."[2] The natural inference from this very plain sentence is that there are some sins of such a nature that they shall be forgiven in the life to come. And if there be, those who are charged with them must be in a state of imprisonment until that happiness takes place. They cannot be in heaven, into which "nothing defiled can enter." They cannot be in hell, "out of which there is no redemption." They must, then, be in an intermediate place, where

---

[1] Ps. cix. 1, 2.   [2] Matt. xii. 32.

atonement and hope co-exist. This can be no other than purgatory.

"For other foundation no man can lay, but that which is laid; which is Christ Jesus. Now if any man build upon this foundation, gold, silver, precious stones, wood, hay, stubble: every man's work shall be manifest: for the day of the Lord shall declare it, because it shall be revealed in fire: and the fire shall try every man's work, of what sort it is. If any man's work abide, which he hath built thereupon: he shall receive a reward. If any man's work burn, he shall suffer loss: but he himself shall be saved, yet so as by fire."[1] There are some difficulties in this passage; but there are two affirmations which are devoid of all ambiguity. 1st. Some labourers in the vineyard shall "*suffer loss*" upon or after the day of judgment, in consequence of the imperfection of their works. 2nd. They shall attain salvation *after being first subjected to the influence of fire.*

These two affirmations manifestly establish the existence of temporary punishments in the next world. If it were only said, "he shall suffer loss," and the second assertion were not subjoined, we might escape that inevitable conclusion, as the sense might be, he shall suffer the loss of that reward which his work would merit if it were performed in a more perfect manner—if, instead of being "hay" or "stubble," it were "silver" or "gold." But as the two assertions are conjoined they are obviously identical, or one is explanatory of the other. Now the latter affirmation is a clear admission of the doctrine of purgative fire. "He shall be saved," not absolutely and unconditionally, but through a certain medium. "He shall be saved, *yet so as by fire.*" If he were to be saved *through fire*, it might be argued that the fire here referred to is the same as that referred to in the 13th verse, that is, the judgment of God. But no; he is to be saved *by fire*. Fire is made the instrument of his salvation. Observe, the builder of "hay" and "stubble" on the founda-

[1] 1 Cor. iii. 11, 15.

tion of Christ Jesus, is not to be treated in the same way as the builder of "silver," "gold," "precious stones." Both are to be judged, for "the fire shall try every man's work." But one is "to be rewarded;" the other is to be "saved by fire." If the meaning of being "saved by fire" was being saved by judgment, both would be saved by fire. But both are not saved by fire—but the builder of "hay, wood, stubble." The meaning of being "saved by fire," then, is not being saved by judgment, but saved by igneous and purifying punishment. And this is evidently the "loss" which the imperfect labourer in the Lord's vineyard shall suffer, namely, a loss for a time of that eternal reward, that is, the vision of God and the fruition of heaven, which on the day of accounts the Lord shall render to the perfectly just and sanctified.

The doctrine of purgatory is involved in the teaching of St. Paul.

But perhaps the clearest passage touching upon the doctrine of temporary punishments was contained in an ancient book of great authority, which it was competent for the primitive Church to consult. I abstract for a moment from the question as to whether the second book of Machabees was regarded as inspired. It is enough for my purpose that it was held to be integral and veracious as a history. It narrated correctly the religious acts and warlike exploits of Judas Machabeus, the leader of the people of God. Well, then, if primitive Christians opened this book of Machabees at the 12th chapter, they read the following passage:—"Then they all blessed the just judgment of the Lord, who had discovered the things that were hidden. And so betaking themselves to prayers, they besought him, that the sin which had been committed might be forgotten. . . . . And (Judas) making a gathering, he sent twelve thousand drachms of silver to Jerusalem for sacrifice to be offered for the sins of the dead, thinking well and religiously concerning the resurrection. (For if he had not hoped that they that were slain should rise again, it would have seemed superfluous and vain to pray for the dead.) And because he considered that they who had fallen asleep with godliness, had great grace laid up for them. It is therefore a holy and wholesome thought to pray for the dead, that they may be loosed from their sins."[1]

Let us consider for one moment the circumstances that originated the prayers and sacrifices referred to in this text. A few of the Jews had been slain[2] in battle, fighting on the side of the Most High. They had been slain for a violation of the law. "And they found under the coats of the slain some of the donaries of the idols of Jamnia, which the law forbiddeth to the Jews: so that all plainly saw, that for this cause they were slain."[3] Their crime, which consisted in carrying off a few votive offerings, consecrated to idols, would not appear very grievous; nor was it judged to be so by Judas, who, this crime notwithstanding, "considered," the writer tells us, "that they had fallen asleep with godliness." Their salvation, therefore, was not to be despaired of. And, under these circumstances, what does this most holy man, thoroughly learned in the law? 1st. He joins with the army in prayer that their sin may be forgotten. 2nd. He sends money to Jerusalem with the view of having sacrifice offered for their sins. Clearly he believed that they were not in hell or heaven, but in some middle state, where they could be helped by the suffrages of their brethren on earth. This state can be no other than purgatory. Judas believed in the existence of purgatory; and to the authority of his name is added that of the sacred compiler of his exploits, who did not hesitate to affirm, in the widest sense, a doctrine, which, if false, he durst not insert in this book. "It is therefore a holy and wholesome thought to pray for the dead, that they may be loosed from their sins."

So the early Church, instructed by the Old and New Testaments, could not be insensible to a sort of idea that was running through the sacred writings—that, one time,

[1] 2 Machabees xii. 41—46.   [2] 2 Machabees xii. 34.
[3] 2 Machabees xii. 40.

came above the surface, and disappeared almost before it was apprehended, as when it is said: "Lay out thy bread and wine upon the burial (super sepulturam) of a just man"[1]—that anon appeared to the eye in its integrity, but surrounded by a haze of conflicting interpretations, as when Paul teaches that, "In the name of Jesus, every knee shall bow, of those that are in heaven, on earth, and *under the earth*"[2]—but that sometimes came out of the deep waters of sacred truth, so plain, so transparent, that no one could deny its evidence, as when Paul told the Corinthians that some persons shall be saved by fire, or Judas commanded the Jewish priest to offer sacrifice for the remission of the dead.

DIVISION IX.

THE CHURCH TRIUMPHANT.

§ 1. *Veneration of Saints.*—If St. Francis Xavier appeared upon earth, a well-disciplined Catholic would most assuredly take off his hat in passing or meeting him, in testimony of respect for his zeal for the salvation of souls. If St. Paul came down amongst us he would go farther, and he would consider himself perfectly blameless before the world in kissing through a religious motive that mouth which confessed Christ, or those feet which carried him to martyrdom. If St. Rose of Lima, sweet soul, was allowed to revisit the militant Church, which she had so much edified in her day, would the Catholic be regarded as superstitious, if with his hand to his heart he bowed most profoundly in her presence in testimony of his profound veneration for her innocence without blemish, and the unspotted purity of her life?

As a Catholic he would be rational and consistent with

---

[1] Tobias iv. 18.   [2] Philip. ii. 16.

his principles in so demeaning himself in presence of sanctity confirmed and crowned. Yet who on this earth renders more homage to superior qualities than the Protestant? Protestant countries are in most cases highly aristocratic. Protestants are worshippers of nobility and rank. Protestants, in fact, in common with Catholics, are prepared to give civil respect to civil qualities, be they internal, as genius, talent, acquirements in literature or science, or external, as nobility, rank, official position. They esteem it an honour to be allowed to kiss the hand of royalty, and they are but too happy to "salaam" to its representative in the person of a viceroy. Among them every man has his rank, and according to its grade he takes up his position, and receives more or less deference on public official occasions. Prostration is out of fashion in the courtly usages of the West at the present day, but marks of respect, humiliating enough, are still the order of the day at Potsdam and St. James's, as well as at the Tuileries or Vienna. Civil qualities deserving of respect, receive respect. So it ought to be; common sense so dictates; genius is worshipped, and valour receives its ovation; royalty is revered;—quite reasonable and just. But what about Paul, or Francis, or Rose of Lima? This much, that if Protestants feel themselves justified in venerating and literally worshipping civil qualities, they ought to feel themselves justified in worshipping religious qualities; for if the favour of the king gives a claim to respect, the favour of God ought to give a claim to respect; if an official position in an earthly court entitles the possessor to be saluted, reverenced, a position in the court of heaven ought to entitle its possessor to be saluted, reverenced. If talent be a foundation for esteem, grace is a foundation for esteem; if genius legitimately demands veneration, glory legitimately demands veneration. And hence it would appear that it is practically illogical in the Protestant to grant to Alexander or Frederick William what he would refuse to Francis or Paul.

So that, standing on rational grounds, there is no escape from saint veneration, unless one be disposed to shuffle off on the plea of inconsistency. The general principle is, that all superior qualities are to be respected. Can it be denied that confirmed sanctity is a superior quality? or that the possession of the glory of heaven is a superior quality? Hence, in the supposition of their being known to exist in a given individual, this individual ought to be venerated; or what amounts to the same, in the supposition that St. Paul or St. Francis visited the scene of their former labours, every Christian sound at heart and rational in principle, ought to love and worship them in a manner proportioned to their rank. But to come to realities. Paul and Francis Xavier do not appear upon earth, but they assist continually before the throne of God. The question is, Are they and others like them, who "have washed their robes and made them white in the blood of the Lamb," to be venerated by the faithful upon earth, though they exist and be in heaven only? If they were among us, holy and blessed as they are now, it would be reasonable to venerate them. Does it become unreasonable to venerate them because they are located in the Kingdom of God? It would appear to me that there can be only two objections made against the veneration of the saints in heaven. The first should arise from the existence of a positive divine law prohibiting such veneration, and this should be found in the Sacred Scriptures. The second should arise from the inutility of this devotion, in consequence of the inability of the saints in heaven to witness the devotional acts of the faithful on earth. In other words, if we cannot exhibit to the glorified servants of God that respect which we are allowed to show to the king, to the representatives of government, to our superiors in authority, to men of talent, to warriors, to those, in a word, who are distinguished by any great quality, innate or adventitious, the prohibition must arise from the nature of the case as between the living and the dead, or from the positive decree of God.

There was no positive ordination to prevent the members of the Primitive Church from venerating the saints.

If they looked to the inspired writings of the Old Testament there was no prohibition there. If angels in human form, as narrated in the historic books, sometimes prevented the servants of God from worshipping them, it was because the form of worship tendered was suited only to the Deity, or because it was offered under the false impression that God himself was present in their persons. If they examined the relations between the Essential Being and His creatures there was still no objection; for, from the nature of the case, the worship of God and the worship of His creatures must be fundamentally and radically different. To worship God is to render unlimited homage to infinity. To worship a saint or angel is to do homage to the works of God in a finite degree, proportioned to their excellence or value. Abstracting from the consideration that the worship rendered to the gifts of grace essentially redounds to the honour of God, and naturally ascends to the giver of them, there can be no more conceivable collision between Divine worship and the religious veneration of a saint, than there is between the acts of Divine and of kingly allegiance. But, secondly, devotion to the saints must be a useless practice even in the supposition of its not being positively prohibited in the Sacred Scriptures? The saints are at a distance. They can neither see nor hear their clients, nor be conscious of the praises of the Church on earth. So argue the opponents of Catholicity; but the Revealed Word is plainly opposed to them. St. Paul informed the primitive Christians that they were very near the saints. They were not to regard the saints as separated from them by a vast chasm, but as united to them by the closest bonds. In coming to the Church and embracing the Christian faith they entered the society of the saints and angels: they associated themselves as effectually with the spirits of the just in heaven as they did with the first-born of the Church upon earth. The words of the Apostle are conclusive on this point. He told the Hebrew Christians that as their ancestors, when Moses received the law, approached to the "tangible mountain" (Sinah) and the "burning fire," the "whirlwind," the "darkness," the storm, the "sound of a trumpet," "the voice of words," so they in receiving the Christian faith "came to Mount Sion, and to the city of the living God, the heavenly Jerusalem, and to the company of many thousands of angels, and to the church of the first-born, who are written in the heavens, and to God the judge of all, and to the spirits of just made perfect." Heb. xii. 18, 23. Yes! came as effectually as their ancestors;— came, not figuratively but literally, for their ancestors came so to Sinah;—came, not in hope or expectation, but in fact, came, arrived at the society of the saints and angels already. It would not be just to say that they so came if there was no communication between the Church militant and the Church triumphant. And if, according to their great doctor, St. Paul, there was a close and intimate connection between the two Churches, the sole obstacle to the veneration of the saints was removed for the early Christians.

But there were other passages equally encouraging. If the angels in heaven are conscious of events occurring in the Church upon earth, the saints may be presumed to be conscious of them likewise. If the saints and angels above be conscious of one event occurring in the Church below, there can be no difficulty in supposing them conscious of the Church's history in detail. If the blessed citizens of heaven rejoice in the victories of God's servants over the Prince of Darkness, why may they not sympathize with them in their struggles, and receive their respectful salutations with joy? Now the Primitive Church saw clearly that some events occurring among the flock of Christ are chronicled in heaven, and announced among the angelic choirs. The words of the Redeemer were the vouchers for the fact. "So I say to you, there shall be joy before the angels of God on one sinner doing penance." Luke xv. 10. It is not one angel who may have been a messenger from God to man that shall rejoice, but all the angelic body. Nor is it for the conversion of a particular sinner that they shall rejoice, but, as the sentence is a general one, it appears that the conversion of every sinner shall be a subject of joy to them. They shall all rejoice, and in every individual case of conversion that occurs. Their knowledge on this particular subject must be very extensive indeed, as an infinity of such cases must happen from time to time. The Primitive Church understood this, and perhaps saw in it a further illustration of the communion of saints, so plainly indicated by St. Paul in his Epistle to the Hebrews, and it had some reason to surmise that perhaps a regular line of angelic couriers is established between the inner and outer tabernacle, between the "Holy" and the "Holy of holies," between heaven and the Church, to transmit from every continent, and nation, and city, and village, and house, from every spot upon the earth tenanted by Christian men, the records of the Church, from the operations of its entire body to the most minute actions of its individual members, and to read them out before the whole court of heaven,—supported in this inference to some extent by another sentence pronounced by the Redeemer, "See that you despise not one of these little ones; for I say to you that their angels in heaven always see the face of my father who is in heaven." Mat. xviii. 10. If the angels were constantly travelling between heaven and earth, there was no repugnance in the supposition that they carried to the ears of the saints the pious devotions of their clients in the Church; so that at the very least one of the great objections to saint veneration was annihilated by the doctrine of the Redeemer.

Hitherto the Scripture passages cited afforded a negative demonstration. In comparing three texts of the Gospel according to St. Luke, an example was discovered, which stamped the practice of venerating the saints with the seal of inspired authority. The saint therein referred to is the first of the saints—the mother of the incarnate Word. An angel saluted her with profound respect. Her cousin Elizabeth saluted her in similar terms, which she must have learned from Divine inspiration; and then, in prophetic vision, she predicted that the same form of respectful salutation should be addressed to her by all the generations of the children of God. "Hail, full of grace," said the angel to her, "the Lord is with thee; blessed art thou among women." Luke i. 28. "Blessed art thou among women," said Elizabeth, "and blessed is the fruit of thy womb." Luke i. 42. "Behold," said the virgin mother, "from henceforth all generations shall call me blessed." Luke i. 48. Here are the same words repeated; sung out almost in chorus by Gabriel and Elizabeth, taken up by the faithful, and wafted through all time. Words they are, too, of great meaning; conveying the greatest compliment, if I may so speak, that can be addressed to a human being, because they single out one woman from all the members of her sex, past and to come, and pronounce her holy and happy above and beyond them all; words, too, which imply a worship as profound as any that can be rendered to a creature; words, the spirit of which must be imbibed, and the tenor of which must be repeated as of precept. There is no worship in words? Fully as much as in actions. There is a sort of worship, and must be in every term which recognizes the sanctity of the being to whom it is addressed, and is used for the purpose of expressing internal homage to such being. In common expressions there may be an "actus cultus duliæ;" and if this be so, what must we not say of words such as these, come down from heaven, announced by an archangel, to be repeated as of precept by the Church to the end of time. The blessed Virgin does not hear them? We infer that she does from the obligation of repeating them in compliment to her. What advantage are they to her? They add to her accidental glory. What significance had they for the members of the Primitive Church? This only: that if the blessed Virgin, by reason of her sanctity and the intimate relation she assumed to the Saviour of the world by Divine maternity, was to be venerated, and respected, and saluted as of necessity by Christians of all ages, the faithful of Christ were justified in venerating other saints, and worshipping them though in an inferior way, for they too are holy and confirmed in holiness, and united to the Saviour by grace, and glory, and everlasting love.

§ 2. *Prayers to them.*—Seated near the throne of God, and remaining perpetually in his divine presence, familiarised with the Divinity, if I may use the expression, by uninterrupted union and unvarying contemplation, the saints would appear from their position to be appropriate advocates between the heavenly Father and his struggling children upon earth. Primitive Christianity had been taught to believe that there is but "one mediator of God and man, the man Christ Jesus."[1] The primitive Christians had been again and again informed that there are numberless intercessors between God and man, in fact, that every member of the Church may be an advocate or intercessor for his brethren. "Pray for us," said St. Paul to the Hebrew Christians.[2] "We give thanks to God and the Father of our Lord Jesus Christ," said he to the Colossians, "praying always for you."[3] "Pray for one another, that you may be saved,"[4] said St. James. "This also we prayed for, your perfection."[5] "And this I pray that your charity may more and more abound in knowledge and in all understanding,"[6] &c., &c. The literal meaning of the word mediator is one who comes between two or more for purposes of arrangement or conciliation. Assuredly if a Christian pray to God for his fellow-Christian he comes between him and God for purposes of conciliation, and is, therefore, a mediator between God and man. Yet St. Paul says that there is but *one* mediator between God and man. Hence it is clear that in this sentence the Apostle employs the word mediator in a special and particular sense, employing much more than its literal meaning. I fancy the strong intellects of the primitive Church would have reasoned so. I don't believe Silas, or Apollo, or Ignatius, or Clement, would have fallen into the sophistry of some modern controversialists, who thus deliver themselves of a potent "eureka." If the saints could intercede for us they would be mediators.

---

[1] 1 Tim. ii. 5.
[2] Heb. xiii. 18.
[3] Coloss. i. 3.
[4] James v. 16.
[5] 2 Cor. xiii. 9.
[6] Philip. i. 9.

There is but one mediator, Christ Jesus, according to Paul. Therefore, intercessory prayer is beyond the province of the saints. Oh! how would not that man, powerful in the Scripture, who had learned logic, too, in the Roman schools, reply to such imbecility by a comparative argument as follows:—If the faithful on earth can intercede for you, they, by the fact of doing so, become mediators between God and man. But there is but one mediator between God and man, Christ Jesus. Therefore, the faithful upon earth cannot pray for you. But they can and ought to pray for each other according to inspired passages of the epistles of Paul and of James. Therefore, the argument in both cases is inconclusive, and the inference positively false.

Clearly so, and it is very foolish to play upon a mere word at the sacrifice of truth, and to the abuse of common sense. There is truly but one great Mediator of redemption, and it is from the infinite value of his mediation that the prayers of the faithful upon earth and of the glorified saints in heaven derive their efficacy and value. There are various mediators of intercession; notwithstanding which, the words of the Apostle are clearly and invariably true: "There is no other name under heaven given to men, whereby we must be saved,"[1] but the name of the Lord Jesus.

There was evidently no objection to the practice of invoking the intercession of the saints in the doctrine of "one mediator," and this is the only doctrine put forth in the New Testament which could appear, even for a moment, to come into collision with it. On the other hand, there is a passage in that mysterious book, the Apocalypse, which seems to reveal a state of things in the Heavenly Jerusalem dependent upon this practice, resulting from it, and directly sanctioning its existence. Here it is—
"And when he had opened the book, the four living creatures and the four and twenty ancients fell down before the Lamb, having everyone of them harps and

---

[1] Acts iv. 12.

golden vials full of odours, which are the prayers of the saints."[1]

The Apocalypse is a difficult book; and as there is an immense amount of imagery and mysticism in it, it will no doubt appear strange to some that a doctrine such as we now contemplate should be gathered from its obscure allusions. Yet even in the "Apocalypse" there are passages that can be easily understood. No doubt all is not clear in the text I have cited. For instance, who are the four living creatures and the four and twenty elders? Are they angels or saints? And if they be either, does it not destroy the significance of the passage that they should be seen by St. John under sensible forms? All these difficulties are fully admitted; yet a fact is plainly stated, the bearing of which on the practice under discussion cannot be questioned or denied. These four and twenty creatures, be they angels or saints, fell down before the throne of God, "with vials full of odours, which are the prayers of the saints." Certainly the saints mentioned here are not the glorified saints in heaven, for, in the first place, they don't pray nor require to pray for themselves, and then it would be unreasonable to suppose that they are prayed for by their brethren in glory. If they be not the saints in heaven, they must be those whom St. Paul designates "sancti," "electi," "vocati," viz., the saints of the Church upon earth. And if this be the fact, we have the living creatures, be they angels or saints, presenting the petitions of the faithful before the throne of God, *i. e.*, the saints in heaven offering to God the prayers of the saints on earth. If this be not the sense of the passage, I think we must give up the interpretation of it altogether, and place it among the "obscura" of the Apocalypse. Now if the saints pray for us, or, what is the same thing, if they present our petitions before God, it is obvious that we may pray to them—it is clear even that we ought to pray to them, for, hurried about among the distracting cares of life, and buffeted by the waves of temptation and

[1] Apocalypse v. 8.

error, all the time—sinful and not worthy to come before the majesty of God in the form of petitioners, we ought to be, above all, anxious to present our addresses in the most effectual way to the source of light and strength. Our own interest should urge us to secure the advocacy of the citizens of heaven, of the courtiers of Divine Majesty, so dear to him, so holy, so blameless as the glorified saints.

Thus the early Christians, reading the Scriptures honestly, saw no objection there to the practice of praying to the saints. Not only this, but they found some foundation for the exercise in an event recorded in the mysterious vision of St. John. When the Scriptures were written, few members of the Church, at least few of its pillars and ornaments, had yet gone to glory; and hence we shall not find positive examples of addresses to the saints until the first age has passed away, carrying with it the firstfruits of faith and grace, and depositing them in the kingdom of God.

§ 3. *Their relics.*—I believe we cannot deny that the primitive Church had some reason founded on the Sacred Scriptures for paying respect and reverence to the bones or body of, suppose, an apostle or sainted bishop after his demise. The faithful had ocular demonstration of miracles wrought by contact with these bodies while they were still animated by the soul. They had seen the shadow of the body of Peter delivering from their infirmities the sick whom it overshadowed. "And the multitude of men and women who believed in the Lord was more increased. In so much that they brought forth the sick into the streets and laid them on beds and couches, that when Peter came, his shadow at the least might overshadow any of them, and they might be delivered from their infirmities."[1] They had seen, too, diseases and evil spirits expelled by the contact of aprons and handkerchiefs which had touched the body of Paul. "And God wrought by the hand of Paul more than common miracles. So that there were

---

[1] Acts v. 14, 15.

brought from his body to the sick handkerchiefs and aprons, and the diseases departed from them, and the evil spirits went out of them."[1] Perchance, too, some of them remembered a fact that had been recorded of the bones of the prophet Eliseus by the inspired writer of the Fourth Book of Kings. "And some that were burying a man, saw the rovers, and cast the body into the sepulchre of Eliseus. And when it had touched the bones of Eliseus, the man came to life, and stood upon his feet."[2] Such facts as these were calculated to create in the minds of the primitive Christians sentiments of respect and reverence for the remains of the holy ones of the Church deceased; and accordingly we find that when Stephen died for the faith, his body was not immediately consigned to the tomb, but religious ceremony would appear to have accompanied his obsequies. If his deceased body was valueless in the eyes of the Church, we should expect that his funeral would be a matter of indifference to the faithful. Sinners or infidels might carry him to the grave, or the Jewish rabble that had stoned him. But no! it would appear from a passage in the Sacred Scripture that this office was reserved for the sanctified members of the Church. "Devout men took order for Stephen's funeral, and made great mourning over him."[3]

Particular facts may be apposite illustrations of a general truth. They do not demonstrate it conclusively. The miraculous properties of the bodies of Peter and Paul and Eliseus do not prove, nor are they intended to prove, that the body of every saint is necessarily a miracle-working instrument, nor does the fact recorded of Stephen evince beyond dispute that the corpse of every one who fell for the faith was honoured and watched over by the pious. Yet these facts are suggestive of what may have been the practice of the primitive Church in reference to the treatment of the remains of her saints and martyrs, and of the grounds on which such practice was founded.

If we look for a demonstrative proof, that the primitive

---

[1] Acts xix. 11, 12.   [2] 4 Kings xiii. 21.   [3] Acts viii. 2.

Church honoured the relics of the saints, we shall find it in a magnificent passage of St. Paul's first epistle to the Corinthians, where, speaking of the bodies of the elect, he says, "It is sown in corruption; it shall rise in incorruption. It is sown in dishonour; it shall rise in glory. It is sown in weakness; it shall rise in power. It is sown a natural body; it shall rise a spiritual body."[1] It (that is to say, the body of the saint) is, according to the Apostle, the same body in this life, and in death, and after the resurrection: its qualities only are changed. It puts off corruption, weakness, inertness; it assumes agility, glory, power, incorruption; but it is the same body all through. Take it in its worst state, when it is yielding to the gradual approach of decomposition, or when it is reduced to a mass of dry bones. It was the temple of God while the soul animated it: Christ came to it and his eternal Father, and they dwelled in it. So it was as to the past; as to its future state, already elected to glory, every particle of matter composing it is destined to be reunited to the soul on the last day, and to live through all eternity in the freshness of immortal life. Is it then to get no honour in its present state? Surely it is superior to the matter surrounding it, in consequence of its certain election to a glorious immortality. Therefore, the primitive disciples of the Redeemer, knowing the doctrine of St. Paul on the subject of the resurrection, were compelled on principle to pay a certain rational amount of religious respect to the relics of their sainted dead, and we would reasonably expect to find them gathering their dust and collecting their shattered bones, and depositing them in holy places near the altar of sacrifice, or at least in the houses of prayer.

§ 4. *Relative Worship, the Cross, &c.*—Worship may be absolute or relative. The distinction is not a technical or gratuitous one, but it arises from the circumstances of the case, and the grounds of such a distinction are dis-

---

[1] 1 Cor. xv. 42—44.

cernible in daily usage. Worship may be absolute or
relative, because the object worshipped may be good and
valuable in itself, or it may be appreciable solely on account
of its connection with some other being. There can be
no great difficulty in catching the nature of absolute worship
and fully understanding the meaning of the term. Examples
of absolute worship abound in social and civil life,
so numerous, so familiar, as to present a clear idea devoid
of all ambiguity. It is only necessary to represent a few
of them to ourselves. A man of surpassing genius is
revered; his genius, his talents are revered; there is in him
the foundation of the reverence he receives, and the object
(his genius) to which it is directed. This veneration of
him, this civil worship he receives is absolute. A statesman
has had every advantage of experience and good training.
An immense acquired knowledge grafted upon a rarely
energetic and practical disposition, has given him uncommon
skill and wisdom in the despatch of public business.
The aptitude, the faculty for business, thus acquired is an
absolute quality inherent in his soul. It is quite clear that
if his skill in public affairs be revered, or if he be reverenced
in consequence of it, the civil worship rendered him
must be absolute worship. Absolute worship, then, is the
reverence paid to a superior quality existing in another, in
his soul, his body, his mind, his intelligence; it makes no
difference provided it so abides with him, that it may be
properly called his own. Relative worship it is not so
easy to understand, though of it, too, examples occur in
civil life, which are strongly significant and suggestive.
In relative worship the veneration rendered does not terminate
at the being to whom it is immediately directed,
but ascends to another being with whom the first is someway
connected. It is, in fact, representative respect, representative
reverence. It is addressed to a being animate or
inanimate, because it represents another, and brings another
to mind, and shows forth some property or quality of
another. Its object is not anything existing in the being
to whom it is addressed, but existing in another to which
the first bears some relation. In truth, it is called relative,

because it is founded on a relation of one thing to another. The relations of things are innumerable; there are the relations of paternity, of friendship, of unity, of authority, of similarity. There are evil relations, which lead to distrust, dislike; good relations, which lead to love, respect. The relations of things become obvious through the senses generally, by the sight, the hearing, the touch. Examples of relative civil worship may be easily adduced. A viceroy represents sovereign authority. If the viceroy be venerated, inasmuch as he represents the King or Queen, the worship rendered to him is relative. A son, in a certain sense, represents his parents. If a son be respected and loved precisely because he is the son of such a father or mother, the civil respect shown him is relative. No doubt both the viceroy and the son may be venerated for their own qualities, irrespective of those whom they represent,—the former for his power and authority, the latter for his faithfulness and industry; but this does not destroy the possibility of making them the channels or "media" through which loyalty and friendship find their way to their proper term.

The distinction of worship into absolute and relative may be applied to spiritual things; and the following will appear to be the result:—1. The worship of God is absolute, inasmuch as the perfections of all other beings are derived from him; the veneration of the firmament, inasmuch as it represents the power of God, is relative. 2. The worship of the sacred humanity of Christ, hypostatically united to the Divinity, is absolute. The veneration of the Cross, the "sacred stairs," the hill of Calvary, inasmuch as they represent the passion, and bring it to mind, is relative. 3. The worship of sanctifying grace or the gifts of glory existing in a saint is absolute. The veneration of the picture of the saint, his girdle, his house, which recall his blameless life, is relative.

With this preface we come to the consideration of the question which presents itself in natural order, after the cussions of the last three sections,—namely, Did relative rship exist in the primitive Church? or could it be tolerated among the faithful of those days, consistently with the doctrine of the ancient inspired writers, or their own apostles or evangelists?

Relative worship is most certainly not forbidden by the first commandment as announced in the Pentateuch. "Thou shalt not have strange gods before me. Thou shalt not make to thyself a graven thing, nor the likeness of anything that is in heaven above or in the earth beneath, or of those things that are in the waters under the earth. Thou shalt not adore them nor serve them."[1] This commandment is susceptible of two interpretations. Its meaning might, on a first view, be taken to be: Make not to thyself images for any purpose. Or, it might be: Make them not for the special purpose of sovereign adoration. On a closer examination of the passage, however, aided by common sense, and a little, ever so little, scriptural knowledge, it would be apparent that the first interpretation is perfectly inadmissible. For, in the first place, the text introduces the prohibition of image-making by the words "Thou shalt not have strange gods before me," and dismisses it with the significant remark, "Thou shalt not adore them nor serve them," thereby showing us clearly that the images here denounced and reprobated are they that are used as gods. Secondly, if the formation of images could be supposed to be universally forbidden here, the Sacred Scripture would be scarcely consistent with itself. In this case it would not be lawful to form the likeness of a cherub, because it is in heaven, nor of a serpent, because it is on earth. The words are, "Thou shalt not make to thyself a graven thing, nor the likeness of anything that is in heaven above, or in the earth beneath, nor of those things that are in the waters under the earth." Yet it was not only lawful, but it was commanded to make a likeness both of a serpent and a cherub, —ordered by God himself. "Thou shalt make also two cherubims of beaten gold on the two sides of the oracle."[2]

[1] Exodus xx. 3, 4, 5.   [2] Exodus xxv. 18.

"And the Lord said to him: Make a brazen serpent, and set it up for a sign: whosoever being struck shall look upon it, shall live."[1] Finally, common sense repudiates such a general prohibition, unless it could be supposed to be a part of the ceremonial law of the Jews, and if it be supposed to be so, it was abrogated on the advent of Christianity.

The first commandment, therefore, prohibiting the formation of idols and their worship only, does not touch the question we have proposed to discuss, namely, Did relative worship exist in the primitive Church, and did the faithful of these early times revere the pictures and images of departed saints or the mementos of the passion of Christ?

Writers of certain opinions would fain make us believe that there is something so intrinsically absurd in saluting a statue or bowing to the Cross, that sound Christianity in all ages must have recoiled from such practices. "A pretty idea," said an American gentleman, in my hearing, as he stopped to take breath opposite a little picture of St. Francis on the hill-side, as he mounted towards the valley of Chamounix; "pretty, but unmeaning." An English novel-writer of distinction gives us, in his own graphic way, a description of a scene in which an Italian desperado, "at the sound of the angelus turns towards 'a little doll' (an image of the blessed Virgin) fastened to a tree, salutes it, blesses himself, mutters some prayers, and returns to his daily avocation." Such a fund of indignation does the practice of relative worship in Catholic countries excite in the minds of certain travellers that they feel themselves called upon, in the name of Christianity, to sneer at the chains of St. Peter, to scoff at the blood of St. Januarius, to talk out and laugh in ascending the "scala sancta;" and I am sure, if they were not restrained by a salutary fear, they would take a morbid pleasure, on their travels abroad, in overturning the crucifixes which cover French territory, or tearing down the images which adorn the town, houses, and farmsteads of Bavaria.

---

[1] Numbers xxi. 8.

So much enlightenment is not appreciated; for, notwithstanding the Anglo-Saxon howl of derision, simple people, living on the slopes of Styria, or perched upon the green plateaux which circle the base of the glaciers of Savoy, reanimate their love for the Redeemer when they uncover to the crosses which stand on the brink of the precipice, while scholars, astute and wise, living peaceably among their books in the universities of Spain and Belgium, Austria and the Rhine provinces, Italy and France, defend on rational grounds, abstracting from authority, the thesis, that the relative veneration of religious objects is not repugnant to any duty arising out of the subjection of man to God.

I will take it for granted that primitive Christianity, so recently enlightened, and so near the source of truth, saw things without crookedness, prejudice, or hurry, and reasoned upon them calmly and logically.

If relative worship be unreasonable and repugnant to man's duty as a creature, it must detract from the worship of the Creator. Yet, no! it rather promotes the worship of God; it leads unenlightened minds to him, by sensible objects, which produce upon them a greater impression than intellectual motives; it leads learned minds to him, by arresting them in their profound reflections, and recalling their thoughts, wandering too often and dissipated, to the single contemplation of his goodness or his love. Nor can it be fairly said that it is calculated to fix the mind of the Christian on the visible and created, and withdraw it from the innate and unseen. It would be so, in the supposition that Christians were of excessively gross apprehension, and perfectly uninstructed in the nature of relative veneration; but the Church of God is solemnly bound to see to the religious instruction of all her children, and for those who are moderately acquainted with the Christian doctrine, idol-worship is about the least danger to be apprehended. But abstracting from its consequences, let us consider it in itself. Image veneration is seated in the bosom of every family where sympathy and union flourish, and respect for the ties of kindred. How often will you find the picture of a deceased parent, brother, or sister, occupying the most honourable position in a dining-room! How often are the mementos of a deceased friend, in the form of ornaments, letters, keepsakes, preserved with religious care! But there is no danger of adoring them? Certainly not; but there is likewise no danger of adoring a statue of the Madonna, or a crucifix, unless a man is bereft of reason. Then the veneration given to such mementos of family affection is social or civil, whereas in the case of the crucifix and picture of the saints it is religious? Quite true; but if there be an obligation never to respect or venerate the created gifts of God, neither friends nor their mementos ought to be treated with a particle of veneration; and if, on the other side, the worship of the natural and created gifts of God, absolutely or relatively, be allowed, there can be no objection, founded on the relation of man to God, to the relative and absolute worship of the supernatural gifts of God, such as grace and glory, for they, too, are created.

It would not be unreasonable in the primitive Christians to venerate the instruments of the passion of Christ, or the scourges, racks, or gibbets, which had carried the martyrs to their crown. But, better still, there was scriptural usage in favour of such practices; and the conduct and teaching of a great apostle sanctioned them at that day, even as the usage of the Jewish Church had sanctioned them in an age then passed. The pronunciation of a name is a creation of the lips, tongue, and palate, as the formation of a statue is the creation of the hands. A name represents Christ as a statue represents him, that is to say, sensibly. There is as much of a relation between a name and him to whom it belongs, as between him and a statue that is made to represent him. The worship or veneration of a name is, then, about the same thing as the veneration or worship of a statue. Each is the relative worship of a sensible thing. If the worship of a name be allowed, there can be no objection to the relative worship of a statue or representation. Now listen to St. Paul speaking of the name of the Redeemer. " He (the Redeemer) humbled himself, becoming obedient unto death, even the death of the cross. For which cause God also hath exalted him, and hath given him a name, which is above all names, that in the name of Jesus every knee shall bow, of those that are in heaven, on earth, and under the earth."[1] To bow the knee at the mention of the name of Jesus is undoubtedly to render to it a very marked veneration; and if St. Paul's words here enjoin that such a tribute of respect is to be given it, they directly sanction the practice of relative worship. But no! they do not proclaim a precept, says an objector, they simply announce a fact. The meaning is not—Christians, both living and dead, must adore at the mention of the sacred name, but Christians shall bow the knee in his name, that is, invoking God through his merits, adoring him as their head and the author of their salvation. Any one, however, can perceive that both meanings are included in the text; and there can be no reason why the more obvious and literal should be rejected. The Father, according to St. Paul, honoured the Son for his obedience and voluntary sufferings. But how? The Apostle answers by giving him a name—Jesus or Saviour. But in giving him the name Jesus how does he honour him? Because of the great sacredness of this name, for "every knee shall bow in it." But how shall every knee bow in the name of Jesus? Evidently in two ways. 1st. By bowing under its protection. 2nd. By bowing when it is mentioned. And in both cases the Saviour's name is worshipped, while he is absolutely adored. This language of the Apostle so understood was not to be wondered at, when the injunctions of the Old Testament touching the name of God were duly considered by the Philippians. "Thou shalt not take the name of the Lord thy God in vain, for he shall not be unpunished that taketh his name upon a vain thing."[2] 1st. It was not to be mentioned without respect and reasonable cause. 2nd. Its very sound was to be a source of awe and

---

[1] Philip. ii. 8—10.   [2] Deut. v. ii.

reverential fear. "If thou wilt not . . . fear his glorious and terrible name, that is, the Lord thy God, the Lord shall increase thy plagues."[1] 3rd. So holy was it that its publication was withheld from the patriarchs, and it was not communicated until the time of Moses. "I am the Lord that appeared to Abraham, to Isaac, and to Jacob, by the name of the Almighty; and my name 'Adonai' I did not show them."[2]

The respect evinced by the Apostle for the sufferings of his Saviour, where he says, "But God forbid that I should glory save in the cross of our Lord Jesus Christ, by which the world is crucified to me and I to the world,"[3] is immediately directed to the instrument of them—the cross. The cross is venerated by him in an outward glorying in it, which, though it consist of words only, is an external act, or rather a series of external acts of respect. And to venerate the cross as the instrument of the passion, by any suitable act or word, is to render to it a relative worship.

If in the early Church a question arose as to the lawfulness of depositing in a holy place the girdle of James the greater, or railing off from the public the spot on which Stephen shed his blood, reference was naturally made to the Old Testament, and usages bearing on the points presented themselves in the ancient history of the people of God. There was the manna—how religiously it was kept! "Take a vessel," said the Spirit of God, "and put manna into it, as much as a gomer can hold; and lay it up before the Lord, to keep unto all generations."[4] There was, too, the rod of Aaron. "Carry back the rod of Aaron into the tabernacle of the testimony, that it may be kept there for a token of the rebellious children of Israel."[5] There were, besides, the tables of the law, all of which, as St. Paul affirms, had the high honour of being deposited in the ark of the covenant. "And after the second veil, the tabernacle, which is called the holy of

---

[1] Deut. xxviii. 58.   [2] Exod. vi. 1, 2.   [3] Gal. vi. 14.
[4] Exod. xvi. 33.   [5] Numb. xvii. 10.

holies, having a golden censer, and the ark of the testament covered about on every part with gold, in which was a golden pot that had manna, and the rod of Aaron that had blossomed, and the tables of the testament."[1] The acts of depositing and retaining in so sacred a place these mementos of the exercise of divine power would appear to involve a religious and relative worship to them. For what, after all, is the veneration of a relic, if it consist not in separating it from secular and profane usages, of regarding it with reverence, and treating it with respect and honour? And there would appear to be a difference only nominal between the operation of "kissing the sacred remains of a saint, wrapped up in silk and gold," and depositing the same remains in a place so sacred as the ark of the covenant, so inapproachable as the "holy of holies," where no one presumed to enter but the high-priest, and he but once a year.

Great as was the reverence that surrounded the manna and the rod of Aaron, it was not so palpable, or illustrative, as that which a Divine ordinance demanded for the "ark of the covenant." The multitude was not to approach it. It was death to touch it, even in what would appear to be a case of necessity.. The ground within a certain distance of it was hallowed by its presence, and must not be trespassed upon by the feet of the unconsecrated. "When you shall see the ark of the covenant of the Lord your God, and the priests of the race of Levi carrying it, rise you up also, and follow them as they go before. And let there be between you and the ark the space of two thousand cubits: that you may see it afar off, and know which way you must go: for you have not gone this way before; and take care you come not near the ark."[2] "And when they came to the floor of Nachor, Oza put forth his hand to the ark of God, and took hold of it, because the oxen kicked and made it lean aside. And the indignation of the Lord was enkindled against Oza, and he struck him for his rashness, and he died there before the ark of God."[3] The

[1] Heb. ix. 4.   [2] Josue iii. 3, 4.   [3] 2 Kings vi. 6, 7.

veneration enjoined and sanctioned in these passages was unquestionably of a very high order. It was relative of course; but it was eminently religious. It was negative—"Take care you come not near the ark." It was positive—"Let there be between you and the ark the space of two thousand cubits." If it were said nevertheless that it did not involve such acts as the Catholic Church sometimes rendered to holy things, bowing, for instance, or uncovering the head, it was easy to cite from the history of Moses, a case that illustrated that point precisely—where the Spirit of God speaking from the burning bush said to that holy man, "Come not nigh hither: put off the shoes from thy feet: for the place whereon thou standest is holy ground."[1]

The relative religious veneration of inanimate things connected in some intimate way with God and his saints, and the absolute adoration of the power and goodness, the mercy and providence of God, in such objects as shewed forth these Divine perfections, were not repugnant to reason or common sense,—were not inconsistent with the relations of man to God, and his utter subjection to the dominion of His providence, and so far from being opposed to any positive Divine law, they had numerous sanctions in the inspired Scriptures of the Old Testament. It therefore is of little importance whether examples of relative worship occur in the pages of the New Testament, for we may be assured that the primitive disciples of the Lord, acting upon the dictates of reason and the suggestions of revelation, render to all things their due—civil respect to whom civil respect is due, religious veneration to objects that demanded it, "fear to whom fear," honour to whom honour;" and we need not argue upon the point to understand thoroughly how different was their conduct from that of those who, while they treasure the mementos of sinners, scoff at the mementos of the saints and friends of God.[2]

There is a city in Italy disinterred after lying for a

---

[1] Exod. iii. v.   [2] See Appendix B.

decade and a half of centuries hidden in the bowels of the
earth, into which we can now descend to study the arts
and usages of ancient Rome, and almost to converse with
the spirits of those who once tenanted its houses, and trod
its desolate streets. Does it not appear that by descending
a little into the deep mines of truth contained in the
sacred writings, by sifting and examining, and throwing
off the dark coverings which hang over certain passages,
we find ourselves among the primitive disciples of the
Lord, where a light is shed over all the institutions of that
City of the living God, in which we can clearly discern the
manners and usages, the belief and discipline, the worship
and conversation of the immediate disciples of the Lord?
There we see an altar, and a real sacrifice offered upon
it, and veritable priests standing by it, and distributing
the fruits of it—the very victim offered to the assembled
people of God. Prayer and instruction, hymns and many
tapers, prophecy and tongues accompanying the oblation,
and serving as so many ornaments to embellish the dwelling
of the great King. Much pomp, or state, or consequence?
No, not much; but poverty honoured and commended—
the poor to sit near the rich in the congregation—the rich
to renounce the goods of this world, and to become dependants living on the alms of the Church. Marrying
and getting married? Yes! in many cases, but more
exalted still the state of perpetual continency embraced
for the love of God, as removing many obstacles to the
contemplation of His infinite perfections. And the congregation in common, how spiritually favoured! Every
individual washed from sin (Abluti estis), confirmed, anointed, sealed, and, as a result, endowed with the pledge
of the Spirit in the heart—("Now he that confirmeth us
with you in Christ and that anointeth us is God, Who
also hath sealed us and given the pledge of the Spirit in
our hearts;"[1])—the sinner released from his actual sins
before God, by a ministry of reconciliation, exercised by
the Ministers of the Church on earth—the dying anointed

---

[1] 2 Cor. i. 21, 22.

with oil—the dead in the love of God "wept over and honoured by the pious," their relics preserved, their memories honoured, their intercession invoked — the suffering dead prayed for—and high above all, as it will be before the coming of the day of the Lord, "the sign of the Son of Man," the cross, venerated as the symbol of redemption, gloried in as the instrument of God's incomprehensible love for His creatures.

Part the Second.

THE PERPETUATION OF THE FAITH AND PRACTICE DELIVERED TO THE FIRST SAINTS.

Anno 110—216.

Part the Second.

DIVISION I.

IDENTITY OF CHRISTIAN FAITH.

The second century of the Christian era is a comparatively dark period, thrown in between two periods of light; and it is not to be wondered at if controversialists, unable to maintain from direct historic evidence, the non-revelation of doctrines cherished by their adversaries, should refer the introduction of them to such a period as this, where direct rebutting evidence is not discovered without difficulty, and the materials of positive proof are few indeed, and not very strong or convincing. The Church of this period has been a favourite theme with the adversaries of the Catholic Church. They discover here an orthodoxy at first, and there a heterodoxy of belief and practice. It grew and it grew not. It flourished and it died. It believed—it doubted—it denied the faith: and all within the short space of one hundred years. Such is the Protestant view. Let us consider the facts of this important case as they can be culled from the writings of the time.

Was the faith of the Church the same at the beginning and at the end of this period we now examine? Here is the question as to the identity of faith. Or in other words, did the Church in the middle of the third century, hold a body of doctrine substantially different from that which it held while the Apostles were still presiding over it, and guiding it by their counsels and inspiration? It must be admitted by all parties that a certain body of revealed doctrine was delivered by God to His Church. Certain men of the old dispensation were inspired; who they were is a question with which we have nothing to do here. Certain men of the new dispensation were inspired; whether they wrote all that God revealed to them, or whether they delivered a portion of it unwritten to the Church, is a question we do not now discuss. That certain holy men of the old and new dispensations were heavenly-taught men is a fact admitted by all: and that these men—the Prophets of the Old, and the Apostles of the New Testament, delivered their heavenly doctrines to the people of God under divine inspiration is, a fact that is equally incontrovertible.

The body of revealed doctrine was certainly not the same at all times—for instance, it was greater in the time of St. Paul than it was in the time of Isaias. It had been gradually growing from the time that Moses wrote the book of Genesis: and it went on accumulating word upon word, and fact upon fact, and book upon book, until some period approaching the death of the last of the Apostles, when it formed one comprehensive body of doctrine, which was the property and the possession of the Church of God on earth. Did the Church retain this body of doctrine unchanged during the second century of its existence? Here is the important question that we have now to examine, and from the answer to this question there will be a great result deducible, for it will determine the validity of the claims of parties sufficiently hostile to identification in faith with the professors of primitive Christianity. This question involves a twofold inquiry. The Church might be supposed to lose the deposit of faith —1st, By becoming absolutely oblivious of some revealed doctrine committed to her keeping. Or 2nd, By erring as to the meaning of some such doctrine, though perhaps retaining its forms. Or, in other words, the Church might be supposed to get into a state of simple nescience in reference to certain articles of faith, or into a state of palpable heresy. Heresy is criminal—oblivion is not necessarily a crime. The Church might be an oblivious Church: and yet not necessarily unorthodox in faith. But if the Church lost the faith, by erring as to the meaning of any revealed article committed to her care, she would by this very fact cease at once to be the heavenly-taught Church of Christ.

We do not inquire here whether the Church of the two first centuries was oblivious of the faith or not; but we want to discover, whether the Church was orthodox or unorthodox. The adversaries of the Catholic Church who identify the integrity of faith with the integrity of the sacred Scriptures, and who gladly acknowledge that the Scriptures were preserved in their integrity during the two first centuries, do not bring any charge of obliviousness against the Church of this period. They impute to her a crime—the crime of having erred from the faith—the crime of having believed, of having doubted, of having denied. Catholic divines, while admitting that the explicit belief of the Church might undergo some change from circumstances, and might be greater at one time than another, are still unanimous in asserting that the adequate belief of the Church has been always one and the same. Catholics and Acatholics argue the question on different grounds, and they regard the question of the Church's obliviousness from an entirely different point of view; but they are both agreed as to the result, namely, that the Church of this period handed down to the Church that succeeded it, a body of doctrine, co-extensive with that which it received from the Apostles; or, in other words, both admit alike, that the Church did not become nescient from obliviousness of any article of the faith committed to her during the course of the two first centuries.

But we have said that the Church might be supposed to lose the faith, by erring as to the meaning of some article of it, though perhaps retaining the form of words in which such article was originally conveyed: and it is in reference to the truth or falsehood of this supposition as regards the Church of the second century that the identity of faith becomes here a matter for discussion. The question we ask is as follows—Did the Christian Church during the course of the second century of her existence, err as to the meaning of any article of faith committed to her? Did she substitute truth for falsehood—a shadow for the substance, a human lie for the revealed Word of God? Did she, for instance, in reference to the Holy Eucharist, substitute a real presence for a figurative presence; or in reference to orders, did she conceive an inherent virtue, operative of grace, in the rite, whereby it was administered, in lieu of a mere denominating influence, or a simply consecrating power? Did she, in one word, understand any revealed dogma touching grace or ceremony, sacrifice or election, mediation or sacrament, redemption or salvation in the middle of the third century in a sense different from that sense, in which such articles were understood by the Apostles, and received by that Church over which the Apostles personally presided? If a truth were clearly deducible from a revealed dogma, it might be for the Church to draw the deduction; and if the Church defined or assumed as a doctrine to be believed an obvious inference from revelation, it would not follow as a consequence, that the Church had changed her faith.

Particular propositions are contained in general propositions distributively taken; and if the general proposition be truth, the truth of the particular proposition will follow as a consequence from it. If it be true that all men are mortal, it will necessarily follow that every individual is a mortal man. If it be laid down that every soul of man is immortal, we may lawfully conclude that John, or Thomas, or Paul, is endowed with an immortal soul.

What we say of propositions in general, we may say of revealed propositions. If a universal proposition be revealed, a particular proposition contained in it may not be strictly a revealed proposition, but unquestionably it will be a true proposition; and when the Church by an accurate process of reasoning derives a particular proposition not revealed in terms from a general revealed proposition, and adopts the former as an article to be believed, she does not add to the deposit of faith, nor pretend to a new revelation. The doctrine of the Church might be added to, the faith of the Church remaining the same. The body of revelation might be developed without losing a particle of its identity.

We do not inquire here whether the Church added to the revelation by deduction or legitimate inference, but we wish to ascertain if she added to it in such a way as to make the body of doctrine assumed as revealed, in the end of the third century, different from the deposit of faith which had been committed to her keeping in the first.

Wherefore the original question as to the identity of the Church's faith, divested of all obscurity, reduces itself to the simply inquiry—Did the Church fall into an error in faith during the period which elapsed between the death of the Apostles and the middle of the second century? Did she falsify any article committed to her, or did she add falsehood to revelation, for, if she did, the identity of faith was lost, and if she did not, the faith of the third century, so particular, so manifest in all its parts, so catholic, so fully identical with our own, is proved to have come down by direct tradition from the very source of light and truth—the Redeemer speaking upon earth and the Apostles speaking in his name.

DIVISION II.

WHAT THE CHURCH BELIEVED ON THE SUBJECT.

A CANDID examiner of the ecclesiastical documents of the first and second century cannot fail to be struck by the evidence there afforded of the pertinacious adherence of the Church to the doctrines which she believed to have come from the Apostles. The Church believed in her own orthodoxy, and the Christian controversialists of the very earliest age constantly referred to the traditionary teaching of the Church as a guarantee against all errors, and a tribunal from which there was no appeal. The Church believed that she did not err in faith. Individual writers believed that she could not err in faith; and, amidst the mental activity of the time and the manifestly exalted piety of the primitive Christians, it is difficult to suppose that, with such a belief of individuals and the Church, an actual error could have crept in and pervaded the mind of a community so extensive and composed of such various and, under many respects, discordant elements.

Individuals and the Church were fully persuaded of their thorough orthodoxy during the entire of the second century; and this conviction is often manifest in the words and conduct of the most illustrious ecclesiastics of that period. Hear how one of them, a Phrygian bishop who lived in the beginning of the second century, identifies his faith with the faith which the Apostles taught. The fragment from which I quote is preserved by Eusebius. "For me, I have little regard for those who speak much, but I love those who speak the truth; nor for those do I care who ventilate precepts that are strange to me, but for such as relate the precepts which the Lord has confided to us, and which proceed from truth itself. If any one comes the way who has been a disciple of the ancients, I interrogate him as to their discourse. What Andrew said, or Peter, or Philip, or Thomas, or James, or John, or Matthew, or any other of the disciples of the Lord, or what said Aristion, or the presbyter John, the ancient disciple of the Lord. For to me it appears that what I read in books doth not profit me so much as that which I have learned from the living word of mouth."[1] Papias was a bishop, and probably an old man, when he expressed himself in these words. He was a contemporary of Polycarpe and Ignatius; and possibly had often conversed with "the

---

[1] Euseb. His. iii. cap. ult.

light of the Churches of Asia,"[1] and his affections were obviously with an age that had just passed, and with men that were now no more. He cherished a memento of them—their faith. He ruminated upon it. He made it his own. He kept it fresh in his memory by talking often about it. He is a living link in the chain of the succession of apostolic doctrine, and a valuable witness to the faith of the Churches of Asia in the beginning of the second century of the Christian era.

Farther on in the century, we discover a passage of similar import in a treatise written against the heretic Florinus, by Irenæus, the bishop of Lyons. The passage is a very beautiful one, and I give it at length from the Ecclesiatical History of Fleury. "These dogmas, Florinus, to speak with moderation, are not sound doctrine. These teachings do not accord with the Church; and they involve those who embrace them in impiety of the deepest die. The heretics themselves, who are outside the Church, have never ventured to advance such doctrines as these. These are not what we have been taught by the presbyters, our predecessors, who have conversed with the Apostles themselves. For, when I was yet a child, I saw you in Asia Minor, at the house of Polycarpe, whose esteem you sought, though you had even then a considerable employment at court. I have a clearer recollection of that time than of this which has just passed. For early recollections grow with the soul and entwine themselves about it; to such a degree (in my case) that I could tell of the place where the blessed Polycarpe sat when he spoke, of his employments, of his manner of life, of his external appearance, of the discourse which he made to the people. How he told us that he had lived with John and with the others who had seen the Lord. How he remembered their discourse, and that which he had heard them say touching their Lord, his miracles, and his doctrine. Polycarpe related all this conformably to the Scriptures, having learned it from those who with their own eyes had

---

[1] St. John.

seen the Word of Life. God gave me the grace at the time to listen to these discourses with profound application, and to write them, not on paper, but on my heart, and, by the mercy of God, I ruminate upon them even now continually."[1] It is worth while to observe the drift of the argument of Irenæus. The principles of Florinus cannot be admitted. They do not agree with the teaching of the Church. They are contrary to the teaching of Polycarpe, who conversed with the immediate disciples of the Lord. They are absolutely irreconcilable with the traditions still firmly adhered to by those who had the happiness of being present at the discourses of the orthodox bishop of Smyrna. The point in dispute between Irenæus and Florinus was an elementary one, it is true, and one which did not require any great research or strained effort of memory to have its falsehood detected and uncovered; but the principle on which the argument of the Christian controversialist is founded, supposes a traditional orthodoxy in the individual and the Church, and assumes, as a certain fact, that such orthodox traditions should be a standard to which heresy should be compared, and a test by which error should be vanquished.

As we go on through the century other remarkable testimonies to the same effect meet us from time to time. There is a very striking one on the inerrancy of the Church, in the treatise of Theophilus, the bishop of Antioch, against the pagan philosopher Autolycus. It was written towards the end of the second century. The passage is as follows:—" And as in the sea there are some habitable islands, well-watered, fruit-bearing, furnished with harbours, so as to be an asylum to those who are tossed by the tempest, so, to the world surging and agitated by the waves of sin, hath God given synagogues, that is to say, holy churches, in which the doctrine of truth is preserved, as in the station of these well-harboured islands to which they fly, who desire to attain salvation, become lovers of truth, and desirous to escape the anger and the judgment of God. But

---

[1] Fleury, "Hist. Eccles." lib. i. 17. ed. Paris, 1840.

as there are other islands rocky and parched, fruitless, full of wild beasts and uninhabited, doomed for the destruction of navigators, and those who are overtaken by the tempest, where ships are wrecked and they who approach the shore are lost, so are the doctrines of error, heresies, I mean whither they who approach entirely perish; nor do they follow the word of truth, but as pirates, when they have filled the ship, drive it to the before-mentioned places that they may destroy it. So happens it to those who have wandered from the truth, that they are engulfed by error."[1] Here is an evident affirmation of the perfect orthodoxy, not of individuals but of entire communities, or to speak more correctly, of particular churches abiding within the bosom of the then wide-spread Church of Christ. And what an orthodoxy, how perfect, how comprehensive, how minute, how detailed, how living, active, and efficacious. These churches, furnished with everything that can render them delightful habitations for men destined for heaven, with the salutary waters of grace, and the fruits of a pure morality, free of the storms of heresy, and secure from the incursions of the devouring ministers of error, opening wide their arms to receive sinners and unbelievers, and to protect them from the judgments of God, constituted by God, appointed for a sinful world, preserving the doctrine of truth.

I will add one more passage bearing on this subject, which I extract from the first book of the "Stromata" of Clement, of Alexandria, and which may very appropriately be subjoined here, as it was written posterior in point of time to those I have hitherto quoted. The books called the Στρωματα were written about the beginning of the third century. He is describing the reason why he compiled this work. He says, "But this work, artfully put together, has not been compiled through a motive of ostentation; but here I have stored up mementos for my old age, an antidote against oblivion, truly an image and a reflection of those clear and animated discourses, which it hath been

---

[1] Theop. ad Autol. lib. iii. parag. 14, ed. Maran.

vouchsafed me to hear, and of men of happy memory, who were unquestionably of the greatest worth. Of these one was in Greece, of the Ionic sect; the other in Magna Grecia; of whom the one was born in Cœlesyria, and the other was a native of Egypt. There were others from the East, one of whom was an Assyrian, and the other of Hebrew origin. But when I met with my last master, and he of transcendent powers, I ceased to seek any more, and abode with him living in retirement in Egypt. Verily the Sicilian bee, culling the flowers of the meadow of the Prophets and Apostles, he infused into the minds of his audience a knowledge clear and incorruptible. But they (who heard him) preserving the tradition of the blessed doctrine straight from the holy Apostles, Peter and James, and John and Paul, as if a son received it from his father (but few are like to the fathers) have survived by the will of God to our day, to deposit the apostolic seed which they have received from their elders."[1] The substance of this passage is, that Clement of Alexandria, in his search for truth, and in his desire to improve his mind, had put himself under the direction of many masters, the majority of them pagan philosophers; and that finally he had met with a Christian teacher, whose instructions left him nothing more to desire. He preserved the doctrine he had heard, and others preserved it too; and there were living in his day men who had immediately succeeded the apostles, and who kept the blessed doctrine which had been delivered to them; and this doctrine was deposited in the church as a seed which was to bring forth fruit unto eternal life.

These passages, which we may fairly assume as conjointly affording correct evidence as to the general belief on the orthodoxy of the Church from the death of the Apostles to the third century, ought to be of considerable weight in affirming the question as to the preservation of

[1] Clem. Alex. Strom. lib. i. parag. 17, edit. post Pott, Wirceburg, 1799.

the deposit of faith. They are not the "dicta" of a particular school or a particular class, or of men of the same locality; they were spoken by men of different countries, the representatives of the faith of churches widely separated; one of them a Phrygian bishop, another an Egyptian priest, a third the bishop of Antioch, a fourth the bishop of Lyons. They are rays of light emanating from different periods and different parts of the Catholic Church, but converging to one point, when they reveal to us a conviction of the actual inerrancy of the Christian people. They do not by any means decide the question peremptorily; this is quite obvious. No one of these writers, for instance, undertakes to say in terms that the Church of the second century did not lose the meaning of any dogma committed to her, and substitute a false meaning in its stead, or add to the deposit of faith by introducing a falsehood as a revealed dogma. They wrote these passages casually, and in treating of other subjects besides the preservation of the deposit of faith. One of them, Irenæus, is arguing against a heretic, who introduced a god as the author of evil, and consequently admitted the existence of two principles. He appeals for the decision of the question to the traditions which had come down from the Apostles; and the object of this appeal would be sufficiently attained if these tradition were correct on the elementary principle of the unity of God. The others speak generally, without giving us grounds to judge of the comprehensiveness or details of the body of traditional doctrine to which they refer, nevertheless the fact of their affirming that the doctrine of the Apostles had been delivered to the Church, and was preserved in the Church, and that there were men in the Church who had listened to the Apostles, and the additional fact of their referring to these truths, with a view to the refutation of heresies, or with a view to the exaltation of the Church, are sufficient proofs, even abstracting from the tenor of the words they used, that it was their firm conviction that the deposit of faith was preserved in its integrity undefiled. They believed in their own perfect orthodoxy; they believed in the orthodoxy of the Church;

though widely separated, their Churches were in communion with each other. Their words would appear the echo of a general conviction that the Church was perfectly sound in faith. Might this conviction be without foundation? We shall seek for the answer by considering other facts which are detailed in the documents of the age.

DIVISION III.

HOW THE CHURCH ACTED IN REFERENCE TO THE DEPOSIT OF FAITH.

REGARDING the subject in a purely human view, it must appear surprising to us, that individuals and communities, bishops and priests, and even the whole Church could have come to so absolute and unwavering a conclusion as to their perfect adherence to the doctrine delivered to them, when the truths were so new, and some of them so obscure, when the subjects were so varied, and when the points of faith were so detailed, and the articles so numerous. It would not be difficult perhaps to transmit the leading facts of Christianity from generation to generation, for the space of a couple of centuries; but how could its numerous episodes, its histories, its precepts, its examples be recollected, retained, and observed? The Church, nevertheless, believed, in the second century, that it had retained the revelation in its integrity, and without going beyond the human view of the subject, we need not search very deep to discover that the Church had good reason for entertaining such a belief.

Christianity is, in a great measure, a practical science. It might be humanly impossible for a large community to retain in its mind the elements of a vastly extensive speculative science for a long period of time; but if the leading facts of this science be practical dogmas, the difficulties to the recollection of it are to some extent removed, for it is daily brought before the mind in the public ceremony or the private observance, and it is daily represented to the eyes—it is tasted as it were, it is heard, it is touched daily.

Christianity is a practical science. It is likewise a speculative science: but it is by no means reasonable to suppose that all the speculative parts of Christianity were explicitly believed, or explicitly handed down from bishop to bishop, and from church to church during the term of the two first centuries.

The bishops believed they were orthodox, and the Church, the priests and the laity, believed in their own perfect orthodoxy: and in believing so they did not believe that they were perfect masters of the whole science of Christianity in all its details, just as a school-boy would be convinced that he knew all the demonstrations of geometry or astronomy; but their conviction of their orthodoxy amounted to this: they had not added error to the deposit of faith delivered to them, nor had they taken from it, by introducing a false untransmitted meaning for any article it contained; but they had it there in its integrity—its practical dogmas, unchanged since they came from the mouths of the Apostles—its speculative dogmas, as far as they were explicitly believed, neither changed, impaired, nor augmented.

This was the substance of the Church's belief in her own orthodoxy; and there are two classes of facts in the history of these centuries to which the Church might refer with pride, as affording convincing proofs that this belief was not without foundation. The first consisted of the actual evidences of her faithful adherence to the tradition on all occasions. The second consisted of the evidences, that she had always repudiated error.

1st. From the very days of the Apostles, the faithful and the bishops of the Church had been exhorted unceasingly to "hold fast" to the doctrine that had been delivered to them. Nothing in language could be stronger than the advices on this subject, which are found in the

earliest Christian writers. "Remember your prelates,"
says St. Paul, in his Epistle to the Hebrews, "who have
spoken the Word of God to you: whose faith follow, considering the end of their conversation;"[1] and again in
the Epistle to Timothy, the same Apostle says: "Hold
the form of sound words, which thou hast heard of me in
faith, and in the love which is in Christ Jesus: keep the
good thing committed to thy trust by the Holy Ghost
who dwelleth in us."[2] "O Timothy," he adds in another
place, "keep that which is committed to thy trust, avoiding the profane novelties of words, and oppositions of
knowledge falsely so called."[3] In the Second Epistle to
the Thessalonians he says: "Therefore, brethren, stand
fast: and hold the traditions which you have learned,
whether by word or by our epistle."[4] The object of some
of the Apostolic exhortations appears to be to compel them
to advert to the truth they had received, to keep it fresh
in their memories. Thus St. Peter—"Behold this second
epistle I write to you, my dearly beloved, in which I stir
up by way of admonition your sincere mind. That you
may be mindful of those words which I told you before,
from the holy Prophets, and of the Apostles, of the precepts of the Lord and Saviour."[5] And St. John—"I
have not written to you, as to them that know not the
truth, but as to them that know it;"[6] scil., to stir up their
knowledge of it. "As for you, let that which you have
heard from the beginning abide with you. And you have
no need that any one should teach you: but as His unction
teacheth you of all things, and is truth and is no lie, And
as it hath taught you, abide in Him."[7]

The Apostles exhorted the faithful and the bishops whom
they had constituted to unity in faith, and to adhere strictly
to the doctrines that had been delivered to them: and the
views of their successors in the episcopacy were, as far

[1] Heb. xiii. 7.
[2] 2 Tim. i. 13, 14.
[3] 1 Tim. vi. 20.
[4] 2 Thess. ii. 14.
[5] 2 Pet. iii. 1, 2.
[6] 1 John ii. 21.
[7] 1 John ii. 27.

as we are able to judge of them, equally strong and decided. We have not many documents of this second age: but the few that have come down to us are full of admonitions to the faithful, to preserve the faith in its integrity. In the Epistles of Ignatius, the Bishop of Antioch, this lesson is forcibly inculcated. In his Epistle to the Church of Magnesia he has the following words:—"Wherefore study to confirm yourselves in the dogmas of the Lord and the Apostles, to the end that everything you do may succeed with you, by the flesh and the spirit, by faith and charity, in the Father and the Son, and the Holy Ghost, in the beginning and the end."[1] And again, in his Epistle to the Church of Ephesus—"Wherefore it becometh you to run according to the judgment of your bishop, which you do."[2] And in his Epistle to the Trullians—"Refrain from such (heretics); which you will do, if you remain united to God, Jesus Christ, and the bishop, and the precepts of the Apostles."[3] In the Epistles of Polycarpe, the Bishop of Smyrna, the same precept is strongly enforced—"Wherefore, giving up vanity and false doctrines, let us return to the doctrine that has been delivered to us from the beginning."[4]

These were the sort of exhortations which were wont to be made to the Church, faithful and clergy, by the Apostles and those who succeeded them. Did the Church profit by these exhortations? Did the people of God, on all occasions during the first and second centuries, exhibit a zeal for the faith, and an anxiety to preserve it in its purity? Did they actually preserve it in its integrity, unchanged, as they had received it from the mouths of the Apostles? The Church of the third century could answer all these questions in the affirmative. She could point to her thousands of martyrs who had suffered in Rome torments the most cruel and excruciating, deaths the most barbarous and revolting, for the profession of the

[1] Ignat. Ep. ad Magnes. No. xiii. ed. Cot.
[2] Ep. ad Ephes. No. 4, tom. ii. *ibid*.
[3] Ep. ad Trul. No. 8, *ibid*.
[4] Pol. Ep. ad Phill. No. 7, p. 188, *ibid*.

common doctrines of Christianity. Could they, before whose orthodoxy the rack lost all its terrors, and the boiling cauldron and the fire, and the teeth of lions, were but a sport, have knowingly sacrificed even a single point of that faith which had been revealed by that God whose love was so lively in their hearts? And she could point to the martyrs of Africa as zealous preservers of the doctrines of the Apostles; these men, who rather than deliver up the sacred Scriptures to be burned, marched with a smile to the scaffold, and bent their heads under the axe of the executioner with a prayer of thanksgiving on their lips. And she could point to the extent of her communion as a perfect proof of her orthodoxy, countries the most distant, nations the most opposed and even hostile, peoples the most different from each other in disposition, in talents, in education, all reposing in peace within her bosom. Could they all have fallen into error together? Impossible. Could they have fallen into error one by one? In that case, there must have been endless confusion and strife, and controversy of which there was positively no record preserved. Could error have been infused in the source? Could the doctrine have been poisoned before it came to them? Then the Apostles themselves must have lost the faith. Yet there were the different Churches, Antioch and Rome, Smyrna and Alexandria, Carthage and Corinth, Jerusalem and Crete, Lyons and Milan, united in the same communion, practising the same religious rites, professing the same faith. Their unanimity was an evident proof of their orthodoxy. And the Church too could point to the position she had always held in respect to infidelity and the sects of error. She had stood alone, distinct from them all since the beginning. She had never identified herself with heathen rites. She had repelled heretics and cast them out from her. She had stood aloof from all dangerous polemics, and in all doubts and difficult questions which had been raised she had shut her ears to seduction, sophistry, and as her writers said, she had fled away and taken hold of the doctrine that had been delivered to her from the beginning. Oh yes!

the Church had been well lectured on the necessity of preserving the tradition entire, and in the third century she could point with thanksgiving to God, to facts such as these, as a proof that she had adhered to it with tenacity.

2. The uniform conduct of the Church in reference to heresy and heretics was another fact which put her orthodoxy beyond all dispute. To arouse the attention of the bishops and the faithful, and to prepare them for conflicts with error, the Apostles, in the Epistles which they addressed to their converts, took occasion to remind them often that false teachers would rise up and endeavour to seduce them from the faith. "Now the Spirit manifestly teaches," said St. Paul to Timothy, "that in the last times some shall depart from the faith, giving heed to spirits of error, and doctrines of devils, speaking lies in hypocrisy and having their conscience seared."[1] And in his second Epistle to the same bishop, he repeats the same prediction, and associates with it a more full description of the class to which he refers. "Know this also, that in the last days shall come on dangerous times. Men shall be lovers of themselves, covetous, haughty, proud, blasphemers, disobedient to parents, ungrateful, wicked, without affection, without peace, slanderers, incontinent, unmerciful, without kindness, traitors, stubborn, puffed up, and lovers of pleasure more than of God, having the appearance of godliness, but denying the power thereof. . . . . Now as Jannes and Mambres resisted Moyses, so these also resist the truth, men corrupted in mind, reprobate concerning the faith."[2] And then, in various passages through his Epistles, St. Paul points out the manner in which the bishops of the Church were to deal with these perverters of the doctrine of Christ, and the sum of his instructions on this head amounts to this: They were not to enter on long and useless controversies with them; they were not to contend with them in words, to strive as it were for the mastery in disputation; but they were to admonish them calmly, and seriously, and learnedly; and

---

[1] 1 Timothy iv. 1, 2. [2] 2 Timothy iii. 1 *et seq.*

if their admonition produced no effect, they were to avoid them and to withdraw from their society.

First. They were not to expose themselves even to remote danger of seduction by prolonged discussions with heretics. "But shun profane and vain babblings, for they grow much towards ungodliness, and their speech spreadeth like a cancer."[1] "And avoid foolish and unlearned questions, knowing that they beget strifes."[2] "Not giving heed to Jewish fables and commandments of men, who turn themselves away from the truth."[3] "But avoid foolish questions and genealogies, and strivings about the law, for they are unprofitable and vain."[4]

Secondly. The bishops were nevertheless to convince them of their errors in gravity and in strength of argument. One of the qualifications of a bishop as laid down by St. Paul was, "That he may be able to exhort in sound doctrine, and to convince the gainsayers."[5] "But the servant of God must not wrangle, but be mild towards all men, apt to teach, patient, with modesty admonishing them that resist the truth; if peradventure God may give them repentance to know the truth, and they may recover themselves from the snares of the devil, by whom they are held captive at his will."[6]

Thirdly. They were to avoid them, and to renounce all communication with them, in case that their exhortations produce no effect. "A man that is a heretic after the first and second admonition, avoid. Knowing that he, that is such a one, is subverted and sinneth, being condemned by his own judgment."[7] "Whosoever revolteth, and continueth not in the doctrine of Christ, hath not God. He that continueth in the doctrine, the same hath both the Father and the Son. If any man come to you, and bring not this doctrine, receive him not into the house, nor say to him, God speed you. For he that sayeth to him, God speed you, communicateth with his

---

[1] 2 Timothy ii. 16.
[2] 2 Tim. ii. 23.
[3] Ep. ad Tit. i. 14.
[4] Titus iii. 9.
[5] Titus i. 9.
[6] 2 Timothy ii. 24, *seq.*
[7] Titus iii. 10, 11.

wicked works."[1] "Now, I beseech you brethren, to mark them who make dissensions and offences contrary to the doctrine which you have learned, and to avoid them."[2]

Here were the sort of exhortations in reference to the disseminators of error, which the disciples of the Apostles were accustomed to hear. Assuredly they could not be more strongly lectured against the dangers of seduction; and if they followed the advice given them in such passages as these, they would be securely fenced within the fold of perfect orthodoxy.

The lesson was repeated in the age immediately following, and in terms scarcely less strong and decisive. "Wherefore, I beseech you," says the bishop of Smyrna in one of his letters, "not I though, but the charity of Jesus Christ, to use Christian nutriment alone, and to abstain from the foreign herb, which is heresy: heretics who even involve Jesus Christ with the wicked, in consequence of the dignity which they have obtained, in receiving the true faith. . . . . Wherefore guard yourselves from such; which you will, if you be not puffed up and remain undivided from God and Jesus Christ, and your bishop and the precepts of the Apostles."[3] "Children of light and truth," he says in another letter, "avoid divisions and false doctrines. And where the bishop is thither let the sheep follow him."[4] Again, in his epistle to the Ephesians—"But if they who according to the flesh have wrought such things, are punished with death, how much more if a man by false doctrine corrupt the faith of God."[5] But who were these heretics, according to the apprehension of these early Christian writers, whom the faithful were exhorted to avoid? They were "they," according to Clement of Alexandria, "who had left the primitive Church."[6] "Now," this father adds, giving a further description of them, "who falls into heresy passes through

---

[1] 2 John i. 9. [2] Rom. xvi. 17.
[3] Ign. ad Trul. No. 7, 8, p. 23, ed. Cot. [4] Ign. ad Phill. ii. ed. Cot.
[5] Ign. ad Ephes. No. 16, ed. Cot. [6] Clem. Alex. Strom. lib. i. p. 119, ed. Wirceburg, 1777.

a desert without water, having left the true God, abandoned by God, seeking water where there is no water, travelling a land uninhabitable and thirsty, gathering with his hands fruits which cannot come to perfection.[1] Again, commenting on the passage in the Epistle of St. Paul to the Ephesians—" until we all meet in the unity of faith," &c., he says, "But we children, avoiding the winds of heresy, which would puff us to inflation, and giving no faith to those who teach us other than the fathers, will then be advanced to perfection when we constitute the Church, having been associated with Christ the Head."[2]

What a deep impression must not such exhortations have made upon the minds of the faithful—clergy and people—and so often repeated—what profound effects must they not have produced in reference to error and its abettors! It was useless to talk in those days of civility and courtesy to heretics. Pagans could be borne with patience, but there was positively no patience nor toleration for the wilful perverters of the faith or doctrine of the Church. St. John meets Cerinthus at a bath, and immediately starts back and says to those who accompany him, "Let us, my brethren, make haste and begone, lest the bath wherein is Cerinthus, the enemy of truth, should fall upon our heads."[3] Polycarpe encounters the heretic Marcion at Rome, and, in reply to his question, Dost thou recognize me? answers, "Yes; I recognize you as the eldest son of Satan."[4] But the effect of such exhortations as I have quoted was not confined to exciting a detestation of heretics in the minds of the preachers and their flocks; they aroused the dormant, they stimulated the vigilant, they made all active and watchful, they set whole nations in confusion, and whole Churches in motion at the slightest

---

[1] Clem. Alex. Strom. lib. i. p. 119, ed. Wirceburg, 1777.

[2] Pedag. p. 221, lib. i. *ibid*.

[3] Iren. lib. iii. cap. 3.—Euseb. lib. iii. cap. 28, p. 123, ed. Cantab.

[4] Iren. lib. iii. cap. 3.

approach to novelty in doctrine, or the remotest suspicion of unsound views.

Any one who reads the documents of these centuries cannot fail to be struck by the excitement caused by questions even of a speculative nature, and which did not immediately involve a doctrine of faith. There was the question as to the fit time for celebrating Easter. The whole Church was divided about it. It was deemed of such importance in the East, that we find the bishop Polycarpe[1] undertaking the long and, in those days, hazardous journey to Rome to confer with Anicetus about the decision of it. And yet it was a mere matter of discipline, which in neither view that was taken of it could involve a departure from the revealed word of God. In the case of Montanus, who, with the two women, Priscilla and Maximilla, pretended to a new revelation, the excitement amounted to an absolute frenzy—bishops, priests, and the people were all equally in motion. "The faithful of Asia," says Fleury, "assembled often in many places to examine these pretended miracles."[2] Then we find a council held. And then a letter[3] condemning the errors of the heretic circulated among the Churches of Asia Minor. So far as we can learn from the documents which have come down to us, there has been no age in the Church's history during which the bishops were more watchful, or the controversialists of the Church more prompt in attacking error. They spared no one. Past services were forgotten. To become a heretic was to forfeit all right to mercy or compassion. Tatian, who had been a champion of orthodoxy, fell into error. And immediately he was attacked on all sides. "His errors were combated," says Fleury, "by Musanus, Apollinaris, bishop of Hieropolis, and Clement of Alexandria."[4]

We have evidences, therefore, in the first and second centuries, that the members of the Church were constantly

---

[1] Euseb. Hist. lib. iv. c. 14. [2] Hist. Eccles. lib. iv. s. vi. ed. Paris, 1840.
[3] Euseb. Hist. lib. v. c. 19. [4] *Ibid.* lib. iv. s. viii. p. 155.

aroused to a sense of the danger to which the faith was exposed, and that they were frequently warned to avoid heresies and heretics. Were these advices complied with? Amongst other facts, the Church could refer to such as I have just now adduced, in proof that they were. Heretics were shunned—avoided. Errors were combated—defeated. "The watchmen" were always "on the walls" telling the "hour of night," and proclaiming that "all was well." Viewing the subject in the most impartial spirit, we shall find it difficult to conceive how the introduction of a substantial error in the Church's belief may be reconcilable with such facts as these.

It may be argued that as the heresies of the two first centuries principally arose out of combining Christianity with the principles of Judaism or Paganism, and as for the most part they entered into the field of philosophy, leaving matters of daily practice and ordinary belief untouched, the opposition with which they were encountered does not afford an absolute proof of the orthodoxy of the Church in detail. The objection would amount to this:—While Saturninus was throwing the Syrian Churches into confusion by his curious theories with regard to the creation of the world and of man, what was there to prevent the Church of Antioch, for instance, from gradually changing her belief on the subject of penance and the Eucharist? The difficulty is an important one. It has been often urged in substance by Protestant writers of a certain school and sect. It may be even put in a stronger form than this in which we commonly find it—thus: The heresies of the two first centuries, individually or collectively, did not regard all or one-half of the articles of faith alluded to in the sacred Scriptures. There were numberless points of doctrine which they left entirely untouched. There were many heresies, it is true. There was strong opposition to them—admitted. In the circumstances of these ages it would have been impossible to introduce a general error with regard to the origin of good or evil, or the mission of the angels or the creation of the soul. But what, in the name of common sense, had the dispute about the αβραξας to do with the doctrine of the invocation of Saints, or the δυναμις with holy water, or the φρονεσις with purgatory, or the νους with the sacrifice of the mass? There was much error and strong opposition to it, but the very articles into which error might be most easily infused were almost entirely out of the field of polemics.

Nevertheless her manner of speaking about heretics, and the mode of treatment which she adopted towards all the abettors of error, put the perfect orthodoxy of the primitive Church in the strongest possible light. The exhortations of the Apostles and their successors to the members of the Church, warning them to avoid error, are couched in general terms. It is not one error they are to avoid, but every error. It is not falsehood on the subject of the creation that they are to reject, but everything contrary to the doctrine that has been delivered to them. They cannot make any change in the doctrines of faith which have been delivered to them; they are even to hold the very form of sound words in which these doctrines have been dictated by the Holy Ghost. Then it is not true to say that the majority of the doctrines of the Church were unassailed by the heretics of these ages. The heretics divided from the Church on general questions touching the foundations of religion, but they did not stop here. They renounced the practices of the Church. They perverted the discipline of the Church. They abandoned its ancient usages; and, in the opinion of the controversialists who attacked them, they were not less heretics for their speculative errors in the questions on which they first split, than for their abuse in practice of the rites of religion[1] and their introduction of untransmitted forms in the worship of God.[2] From Irenæus and Epiphanius we learn that the unity of marriage and the merit of virginity were denied;[3] the lawfulness of polygamy maintained;[4] the perpetual virginity of the Blessed Virgin impugned.[5] One sect denied that

---

[1] Iren. de Heres.
[2] Clem. Alex. Strom. lib. i. s. xix. p. 121, ed. post Pot.
[3] Nicholaites. [4] Ebionites. [5] Cerinthians.

marriage was lawful; and the same sect prohibited the use of wine in the Eucharist.[1] Another sect allowed a first marriage, but pronounced a second marriage unlawful; and, at the same time, denied that there existed in the Church a power of remitting certain enormous sins.[2] On principle, the followers of one sectary abstained from animal food,[3] and equally on principle the followers of another[4] partook of meat offered to idols. There was a class of heretics who held that faith and good works were necessary for some, and that others could not better secure salvation than by giving way to the criminal desires and passions of the flesh.[5] Cerdon denied the resurrection of the flesh, and rejected the Gospel of St. Luke as not authentic. Appelles introduced a new revelation in the treatises, called Φανερωσες, which he circulated amongst his followers. On the subject of baptism alone there were many errors. One heretic would have his followers baptized in his own name.[6] Another rejected the ordinary baptism as useless, pretending that his followers, according to the Scripture, should be baptized after a new and extraordinary manner by fire and the Holy Ghost.[7] There was scarcely a point of belief or practice of the Church which was not, some way or the other, touched upon by the heretics. Fasting[8]—the sacrament of confirmation[9]—the Persons of the Trinity[10]—martyrs and their relics[11]—the divinity of Christ.[12]

The controversy which was carried on in these first centuries, therefore, did not regard primary or elementary points alone, nor was it occupied merely with the opposition between Christianity and philosophy on such questions as the nature of God and the creation of matter, but it entered into the most subtle disputes on the plan and method of the redemption—the ceremonies and usages of religion—public observances and individual

[1] Marcionites. [2] Montanists. [3] Saturninians.
[4] Followers of Basilides. [5] Valentinians. [6] Menander.
[7] Hermogines. [8] Montanists. [9] Novatians.
[10] Sabellians. [11] Novatians. [12] Theod of Byzan.

practice—morals and worship—discipline and belief. The guardians of the faith were well practised in every description of spiritual warfare. They were men of acute observation and philosophical minds. Many of them had learned dialectics in the Roman schools, and were adepts in disputation before they embraced Christianity. The bishops among them were the seniors of the Churches over which they presided, selected for this office in consequence of their irreproachable lives, their thorough acquaintance with the doctrines of Christianity, their facility in communicating knowledge, and their ability to confute error. It is useless to say that there are no records of their having disputed on such questions as the spiritual efficacy of extreme unction or the intercessory power of the saints. They were occupied with questions fully as detailed and obscure, and if errors were broached on these points, they were equally competent to meet and refute them. They were watching for novelty. They were in readiness to attack and dispute everything that savoured of error. They were learned. They were subtle. They were zealous. It is difficult to understand how the Church in these times, so well lectured to beware of heretics and defended by such champions as these, could have fallen into error on any point of the revealed doctrine committed to her. Certain it is that she did not fall wilfully. But was there an intrinsic weakness in the constitution of the Church, by which she might have lost any portion of the deposit of faith, innocently, it is true, but fatally for the interests of posterity?

DIVISION IV.

INFALLIBILITY OF THE CHURCH IN THESE AGES.

§ 1. *The Old Testament.*—Let us make the supposition that, through a fallibility inherent in her constitution, the Church had fallen into error before the days of Tertullian. General errors have many times pervaded society. The Church had fallen and had lost the faith; tried to preserve it entire, but was not able, lost a portion of it, and she lost it in all her members—the priests, the bishops, and the laity. It was the Church that lost it, too, and not a particular congregation. It was not the Church of Jerusalem, or the Church of Alexandria, or the Church of Corinth, but the aggregation of all the particular Churches that then existed. It was the Church of Christ—that congregated mass of all believers which constituted what the Scripture designates "the kingdom of God on earth." An error in some particular dogma originated with some teacher, or bishop, or it began to manifest itself in a religious practice in some particular locality, and from this centre it had gone out, in ever-widening circles, over the surface of the Church, until it had settled down in the minds of all and become a fixed conviction, and other storms blew over and agitated that multitude, but, so far as the truth lost, the error received, it was unconscious, calm, unruffled as the ocean reposing under a summer sun.

The supposition made, reduces itself to this: The mass of Christians, and of that class of Christians which we look upon as "the orthodox," believed, in the third century, some article to be "of faith" which was not "of faith," something to be revealed which in fact was a falsehood, something to be the word of Christ which was the suggestion of the enemy of God. Could such a supposition be admitted consistently with the view of this Church which we are constrained to adopt from the Scriptures?

The scriptural idea of the Church is—a congregation of people collected from all the nations of the earth: "The kingdom of heaven is like to a net cast into the sea, and gathering together all kinds of fishes."¹ A vast society in which wanderers might come to dwell: "The kingdom of heaven is like to a grain of mustard-seed, which a man took and sowed in the field. Which is the least indeed of all seeds; but when it is grown up, it is greater than all herbs, and becometh a tree, so that the birds of the air come and dwell in the branches thereof."² A dominion extending over the whole world: "He (the Messiah) shall rule from sea to sea, and from the river even to the uttermost bounds of the earth."³ This Church to be perpetual —never to fail, never to fall away—different from human societies, which, sooner or later, break up and form new combinations—this vast assemblage of true believers to remain in its integrity until the end of time: "But in the days of those kingdoms, the God of heaven will set up a kingdom that shall never be destroyed, and his kingdom shall not be delivered up to another people; and it shall break in pieces and consume all these kingdoms; and itself shall stand for ever." ⁴ These two characteristics of the Church—universality and perpetuity—are referred to again and again in the scriptural prophecies which foretold the reign of the Messiah. Universality: "Ask of me, and I will give the Gentiles for thy inheritance, and the uttermost parts of the earth for thy dominion."⁵ "All the ends of the earth shall remember and shall be converted to the Lord. And all the kindred of the Gentiles shall adore in his sight."⁶ "Behold! I have given thee to be the light of the Gentiles, that thou mayest be my salvation even to the farthest part of the earth."⁷ "Then was the iron, the clay, the brass, the silver, and the gold, broken to pieces together, and became like the chaff of a

---

¹ Matthew xiii. 47.   ² *Ibid.* 31, 32.
³ Psalm lxxi. 8.   ⁴ Daniel ii. 44.
⁵ Psalm ii. 8.   ⁶ Psalm xxi. 28, 29.
⁷ Isaias xlix. 6.

summer threshing-floor, and they were carried away by the wind, and there was no place found for them; but the stone that struck the statue became a great mountain, and filled the whole earth." [1] Perpetuity: "And I will make a covenant of peace with them, it shall be an everlasting covenant with them, and I will establish them and will multiply them, and will set my sanctuary in the midst of them for ever." [2] "If my covenant with the day may be made void, and my covenant with the night, that there should not be day or night in their season; also my covenant with David my son may be made void, that he should not have a son to reign upon his throne, and with the Levites and priests, my ministers. As the stars of heaven cannot be numbered, nor the sand of the sea be measured, so will I multiply the seed of David my servant and the Levites my ministers." [3] "Thou shalt no more have the sun for thy light by day, neither shall the brightness of the moon enlighten thee; but the Lord shall be unto thee for an everlasting light, and thy God for thy glory." [4]

The Church was to be perpetual and universal. The prophetic books of the Old Testament exhibited these properties of the Church in glowing terms many hundred years before the Redeemer came upon earth. It might be almost said that there is a degree of exaggeration common in poetry and highly-wrought figurative language in the manner in which these characteristics are attributed to the Church in the Psalms and the prophecy of Isaias. They are, however, so often recurred to, and so strongly insisted upon, they occur in so many passages, they appear under so many types and figures, as leave us no room to doubt that they enter into the very essence and constitution of the Church. There would be no Church of Christ if there was not a perpetual Church. There would be no Christian Church if it was not universal and catholic. The Church would be small at first naturally; the prophets represent her as growing rapidly, opening out her arms and

---

[1] Daniel ii. 35. [2] Ezech. xxxvii. 26.
[3] Jeremias xxxiii. 20, 21, 22. [4] Isaias lx. 23.

receiving the Gentiles far and near, and then retaining them in her bosom, or if losing some of them from time to time, receiving others by fresh conquests, and always comprising so large a body of believers as to be morally diffused through the world.

Such is the idea of the Christian Church suggested by the Old Testament—universal, perpetual, perpetually universal, and universally perpetual. The books of the New Testament reproduce the idea of universality and perpetuity in terms equally significant. At one time it is a net cast into the sea and gathering together of all kind of fishes, universal. At another time it is a tree greater than all herbs, in which the birds of the air come and dwell, still universal. And then, on the other hand, the Holy Ghost is to remain with it "for ever," perpetual; and Christ to be with it, "even to the consummation of the world."

Supposing the Church to be constitutionally—its constitution being derived from the will of God—perpetual and universal, two questions naturally arise :—1. Is there consequently any difficulty in supposing the Church to be infallible? And, 2, Does the property of infallibility follow naturally, if not necessarily, as a consequence of perpetuity and universality? 1. The Church being supposed to be universal and perpetual, and perpetually universal, it follows as a necessary consequence that the very existence of the Church is supernatural and out of the ordinary course of things. Perpetuity does not naturally belong to any human society. The greatest empires have had a beginning and an end, and the history of antiquity is but the record of the birth, the decadence, and the dissolution of society in every variety of combination. Religious societies, on the whole, have had more permanence than civil societies. Yet even religious societies, with the strong attachment of men and nations to established forms of religion, have had their day of absorption or annihilation. So that if we could discover a religious society constitutionally free from the principle of decay, we would be compelled to admit that the finger of

God is there, and in reason we could not refuse to recognize the existence of an invisible and supernatural agency working in this society and consolidating it, not the ordinary operation of Providence in the conservation of created things, but an operation extraordinary, out of the course of nature, miraculous. As regards religious society the absence of the principle of dissolution common to all human things, argues the presence of the Spirit of God working supernaturally in it.

If this society be Catholic and universal in principle, the argument in favour of its supernaturality receives still greater force from the fact. For, what has not a religious society pervading all nations to encounter? Obstacles which naturally it could not perpetually overcome. If we examine in detail the systems of religion, which have existed in antiquity, or which pervade the Eastern nations at the present day, we will find that they have in many respects accommodated themselves to prevailing tastes and notions. Superstition or infidelity, or call it what you will, would assume as many forms as there are races specifically distinct. Bloody rites and perhaps even human sacrifice would suit the morbid taste of the extreme Northern. Flowers and music, and sensuality, would assume a place in the religious system of the South. We would have a visible religion among the nations of lively imagination — a religion almost invisible among deep-thinking nations given to study and business. Religion would vary, the tastes of nations would develope new rites; the sympathies of nations would draw forth latent properties, perhaps even the whim of nations as of individuals would build up and take down, would create and destroy.

The Church, therefore, as it was destined by the will of God to be a universal religious society, had many repugnances to contend with—numberless prejudices to overcome. It had to enter into every nation, and to beat down opposition everywhere, and to maintain its universal sway despite the rebellious tendencies of the world.

Could the Church accomplish this double mission without a special assistance on the part of God—without a supernatural protection—without an almost miraculous co-operation? The Christian Church is a society essentially in opposition to human passion and the corrupt tendencies of human nature. Its faith, in some instances surpassing the comprehension of man—its discipline restraining—its morality severe. Could such a society maintain its morally universal and perpetual supremacy without an extraordinary action of the Divinity on the minds of its members as a body? Evidently it could not. Therefore, in promising universality and perpetuity to His Church, God pledged himself to assist and protect it by an unusual and supernatural "concursus"—no other than a supernatural action on the minds of its members. And this "concursus" being once admitted, the infallibility of the Church is a natural, an almost necessary consequence. For what in reality is the essential idea of the Church? It is the assembly of the followers of Christ. But something more: it is the assembly of the believers in Christ. Still more, it is the assembly of those who believe in the doctrine of Christ. Faith, belief, enters into the very idea of the Church. Faith in what? In God, in the Trinity, in Christ? Would this be enough? Would any one say that it would be the Christian Church if its faith were limited to these articles? Therefore faith in the doctrine of Christ, too, is essential to the Church? (How far is this faith to extend? To how many articles? We won't now define—but unquestionably faith in a certain body of revelation enters into the very essence and idea of the Christian Church.) A supernatural "concursus" of the Divinity preserves this Church universal; and therefore preserves its faith universal. The same Divine "concursus" preserves the Church perpetual, and hence preserves its faith perpetual. And faith preserved universally and perpetually in the Church is unquestionably the gift of infallibility.

Infallibility, or at least inerrancy to some extent, must be admitted to belong to the very constitution of the Christian Church. Otherwise, the Church might continue "the spouse of Christ," and lose its faith in the character and mission of the Redeemer. The sceptic who will deny to the Christian Church the privilege of infallibility in every sense, is driven to one of two conclusions—he denies the perpetuity of the Church, or he affirms that Christianity is not incompatible with the profession of Buddhism or Mahomedism.

The Church must be infallible; but this is not enough: its infallibility must not be natural, but supernatural, or, in other words, it must be a special gift conferred by God upon his Church which could not naturally belong to it as a society. This latter conclusion follows from two facts, one of which may be assumed, and the other of which has been proved, namely, 1st, that a certain body of doctrine is essential to the very existence of the Church; and, 2nd, that this believing Church must be universal and perpetual. The only question, therefore, which it can be reasonable to discuss, as regards the Church's infallibility, is, how far does it extend? what doctrines does it regard? does the infallibility of the Church extend to all the articles of faith committed to her? so that the Church cannot err as to the meaning of any of them.

We recur again to the prophetic view of the Church. It is strikingly complete in all its details, and this subject of its infallibility is exhibited there in vivid and attractive colours. "Oh, poor little one," God says by His prophet, speaking of the Church, "tossed with tempest, without all comfort, behold I will lay thy stones in order, and will lay thy foundations with sapphires. . . . . . All thy children shall be taught of the Lord; and great shall be the peace of thy children."[1] The prophet describes the diffusion, the stability, the illumination of the Church in these and the following verses, and a little further on he continues: "No weapon that is formed against thee shall prosper: and every tongue that resisteth thee in judgment, thou shalt condemn."[2] Perhaps it is hardly fair to connect these two verses together in the relation of cause and effect; or, in other words, to affirm, that therefore shall

[1] Isaias liv. 11—13. [2] *Ibid.* verse 17.

the Church condemn in judgment, because she " shall be taught of the Lord." This inference, if strictly drawn from the words of the prophet, would establish for the Church a very general infallibility; and possibly such inference is not warranted by the context. But let us take the texts separately, and even so taken they appear to prove a general inerrancy in matters of faith. The Church is " taught of the Lord,"—" all her children taught,"— " every one that resisteth her in judgment, she shall condemn." All are taught, and she condemns all gainsayers— a general teaching—a general condemnation—it looks like a general infallibility. The last passage (verse 17) represents the Church as contending with certain opponents— contending with them, and at the same time sitting as judge of the controversy. What could this controversy regard? Possessions, riches, pre-eminence? But God never promised the Church the victory in such contentions as these. There is a battle-field, and there is a contention, and this contention must regard the property of the opposing world—that is to say, riches, possessions, pre-eminence, or it must regard the property of the Church, morality and faith. The Church is judge. Therefore the controversy must be about spiritual goods, morality and faith. This appears to be the meaning of the passage— the Church is judge in controversies regarding faith and morality; and as she condemns those who oppose her, and this by a power founded on prophecy, her sentence must be a true one and her condemnation just, and as she justly and truly condemns all who oppose her in faith, without any exception or limitation, her inerrancy must be general, and her infallibility coextensive with the deposit of faith committed to her keeping.

This appears to be the scope and meaning of the words of the Prophet Isaias in these verses which are taken from the 54th chapter.

There is another allusion to the Church in the 59th chapter of the same prophecy, which throws additional light on the subject of the Church's general infallibility. The words are of God to the Church: " This is my covenant with them, saith the Lord. My spirit that is in thee, and my words that I have put in thy mouth, shall not depart out of thy mouth, nor out of the mouth of thy seed, nor out of the mouth of thy seed's seed, saith the Lord, from henceforth and for ever."[1] The passage is a significant one. The words of God which he has put into the mouth of his Church, manifestly, the doctrine which he has taught his Church, shall not depart out of its mouth for ever, obviously, shall never be lost. In other words, the faith once taught to the Church shall never degenerate into error: and this is confirmed by a solemn oath and covenant. The Church is therefore generally infallible.

So far the writings of the Old Testament. We turn now to the writings of the New Testament; and we are anxious to discover if they afford us grounds for the satisfactory solution of the question we now examine; namely, is the Church generally infallible in all matters appertaining to faith?

§ 2. *The New Testament.*—To deny the infallibility of the Church is to give up its spirituality and supernaturality, and to reduce it to the level of any human society. Protestants of the various denominations, who give up the infallibility of the Church, do away with the spiritual life, grace, the dwelling of the Holy Spirit among the disciples of Christ, the love of God for his spouse. If faith be gone, or can go in part, there is no reason why it may not go entirely, and with it all supernaturality. If the Church be pronounced fallible in principle, the majority, nay all its members, may err on fundamental points of doctrine, its governing and teaching body may err, and all together may fall under the anathema of the Sacred Scriptures, scil. "Whosoever believeth not shall be condemned." A controversialist on the side of liberal opinions will meet me with the rebutting answer—all cannot be lost; for the Church preserves the Scriptures. But who does not see that such a reply is vain? It does not affect the

---

[1] Isaias lix. 21.

original position. If the Church be fallible in principle, then the Scriptures themselves are not proved to be the revealed word of God. All is gone in this supposition, the written word, the unwritten word, and "there is no faith upon the earth." For to confine ourselves to the Scriptures, whose supposed authenticity, integrity, veracity, and inspiration, is the groundwork of the entire Protestant argument against the infallibility of the Church, does human reason individually or collectively prove the Sacred Scriptures to contain one particle of revealed truth? No: unless human reason proves that the Scriptures are inspired. But could human reason prove the Scriptures to be inspired? No: unless human beings had the capacity and privilege of contemplating the workings of the minds of Sts. Peter, Paul, Luke, Mark, John, James, Jude, and Matthew, when they penned down the books of the New Testament, and of discovering there two facts, scil.; the first, that they wrote what they heard from Christ or the Holy Spirit; the second, that they were moved by the Spirit of God to commit these revealed words to writing. For an inspired book is a book that is made up of revelation penned down under an impulse of the Spirit of God. Reason can prove that the Sacred Scriptures are the authentic works of the writers to which they are ascribed; an authentic book may be a tissue of falsehoods. Reason can prove that the Scriptures are integral; a book may preserve its integrity though some of it be lost, and many minor errors introduced into it. Reason can prove that the Scriptures are veracious; but surely such a proof extends to certain leading facts only, otherwise it must be assumed that the Apostolic Church, by whose assent the truth of these writings is rationally demonstrated, was acquainted beforehand with the whole body of revelation. To this tripartite proof the office of reason is confined. Its arguments are so far satisfactory. But if reason attempts to demonstrate the inspiration of the Sacred volume, it goes beyond its sphere and treads on forbidden ground, and the only fact it can establish is, that the Apostles said they were inspired when they wrote the Sacred

Scriptures. Perhaps they were deceived in thinking so; perhaps they deceived the world!

On the other hand, in the supposition of an unerring Church, how safe are the ground-works of religion, and how satisfactory to the rational mind is the whole economy of Christianity. The Church is proved infallible, not by the Scriptures supposed to be inspired, but by the Scriptures as an authentic, veracious, and integral volume, and also by a general belief of ages, which could only come from the Apostles and Christ. Then this unerring Church gives us the Sacred Scriptures as the inspired word of God. Faith is in this supposition safe in its origin and subsequent career through the troubled sea of an erring world.

If the infallibility of the Church be supposed to be such that the body of its members morally speaking, or the great majority of them, cannot fall into a substantial error in faith, it will follow as an easy consequence that the body of the Church which teaches with authority, the governing body, cannot put forth a falsehood. On the other hand, if the active infallibility, or the inerrancy of the teaching body be proved, the passive infallibility, or the inerrancy of the body thought, is a natural and rational inference. So that, in reality, the proofs which are adduced in favour of the passive and active infallibility mutually prop up each other, or, to speak more correctly, they coalesce into one convincing argument of the proposition we are now considering. The question we have now to answer is, what does the New Testament say of the infallibility of the Church in reference to its assembled bishops, and in reference to its flocks dispersed?

In favour of the infallibility of the bishops the texts are as follows:—

" Going therefore, teach all nations; baptizing them in the name of the Father, and of the Son, and of the Holy Ghost; teaching them to observe all things whatsoever I have commanded you; and behold I am with you all days, even to the consummation of the world." [1] Words

---

[1] Matthew xxviii. 19, 20.

addressed to the Apostles, commanding them to teach the whole doctrine of Christ—"All things whatsoever I have commanded you"—promising them the presence and protection of Christ while teaching, and therefore exemption from error. "Behold I am with you all days." The command and the promise are to be extended to that body which is, morally speaking, one with the Apostles, which is the apostolic body continued, namely, the episcopal body of the Church at all times, for both command and promise extend to all times and periods, "even to the end of the world." This is the interpretation always given to the passage by the Church, for the usage was from the earliest ages, that the bishops assembled in council do decide matters of faith definitively.

"And I will ask the Father, and he shall give you another Paraclete, and he shall abide with you for ever, the spirit of truth. . . . ."[1] "But when he, the spirit of truth, is come, he will teach you all truth."[2] Two sentences addressed to the Apostles to the effect that the Holy Ghost was to teach them generally, "He will teach you all truth," and to dwell permanently with them, "that he may abide with you for ever." The permanent dwelling implies obviously the permanent preservation of truth amongst them, and hence their infallibility as a body. The double promise extends to the governing body to succeed them, namely, the episcopal body to the end of time, for it is a promise that requires fulfilment "for ever."

Texts illustrative of the infallibility of the Church as a whole:

"But if I tarry long, that thou mayest know how thou oughtest to behave thyself in the house of God, which is the Church of the living God, the pillar and ground of truth."[3] "The Church of the living God" here referred to, is clearly not the material edifice. The brick-and-mortar edifice could not be in any sense "the pillar and ground of truth." Nor is it the particular Church of

[1] John xiv. 16, 17. [2] *Ibid.* xvi. 13. [3] 1 Tim. iii. 15.

Ephesus, which Timothy governed at this time, or the national Church, made up of the aggregate of the Churches of Asia Minor, the general superintendence of which was committed to him; but "the Church or assembly of the living God," that is, the combined assembly of all the children of God. This general Church is, according to St. Paul, "the pillar and ground of truth." This was its character then. It was, too, a perpetual Church. Therefore its character always. Now, interpret the words "pillar and ground of truth" as you will, errancy, fallibility, actual error in faith, are inadmissible in that body of which they are predicted as perpetual qualities.

"And I say to thee; that thou art Peter, and upon this rock I will build my Church, and the gates of hell shall not prevail against it."[1] We have here—1st. The Church universal built upon a rock—manifestly a man having spiritually, and by a divine gift in reference to it, the consolidating and supporting qualities of a rock in regard to the material edifice standing upon it. 2nd. So strong, therefore, as to resist successfully the efforts, attacks, &c., of the opposing kingdom of hell or the devil. What' are the assaults of the devil against the children of God? Twofold—scil.—against their morality and their faith. The Church, victorious in both conflicts, is, therefore, infallible.

It appears almost childish to attempt to demonstrate the infallibility of the Church from insulated and detached passages in the Scriptures of the New Testament. Our idea of the faith of the Church ought rather to be taken from the whole volume—the economy of its founders—the general characteristics put forth—the combined bearing of passages. There is the whole Church "compacted and knit together," like the joints of the human body. The faith of it is one, even as God is one. It is "built upon a rock," not to be shaken to pieces by the storms that agitate the world; supporting truth like a pillar, and the solid foundation on which truth is built; "taught all

[1] Matthew xvi. 18.

truth" by the Holy Spirit "for ever." Whoever "will not hear this Church" is to be regarded "as a heathen and publican."¹ Here are the combined characteristics of the Church put forth in the sacred volume. A Church such as this, was the Church the Apostles founded, and it was to be permanent. Now, for argument sake, let us suppose this Church fallible and liable to fall into substantial errors in matters of faith. What is the consequence? All these scriptural characteristics disappear at once. Is it "built upon a rock?" No! but upon the fickle and fallible minds of mere human beings, unaided, unenlightened, unprotected, consequently deceiving and deceived; and surely such a foundation of an assemblage of believers, such as the Church, is not a rock, but a foundation of sand. Is Christ with such a Church "all days, even to the end of the world," and is the Holy Spirit abiding with it "for ever?" No! unless the two persons of the Holy Trinity are there to witness and sanction its infidelities. Has it a right to teach and to be heard? No! for its children may naturally object to receive its teaching on the principle that it teaches error. A fallible Church, therefore, is not the Church of the sacred Scriptures.

Then, if we look to the economy of the Apostles in founding the Church, their very mode of proceeding is a standing argument of its infallibility. For by the stupendous miracles they wrought, they not only proved the truth of the particular doctrine they first put forward, which was the incarnation of the Son of God, but they proved their own Divine mission to teach and to teach truly the whole body of revelation. Or, in other words, they proved their own infallibility. This is clear from the Scriptural history of the Primitive Church. The founders of the Church were infallible; but, some one will say, infallibility died with them. Therefore, I say, the Church, from being a Divine and Heaven-protected institution, became a mere human society. Its constitution was fundamentally altered when the Apostles were withdrawn from it. But, my

---

¹ Matthew xviii. 17.

opponent will continue, this human society was still Divinely taught, because it had received the revelation committed to writing by the Apostles before they left it. Then I reply, its destination was to battle about the meaning of the sacred Scriptures to the end of time, for it held the truth, but had no commission to teach it, and indeed could not teach it, so as to give any security for the truth of the articles delivered.

In the hypothesis of fallibility, therefore, there is an end to all stability and unity and spirituality in the Church, even though we suppose it to hold the sacred Scriptures, and them to contain all truth. It consists of a body of believers, whose sole bond of union is their agreement on one point, viz., that all truth is in the sacred Scripture. We have only to read attentively the prophetic descriptions of the Church in the Old Testament or the Apostolic descriptions in the New, to be fully convinced that such a Church does not in any way realize the pictures of revelation.

Part the Third.

HOW THE EARLY PATRISTIC WRITINGS REPRODUCE THE SCRIPTURAL PICTURE OF THE CHURCH OF GOD.

Anno 200—300.

Part the Third.

INTRODUCTION.

CONTROVERSY.

THE progress of Christianity into the Pagan world, and its detailed conflicts with Judaism, developed new species of controversy, and mutually the success of Christian controversialists, in hard-fought polemical battles, was, under Divine Providence, one of the great causes of the propagation of the faith in the second and third centuries. At an earlier period the Apostles endeavoured in a summary way to beat down and crush the physical and moral strength of Grecian and Roman Paganism by the demonstrative force of stupendous miracles, while they confuted Jewish arguments by an appeal to the fulfilment of prophecy. They did not, however, stop here; they condescended to argue out the case with Jews and Pagans, and to answer their objections by facts and logic. For example, St. Paul was accustomed to enter the Jewish synagogues, and to dispute with the priests and scribes on the sense and significance of Scripture passages. He pleaded the cause of Christianity in strong and lucid language before Felix and Agrippa; and in the following short and beautiful discourse addressed to the supreme council of Greece, he fearlessly attacked Polytheism and idolatry, and boldly affirmed the unity and omnipresence of God, insinuating all the time the reasonableness and necessity of faith, and suggesting as a motive for the acceptance of his preaching the fear of the judgment to come. "Ye men of Athens, I perceive that in all things you are too superstitious. For passing by and seeing your idols, I found an altar also, on which was written, 'To the unknown God.' What, therefore, you worship without knowing it, that I preach to you. God, who made the world and all things therein, he, being Lord of heaven and earth, dwelleth not in temples made with hands. Neither is he served with men's hands, as though he needed anything, seeing it is he who giveth to all life and breath and all things. And hath made of one all mankind to dwell upon the whole face of the earth, determining appointed times and the limits of their habitation. That they should seek God, if happily they may feel after him or find him; although he be not far from every one of us, for in him we live and move and are: as some of your poets said, 'For we are also his offspring.' Being, therefore, the offspring of God, we must not suppose the Divinity to be like unto gold, or silver, or stone, the graving of art and device of man. And God, indeed, having winked at the times of this ignorance, now declareth unto men that all should everywhere do penance. Because he hath appointed a day wherein he will judge the world in equity, by the man whom he hath appointed, giving faith to all by raising him up from the dead."[1] It was not only in his spoken discourses that St. Paul disputed and argued with the opponents of the Christian faith; but in his epistles addressed to the Churches he had founded, and in his written instructions to Timothy and Titus he takes occasion, from time to time, to attack the popular erroneous notions of the day, and to overthrow the false principles of philosophy. The epistles to the Romans, Hebrews, and Corinthians, are full of controversy, and in his epistle to Titus he points out as one of the essential characteristics of a bishop, an aptitude "to exhort in sound doctrine and to *convince the gainsayers.*"

Following in the footsteps of the Apostles, the priests and bishops of the second century, their successors in the

---

[1] Acts of the Apostles xvii. 22—31.

ministry of the gospel, were zealous lecturers on polemical subjects and prompt and earnest disputants on the side of Christian truth as against the sophistry of the Greeks and the captious bitterness of the Jews. The learning of the Gentile world had been transferred into the Church of God. The "spoils of Egypt" had come in by masses. Men who in Paganism had learned everything that could be learned, and whose minds were stored with the science of Rome, and the literature of Greece, and the legendary lore of the East—men who were the ornaments of their epoch had become converts to Christianity; and thenceforth their active minds and great acquirements were devoted to the defence of the principles they had embraced and the refutation of the errors they had abandoned. Several reasons can be assigned for the ever-increasing number and importance of controversial treatises and discourses during the age succeeding the apostolic. 1st. Though miraculous effects were still produced in favour of truth, they were less frequent and, on the whole, less startling than the miracles wrought by the twelve. Miracles are the greatest argument in favour of the gospel. Whilst the Apostles were living, arguments for Christianity were almost unnecessary, for miracles were being wrought constantly. The Apostles being now dead, and miracles having become of less frequent occurrence than in their day, the necessity for availing of the natural and ordinary means of impressing, defending, and enforcing truth, namely, by appeals to reason, history, and experience, was much increased. To be sure, the primitive miracles could be always adduced, as affording irrefragable proof of the divine origin of Christianity; yet as, from its nature, a miracle is not so moving when attested as when operated, we are perhaps justified in attributing, partly to the comparative decadence of actual miracles, the sober earnestness with which the Christian disputants of the second century sat down to examine the foundations of Pagan mythology and the grounds of Jewish prejudice. 2nd. Another cause of the controversy of the second century was the close contact of Christianity with Paganism and Judaism, arising from the

P

actual diffusion of the Christian religion. The priests and bishops of the Church were confronted with Jewish rabbis and Pagan sacrificers in every town and village. They met in conversation; they were fellow-citizens; civil, if not social intercourse united them in the same community; living house by house, and walking side by side. Religion, and its changes, the abandonment of the worship of the gods, and the adoption of the worship of the "Crucified," were the topics of the day. They were discussed in every society. The discussion of them enkindled the fire of party feeling. Jews and Pagans attacked the Christians, and the latter were forced to defend themselves: they did so with effect, and even carried the fire into the camp of the enemy. Treatises against Christianity were composed and circulated on the side of Paganism; and then the great converts and bishops of the Church arose up in the might of their powerful intellects and intimate acquaintance with both sides of the question, and poured out upon their opponents a torrent of raillery and invective, accompanied with the most brilliant demonstrations of truth and the most telling confutations of error. It was absolutely necessary that more frequent controversies about religion should be the result of the wider diffusion of the faith. It was consonant to the zeal and piety of the Christian controversialists to labour assiduously by the composition of learned works to put before the multitudes a strong protest against fables, sophistry, and pretence, that were leading them to spiritual ruin. 3rd. Calumnies of a most gross and grievous character had been put in circulation against the practices and doctrines of Christians: it was necessary to meet them, and to prove their falsehood by a full and candid exposition of Christian truths; and in expounding the pure morality of the gospel to all classes of opponents, it was not to be expected that ecclesiastical writers would overlook the opportunity of contrasting creeds and principles. Calumny had become the foundation of State prosecution; while subverting the grounds of calumny, it was natural that the maligned and injured Christians should endeavour to show that absurdities and crimes of the most glaring kind were not only tolerated in the Pagan systems, but positively countenanced and approved. To stop the mouth of calumny it would have been absolutely sufficient to say we are not guilty; but it was a much more telling and forcible reply to affirm, while proving the fact, "You are yourselves guilty of the very crimes you impute to us."

Such causes as these, and many others to which it is now unnecessary to refer, contributed to foster and enlarge the controversial spirit of Christianity in early times; and it is to their conjoint operation that we are to trace the origin of the powerful and subtle polemical writings that issued from the bosom of the Church in the form of "orations" and "apologies" in the second century.

To these treatises, and the arguments they embody, we must briefly direct our attention before entering upon the third and last part of our historical researches.

DIVISION I.

POLEMICAL WRITINGS.

§ 1. *The Jews again.*—The members of the Jewish race were quite content with their knowledge of God; and they rested in the belief that all perfection consisted in the faithful discharge of the duties imposed by their moral and ceremonial laws. Here was their strong fortress. Had not their prophets been inspired? Had not the Lord selected them as His peculiar people from all the nations of the earth? Had not He promised to multiply the seed of their patriarchs "as the stars of heaven, or as the sands on the sea-shore?" On such assumptions as these, the Jews might have rejected or even refused to hear the arguments of the Christian writers and preachers, only that the question of the Messias, the great question dilated and insisted upon by Christianity, was raised again and again, and largely discussed in their own prophetical books. The Messias, then, they must prepare for: the Messias they must receive. Yes! but they had made up their minds not to receive any claimant to that dignity, who came not in the form of a temporal king, and surrounded by the glory of a conqueror.

Now, if it could be demonstrated to the Jews, that the prophecies touching the Messias had all been fulfilled in Christ, that the circumstances that attended the birth and preaching of Christ accorded with the vivid pictures of Isaias and Jeremias, that his career upon earth, his sufferings and death had been in all their leading circumstances foreseen and foretold; they had no rational grounds for refusing to acknowledge him as their Messias, and it would be both impious and unpardonable to hesitate about receiving his doctrine. All these points were demonstrated clearly and with flashing evidence; and as it had been the constant effort of the Apostles to establish them in the first century—Peter in Jerusalem, Paul in Asia-Minor, the others in the synagogues of more remote lands—so now it became a labour of love for strong Christian minds deeply imbued with Scriptural learning, to evolve them before an obstinate and deluded race in language clear and copious, in argument the force of which it was difficult to withstand.

"The dialogue of. St. Justin with the Jew Tryphon," which appeared about the middle of the second century, contains the Christian-Jewish disputation in all its details, and it may be taken as a fair illustration of the manner in which the Church brought conviction to the minds of one class of her opponents, answered their objections, and cleared up their doubts. The object of the Christian controversialist in this work, is, as he says—" to demonstrate that we have not believed fables, nor stories destitute of proof, but full of the Holy Ghost, overflowing with

virtue, and blooming with grace;"[1] or, in other words, to demonstrate the solid grounds of Christianity against the Jews receiving the Scriptures. He begins by laying down the proposition, that Jews and Christians agree in believing in the same God. " Nor, Tryphon, shall there ever be another God, nor has there been from eternity, but He, who has made and ordered the universe. Nor do we believe that there is one God for us, another for you; but the same who led forth your fathers from the land of Egypt in a powerful hand, and an outstretched arm."[2] They agree too, he subjoins, in hoping in Him, but not after the same manner. " But we hope, not through Moyses or the law; for so we would act in the same manner as you.[3] . . . . . We are of the race of those who are led to God, through this crucified one, Christ, as will be shown by me in the sequel of this discourse."[4] Having touched upon the grounds of the Christian's hope, he proceeds to demonstrate the Scriptural foundation of them by long extracts from the prophecy of Isaias, after which he winds up as follows:—
" Of these, and other sayings of the same prophet, Tryphon, some are spoken in reference to the first coming of Christ, in which he is foreshown as about to have an inglorious, and ill-favoured, and mortal appearance: the others, in reference to his second coming, when he shall present himself in glory from the clouds, and your race shall see and recognize him, whom they have pierced, as Osee, one of the twelve prophets, and Daniel, have foretold."[5]

St. Justin associates with his proof from Isaias of the identity of Christ with the promised Messias, an explanation of the necessity of penance and baptism. The latter rite, he says, has been now substituted for circumcision. But his adversary will naturally inquire, why has God instituted circumcision if if be not necessary to justification?

---

[1] St. Just. Mart. "Dialogus cum Tryp. Jud." No. 9, p. 33, tom. ii. "SS. Patrum Opera Polemica," Wirceburg, 1777.
[2] *Ibid.* No. 11, p. 35.   [3] *Ibid.* No. 11, p. 37.
[4] *Ibid.* No. 11, p. 39.   [5] *Ibid.* No. 14, p. 47.

To meet this difficulty, the apologist again reverts to the prophetical writings, and shows from them, that the law of the sabbath, the distinction of meats, and circumcision were instituted, not to confer justification, but to distinguish the Jewish race from other nations, and thereby to preserve them from idolatry. "Which if we are unwilling to allow, we fall into an absurd conclusion, as if God was not the same in the time of Enoch and those other just ones, who had not the circumcision of the flesh, and observed not the sabbath and laws of that kind, as being instituted by Moyses: or (as if) he wished not the same justice to be practised by the human race at all times; to assert which is clearly absurd and foolish." [1]

The grand point in the argument of Justin with Tryphon, as indeed it must always be in the disputes of Christianity with Judaism, was the proof of the Divinity of Christ. To this the apologist addresses himself at great length. At first, however, he does not openly affirm it; but by citing Scriptural passages, which show forth the power, majesty, and dominion of the promised Messias, he leaves his opponent to infer that he can be no other than the Son of the Most High, and God equal to his Father. To this inference, clear though it be, Tryphon is perfectly blind. So far is he from admitting it, that he takes occasion from the tenor of the words of Scripture adduced, to raise the following objection to the character and mission of Christ. "These," he says, "and other Scriptures of the kind, compel us to expect one glorious and great, who, as the Son of Man, receives an eternal kingdom from the Ancient of Days. But this Christ of yours, whom you so name, was without honour, without glory, so as to incur that last degree of execration that is sanctioned in the laws of God." [2] This objection of Tryphon's leads St. Justin to prove that, according to the Prophets, Christ was to come twice; that he was to come in humiliation and to

[1] St. Just. Mart. "Dialogus cum Tryp. Jud." No. 23, p. 65, tom. ii. "SS. Patrum Opera Polemica," Wirceburg, 1777.
[2] Ibid. 32, p. 83.

come in glory; that he was to come to suffer first for the salvation of mankind, and that he was to come a second time to judge the world in power. Upon hearing this proof, Tryphon rejoins, without distinctly admitting the validity of it. "I am conscious of your views on these matters; wherefore, resuming your discourse where you have broken off, finish it. For to me it appears something wonderful and indemonstrable. For what you say, that this Christ has been God before all ages, and afterwards has been born and made man. . . . . This appears to me not only repugnant, but absolutely absurd."[1] This rejoinder elicits from Justin a long and brilliant demonstration of the Divinity of the promised Messias from the writings of the Old Testament, an argument which gradually gains in strength as it goes on, creating first bitter recrimination in the mind of his opponent, then embarrassment, and finally almost conviction. From the interruptions and admissions of Tryphon, we may judge of its force. At first he denies the pertinency of the passages of Scripture introduced. "All the prophetic words adduced by you are ambiguous, nor do they contain anything decisive of that which you wish to prove."[2] After some time he is compelled to admit that there is in these ancient prophecies something illustrative of the superhuman character of the Messias; something, in fact, which might almost justify external nations in believing him to be God. His words are: "For you, who are of the Gentiles, who also from his name are called Christians, be he acknowledged Lord, and Christ, and God, as the Scriptures signify. But for us, who are the worshippers of God, by whom even he has been made, there is no need to confess or adore him."[3] Further on he confesses himself perplexed by the multitude and probativeness of texts, as to the sense he ought to put on those other passages of Scripture in which the undivided power and majesty of God are

---

[1] St. Just. Mart. "Dialogus cum Tryp. Jud." No. 48, p. 125, tom. ii. "SS. Patrum Opera Polemica," 1777.
[2] *Ibid.* No. 51, p. 133.   [3] *Ibid.* No. 64, p. 173.

affirmed, which is almost equivalent to an admission of
the conclusiveness of the Christian controversialist's proof.
"Moved," he says, "by the authority of so many Scriptures,
I am doubtful as to what I ought to say of that Scripture,
by which God through Isaias, declares that he will not
give his glory to another, in these words : ' I am the Lord
God ; this my name, and my glory and power, I will not
give to another.' "[1]

In proving the Divinity of Christ from the sacred
Scriptures, St. Justin takes occasion to refute the Jewish
interpretations of the prophecies : thus he shows that
several passages which were commonly held to have been
spoken of Solomon or Ezechiel, could not be applied to
them : these passages were verified in Christ, and the
glories they announced were those of his spiritual kingdom.
The pascal lamb and the emissary goat are figures
of Christ : the oblation prescribed for those who have
been cleansed from leprosy is a figure of the Eucharist,
which too he affirms to be the "clean oblation" alluded
to by the prophet Malachy. An objection of Tryphon's to
the effect that the Messias had not come, because Elias has
not yet appeared, leads him to prove that John the Baptist
was the Elias referred to by the Prophets. "Then (to
use his own words) resuming the discourse, interrupted at
an earlier period in which I was demonstrating that He
was born of a virgin, and that this generation of a virgin
was foretold by Isaias, I quoted the prophecy anew after
this manner:—' And the Lord spoke again to Achaz,
saying .... Behold a virgin shall conceive and bear a
son.' .... Then I added, it is clear to every one, that
in the race of Abraham according to the flesh, no one
hath existed, but this our Christ, who was born of a virgin,
or was said to be so born."[2] From various figures in the
writings of the Old Testament, Justin makes it quite clear
that the Messias was to die upon a cross : and then he

---

[1] St. Just. Mart. "Dialogus cum Tryp. Jud." No. 65, p. 177, tom. ii. "SS. Patrum Opera Polemica," Wirceburg, 1777.

[2] *Ibid.* No. 66, p. 179, 181.

proceeds to a full and learned exposition of the 21st Psalm, in which he proves that the various prophecies therein contained were literally fulfilled in the circumstances of the sufferings, crucifixion, and death of the Redeemer.

Again, he reverts to the two comings of Christ, and evinces them at great length from the Scriptures; whence he passes to the rejection of the Jews and the call of the Gentiles, sharply and strongly rebuking the former for their ingratitude and obstinacy. He concludes by insisting on the necessity of doing penance, and bringing forth fruits worthy of penance; and he exhorts Tryphon and the members of his race to have recourse to Christ, as the author of justification and salvation, and to abandon their present teachers.

It was after this manner that the Christians of the second century argued against the Jews. They did not go outside the Scriptures to look for materials whereof to build their "tower of strength against the face of the enemies" of the God-man; but entering boldly into the discussion of topics which heretofore were the exclusive property of the descendants of Abraham, following tradition step by step to its source in the prophetical writings, comparing the sayings of the different "inspired ones," selecting facts, arranging them, and generalizing conclusions, they heaped up an amount of evidence in favour of the Christian religion, so subtle in texture that it was absolutely impenetrable, so clear, so brilliant, that it shot its rays into the most recusant minds, and carried conviction to judgments clouded with prejudice. Yet it would be wrong to suppose for a moment that the Jewish doctors of this period were devoid of ingenuity and learning. They had their own interpretations of Isaias and Daniel, and their own views with regard to the character of the Messias, and they used them with some effect in controverting the positions of such men as Justin the Apologist. But the greater the opposition the more signal was the victory of the Christian disputant. And the most eminent Jew, returning from a conflict with a Christian of similar attainments, should say, if he spoke with candour, like Tryphon at the conclusion of the dialogue so often quoted. " Indeed, I confess myself much delighted with this discussion .... For I have found more than I expected, or than even could be expected." [1]

§ 2. *Detailed Conflict with Paganism.*—The conflict with Paganism was of an entirely different character from that we have just been considering. It was taken up with the discussion of elementary principles.

Every religious system ought to be traceable to Divine institution. The origin of every religion in detail ought to be referable to a positive ordination of the Divinity, or should be discoverable in the essential relations existing between contingent beings and the necessary Being, more or less clearly seen by the light of human reason. In other words, religion ought to be natural or revealed. The systems of Greek and Roman paganism were too much detailed and complicated; they professed to know too much of the nature and attributes of God, and of the relations of man to the other life to be even in the opinion of their deluded followers the mere externations of natural religion. Consequently, they must have originated in some positive teachings, and if they came from God, they must have come by the way of revelation. Now, with the exception of some vagaries about the Sibylline volumes, paganism in the second century did not pretend to revelation. Then it was not a revealed religion. It was not a natural religion. Therefore, it had not come from God in any way, but was a mere tissue of fables, invented by the poets and philosophical writers, and wrought into varied forms, to minister to the tastes, or please the passions of the multitude, to terrify, to startle, to amuse.

This was, in reality, the position of paganism, and it was well understood by the Christian controversialists of the second century. Hear how one of them urges the Greeks on the origin of their theology. " Who then, O

---

[1] St. Just. Mart. "Dialogus cum Tryp. Jud." No. 142, p. 361, tom. ii. "SS. Patrum Opera Polemica," Wirceburg, 1777.

Greeks, do you assign as the teachers of your religion? The poets? But it is vain for you to allege the poets, to those who are versed in the poets; for they know their absurd ideas about the origin of the gods, as I can show you from him who is the most celebrated with you—Homer, the prince of poets.[1] .... But if you refuse to allege the poets, because fiction is their privilege, and they are allowed in fabulous dissertation about the gods to say many things that are far from the truth; who else, I ask, do you think, you have as teachers of your religion, and whence do you say they have received it?[2] The wise men assuredly and philosophers you will say.[3] ...... Wherefore, beginning as it is meet, with the most ancient and the first of them, I will show you in detail that their opinions are much more absurd than the theology of the poets."[4] The writer here alluded to fulfils the double task he proposes to himself in a most telling and forcible manner. He shows in the first place, by copious extracts from Homer, that the religious theories propounded by the poets are most silly and laughable, and of no weight whatsoever; and then he shows, by a reference to their written opinions, that the greatest philosophers of antiquity were quite in opposition on the fundamental principle of all religion, namely, the nature and attributes of the first cause, God.

Apart from their origin, the Pagan systems were tested on their intrinsic merits. The object to which they directed prayer and ceremony was an idol, the work of the hands of man. This was not a service that reverenced with inferior homage an image or statue of the Divine; but it was a sovereign and a supreme worship, the worship of incense and sacrifice, which terminated at a figure in bronze or stone. "Moreover," says Justin, "when often of vessels the most contemptible, they have merely changed the form, and superinduced the likeness of some one—

---

[1] St. Just. Mart. "Ad Græcos Cohortatio," No. 2, p. 19, tom. i. "SS. Patrum Opera Polemica," Wirceburg, 1777.
[2] *Ibid.* No. 3, p. 23.   [3] *Ibid.*   [4] *Ibid.*

these they designate gods; which we not only believe to be irrational, but a positive insult to the Deity, whose name is given to things liable to corruption, and requiring assiduous care, while His glory and form are alike untold by words. . . . . . Oh, infatuation of the smitten mind! to grant to incontinent men the reputation of forming and transforming gods for worship, and to constitute such the guardians of the temples in which they are placed."[1] "What then?" says Athenagoras; "for many, whilst they know not what matter is, or what God is, or what is the distance between them, offer supplication to images formed of matter: must we, too, who discern and distinguish that which is inborn and which is born, that which is and which is not, that which is perceived by the mind and by the senses, and give each its proper name, must we adopt and adore idols?"[2] "To me," says Theophilus, "it appears absurd, that statuaries, potters, painters, founders, should mould, paint, carve, found, and prepare gods, which, when made by the workmen, are held in no repute; but, when they have come to the use of temple or private house, they sacrifice to them; not only they who have bought, but they, who at much pains have made and sold them, with the pomp of victims and libations, come to adore them and repute them as gods, nor see that they are such as when they made them, stone, brass, wood, colour, or such-like material."[3]

It was thus that the controversialists of the second century attacked the worship of idols. They stated the doctrine, if it be fair to denominate it such: they then made it a butt for bitter sarcasm or pleasant raillery. It was useless to argue about it, for there was contradiction in the terms of the proposition, which enunciated, that cold metal had a warm heart to sympathize with human woes, or that lifeless clay could avert from man the

[1] St. Just. Mart. "Apolog. I." No. 9, p. 131, tom. i. "SS. Patrum Opera Polemica," Wirceburg, 1777.

[2] Athenag. "Legatio pro Chris." No. 15, p. 135, tom. iii. *ibid.*

[3] S. Theophil. "Ad Autolyc." lib. ii. No. 2, p. 289, *ibid.*

scourges of pestilence and famine, or rain down favours from the clouds.

From idol-worship, the Christian writers turned to the worship of the gods, which they assailed in language no less severe, and witticism not less pointed.

The gods ought not to be worshipped with supreme adoration, unless they were inborn and increated. If, with human bodies, and human passions, they lived like men— above all, if like wicked men, they plunged into human vices, it was blasphemy to sing Divine praises in their honour. That which eats and drinks and sleeps, which has a birthday and a day of pleasure, which laughs and cries and wrangles, is, to speak moderately, an object unsuited for other than civil respect. To constitute such a being the term of religious worship must be an act of exaggerated profanity. Now, the gods had a beginning, as their authorized histories proved: they were even endowed with bodies, inferior in some respects to those of men; their vices were human vices, nay, some of their vaunted exploits were tinged with every hue of guilt.

1st. They were born, or had a beginning.—" From the beginning," says Athenagoras, as "they (the poets) affirm, the gods were not; but as we are born, so was each of them born: about this all agree. For thus sings Homer: Ωκεανον τε θεων γενεσιν και μητερα Τηθυν (Ocean the origin of the gods and mother Thetis). But Orpheus, who first discovered their names, and narrated their mode of birth and told their exploits, and who with them has a higher reputation of having spoken truth on subjects connected with the divinities, whom Homer imitated in many things, and especially in such as regard the gods: Orpheus, I repeat, determined their primary generation from water: Ωκεανος οσπερ γενεσις παντεσσι τετυκται (Ocean which to all is the source of generation).[1] . . . . This is the primary origin of their reputed gods, as well as of all things. What, therefore, does this amount to?

---

[1] Athenag. "Legatio pro Chris." No. 18, p. 143, tom. i. "SS. Patrum Opera Polemica," Wirceburg, 1777.

That each of those, to whom divine nature is attributed, is understood to have had a beginning. Now, if, when they were not, they were made, as it seems to those who treat of these matters, undoubtedly they exist not. For either a being is inborn and eternal, or, if born, obnoxious to corruption."[1]

2nd. They had bodies of a monstrous and even disgusting appearance.—" But now they describe their bodies, as when they speak of the god Hercules as a flying dragon and hundred-handed, or, as when they say of the daughter of Jove .... that 'she is provided with two eyes in the natural position, two also in the forehead, and a sort of beak in the back of the neck, and horns besides.' "[2]

3rd. Their vices were such, that even in men they would be regarded as unnatural and enormous.—" Again, they describe what they conceive to be their exploits: of Saturn, for example .... how he cast his father from a chariot, and devouring his male children, involved himself in the guilt of parricide; of Jove, for instance, how he bound his father and cast him into Tartarus, as Uranus did his sons: how he warred with the Titans for the sovereign power, and pursued his mother Rhea, flying with horror from marriage union with him. ..... What of decency or utility is in such stories as these, that we should believe Saturn to be a god, or Jove, or Ceres, or the others?"[3]

If such, in their origin, their form, their morals and conduct were the pagan deities (and the instances here given fairly represent the entire class) they were deserving of contempt rather than veneration. From the passions that influenced them, and the crimes they committed, they must be, if they could be supposed to exist at all, monsters in disposition. Tatian, in his treatise against the Greeks,[4] describes the fall of the angels, and takes occa-

---

[1] Athenag. "Legatio pro Chris." No. 19, p. 145, tom. i. "SS. Patrum Opera Polemica," Wirceburg, 1777.

[2] *Ibid.* No. 20, p. 147.   [3] *Ibid.*

[4] Tatian. Assyr. "Contra Græc. Oratio" *passim, ibid.*

sion to affirm again and again, that it was the fallen spirits that personated the heathen gods, and were worshipped under the different names of pagan mythology. If oracles were pronounced in truth, they emanated from the mouths of devils; if prodigies were wrought in the temples, the operation of Satan was there.

Independently of such considerations as the above, it was objected that the entire system of paganism was shifting and indefinite, as scarcely two nations worshipped the same deities, and the number of gods was unlimited.—
" What, now, does it conduce to enumerate the multitude of animals that are worshipped by the Egyptians, of reptiles, of cattle, of beasts, of birds, and of swimming things of the waters. . . . . . But if you cite the Greeks and other nations, they worship stones, wood, and other material things, images, as I said before, of dead men. For Phidias is known to have made at Pisa Olympic Jove for the people of Elis, and for the Athenians Minerva in the citadel. It is worth your while, man, to know how many Joves there are. In the first place there is Jupiter called Olympian; then Jupiter 'Latialis;' Jupiter 'Cassius,' Jupiter 'Ceraunis,' Jupiter 'Propater,' Jupiter 'Pannychius,' Jupiter 'Polinchus,' Jupiter 'Capitolinus;' and that great Jupiter, who was son of Saturn and king of Crete, has a tomb in Crete: for the rest, I know not if they have been dignified with tombs. But if you put forth the mother of those whom you call gods, I would not presume to mention her actions, or those of the ministers by whom she is served, or the taxes and tributes that she and her sons pay to the king. These are not gods at all, as I said before, but idols and impure demons. So shall they be who make them and place their hope in them."[1]

This multiform and conclusive reasoning of Christian writers in the second age of the Church, shadowed forth the dissolution of Paganism in all its forms. The worship of the gods ought to disappear, because it was silly, irra-

---

[1] St. Theop. ad Autol. lib. i. No. 10, p. 279, tom. i. "SS. Patrum Opera Polemica," Wirceburg, 1777.

tional, and unsustained by any argument or authority. Paganism must be banished from the world, and the people of Rome and Greece must look out for some other object of adoration besides horses, statues, or demons, and some other code of morality, besides the lax and immoral principles inculcated in the lives of their deities. This was the conclusion of the indirect argument for Christianity, which consisted in an enumeration of the shortcomings, sins, and absurdities of Paganism, and the vanities of the worship of idols.

In directly impugning the fables of Paganism, the controversialists of these early times, indirectly and by inference, demonstrated the truth of the gospel history and the Divine origin of the Christian religion. The question of truth lay between Paganism and Christianity only. If the former was sustainable on rational grounds, the truth of the latter was inadmissible. If the latter was true, the former was deluding and erroneous. And Paganism had been shown to be false in its origin, its nature as a religious system, and its operations. Therefore Christianity was to be taken as the true epitome of the history of man and the world, of the relation of both to God, and the connection between the seen and the invisible.

Direct proofs of the truth of Christian revelation are not wanting in the polemical writings of the second century. They are to be found in the works of the apologists and others, lucid, nervous, and fraught with the most varied information. We may instance, as a volume that contains them, the three books addressed by S. Theophilus of Antioch to Autolycus. In these remarkable treatises, the harmony of the Mosaic account of the creation is evinced at great length.[1] It is compared with the narrations of Plato, Homer, and Hesiod. Its truth is proved from the fact of its coincidence with the results of observation and experience. It accounts for the origin of the most ancient

---

[1] St. Theop. ad Autol. lib. ii. per totum, tom. i. "SS. Patrum Opera Polemica," Wirceburg, 1777.

kingdoms and cities, the diversity of languages, and the successions of the most protracted lines of kings. We said awhile ago, that Paganism in the second century scarcely pretended to revelation. Theophilus puts in its claim; but he affirms at the same time, that all the religious truths propounded by Pagan authors were learned by the Greeks from the Egyptians, and thus found their way from the revealed Scriptures into the poetry and literature of Greece. So having proved from the inspired writings the unity of God, the creation of all things by Him, and the vanity of idols, he establishes the same doctrines by quotations from the Sibylline verses.[1] He shows from the poets that man shall be rewarded or punished in the next world, according to his good or bad works in this life. He concludes that "nolentes volentes," the Sibyl, the poets, and the philosophers are of accord with the sacred Scriptures on the fundamental truths of religion.

Nevertheless, the Greek writers have[2] fallen into gross errors in some circumstances of the account they give of the creation. Their chronology is shown to be absurd and contradictory, and, as their oldest writers are recent in comparison to Moyses, of no authority when placed side by side with the narrative of the book of Genesis. Theophilus confirms the Scripture chronology, by collating the periods of the great events of sacred history, with events recorded in the writings of Manethon the Egyptian, and Menander the Ephesian, and he makes mention of documents existing at Tyre, which confirm the Scriptural account of the building of the temple of Solomon.

The whole tissue of his argument is close and varied, and the writer, a good specimen of the Christian dogmatists of the age in which he lived, shows throughout a clear and strong mind, an intimate acquaintance with the Holy Scriptures, the poets and historians of Greece, Egyptian chroniclers and Chaldean traditions.

[1] St. Theop. ad Autol. lib. iii. passim, tom. i. "SS. Patrum Opera Polemica," Wirceburg, 1777.
[2] *Ibid.* lib. ii.

When to the refutations of pagan theories, Christian evidences such as these were added, the result must have been the attraction to the faith of many of the great and thinking minds of the age, as nothing was wanting to satisfy the logician, the man of information, or the searcher after truth, as to the claims of the Christian Church to be the conductor of the human race on the road that leads to the knowledge of God in this world, and the enjoyment of his kingdom hereafter.

§ 8. *Conflict with Philosophic Theories.*—The direct arguments of Christianity were levelled against the errors of philosophy as well as against other opponents. All the great problems of philosophy were solved by revelation. The creation of the world, the nature of the human soul, the end of man, about which philosophy had dogmatized and erred, were all solved by revelation. Matter and spirit, the beginning and end of things, which had afforded such fruitful themes to the devisers of systems of philosophy, still solved by revelation. The light of Christianity shone into the world of ideas and the region of sensations, and expelled the chaotic darkness which philosophy had accumulated there. Thus it was, that Christianity and philosophy as it then existed, dealing with the same important subjects, and solving them in an entirely different way, the direct and positive arguments which evinced the truth of Christianity as a whole, refuted in detail the philosophic theories which were opposed to revealed doctrines. Christianity demonstrated itself not by halves or piecemeal, but in its entirety, and to the utmost extent of its revelation, and therefore its refutation of philosophical broachings was co-extensive with the errors contained in them. It may then be said with truth that the first great arguments against the philosophic errors of the first centuries of the Christian era, were the demonstrations of the authenticity, integrity, and veracity, of the Sacred Scriptures, the proofs of the Divinity of Christ, and the inspiration of his Apostles, of the inerrancy of the Church, and of its commission to teach truth to the world.

The position first assumed by Christianity in respect to all opponents was the high ground of authority, and therefore we can scarcely expect that she should descend into the arena of the schools to contend about particular questions on which she and the philosophers disagreed. To do so, in fact, would be to demonstrate from natural principles, as revelation did not generally suggest the " ratio " of the facts she propounded, nor derive them from the human mind warped too often and erring, but from the mind of the Divinity undeceiving and undeceived. To argue with Plato about his theories, was to become a philosopher. Christianity, as such, was no philosopher. To contend about the rational truth or falsehood of the immortality of the soul with some, or its increation with others, was to philosophize. There was one case in which Christianity in these early ages regarded it as a duty to contend with the philosophers on their own principles. It was as follows:—Christianity having demonstrated itself, proposed some dogma to be believed as of faith. Philosophy denied its truth, because it was repugnant to reason. Take a particular proposition for an illustration. "The dead shall rise again," says Christianity; "the trumpet shall sound and the dead shall rise." "No," says philosophy, " the dead shall not rise; absurd, it cannot be." Christianity in this and similar cases was not strictly bound to philosophize, because there was no conclusive argument from reason against the possibility of the resurrection. There were, however, plausible arguments, and consequently Christianity regarded it as important to become a philosopher for a moment, in order to eradicate philosophical errors more thoroughly, and to prevent the scandal of the weak. So in this case thus commenced the Christian controversialist. "Who deny the resurrection of the dead or doubt about it . . . . either do not attribute the origin of man to any cause (which is easily refuted), or ascribing to God the cause of things, and regarding this dogma as a primary principle, demonstrate from it the credibility of no resurrection. This they will accomplish, if they can prove that God *cannot*, or *does not wish*, to put together bodies that are dead and entirely dissolved, and so to unite them as to form the same man (again). But if they cannot accomplish this, let them cease to be incredulous, and to blaspheme things which it is unlawful to assail. Now, from what I am about to say, it will be clear that there is no truth in their assertions, whether they say that God *cannot* or *will not*. We know for certain that a thing *cannot* be effected by another, either from the fact that he knows not how to do it, or from the fact that he has not sufficient power to bring to a successful issue that which he knows. For, who is ignorant of the means to effect a thing, can neither attempt nor accomplish that which he knows not. But who well knows what is to be done, and whence and how he is to do it, but who has no power to effect what he knows, or powers inadequate to the task, if he have sense and looks to his own capabilities, will not attempt it; or, if he make the rash attempt, will not accomplish that which he designs."[1] The argument so far is clear, consecutive, and strictly philosophical. The resurrection, or non-resurrection of the dead, turns on the power and will of the Creator and Regenerator. If God cannot or will not effect the resurrection of the dead, there will be no resurrection. And if God cannot effect the resurrection, it must be owing to a want of knowledge or of power. But, 1st, God does not want the necessary knowledge. "God cannot be ignorant of the nature of bodies, that are to be recalled to life, to the extent of their entire members or the parts thereof, nor of whither each has gone after its dissolution, nor of which of the elements has taken that which was dissolved and carried it to its proper resting-place. . . . For it is quite clear that He, who before the formation of every individual well knew the nature of the elements of which is the human body, and the parts of the elements from which He was to gather what appeared suitable to him for the construction of the body, cannot be ignorant whither, after the same has

---

[1] Athenag. de Resurrectione Mortuorum, No. 2, pp. 199, 200, tom. iii. "SS. Patrum Opera Polemica," Wirceburg, 1777.

fallen asunder by dissolution, has migrated each of those materials which he employed in finishing and perfecting the individual."[1] 2d. God does not want the necessary power, in proof of which he adds:—" Their generation by him is an argument of his power to bring bodies to life again. For if, when they did not exist he made them, and in the first creation, their primary matter, how can it be that he will have greater difficulty in raising them up when they have fallen to decay; for one is as easy as the other."[2]

God then does not want the power, nor the knowledge necessary to bring about the resurrection of the dead. If God have the power and the knowledge required, there is no repugnance in the assumption that the dead will rise again. Here terminates the reply to the philosophical difficulty against the resurrection. Then the argument of Athenagoras contracts itself into a brief, but forcible conclusion. God has the knowledge; God has the power; God has the will to resuscitate the human body. Nothing is wanting on the part of God; therefore, the dead shall rise again.

This one case illustrates a thousand others, in which Christianity stood on the defensive, and proved in philosophic argument that the doctrines she propounded were not repugnant to reason, or inconsistent with principles known by observation or experience. Still Christianity was no philosopher, and in all such cases as these she but answered the objections raised by the schools, and urged so strongly by the sophists and dogmatists of the age, that it was expedient to give them a hearing.

The great argument of Christianity against the philosophy of the first and second centuries, like that against their idolatry and polytheism, consisted in an enumeration of discrepancies, contradictions, and manifest absurdities. Philosophy, as a whole, was open to attack on the side of its inconsistencies and the disputes of its various sects.

---

[1] Athenag. de Resurrectione Mortuorum, No. 2, pp. 199, 200, tom. iii. "SS. Patrum Opera Polemica," Wirceburg, 1777.
[2] *Ibid.* No. 3.

There was scarcely a moral point that philosophers had not sullied, or a metaphysical one that they had not obscured; and here was the position of an aspirer after a happy end, who looked for light and guidance from pagan philosophy, as it existed then or in times past. In the first place he wanted to know something about his soul—what it is, or where it came from. Then it was necessary to ascertain whither it was going; and on this turned the question that philosophy should answer, what is the happiness of the soul. But this was not all. The world in which man has been placed must have had a beginning—who created it? And God, who placed man in this world, must have laid down certain rules for his guidance, founded on the essential relations between creatures and their Creator. What are these rules? What are the perfections and attributes of the Deity? Here were important questions that philosophy must answer now, plainly and consistently, if she hoped to maintain her position as the teacher of morals and the guide of man on the path that leads to happiness. How had she answered them? Her teachings on all these subjects were full of opposition and confusion.

1. On the nature of the human soul philosophers had differed most materially, and there was no kind of unmeaning theory that they had not advanced to account for its existence and future state. "For some of them," says Hermias, "say that the soul is fire, Democritus for instance; others air, as the Stoics; others mind; others motion, as Heraclitus; others, an exhalation; others a virtue that flows from the stars; others, as Pythagoras, a number endowed with the power of motion; .... others, an element of the elements; others, harmony, as Dinarchus; others, blood, as Cretias; others, spirit; others, unity, as Pythagoras; and the ancients, something different.[1] . . . Some of them affirm that its nature is to last for a short time; others transfer it into the condition of beasts;

---

[1] Hermiæ Philosophi Gentilium Philosophorum Irrisio, No. 1, p. 427. "SS. Patrum Opera Polemica," Wirceburg, 1777.

others cut it into atoms. Some allow it to return to bodies thrice; others allow it a duration of a thousand years."[1] Having thus stated the opinions of philosophers on this subject, Hermias jestingly, but pointedly adds:—
"Now I am immortal, and I am glad; now, on the contrary, I become mortal, and I weep; soon I am dissolved into corporal elements, I become water, I become air, I become fire; a little after, neither air nor fire; one makes me a wild beast, another makes me a fish. In my turn I have dolphins as my brethren, and when I behold myself I am afraid of my body, and I know not what name I should call it, a man, or a dog, or a wolf, or a bull, or a bird, or a serpent, or a dragon, or a chimera. For by the studious of wisdom, I am changed into all the animals, terrestrial, aquatic, winged, multiform, rural, tame, mute, vocal, wild, rational. I swim, I fly, I am carried up in the air, I creep, I run, I sit. Besides Empedocles comes forward and makes me a tree."[2]

2. The philosophers were equally at sea with regard to the beginning of things and the nature of the first cause. "When philosophers," continues Hermias, "cannot agree about the nature of man's soul, much less can they speak truth about the gods and the world. . . . . Certainly, in their account of the beginning of natural things there is the greatest discrepancy. When Anaxagoras catches me, he teaches as follows: The beginning of all things is mind, and the same is the cause and mistress of all, and gives order to the confused, and motion to the motionless, and difference to the conjoined, and beauty to the unsightly. When Anaxagoras so speaks, he is my friend, and I submit to his opinion. But Melissus and Parmenides oppose; of whom the latter, in poetic metre proclaims, that *what is*, is one and eternal, and infinite and immovable, and like itself in every respect. Wherefore again, I don't know why, I yield to this theory, and Parmenides expels Anaxa-

---

[1] Hermiæ Philosophi Gentilium Philosophorum Irrisio, No. 2. "SS. Patrum Opera Polemica," Wirceburg, 1777.

[2] *Ibid.* No. 2, p. 429.

goras from my soul. But when I think that I have lighted on a stable theory, Anaximenes taking his turn, vociferates against them. I tell you everything that is, is air; which condensed and concrete becomes water; but if rarified and diffused, ether and fire; returned to its own nature, liquid air; but if condensed, he says, it is changed. Again, I pass over to this theory, and Anaximenes is my beloved. But Empedocles is eager in his opposition, threatening and roaring aloud from Ætna; the beginnings of all things are enmities and friendships, of which the latter gathers, the former scatters, and all things are the offspring of their contention. And I define them to be like and unlike, and infinite and limited, and eternal and created. Well done, Empedocles, I will follow you to the craters of fire."[1] Following up this subject, Hermias passes in review the systems of the creation or origin of things, propounded by Protagoras, Thales, Anaximander, Archelaus, Plato, Pherecides, Democritus, Heraclitus, Epicurus, Clianthus, Carneades, and Clitomachus; and placing them side by side, he exhibits their deformities and mutual repugnances, and having finished his elaborate task, he concludes in the following appropriate words:—"These have I narrated to expose the contrariety of their opinions, and the unlimited and interminable rovings of their speculations, and their end inexplicable and useless, as unconfirmed by evident fact or clear reason."[2]

3. The nature of God and the way to happiness were discussed by the philosophers with even less success than the questions heretofore alluded to. In reply to the question, what is the true happiness of the soul, some philosophers answered: pleasure earthly and sensual. There were others of a more austere disposition, who looked upon pleasure as an evil. "One," says Hermias, "calls pleasure its good; another designates it an evil; another, something mediate between good and evil."[3] In reply

[1] Hermiæ Philosophi Gentilium Philosophorum Irrisio, No. 3, p. 431. "SS. Patrum Opera Polemica," Wirceburg, 1777.
[2] *Ibid.* No. 10, p. 439. [3] *Ibid.* No. 2, p. 427.

to the question, what is the nature of God ? the wildest, most blasphemous and reckless views were put forward. " Some of the Portico," says Theophilus, "altogether deny that there is a God; or, if there be, that he has any concern except for himself. And this is what the folly of Epicurus and Chrysippus has pronounced. Others assert that all things happen fortuitously, and that the world is increated, and that nature is eternal; and they have presumed to say that there is no providence of God at all, but God they think is merely the conscience of the individual. Others again think that the spirit which pervades all things is God. But Plato and his followers, allow indeed that God is innate, and the Father and Creator of all; but then they determine that the innate are two, God and matter; and the latter, they say, is coeval with God."[1]

It was after this manner that pagan philosophy disposed of the most grave and important questions that have ever agitated the soul of man. There was no consistency in its speculations; every principle that it laid down was liable to contradiction, and was met by opposition on the part of men, who were regarded to be fully as wise as those who had advanced it; and so the profession of wisdom, instead of being a rich garden, where the fruits of truth and justice might be gathered, became an arid and bare arena, where to the ignorant and needy nothing was given to feast upon but the combats of intellectual gladiators. Under these circumstances it is only natural to expect that among the polemical Christian writings of the second century, pages and whole treatises should be devoted to the errors and inconsistencies of the various philosophical schools. Nevertheless, we are not to suppose for a moment that the Christian controversialists of these early ages meant to call in question the prerogatives of reason, or wished to expel her from her throne. When they argued from an enumeration of results and facts,

[1] S. Theop. ad Autol. No. 4, p. 293. "SS. Patrum Opera Polemica," Wirceburg, 1777.

that reason, as represented by philosophy, had failed to fulfil her mission, they did not intend to give even the slightest grounds for the conclusion that reason must necessarily err. Reason had erred. Why so? Because reason had speculated recklessly. Passion, whim, and prejudice had mixed themselves up with the investigations of reason, and so it will often be in this world, and thus reason had erred. But was error the result of the operation of reason, or of the co-operation of whim and prejudice? Of the latter undoubtedly, for reason ceases to operate where truth ceases to hold sway.

The force of the Christian argument amounted to this:— Philosophers had advanced every variety of theory on religious subjects; wherefore, they were unsafe guides for those who aspired after immortality. If it was objected to Christianity, that notwithstanding the manifest contradictions of philosophers, some of them had advocated doctrines that agreed with the teachings of Christianity, the answer was ready, that the very man who had spoken truth on one point, had erred on fifty others. Philosophers had erred perseveringly, and so long had they been tried now, and so powerful had been the intellects engaged in the struggle, that it appeared idle to expect from them as religious guides, aught but inconsistency and self-sufficiency, and the advocacy of views and theories hostile to common sense and dangerous to immortal souls.

DIVISION II.

THE SECOND VICTORY.

§ 1. *Progress of the Church.*—The Church, triumphing over her adversaries, continued to widen her domain and extend her dominion. Her first successes had been in the East. The close of the first century saw her reigning over Asia Minor, Palestine, Crete, Greece, and Syria. Advancing to the West, she had seized upon Italy; and she had established her head-quarters, so to speak, in Rome long before the close of the first age of her existence.

Rome, the undying seat of ecclesiastical sovereignty; Rome, attacked, shattered, broken then as in this year 1860-1861; Rome, strong and weak, conquering and conquered, the object of the respect and scorn of the millions, receiving the faith in the first century, became the centre from which it was thenceforth diffused through the infidel nations of the universe. The Church, therefore, starting from Rome, continued her journey towards the far West, during the second and third centuries of the Christian Era, following up victory after victory.

When reading the history of the great schism of the 16th century, we must have been struck by two facts therein recited: 1st, The facility with which some Northern European nations gave up the Catholic faith; and, 2nd, The tenacity with which the nations of the South adhered to it. It did not, perhaps, then strike us that the Southerns were the older children of the Church, while the inhabitants of the North were comparatively neophytes. Yet such is the fact, as we learn from studying the history of the first propagation of the Christian faith in Europe.

Leaving Rome, the Church was not far from the "great sea" of the Scriptures: "Hoc mare magnum et spatiosum manibus." Or, if she preferred it, the great road to the Alps was open to her, by which she might enter Gaul from the south-east. Slow ships from Ostia to the ports of France and Spain were numerous in those days, and conveyances to the land confines of Helvetia and Gaul were not wanting. In either mode of travelling, Gaul and Spain were the first countries encountered by the Church in journeying from Italy towards the west of Europe. It is not for us to say whether the facility of reaching these countries influenced the choice of the primitive propagators of the Gospel, but certain it is, that after Italy, they were the first evangelized in the West.

Even as early as the Apostolic period, we find mention of the intended journey of a great missioner from Rome to Spain, on the business of the gospel. The missioner referred to is St. Paul. In his Epistle to the Christians of Rome, written from the East, he thus announces his project: "When I shall begin to take my journey into Spain, I hope that as I pass I shall see you, and be brought on my way thither by you if first in part I shall have enjoyed you."[1] And a little further on he reverts to it in the following terms: "When, therefore, I shall have accomplished this and consigned to them this fruit, I will come by you into Spain."[2] We are not aware whether circumstances allowed the Apostle of the Gentiles to carry out his design of announcing the faith in person to the Spaniards; but certain it is that long before the close of the second century the Church, issuing from Rome, had travelled along by the Mediterranean, and established large and flourishing Christian colonies in the principal cities of Proconsular Spain, and Gaul.

Nor had the other side of the water been neglected. The province of Africa, lying along the southern shores of the "great sea," had been evangelized at an early period. Its "Coloniæ" and "Municipia" were full of Christians at the opening of the third century. Egypt and Numidia had received the faith, and a line of ancient cities, stretch-

---

[1] Romans xv. 24. [2] *Ibid.* verse 28.

ing along the coast of Northern Africa and to the confines of the Great Desert, were become as remarkable for their orthodoxy and for the learning and constancy of their bishops as they had formerly been for their skill in arms and the martial energy of their kings.

Thus the Church, having during the first years of her existence brought Judea, Asia Minor, Crete, Greece, and Italy under the standard of the Redeemer, pushed on in two conquering and almost parallel columns towards the West, subduing in the first instance the countries surrounding the great midland sea that separates Europe from Africa.

§ 2. *Characteristics of the Church.*—When we designate the entire Christian community by the name *Church* we individualize it. When under this term we speak of the victories, journeys, and reverses of the Christian people, we give them, scattered though they may be, a corporate existence, and we attribute to them a close union as parts of a whole, and as a whole composed of parts—a strict and inseparable unity. The Church travelled from place to place. The Church established herself in a certain town or city. The Church extended herself. Such expressions could not be used with propriety if the Church was a disjointed and dislocated mass of human beings, agreeing in a few fundamental articles of faith, but differing in worship and government. Therefore, in our mode of speaking of the conflicts and victories of the Church in the second and third centuries, we suppose her to be essentially one. Let us see if this supposition accords with the views of the fathers of that period.

The learned, the orthodox Bishop Cyprian may be taken as a fair representative of the belief and practice of his order on all subjects connected with controversy, and, as he wrote as the recognized champion of the Church, his authority as an expounder of her constitution and properties is the highest that can be produced. It will be, then, important and interesting to ascertain in what respect and how far he believed unity to be essential to the body of the faithful. Happily, as regards this subject, his writings are a vein of the richest and most varied illustration. The Church is according to him—"A body whose limbs are distributed through various distinct provinces;"[1] "the Church is one through the whole world;"[2] "the Catholic Church which is one and true;"[3] "Christ prayed that we should be one, as the Father and Son;"[4] "the Church is one;"[5] "in Christ one body, to which our multitude is aggregated;"[6] "the Church is one body;"[7] "Christ attached more importance to the unanimity than to the multitude of his members;"[8] "the unity of the Church deriving from the divine institution;"[9] "the Lord, referring to unity as springing from the divine bounty, said, 'I and the Father are one;'"[10] "one God and one Church;"[11] "one is the house of God;"[12] "one Christ and one Church;"[13] "the body and soul of the flock of the Lord are one;"[14] "the Church is not among heretics, because it is one and cannot be divided;"[15] "the Church cannot be cut asunder or divided;"[16] "unity cannot be in any wise separated or divided;"[17] "the unity of the Church cannot be rent;"[18] "the Church neither rent nor divided, but connected by the bond of priests mutually cohering to each other."[19] In his book on the unity of the Church, St. Cyprian breaks out into the following description, which may be taken as a summary of what he has elsewhere written on the point:—"The Church, too, is one which by enlarged fecundity is spread out into a vast multitude. As the rays of the sun are many but its light is one, and the branches of the tree are many but the strength, founded in the tenacious trunk, is one, and when from the same source many streams flow, unity is preserved in the source, though multiplicity ap-

---

[1] D. Cypr. No. 41, Ed. Paris, 1844. [2] No. 73. [3] No. 124.
[4] No. 213. [5] Nos. 53, 62, 123, 152, 195, 202. [6] No. 108.
[7] No. 201. [8] No. 198. [9] No. 128. [10] No. 153.
[11] No. 202. [12] No. 103. [13] No. 132. [14] No. 58.
[15] No. 139. [16] Nos. 62, 139, 153. [17] No. 151.
[18] Nos. 74. 196. [19] No. 123.

pears to be derived from the abundance of the flowing waters. Take away the ray of the sun from the body, unity will not allow the division of the light; break the branch from the tree, when broken it cannot produce; cut off the stream from its source, separated it dries up. So the Church of God, by diffusing its light, sheddeth its rays through the whole earth; yet the light is one, which is diffused everywhere, nor is the unity of the body impaired. By the greatness of its fecundity it stretcheth its branches through the whole earth: its copiously-flowing streams it widely expands. There is, however, but one head and one source, and one mother fruitful in successive progeny." [1]

Here are Cyprian's views. Here are the views of the third century. The Church is an individual, one in its isolation—one in the unanimity of its members—one by the connecting bonds of sacerdotal and episcopal jurisdiction—one so as to repudiate identification with all heretical societies—one so as to admit of no schism or division of its members—one in body and in soul, that is, in its external aspect and its invisible life—one as Christ is one, as God is one—this one Church all pervading, everywhere. In speaking of the propagation of Christianity in the third century, we were, therefore, justified in individualizing the Christian body, and we but used the language of the fathers of that time when we identified the travels and propagandism of the Apostles and the authorized Christian missioners with those of the Church whose faith, discipline, practices, government, worship, whose very being they carried into strange lands and diffused through the nations of the universe.

It is refreshing in such an age as this to find oneself among the ancient fathers, and to hear sound doctrine flow from their all but inspired lips. When, according to some, the true Church is the aggregate of all Christian societies, however opposed and divided; when, in the opinion of others, it is the Church of Sweden or the Church of Scot-

---

[1] D. Cypr. de Unitate Ecclesiæ, No. 5, p. 501; 2. Curs. Coplet. Patrol. series 1ma. tom. iv. Paris, 1844.

land;—when doctrines are favoured in high quarters which would almost rend from the centre of unity the Catholic Churches of certain great nations;—when, for a small pension or a little place, nominal Catholics decry ultramontanism in order to open the way to schism: "They violated me among my people for a handful of barley or a little bread;"—in such an age of scandals and delusions it is strengthening and consoling to learn from such an authority as Cyprian and his contemporaries that there is but one "house of God" where his faithful children dwell in union, unity, and peace. So, extended as was the Christian Church of the third century over Asia, Europe, and Africa, it was a cemented and cohesive body of believers—governed by the same laws, worshipping at the same altar, using the same rites, holding the same faith; and if we search for the fundamental reason of this unity, so extraordinary, so almost miraculous, Cyprian tells us that it was "built upon Peter;"[1] that "it is built upon one who also received its keys;"[2] that "the foundations of the Church are laid upon Peter;"[3] that "one it hath been founded by Christ the Lord upon Peter in the origin and disposition of unity."[4] Of this one true Church how great was the power and spiritual dominion! "All power and grace are constituted in the Church,"[5] said the same high authority just quoted. "The Church holds and possesses all the power of her Spouse and Lord."[6] How marvellous her fidelity and indefectibility! "The Church is no adultress."[7] The Church is incorrupt and modest."[8] "No event can separate the Church from Christ."[9] "Never, under any circumstances, does the Church recede from the doctrine of Christ."[10]

And if the Church were one and universal—sound in doctrine, and gifted with authority to teach, to direct, to

---

[1] D. Cypr. Nos. 83, 123, 127, 132, 250. Curs. Coplet. Patrol. series 1ma. tom. iv. Paris, 1844.

[2] No. 132. [3] No. 148. [4] No. 125, 127, 131.
[5] No. 145. [6] No. 132. [7] No. 195.
[8] No. 195. [9] No. 108. [10] No. 83.

govern—is it wonderful that the promise of salvation was
limited to her children, and that they who are outside
her communion were pronounced unfruitful and withered
branches, and that all other societies professing to be
Christian were regarded by the orthodox fathers as combinations for the ruin and not for the salvation of souls.
We consequently meet in the writings of St. Cyprian the
most severe denunciations of heresies, associated with
the most fervent praises of the soul-saving power of the
Church. Thus he tells us, on the one hand, that " Christ
is not with those who are assembled outside the Church,"[1]
while, on the other, he affirms plainly that "The Church
alone is the spouse of Christ—that she alone can bring forth
children to God."[2] He goes so far as to say that there
is "no salvation outside the Church,"[3] and that there is
"no reconciliation [*pax*] outside the Church;"[4] that "outside the Church there can be neither loosing nor binding;"[5] that "outside the Church there is no martyr;"[6]
that "they who are outside the Church are dead."[7] In
fine, that "It is not easier to escape [destruction] outside
the Church than without the ark of Noah."[8]

It is regarded as illiberal to speak of exclusive salvation
at the present day. How illiberal, then, must the ancient
fathers appear to the advanced minds of our epoch! To us
it must be satisfactory to find that the Church of the third
century, like our own good mother, her successor in the
direct line, was stern and uncompromising in her principles; and, as the expounder of the doctrine of Christ was
in antagonism with worldly views and heretical opinions,
that she believed in herself, and regarded herself as holy
and the source of holiness, faithful and the mother of all
faithful souls, destined to be universal, and never to change
or fall away; and it must be a fresh stimulus to us to uphold severe doctrine on the constitution and mission of the

---

[1] D. Cypr. No. 198, Curs. Coplet. Patrol., series 1ma, tom. iv.
Paris, 1844.
[2] No. 140. [3] No. 195. [4] No. 129. [5] No. 131.
[6] No. 198. [7] No. 126. [8] No. 195.

Church of God, though haply unpalatable to the world, when we find that in doing so we but pass along to those who will come after us a sentence that has been spoken in the beginning and perpetuated through past centuries by all that have been good and true.

DIVISION III.

THE CLERGY OF THE THIRD CENTURY.

§ 1. *Priests and bishops.*—After leaving the Scripture and the early patristic writings we almost lose sight of the clergy, until the broad pages of Cyprian and Tertullian open out before our view. It was easy to understand St. Paul. It was not difficult to give Timothy and the πρεσβυτεροι of his day the place that he assigned to them. We thought we discovered in the former's position at Ephesus the perfect picture of the Christian bishop's jurisdiction, and the intelligible prototype of the parish priest's power in the ministrations of the latter in the cities of Asia Minor and Crete. However this be, there was much said about the επισκοποι and πρεσβυτεροι; there was much said about them and clearly said by the early Christian writers, which enabled us to obtain more than a partial view of their sacred character and of the position they occupied in the Church. It will be, perhaps, well to sum up the result of our previous lucubrations upon this subject before we push out into the comparatively wide expanse of the pages of patristic writing in the third age, where it will give us quite enough to do to adhere to fixed ideas, and where departure from a certain line of treatment would involve the subject in obscurity, and destroy our prospect of arriving at a satisfactory solution of questions of the greatest interest. Here, then, are the points we have determined upon in the first part of this work:—

1st. All the clergy, including επισκοποι, πρεσβυτεροι, and διακονοι, were ordained by the imposition of hands. 2nd. By the imposition of hands, a permanent and abiding grace was conferred upon the επισκοποι and πρεσβυτεροι. 3rd. Ordaining hands were imposed by the Apostles first; then by men, such as Titus and Timothy, who enjoyed a high position in the Church, and a varied and extended jurisdiction. 4th. Besides ordination, a mission from competent ecclesiastical authority was necessary for πρεσβυτεροι and επισκοποι in order that they should be legitimate ministers of the Gospel and of the Church. 5th. Some of the επισκοποι and πρεσβυτεροι were higher than others; some had more extensive powers with regard to Church government. Timothy and Titus were clearly different from the πρεσβυτεροι of Asia Minor and Crete, whom they ordained. We therefore designated the two former by the name of *bishops*, while we regarded the latter as simply *priests*. 6th. Dioceses and parishes existed not yet in name, but in fact we believed that we discovered them in the extensive and almost absolute sway of the bishops, and in the localized though fixed jurisdiction of the priests.

These six points embrace the sum of what we have determined upon relative to the clergy from a close examination of the writings of the New Testament, and particularly from the Acts of the Apostles and the Epistles of St. Paul.

Another question relative to the names πρεσβυτερος and επισκοπος we raised, but did not fully discuss. We affirmed, and indeed proved, that these two names were used indiscriminately to designate the *same* order of the hierarchy by the apostolic and evangelical writers of the New Testament; and we inferred, that if there were priests and bishops in the early Church, the fact could not be proved from the use of the words πρεσβυτερος and επισκοπος. It is singular that the same indiscriminate use of the two words is made by St. Clement of Rome, the first writer after the Apostles, and then ceases, as subsequent writers, such as St. Ignatius of Antioch, St. Polycarpe of Smyrna, and St. Clement of Alexandria, always employ them to designate two distinct orders. For the better understanding this apparent paradox, it will be useful to bring forward here the words in which those early fathers touch upon the subject.

Clement, of Rome (anno 69) has a passage in his epistle to the Church of Corinth, in which he styles certain clerics of that church επισκοπους and πρεσβυτερους. He thus expresses the object to which the epistle is directed. "I have heard that the most stable and ancient Church of Corinth, on account of an individual or so, excites a sedition against the presbyters [προς τους πρεσβυτερους."][1] Then he shows that the Apostles foresaw such seditions as likely to happen, but he passes from the use of the word πρεσβυτερος to επισκοπος. "Our Apostles, enlightened by our Lord Jesus Christ, have well known that there would be contention for the name of the episcopacy."[2] Farther on he employs the two names in almost the same breath. "For it will be no light crime if we reject from the episcopacy those who worthily offer the sacred gifts. Happy the 'presbyters' who have finished their career piously and fruitfully."[3] It is clear that in these passages he employs the words πρεσβυτερος and επισκοπος as denominations for the same order of the clergy, be that order the priesthood or the episcopacy; and this is his invariable practice. I have said before, and I have clearly proved, that it is the practice of St. Luke, St. Peter, and St. Paul. But when we come to the writers who flourished at the beginning of the second century and through it, we shall find a marked distinction made between the application of the two words.

Ignatius, Bishop of Antioch (anno 106), applies the word επισκοπος to the individual who governed the particular

---

[1] Clemens Rom. Ep. 1ma ad Cor., No. 47, p. 175, ed. Cot.
[2] Ibid.   [3] Ibid.

church of each city to which he wrote, and πρεσβυτερος to the higher order of his clergy. He never confounds the two words; he never applies them to the same person. He speaks again and again of the επισκοπος (in the singular), the πρεσβυτερους and διακονους (in the plural). The quotations in proof of this are numberless. "In such way that with union of spirit you obey the bishop [επισκοπῳ] and the priests [πρεσβυτεροις]."[1] "I have had the advantage of seeing you in Damas, your bishop [επισκοπον] elect of God, and the worthy priests (πρεσβυτερους) Bassus and Apollonius, and my brother the deacon Sotion."[2] "So all ought to respect the deacons as established by order of Jesus Christ: the bishops [επισκοπους] as the image of the Father; the priests [πρεσβυτερους] as the senate of God."[3] "Fly divisions as the source of evils; let all follow the bishop [επισκοπῳ] as Jesus Christ follows the Father, and the priests [πρεσβυτεροις] as the Apostles."[4] "I salute your worthy bishop [επισκοπῳ], your venerable priests [πρεσβυτερους], my brethren the deacons."[5]

Polycarpe, bishop of Smyrna (anno 107) commences his epistle to the Philippians in the following words, which make it quite clear that he regarded the επισκοπος of a church as quite a different person from its πρεσβυτεροι. "Polycarpe, and the priests [πρεσβυτεροι] who are with him, to the Church of God that is at Philippi."[6]

Clement of Alexandria (anno 194) observes the same distinction wherever he refers to the hierarchy. "Many other precepts which are addressed to elect persons are written in the holy books: these to priests [πρεσβυτεροις], those to bishops [επισκοποις], others to deacons."[7] "For here, too, in the Church the steps, bishops [επισκοπων], priests [πρεσβυτερων], and deacons are, as I think, models of the glory of the angels."[8]

[1] Ignat. Ep. ad Ephes., ed. Cot.   [2] Ep. ad Magnes.
[3] Ep. ad Trull.   [4] Ep. ad. Smyrn.   [5] Ibid.
[6] Polycarp. Ep. ad Philip., No. 1, ed. Cot.
[7] Clemens Alex. Pedag., lib. iii. p. 639; "Sm. Pm. Op. Polem." Wirceburg, 1777.
[8] Strom., lib. vi. No. 13, p. 301, tom. iii. ibid.

These texts and passages of those early ecclesiastical writers, give us ample food for reflection, and raise questions of great moment which it would be inexpedient to leave in abeyance, even for a while; and it would be slurring over a serious difficulty if we allowed Cyprian or Tertullian to take up the thread of the early history of the hierarchy, until we have succeeded in reconciling these apparently contradictory statements. Here are two parties about equal in number, arrayed against each other. Paul, Luke, and Clement of Rome (anno 40, 60), affirm that the πρεσβυτεροι are επισκοποι; and, *vice versá*: Ignatius, Polycarpe, and Clement of Alexandria (anno 106, 194), affirm that the πρεσβυτεροι are different from the επισκοποι. Here are surely conflicting statements. Are they reconcilable? and if so, how can they be reconciled? Some have said, by supposing all the πρεσβυτεροι and επισκοποι mentioned in the New Testament to have been bishops. But they are called πρεσβυτεροι? No matter, a bishop is a priest. Then in this supposition we shall have the bishops of the first century designated by two names, πρεσβυτερος and επισκοπος, (*i. e.* bishop and priest), each of which may be applied to bishops at the present day; no priests strictly so called in the first century. And when, in the second century, the exigencies of the Christian Church required the ordination of priests, we shall have the word επισκοπος exclusively used to designate the first order of the clergy, and the word πρεσβυτερος confined to the second. There are grave objections to this theory, to some of which I referred before. 1st. It is hard to suppose that there were no priests in the primitive Church. 2nd. It is still more difficult to believe that the high honour and awful dignity of the episcopacy were conferred upon numberless neophytes in Asia Minor and Crete. 3rd. How can it be said, as it is constantly said, that bishops are the successors of the Apostles, if numberless bishops were created by Titus and Timothy while the Apostles were still living? 4th. In this hypothesis we have to account for the disappearance of many bishoprics erected by St. Paul in Asia Minor, as seven only existed when St. John wrote the Apocalypse. 5th. Besides, St. Clement of Rome states positively that the priesthood was of Apostolic institution.

For these reasons we are inclined to doubt the accuracy of the statement, that all the primitive governors of Christian congregations were bishops, and consequently we must find some other theory whereby to explain the apparently conflicting statements of the writers of the first centuries regarding the επισκοποι and πρεσβυτεροι of the primitive Church.

I have said elsewhere that I believe Timothy and Titus to have been the two first bishops outside the Apostolic body, and that all the men above deacons whom they first ordained, as well as all those whom Paul and Barnabas ordained in the Churches of Asia Minor, were priests. But they are called επισκοποι in the Scriptures: no doubt they are; but the name επισκοπος means literally an overseer, and they were in the strict sense overseers, because they had quasi-parochial jurisdiction. They were placed in towns far away from the Apostles, from Titus, from Timothy, where they governed their little flocks as pastors in a state of comparative independence. But the difficulty remains; if the priests of the first age were properly designated επισκοπους why do Ignatius and Polycarpe studiously designate them priests? Simply because the priests of whom the two latter write and speak are a different class from the priests referred to in the Scripture. The former are the priests of the episcopal towns, those who acted immediately under the bishops; the latter are a class of priests who governed churches at a distance from the episcopal see. It is easy to perceive that the latter might be designated επισκοποι, while the word would be quite inappropriate if applied to the former. This view is, to some extent, confirmed by the farewell address of St. Paul to the clergy of Ephesus. He designated them all επισκοποι, "in which the Holy Ghost placed you bishops [επισκοπους] *to rule the Church of God.*" These clergy were certainly pastors, as we must infer from the text. But it would be absurd to suppose that they were bishops, for this is quite irreconcilable with what we know of the history of the primitive Church of Ephesus. They must therefore have been priests with parochial or quasi-parochial jurisdiction. This system, too, as I have shown elsewhere, afforded an easy clue to enable us to unravel the history of the early Churches of Asia Minor, and to reconcile the apparent discrepancies of contemporary writers. There can be but one serious difficulty against it, that is, that it appears to confound sacerdotal with episcopal ordination; and to this difficulty we shall now address ourselves while we endeavour to search for the primitive usage with regard to the election and ordination of bishops.

§ 2. *Difference between the two first orders of the hierarchy.*—The ceremony of the consecration of a bishop is one of the most solemn that takes place in the Church. Its details are numerous and complicated. The form, the words, the presence of the consecrating bishop, and his attendant bishops, the profession of faith, prostrations, &c., invest it with a character the most imposing. Episcopal orders are a grade beyond priest's orders ; hence the consecration of a bishop involves an additional ordination. The bishop is superior to the priest, not only in his jurisdiction and authority over the faithful, but in the radical powers of his priesthood, derived from his new ordination. The bishop can do in respect to orders what a priest cannot do validly; for instance, he can administer the sacrament of holy orders in all its branches. When, therefore, we advance a theory to account for a state of things in the primitive Church, variously stated by apparently conflicting authors, we must studiously avoid laying down any principle which would confound the ordinations of the clergy of the first and second ranks.

The word επισκοπος, as we can infer not only from its literal meaning, but from the mode in which it is employed in the Sacred Scripture, is to be regarded as designating the authority of an ecclesiastic in respect to Church government exclusively. It does not denote any power immediately derived from ordination. St. Paul explains the nature of the word as used by him, when he tells the clergy of Ephesus that the Holy Ghost placed the επισκοπους among the people "to rule the Church of God." If this be the meaning of the word επισκοπος, it would be quite natural to apply it to priests charged with the care of souls. Curates, bishops' assistants, could not be fairly designated by it, but as in the beginning of the Church, from the very nature of the case, all the priests ordained through distant countries were quasi-parochial, we can easily understand why they were denominated επισκοπους by St. Paul and St. Luke. Nevertheless, the priests of these early times were not of the same rank and power in respect to Church government. The episcopacy of some was limited to a town or city; that, for instance, of the πρεσβυτεροι, whom Titus ordained in Crete; while that of others, like Titus and Timothy, extended over large districts and provinces. Were the επισκοποι of the first and second orders differently ordained? The Scripture does not say. Was the priesthood of the former more elevated than that of the latter? Paul and Luke are silent on the subject. Could the former by virtue of their ordination effect anything which the latter could not do? Here is a little light from inspiration. Timothy and Titus could ordain, while there is a strong presumption that no such power or privilege was communicated to the first επισκοποι ordained by them. So there are but two distinctive characteristics of the bishops of the primitive Church outside the Apostolic body referred to in the New Testament, viz., their extensive power of governing, and their power of ordaining. They made πρεσβυτερους and επισκοπους. They ruled over them and the flocks committed to their charge; but as to their own ordination, the evangelical writers are content to tell us that it was effected by "the imposition of hands," like that of all the ecclesiastics who were assumed into the ministry by the Apostles, and those who shared their jurisdiction. Equally unsatisfactory on the subject of episcopal ordination are the early ecclesiastical writers. Clement of Rome throws no light upon the subject. Ignatius glances at it in a most cursory and figurative manner; from which we can only draw the general conclusion, that he regarded the bishop as much higher than the priest; but whether this elevation arose from his ordination or jurisdiction, he gives no grounds for determining. In one place he distinguishes episcopal authority by the name of "the grace of God," and sacerdotal authority by the appellation "the law of God." Of the deacon Sotion, he says: "He is submitted to the bishop as to the grace of God, and to the priests as to the law of Jesus Christ."[1] Again, he warns the Smyrnians of the superior claims of the bishops on their respect and obedience. "Let all follow the bishops as Jesus Christ follows the Father, and the priests as the Apostles."[2] Then, in his epistle to the Trallians, he affirms that the dignity of the bishop as compared to that of the priest is in the same ratio of excess, as that of the king to his councillors. "All ought to respect the deacons as established by the order of Jesus Christ; the bishop as him who is the image of the Father; the priests as the senate of God, the companions of the Apostles."[3] Thus, in the letters of Ignatius, while the personal dignity of the bishop is upheld, the superiority of his priesthood by divine right is probably affirmed; but yet there is an ambiguity about his mode of expression which must nullify any argument on this subject drawn from his words. We are, therefore, reluctantly compelled to pass on from his works, disappointed that he has not spoken clearly upon one of the most interesting questions that can engage the ecclesiastical antiquary. Justin, Theophylus of Antioch, Clement of Alexandria, Irenæus, pass before us; we open their writings and close them again foiled in our efforts to clear up the point. So the second century passes by; and it is not until the comparatively voluminous works of St. Cyprian and Tertullian appear in the middle of the third, that we are enabled to refute on solid grounds and by strong arguments, the erroneous thesis of some moderns who deny that there are any grounds for believing that

---

[1] Ignat. Ep. ad. Mag.   [2] Ep. ad Smyr.   [3] Ep. ad Trall.

ecclesiastics were newly ordained in the early Church when they ascended from the priesthood to the episcopacy.

Tertullian, in his book on baptism, designates the bishop by the name "high priest," which by analogy would lead us to think that his priesthood was of a superior and unique order, like that of the Jewish pontiff. "The high priest [summus sacerdos] who is the bishop, has the right to give (baptism); then the priests and deacons; not, however, without the authority of the bishop, for the honour of the Church."[1] The argument from this passage in favour of episcopal ordination, is strengthened by the fact that the Jewish high priest was differently ordained from the other Levites who were admitted into the sanctuary. Cyprian is still clearer in his allusion to this point, where, in his eleventh Epistle, he speaks of the insult inflicted upon bishops by the rash conduct of some priests. He makes two affirmations. The bishop is superior to the priest in the radical powers of the priesthood; he is superior in authority and the prerogatives of his see. The passage is as follows:—" Still I hear that some priests, mindless of the Gospel, and thoughtless of what the martyrs have written to us, nor allowing to the bishop the honour of his priesthood and his chair, have begun to communicate with the fallen,"[2] &c. The distinction between the two is obvious. The priests in their unwise benignity are regardless of two things: that is, of the bishop's priesthood, and of his pontifical authority. They do not honour, or rather they disrespect his priesthood. Then his priesthood must be entitled to peculiar respect. Why so? because if it be similar to their own priesthood, it cannot be, as such, deserving of more than ordinary respect. No doubt, because it is altogether of a superior character. Hence it is plain that Cyprian here implies that episcopal ordination elevates the cleric who receives it to a higher grade in the priesthood than his brethren who serve in

[1] Tertul. Liber de Lapsis, c. xvii. p. 1218A; Curs. Complet. Patrol., tom. i. series 1ma. Paris, 1844.
[2] Cypr. Ep. xi. No. 11, p. 257A. *Ibid.*

the ministry in any class from which he may have been taken. In his twenty-seventh Epistle, addressed to "the fallen," Cyprian has a long passage which bears upon the subject of episcopal ordination. Here are the points that may be gathered from it. 1. The honour of the episcopacy is deducible from its institution by Christ. 2. The ordination of bishops places them in the honourable position to which the institution of Christ has elevated their order. 3. Bishops, like their predecessors the apostles, are stones in the foundation of the Church. 4. They become so by ordination and succession to its first founders. "Our Lord, whose precepts and warnings we ought to observe, disposing the honour of the bishops and the management of his Church, speaks in the Gospel and says to Peter: 'I say to you, that thou art Peter, and upon this rock I will build my Church, and the gates of hell shall not overcome it; and to thee I will give the keys of the kingdom of heaven; and whatsoever thou shalt bind upon earth shall be bound also in heaven, and whatsoever thou shalt loose upon earth shall be loosed also in heaven.' (Matt. xvi. 18, 19.) Thence by the revolution of times and successions, the ordination of bishops, and the management of the Church, proceed in such way that the Church be established on the bishops, and every act of the Church be directed by the same superiors."[1] According to this passage bishops are ordained. There is an ordination of bishops as such. If there be, it must be distinct from the ordination of priests. The effect of this episcopal ordination is at the same time depressing and elevating. It places the receiver down in the foundation of the Church, and it raises him into the line of the Apostolic succession. Now, as it is quite evident that no such effects could be attributed to the ordination of priests, it follows that in the mind of St. Cyprian a priest received a further application of the sacrament of orders conferring its proper powers and privileges when received into the

[1] D. Cypr. Ep. xxvii. No. 1, p. 298 B; Curs. Complet. Patrol, tom. i. series 1ma. Paris, 1844.

episcopal body. This much will suffice upon this subject. The mind of Cyprian touching episcopal ordination is further evinced in other passages of his works, but so clear are his *dicta* as put forth in the above extracts, that it is quite unnecessary to follow him through their intricacies.

§ 3. *Episcopal succession.*—In the Church of the early ages there were some episcopal sees that had been filled by the Apostles, or by the immediate companions of the Apostles. The former were designated Apostolic Sees; the latter might be fairly called quasi-Apostolic. From the nature of the case, from the fact that the Church had been growing and extending her dominion from the beginning, it is quite clear that there must have been in the third century an immense number of episcopal sees, which, because they existed in cities unseen and countries unvisited by the Apostles or their companions, could not trace their origin to the distinguished sources just mentioned. In fact, new congregations were being formed, new bishops were being given them; and both were reputed orthodox because they derived their being from an authority within the Church which had received the commission to breathe into them "the breath of life." What this authority was we will not discuss at present. We content ourselves with stating the fact of the existence of Apostolic and quasi-Apostolic Churches in the third age, and of other Churches sound and Catholic, whose bishops were not locally the successors of the Apostles or apostolic bishops, though personally the inheritors of their authority "to rule the Church of God." Tertullian will be our voucher for the truth of this affirmation. The thirty-second chapter of his "book on prescriptions" will furnish the items of its proof. He refers distinctly to the different kinds of Churches that existed in his day which will be found to correspond to the three classes just mentioned. He is arguing with heretics who pretended to antiquity and orthodoxy. He says, "But if any heresies attempt to ingraft themselves upon the apostolic age, and by consequence appear derived from the Apostles because they have existed under the Apostles, we can say: let them therefore make known the origin of their Churches; let them evolve the series of their bishops, descending step by step from the beginning in such way that the first bishop will have as originator and predecessor, one of the Apostles or Apostolic men, who with the Apostles persevered. For it is in this way that the Apostolic Churches give account of themselves: as the Church of the Smyrnians refers to Polycarpe located among them by John; as (the Church) of the Romans proclaims Clement ordained by Peter; in like manner as the others parade those whom, appointed to the episcopacy by the Apostles, they possess—the shoots of Apostolic seed. Let the heretics invent something like this: for after their blasphemy what can they regard as unlawful? But though they invent, they will gain nothing for their cause. For their doctrine, compared to that of the Apostles, by its unlikeness and contrariety, will declare that neither Apostle nor Apostolic (man) was its author; for as the Apostles taught not different tenets, so the Apostolic (men) did not announce tenets contrary to the Apostles, but preached after a different manner (truths) which they heard from the Apostles. So thus after this fashion they will be required to give their evidence by those Churches, which, though alleging no Apostle or Apostolic man as their originator, as being long after their time, as being daily erected, yet agreeing in the same faith, are, by identity of doctrine, put down as Apostolic."[1] The argument of Tertullian in this passage goes to show that heretical conventicles were devoid of Apostolicity of succession and Apostolicity of doctrine. Their bishops were not the descendants of the Apostles or Apostolic bishops, and their doctrine was different from that of orthodox Churches, though some of the latter were of recent formation. According to this argument, Apostolicity is of the utmost importance; no Church can be orthodox

---

[1] Tertul. Liber de Præs., c. xxxii. p. 44 B.C.; Curs. Complet. Patrol. series 1ma, tom. ii. Paris, 1844.

without it. If a Church have not Apostolicity of descent, it must at least have Apostolicity of doctrine. Then each particular Church that is sound in faith and practice must be Apostolic by birthright or adoption. The bishop of such a Church must be the lineal descendant of an Apostolic or primitive bishop, or he must have been assumed into the hierarchy by competent authority in the Church. Ordination was essential; a "mission" was equally essential: both were required not only for the bishops of the recently-erected sees, but for the bishops that fell into the line of direct Apostolic descent. Succession, then, was of much importance, but it did not constitute the bishop, and therefore we have now to direct our attention to the means by which bishops were formed,—to the machinery by which they were taken from among the clergy, and placed on the throne,—and we have to ask these early writers what power in the Christian Church had a right to appoint a bishop; by whom was he elected, consecrated, and confirmed in his See.

§ 4. *Episcopal election.*—We must retrograde a little, to inspect the primitive source of episcopal jurisdiction. The Apostles appointed the first bishops: they selected and ordained them, and gave them jurisdiction to govern a portion of the flock of the Lord. All the Apostles appointed bishops; each of them had received a commission to lay those consecrated stones in the foundation of the Church; and each in his own sphere of labour fulfilled his mission on his own responsibility. No wonder it should be so, for the Apostles were collectively and individually infallible, and in their corporate and individual capacity, endowed with unlimited jurisdiction. Peter was the prince of the Apostles: and from the tenor of his official appointment as such, we find that extensive, perpetual, and predominating powers of government were conferred upon him; such powers, indeed, as from the nature of the case must be exercised by his successors rather than by himself. When, therefore, the other Apostles were removed from this life, we would be naturally inclined to surmise, that the plenitude of their electing powers collapsed to the successor of Peter. Was it to be supposed that the power of appointing bishops died with the apostles? Assuredly not, for the Church was to be perpetual. And if this power of election outlived them, where should we suppose it to go, save into the hands of that line of pontiffs who had received the commission—to bind, to loose, to open heaven, to close it, to consolidate the Church, to prop it up, to support it to the end of time? Antecedently, then, to the examination of all documentary evidence bearing on the subject, we would expect to find Rome consulted on the filling of vacant sees in the third century, and the "fiat" of the Roman pontiff in every particular case determining the right of succession to the episcopacy.

With these ideas before our mind, let us open the pages of Cyprian, and search there for some allusion to the rite by which vacant sees were filled, and the candidate for episcopal consecration selected in the African Church of his day. The custom of Africa will determine for us the usage in force through the provinces of the Roman empire remote from the centre of jurisdiction. In the acts of the fourth council of Carthage, held in the year 254, under the presidency of St. Cyprian, we discover more than an allusion, a rather full and vivid description of the mode of electing bishops pursued by him and his colleagues, and generally approved by the assembled Fathers. It is as follows: "God orders a priest to be made before all the synagogue; that is, he informs and shows that sacerdotal ordinations ought not to take place except under the observation of the assembled people, that by the presence of the people the crimes of the bad be discovered, or the deserts of the good be proclaimed, and the ordination be just and legitimate, after being tested by the voice [*suffragio*] and judgment of all, which subsequently, in accordance with Divine teaching, is observed in the Acts of the Apostles."[1] When Peter speaks to the people regarding the

[1] Concil. Carthag. iv. No. 4, p. 1026. Curs. Complet. Patrol, series 1ma, tom. ii. Paris, 1844.

ordination of an apostle in place of Judas, "Peter," he says, "'rose up in the midst of the listeners: now there was a great crowd assembled.' (Acts i. 15.) And we have observed that the Apostles followed this rite, not only in the ordination of bishops and priests, but of deacons, too, of which it is written in their acts, ' and the twelve called together the whole multitude of disciples, and said to them.' (Acts vi. 2.) It is plain that this form of proceeding so diligently and cautiously,—in calling together the whole people, was observed lest an unworthy member should steal into the ministry of the altar and the sacerdotal grade. For by the prophet Osee, who says, ' they have given themselves a king, but not by me' (Osee viii. 4), God himself declares that unworthy (members) are sometimes ordained, not according to the will of God, but the presumption of man, and that these displease God which do not come of legitimate and just ordination." The first point the fathers of the council establish is the necessity of calling together the people for whom a bishop is about to be elected, in order that they may give their opinion on the moral aptitude of the candidates presented; a provision which we would be disposed to believe of the very utmost importance in the circumstances of these early times. Yet we are not to suppose that the people voted as at an election. They were assembled for the purpose of giving information. Their opinion was asked, but it was a preliminary step to the selection of the bishop, from the names that were brought before the meeting. That they had no voice in the election must appear obvious from the words of Cyprian hitherto quoted. They were there in order ' that the crimes of the bad be discovered, and the deserts of the good be proclaimed" .... " lest an unworthy member should steal into the ministry of the altar and of the sacerdotal grade." Their office was principally obstructive, and it was only promotive to the extent of bearing testimony to the integrity of the candidates. It is scarcely necessary to enlarge on this point, as the functions of the laity and episcopal body, as regards the election, are clearly distinguished by St. Cyprian in the sequel of the passage. He continues: "Wherefore diligently of Divine tradition and apostolic observance, it is to be provided and held, as it is held with us, and generally through all the provinces, that to celebrate the ordinations rightly, the proximate bishops of the same province come together to that people, for whom a prelate [*præpositus*] is to be ordained, to the end that the bishop be selected in the presence of the people that fully knows the life of all, and has by daily intercourse become acquainted with the conduct of each. Which we see to have been observed with us in the ordination of our colleague Sabinus in such way, that by the voice [*suffragio*] of all the brethren and the judgment of the [*judicio*] bishops who had come together at the present, and who have sent you letters about him, the episcopacy was given him, and hands were imposed on him in the place of Basilides."[1] There are three things very carefully distinguished by Cyprian in this passage: 1st. The vote or overtly-expressed wish of the people. 2nd. The judgment of the bishops. 3rd. The ordination of the selected candidate. If some historical writers have affirmed that bishops were in ancient times selected by the people, religious theorists have presumed to say, that the election terminated the act or series of acts by which a bishop was made and located. Cyprian is against them both. The laity did not elect, according to him; they only recommended the candidate. It was the bishops that judged of his aptitude, and according to their judgment appointed or rejected him. Then, when the appointment was made, all was not ended; ordination followed, as in the case of Sabinus. The candidate, having been first elected, was subsequently ordained, and it was then he entered upon his office of "ruling the Church of God." It was from the episcopacy, then, that the jurisdiction of the new bishop was derived, as well as the powers conferred upon him by ordination. The bishops of his province, the neighbouring bishops, were the channels

---

[1] Concil. Carthag. iv. No. 5, p. 1027. Curs. Complet. Patrol., series 1ma, tom. iii. Paris, 1844.

through which grace and legislative right, and the very vital spark of his episcopacy flowed, and it was to them he traced his existence as an "overseer" of the Church of God.

I said a while ago that, during their life-time, the apostles appointed bishops. To them it was reserved, in the plenitude of their jurisdiction, to assume new members into the superior pastoral charge. Timothy, it will be said, appointed bishops. No doubt he did, but by a direct commission from Paul. So did Titus, but in this matter he, too, was an apostolic delegate. The plenitude of jurisdiction in the apostles enabled and entitled them to appoint bishops; and reciprocally so sublime is the office of a bishop that it appeared to require for its creation a full exercise of the highest apostolic powers. The apostles were dead. Their superior governing powers devolved to the successor of Peter. Therefore I remarked before, that we would be naturally disposed to believe that the Roman pontiffs in the third century appointed successors to all bishops deceased, and filled all vacant sees. Yet here is the election of a bishop described by Cyprian, and there is not one word about the action of the Roman pontiff. The whole business is expedited by the bishops of the province. They assembled, proposed the candidates, decided on one, appointed him bishop, ordained him, and dismissed him to his pastoral charge.

Here assuredly is a difficulty. The embarrassment of the position is increased by what takes place in the Church at the present day on the occasion of the vacancy of an episcopal see. There is an immediate appeal to Rome, and the Roman pontiff in every particular case reserves to himself the right of appointing the new bishop, and conferring upon him the jurisdiction necessary for the government of his flock. The preliminary steps devolve upon the canons of the widowed Church. An election is held by the canons. The candidates are selected, and their names are sent to the Holy See, when the Pope, in council, appoints the bishop from among them. In some countries a particular candidate is recommended by the temporal governor of the state from among the three canonically elected; and him the Holy Father generally appoints. The authority to govern a particular Church is supposed to come through and from the head and governor of all Churches—the Pope; and whether in its incipient state it be denominated "election," "postulation," or as here in Ireland, "commendation," it is certain that the acts of the canons, parish priests, and suffragan or metropolitan bishops, who take a part in the selection or presentation of the candidates, are only preliminary, and would be plainly nugatory and ineffectual unless the pontifical authority intervened to complete the work. Here, then, are the difficulties of the case. St. Cyprian, in describing the mode of episcopal appointment in his day, makes no mention of the Pope as an actor or abettor in the scene, whereas, at the present day, the Pope is the principal actor and the efficient promoter, and the final adjudicator and the source of episcopal jurisdiction. And, from the organization of the primitive Church and its subjection to Peter and his successors, we would be strongly disposed to think that, in the earliest ages, the action of the Pope in episcopal appointments was the same as in modern times. Hence, several questions arise. Was the mode of episcopal appointment different in different ages? Was the discipline of Africa in this particular in the third age different from the rest of the Church? Did the Roman pontiff lose one of the greatest of his privileges during the days of the general persecution of the Church, to recover it after the lapse of time, and perhaps ages when he began to possess his domains and to exercise his dominion in peace?

To verify the assertion that the mode of episcopal appointment was always substantially the same, it would not be necessary to prove from history that the Roman pontiff was always the direct and immediate source of episcopal jurisdiction. The appointment would be equally his whether express or tacit, whether it came through an official document, as at the present day, or through a general and well-understood sanction on his part of the acts of the canons and provincial bishops who made it. In the documents of the Church of Africa generally, and in the treatises of Cyprian particularly, we have no mention of the appointment of bishops by the Roman pontiff immediately in the third century; but we have references to his interfering in such appointments, his controlling them, his laying down rules for their regulation, his annulling them where not canonically made, which prove beyond all dispute that his was the supreme power, and give us strong reason to conclude that in making them the provincial bishops acted as his delegates.

In proof of this, as regards St. Cyprian, we have but to cite the sequel of the passage already quoted which has given rise to this controversy. He is, after saying that Sabinus has been duly elected bishop in the room of Basilides. He proceeds as follows:—"Nor can it rescind the ordination lawfully accomplished—that Basilides, after his crimes were detected and his conscience laid bare by his own confession, going to Rome deceived our colleague, Stephen, stationed at a distance, and ignorant of the event and the truth, in such a way that he sought to be unjustly replaced in the episcopal charge, from which he had been justly deposed."[1] There are two points in this passage to which we must, for a moment, direct our attention. The first is, the conduct of Basilides. The second, the terms in which Cyprian speaks of it. Basilides is canonically deposed from the episcopacy in consequence of some grave crimes of which he has been guilty. In these circumstances what course does he pursue? Does he quietly acquiesce in the sentence of deposition? No! Does he appeal to the Pope overtly to give his case a second hearing? No! But he sets off privately to Rome, where he endeavours by misrepresentation to induce the pontiff to annul the judgment pronounced against him by the bishops of his province. Is it credible that he would have put his case before the Pope unless the Pope was in the habit of

[1] Concil. Carthag. iv. No. 5, p. 1028. Curs. Complet. Patrol., Series 1ma, tom. iii. Paris, 1844.

pronouncing on the legitimacy of episcopal appointments? Is it credible that he would have appealed to him unless the Pope was in the habit of hearing appeals from the deposing sentences of provincial bishops? And then the second point, the manner in which Cyprian alludes to this appeal. He does not dispute the legality of it; he does not in speaking of it use a word disrespectful to the pontiff's authority; it is even clear, from the tenor of his words, that he recognizes the usage of such appeals and respects it. If the conduct of Basilides, in appealing to the Roman pontiff, was out of the usual course, Cyprian would have expressed his surprise, his astonishment at it. But quite the contrary, he speaks of it as a matter-of-course usage. Basilides, he says, deceived the Pope, because the facts of the case were not before him, from which we are justified in inferring that Cyprian would not dispute, in legitimate circumstances, the Roman pontiff's right to reconsider, revise, and even annul deposing sentences pronounced against bishops by their provincials. Basilides then practised the right of appeal, and Cyprian admitted it. The facts are assuredly significant as regards the source of episcopal jurisdiction. They are doubly so when we take into account the mode of episcopal appointments anterior to the third century and subsequent to it, in the time of the Apostles and during the last twelve centuries of the Church's history. In primitive times the Apostles appointed bishops; when they died, their right devolved to the successor of Peter. This would be evident from the nature of the authority given by our Lord to Peter, and it is absolutely affirmed by a celebrated Roman pontiff, who lived in the next century to the one we are considering. "Especially as it is manifest that in all Italy, Gaul, Spain, and Sicily, and the adjacent islands no one founded churches, but they whom the venerable Peter and his successors appointed priests."[1] So it was in the beginning, in the first and second centuries of the Christian era, we may

---

[1] Innocent 1mus., Ep. 25, ad Decent. Eugubin apud Constan. col. 856.

suppose. But in the fourth and fifth centuries, how did the matter stand? We must conclude very nearly as in the first and second if we glance through the constitutions that emanated from the Roman pontiffs during these centuries. The letters of Pope Sericius[1] (anno 390), of Zozimus[2] (anno 410), of Leo[3] the Great (460), grant the power to certain individuals to nominate and elect bishops, and lay down rules for the regulation of these elections, clearly showing that at the period they wrote, episcopal jurisdiction was supposed to emanate from Rome.

Now here is the significancy of the passage of St. Cyprian, as regards episcopal appointments in the third century. This passage evinces the right of appeal to the Roman pontiff against the deposing sentence of a provincial council. The privilege of receiving these appeals might belong to him as patriarch of the West, and this might be the sole significance of Cyprian's admission, if we had not the evidence of what took place in previous and subsequent times. Episcopal jurisdiction emanated from Rome immediately or mediately, we cannot say which, in the second century. It emanated from Rome in the fourth and fifth centuries. Cyprian's fact comes to light in the third century; that is, that deposed bishops appealed to Rome against the sentence of deposition. It is evidently a connecting link between the two periods, showing that in his day and in the Church of Africa, the jurisdiction of bishops was held from the Roman pontiff, and proving by an easy inference, that if others immediately elected them, he was the source and the origin of their authority to govern a portion of the flock of Christ. Then the discipline of Africa in respect to episcopal election was not peculiar to that Church. The mode of episcopal appointment was not substantially different in different ages. And the Roman pontiff never, either in

[1] Seric. Ep. 4, ad Anys. apud Coust., col. 642.
[2] Zoz. Ep. 7, ad Patroc. Arelat., col. 961. *Ibid.*
[3] Leo. Ep. 10, ad Episcop. Provin. Viennen, cap. 4, tom. i., col. 336. *Ibid.*

the times of persecution or peace, renounced his divinely conferred privilege of appointing all the bishops of the Church, though from the difficulty of official correspondence and other circumstances, he at some periods,—for example in the third century,—made these appointments mediately; that is, by a tacit sanction of the canonical elections made by the bishops of that province in which the vacant see was situated.

§ 5. *Jurisdiction of Bishops.*—I cannot discover the word "diocess" in the ecclesiastical writers of the Church of Africa in the third century. Nevertheless they furnish us with evidence in various forms of the fixity at that time of episcopal jurisdiction, and by divers facts which they exhibit, they prove beyond controversy that the bishop governed a limited territory, beyond which his authority did not extend, and within which no other bishop had a right to intrude, except in certain cases regulated by the canons, or by the constitution of the monarchical Church. The bishop, in fact, had his *diocess*, though called by another name, and there he governed absolutely, with the limitation of a certain amount of subjection to his metropolitan, his patriarch, and the head of the Church, the Pope.

It is difficult to determine when the word "*diocess*" began to be applied to the territory governed by the bishop. We know that under the emperors the provinces of the Roman empire were subdivided into διοικήσες. Every ἐπαρχία, or province, had its διοικήσες, or territorial subdivisions, and its capital city, generally situated near its centre, which was appropriately called the μετροπολις. The Church had adopted the terms διοικήσις and μετροπολις before the Council of Nice assembled in the year 325. She applied the former to the territory governed by the bishop, and by a word derived from the latter she designated the chief bishop of each province, distinguishing him by the name "metropolitan." We are certain that the metropolitan see of each province was established in its μετροπολις, or chief city; but we are not so sure that the διοίκησις of the Church correspond in all cases with the διοίκησις of the empire. In the prefectures of the East and Illyrium there appears[1] to have been a strict coincidence of spiritual and temporal επαρχια (patriarchate), διοίκησις, and μετροπολις. The matter is not so clear for the patriarchate of the West. Certain, however, it is that, in every case in which it was applied, the word διοίκησις, as used by the Church, designated a fixed and limited division of territory over which and within which a bishop exercised spiritual jurisdiction, and beyond which he had no ordinary power.

Though the district subjected to the spiritual government of a given bishop was not yet designated by the name "diocess" at the time we write, it was no less fixed, limited, and separated from the territory of other bishops then than now. This is obvious from the *unity* of the episcopacy so often affirmed by St. Cyprian. For if there were but one bishop in each episcopal see, the limits of such a see must have been ascertainable and determined. This will appear perfectly evident if we make a supposition to the contrary. There was but one bishop of the diocess of Sicca. The bishop of Carthage entering there was a stranger. If he ministered there his ministrations were illicit, and his acts were invalid if he attempted to exercise jurisdiction over its clergy. All this time the diocess of Sicca consisted of a town or city, a country district, and some villages—the two latter unlimited, unnumbered, undefined. The supposition is palpably absurd and repugnant to Cyprian's teaching, for if there were some districts of the spiritual territory of Sicca undefined, neither its bishop nor the Church at large would object to their appropriation by a neighbouring bishop, legitimately constituted and ordained; and thus it might come to pass that Sicca would have three or four bishops, whilst Cyprian says it should have but one. We will best understand Cyprian's mind on this subject, and the length to which his writings go in establishing the existence in his day of

---

[1] Engelhardt, Hist. Eccles., tom. i., pp. 512—17.

what we now call dioceses, by quoting here some passages from his correspondence on various subjects, and his letters in particular to the Pope Cornelius.

He affirms the unity of the episcopacy. "Thence have arisen, and daily arise, schisms and heresies, whilst the bishop, *who is one* and governs the Church, by the pride of certain persons, is despised, and the man honoured by the divine bounty is pronounced unworthy by men."[1] The meaning attached by Cyprian to the expression, "the bishop is one," is evinced by various passages in his writings. 1st. He says, speaking of the ordination of the Pope Cornelius, that his legitimate ordination and collocation excludes the possibility of a second bishop of Rome. "Which [chair] being occupied by the will of God, and strengthened by the consent of us all, whoever now wishes to be constituted bishop is of necessity constituted without, nor has he ecclesiastical ordination who holdeth not the unity of the Church."[2] And 2nd. He reprobates the intrusion of a second bishop into a see already filled as contrary to the law of the Gospel; in fact, to constitute a second bishop is to constitute a second Church. "For the insufferable sadness of a heart smitten almost prostrate grieves, contristates, and affects me, when I discover that, contrary to ecclesiastical discipline, contrary to the Gospel law, contrary to the unity of the Catholic institution, you have agreed to place another bishop there, that is to say (a thing that is neither right nor lawful), to erect another Church, to divide the members of Christ, to lacerate with emulous contention the rent soul and one body of the flock of the Lord."[3]

These two illustrations show us the mind of Cyprian with regard to the unity of the episcopacy; scil., the bishop is one in such a way that he possesses his see to the exclusion of a second bishop, who, by the very fact of his

---

[1] D. Cypr. Ep. lxix. No. 5, p. 404, tom. iv. Curs. Com. Patrol., series 1ma. Paris, 1849.

[2] D. Cypr. Ep. x. ad. Anton. No. 8, p. 773, tom. iii., *ibid.*

[3] Ep. xliv., p. 340, tom. iv., *ibid.*

claiming a see already occupied, is placed outside the Catholic Church, violates the Gospel law, and erects a schismatical conventicle.

The episcopal see, then, is one even as its bishop is one; and if it be one, it must possess the essential characteristic of territorial unity, that is to say, isolation. It must be separated by a defined boundary line from the jurisdiction of other bishops. It must, in fact, of its very nature be a διοίκησις, or section of territory cut off from some whole, and enjoying an individuality palpable and distinguishable. Consequently the bishops of Africa in the days of St. Cyprian, ruling over such dioceses possessed limited territorial jurisdiction. They were the bishops of a certain place and of the Christians residing within it. They were in their sees bishops of the Catholic Church, as distinguished from the bishops of the Novatian Schism, who were bishops only in name. Collectively with their head, the bishop of Rome, they succeeded to the plenitude of the Apostolic power, but individually to a limited share of the power of one Apostle. In this respect since the first age of the Church a change had taken place. The Apostles ruled over nations and provinces, and roamed at large through the world propagating the faith and instructing and confirming the faithful. Their successors, the bishops of the Catholic Church, divided amongst themselves the countries that had been Christianized, and each undertook to be accountable to God and his Church for the instruction, supervision, and direction of that portion of the flock of Christ that dwelled within the territory to which he had been appointed by the legitimate mode of election which raised him to the dignity of the episcopacy.

§ 6. *Jurisdiction of priests.*—There were no such things as parishes, properly so called, at the beginning of the third century. Attached to each city diocess there were rural districts no doubt, and villages and towns of a secondary class. In these towns and villages, and through the country, there were Christian congregations at a considerable distance from the episcopal see. The questions that here suggest themselves are—How were these congregations governed? Who were their immediate spiritual superiors? Were they directly subjected to the bishop, or did another ecclesiastic come between him and them, who was responsible to the Church for their direction?

If these questions were raised at a somewhat more advanced period, we would be able to give them a satisfactory answer. We would be able to say that remote rural towns were immediately subject to an order of priests who had the charge of several of them simultaneously and permanently. The Council of Ancyra, held in the year 314, lays [1] down certain rules for the limitation of the jurisdiction of χωρεπίσκοποι, the name by which these priests were distinguished. We would be able to point to the formal recognition of the existence and rights of rural parishes and pastors by the Council of Chalcedon, held in the year 451. But not having to do at present with the fourth or fifth, but with the third century, we must bring before us the documents of an earlier age, and search among them diligently for some "data" which may afford a plain or even a plausible answer to the important queries above.

The "quasi-parochi" of the first century seem to have disappeared long before the commencement of the third. Their places were filled by bishops. It was in Asia Minor and Crete that we first discovered these "quasi-parochi," and from comparing the allusions to the Churches of Asia in the Apocalypse with the letters of St. Ignatius the Martyr, we found that the number of episcopal sees there was steadily increasing. So it becomes sufficiently clear that most of the towns originally governed by priests were, after some time, raised to the dignity of episcopal sees. This appears to have been the general rule; nevertheless, there were some places inconsiderable in themselves and in the number of Christians they contained. There were some such in the beginning, and as time went on the number of them

---

[1] Con. Ancyr., can. 13, Harduin, tom. i., p. 275.

increased, where it would have been quite superfluous to locate a bishop, and even it is quite certain that no bishop was appointed. How, then, were such places directed? Who was their ordinary governor?

From a passage in the first Apology of St. Justin, it is evident that the country districts surrounding the episcopal town were immediately governed by the bishop. "On the day of the Sun," he says, "as it is called, all, whether living in the city or the country, come together to the same place, and the commentaries of the Apostles and the writings of the prophets are read."[1] There was no "parochus" in the country parts near the episcopal see. This much is clear from St. Justin. But what of the remote districts and towns? It would appear from some passages in the writings of St. Cyprian and other documents of this age, that they were governed by priests and deacons, who had the immediate charge of them, but who were totally dependent on the bishop, and possessed no ordinary but delegated jurisdiction. The following passage in a letter of St. Cyprian to martyrs in prison, proves to us clearly that some of his priests were located at a distance from himself when they performed sacerdotal offices. "And I had trusted that the priests and deacons *who are there present*, warned you and instructed you most fully on the Gospel law, as in times past it hath been done always by our predecessors."[2] But these distant priests did not possess ordinary jurisdiction. This must be quite evident to any one at all acquainted with the letters and other writings of Cyprian. All his priests and deacons were absolutely in his power, and he controlled or removed them as the exigencies of his diocess required. Consequently, neither in the remote districts of the diocess, nor in those immediately bordering on the episcopal city, had the parochial system been established in the middle of the third century. And the answer to the question—what

---

[1] Just. Apol. i., No. 67, p. 83, ed. post Maran. Paris, 1742.

[2] Div. Cypr. Ep. x., p. 254. Curs. Complet. Patrol., series 1ma, tom. iv. Paris, 1844.

was the jurisdiction of priests in this age? should be, it was the jurisdiction of bishops,—vicars at present who have no ordinary rights from the Church, but who depend entirely on the bishop who may transfer them, limit their jurisdiction, or deprive them of all jurisdiction, and reduce them to the rank of irresponsible ecclesiastics, without functions to administer or a flock to tend.

§ 7. *The Roman pontiff—the head and governor of the Church.*—Before attempting to evince the pre-eminence of the pontifical dignity and authority of the bishops of Rome from the writings of the third century, we must advert to certain facts in connection with the same which occurred in a previous age.

Eusebius[1] tells us that St. Peter came to Rome and established his see there A.D. 42, in the second year of the reign of the Emperor Claudius. So the pontiffs of the Roman Church were the successors of Peter in the direct line. Peter, as we said in a previous part of this work, was made the foundation of the Church, the pastor of its sheep and lambs, that is, the whole flock; he received its keys, with the power of binding and loosing, accompanied with the promise, that whatsoever he should bind upon earth should be bound in heaven, and whatsoever he should loose upon earth should be loosed in heaven. Peter, from the infallibility and power of the other Apostles, had not the necessity or opportunity of exercising all his great powers in respect to the entire Church. So at least it is probable from the circumstances of the case. Consequently, we said elsewhere, that the exercise of the pontifical authority in all its magnitude—the exercise of it in respect to co-ordinate bishops, the decision of questions of faith, general discipline, the termination of controversies, was to be looked for among the successors of Peter in the see of Rome. Now Peter had passed away two centuries before the period at which we are arrived; and we want to know before entering upon the details of pontifical power in the

---

[1] Euseb. iii. Hist.; Euseb. Chron. an. 43.

third century, if there are any evidences of its existence or exercise in the time that elapsed since the year 65, in which Peter sealed his confession with his blood.

There are several events recorded in the ecclesiastical history of the first and second centuries which serve as connecting links between the Scriptural evidences of the primacy of Peter and the testifications to the primacy of his successors which occur in the writings of Tertullian and St. Cyprian.

1. The first that occurs, and it is even within the apostolic period, is the epistle of Pope Clement to the Corinthians. This epistle was written a short time after the martyrdom of St. Peter. It is to be noted, that it was not an unsolicited letter; but a reply to certain questions put by the Church of Corinth to the Church of Rome. This is evident from the words of the opening paragraph: "On account of calamities, we seem to have been slow in turning our minds to those questions you proposed to us, beloved."[1] Then the Roman pontiff instructed the clergy, bishop, and people of Corinth on their Christian duties, and this at their own solicitation. Why did he do so—because the Church of Corinth was an Apostolic Church and older than the Church of Rome?

2. The letter of the martyr Ignatius to the Church of Rome contains some expressions which imply a recognition, on his part, not only of the superior dignity of that Church, but of its superior powers to teach. His salutation at the beginning of this letter is longer and more profoundly respectful than those which he sends to the other Churches, to which he wrote about the same time. "Seeing that having asked of God, I have obtained the favour of seeing your Divine face [τα ἀξιοθεα πρόσωπα]."[2] Subsequently, he adds, "You have never been envious in any respect; you have taught others [αλλους ἐδιδαξάτε]. And I wish that such things may be done, as teaching you have commanded [α μαθητευοντες εντελλεσθε]."[3]

---

[1] Clemens. Rom. ep. 1ma, parag. 1, p. 146, ed. Cot.
[2] Ig. Ep. ad Rom., No. 1, p. 25, tom. ii., ed. Cot. [3] Id. No. 3, p. 27.

According to Ignatius, the Roman Church taught others and gave precepts to others; and those others whom it taught were obviously not its own subjects, as in that case they would require no special reference. Now, why did the Roman pontiff teach other Churches, as those Churches had individually their own pastors, who were charged with their instruction, and were responsible for their morality and faith?

3. The flight of Marcion to Rome, when for immoral practices he had been driven from his native Church, is not without significance, as regards the pre-eminence of that see. For it appears that he addressed himself there to "those whom the disciples of the Apostles had instructed," and sought to be admitted to their society. Why did he not direct his steps in preference to some one of the noble churches in the East, which were much nearer to him than the Church of Rome, for he came from Synope, a city of the province of Pontus?

4. On the occasion of the dispute regarding the time of celebrating Easter, the illustrious bishop of Smyrna, Polycarpe, went to Rome for the purpose of conferring with Anicetus, who then filled the papal chair, on the decision of that important question. This was about the middle of the second century. It is true that those illustrious bishops did not agree on the point, each maintained the usage of his own Church, and Polycarpe refused to conform to the decision of Anicetus. Still it may be again asked, why did Polycarpe undertake a long journey to consult Rome in preference to Antioch, Alexandria, Jerusalem, or the illustrious Churches of Asia and Greece?

5. About the year of the Christian era 172, the heresy of the Montanists broke out in the East. The first effort of the heretics, after they had been condemned in Asia, was to endeavour to obtain from the Pope letters approving of their errors, in order that, through their agency, they might recover the character and position they had lost. But why apply to the Pope? Why solicit his interference in a matter which was outside his diocess, district, and nation? a matter, too, of faith which had been discussed

"by the faithful of Asia," and decided by the bishop of Antioch?

6. Towards the close of the second century, Irenæus wrote his treatise against heretics. In this learned production he has a candid admission of the superiority or, as he designates it, "the powerful primacy" of the Roman Church as compared to the other Churches of Christendom. He is about to prove the truth of tradition in matters of faith by the succession of bishops in the different Churches. "But," he says, "because it would be too long to count the successions of all the Churches, we will content ourselves with pointing out the tradition of the greatest and the most known Church in the entire world, founded and established at Rome by the glorious Apostles Peter and Paul. By this tradition, which it received from the Apostles, and this faith, announced to men and preserved to our time by the successions of bishops, we confound all those who form illegitimate congregations in any way, through self-love, through vain-glory, of their blindness, or through malice. For it is with this Church, on account of its powerful, primacy, that every Church ought to agree—that is to say, all the faithful, wheresoever they be—in which the tradition of the Apostles has been preserved by the faithful of all countries."[1] Why must all Churches conform to the Roman Church in faith? Irenæus answers, because the tradition of the Apostles has been preserved there in its integrity. But the question recurs—Why should the tradition be preserved there more safely than in the other great Churches of the universe?

The questions arising out of such facts as these are worthy of attentive consideration. Why did Clement, at their own solicitation, instruct the Christians at Corinth? Why did the Roman Church teach and give precepts to other Churches, as Ignatius affirms? Why did Marcion fly to Rome with a view to be restored to the communion of the Church? Why did Polycarp go to Rome to consult Anicetus on the time of celebrating Easter? Why

---

[1] Iren. lib. iii. c. 3; Euseb. Hist. c. 8; Chron. Alex.

did Irenæus affirm that all Churches must conform in
faith to the Church of Rome, which is the greatest
Church in the entire world? Why all these events and
circumstances, so indicative of the superiority of Rome?
Some one will answer—Rome was a patriarchal Church;
as such it was great and respected, as such it was consulted and appealed to. This is not the reason; for the
events recorded originated for the most part outside the
limits of the ancient patriarchate of Rome. Another says,
Rome was the capital of the Empire, its bishops were
honoured and esteemed in consequence, and its central
position and the convergence to it of the "great roads"
attracted the crowd of ecclesiastics as well as seculars from
the provinces. No doubt it was the capital of the Empire,
but what did it gain by being so in an ecclesiastical point
of view? This much: that during the first and second
centuries it was the theatre of constant and cruel persecutions, which ravaged its flock, took away its pastors and
decimated its clergy without cessation. And as to the
facilities of travelling to Rome for advice, they are to be
made no account of in this matter, for the patriarchal or
metropolitan Church in each province was much more
accessible to the provincials. I will be told, perhaps, that
marks of deference similar to these here recorded were
shown to other illustrious Churches in these ages. This
I must answer by a positive contradiction—they were not.
Respect was shown to Carthage through Numidia and Mauritania, to Antioch through Syria, Cilicia, Cyprus, Palestine,
and Arabia. It was the respect of suffragan Churches to
their metropolitan or patriarch. It was local, limited, and
unaccompanied by any expression that could involve the
admission of universal pre-eminence or authority. Why,
then, I repeat, was the respect shown to Rome so profound, the deference to its decisions so humble, the appeals to its authority so frequent, and the assertion of this
authority so outspoken? Why—because the Pope was the
successor of Peter, and to him, in the person of Peter, it
was said: "Thou art Peter, and upon this rock will I
build my Church, and I will give to thee the keys of the

kingdom of heaven, and whatsoever thou shalt bind upon earth shall be bound also in heaven, and whatsoever thou shalt loose upon earth shall be loosed also in heaven."

One feels somewhat disappointed that St. Cyprian, who is clear and outspoken on nearly all dogmatic points of Catholic divinity, does not treat of the primacy of the Roman pontiff in terms more express and positive, or in a manner less ambiguous, I would almost say perplexing. It is painful to hear him in an epistle to Quintus, on the rebaptization of heretics, make the following pointed allusion to the conduct of Pope Stephen:—" Not even Peter, whom first the Lord chose, and on whom he built his Church, claimed anything insolently or assumed it arrogantly. . . . . . So as to say that he held the primacy, and that present and future generations should obey him, when afterwards Paul disputed with him about circumcision." [1] To be sure, he does not here call in question the primacy of Stephen. He merely states that it is inexpedient for the Pope to appeal to it in his disputes with co-ordinate bishops. Still there is unquestionably a sneer at the exercise of the primacy in this passage, which can only be palliated by the warmth and zeal with which the great Cyprian took up an opinion on which he believed the salvation of millions to depend.

The controversy " de rebaptizandis hæreticis " gave rise to disrespectful allusions to the papacy on the part of others besides the bishop of Carthage. No wonder! the intemperate zeal of polemics has done so even in modern times, when papal law is universally recognized and papal authority is clearly defined. Fermillian, bishop of Cæsarea, wrote a celebrated letter to Cyprian, which is anything but courteous or complimentary when the name of Pope Stephen is introduced. Here is a specimen of its tone in this particular:—"And in this matter I am justly indignant at the open and manifest folly of Stephen, in that

[1] Cyp. Ep. lxxi. No. 3, p. 410, tom. iv., series 1ma, Curs. Com. Patrol.: Paris, 1844.

he who so glories in the place of his episcopacy, and contends that he holds the succession of Peter, upon whom the foundations of the Church were laid, introduces many other rocks and constitutes new edifices of many Churches, while by his authority he is the defender of baptism as administered by them."[1] A little further on he continues: "Stephen, who proclaims that by succession he holds the chair of Peter, is not moved to zeal against heretics, for he grants them not a trifling but the most sublime power of grace."[2]

The disrespectful language of Cyprian, Fermillian, and other orthodox bishops, during the height of the baptism controversy, is under one aspect useful, as it indicates the belief of the Roman pontiffs in the magnitude of their own powers. Fermillian might sneer, Cyprian might grumble at the exercise of primatial authority; but the Pope assumed it, justified it, acted upon it. He was the successor of Peter, and, as such, he would decide controversies of faith. He was the governor of the Church,—as such, he would allow no bishop to oppose him in a matter of general discipline.

Where he speaks of the unity of the Church, St. Cyprian is somewhat more explicit in affirming the primacy of the see of Rome. He affirms again and again that unity is derived from the primacy. Thus, in his 70th epistle he says, "One Church founded upon Peter by the Lord in the origin and disposition of unity."[3] Again, in his 73rd epistle, "For to Peter, upon whom he built the Church, and whence he instituted and demonstrated the origin of unity, he gave this power, that whatsoever he should loose upon earth should be loosed in heaven."[4] In his book "De Unitate Ecclesiæ," he has a striking passage illustrative of the same belief, longer and more outspoken

---

[1] Ep. Fermil. inter Op. Cyp. p. 1169, tom. iii. Curs. Compl. Patrol.: Paris, 1844.

[2] *Ibid.*

[3] Carthag. Concil. sub Cypr. Quint. No. 3, p. 1043, tom. iii. *ibid.*

[4] Cypr. ad Jubaian. No. 7, p. 1114, *ibid.*

than either of those we have quoted. It is as follows:—
"The Lord speaks to Peter, 'I say to thee,' he said, 'that thou art Peter, and upon this rock I will build my Church, and the gates of hell shall not overcome it; and to thee will I give the keys of the kingdom of heaven, and whatsoever thou shalt bind upon earth shall be bound also in heaven, and whatsoever thou shalt loose upon earth shall be loosed also in heaven.' And again to the same, after his resurrection, he says, 'Feed my sheep.' Upon him—one —he builds his Church, and to him he consigns his sheep to be fed, although to the Apostles, after his resurrection, he gives a like power, and says, 'As the Father sent me, I too send you; receive the Holy Ghost. Whose sins you forgive they are forgiven, whose sins you retain they are retained.' Still, to manifest unity, he by his authority ordained the origin of the same unity to take its rise from one. The other Apostles were, the same as Peter, endowed with like participation of honour and power. But from one the beginning proceeds, that the Church of Christ might be demonstrated one."[1]

No one reading such passages as these can have any doubt as to the connection between the primacy and the unity of the Church in the mind of Cyprian. "The Church is proved to be one by the fact of its being built on one." Here is the foundation of his argument. His object is not to show that the Church was one at the time of its foundation, but that the Church is one at the time that he writes. Would the argument be conclusive if it was thus—" The Church is one because it was founded on one"? Scarcely, because it might be answered, "The Church is not necessarily one unless the combining influence of the foundation is still felt." The fact of its being founded on one, then, proves but little for its essential unity, unless the one foundation still exist. Now, the one foundation cannot exist unless the successor of Peter be in power and authority the same as Peter himself. Thus it

[1] Cypr. Liber de Unit. Eccles. No. 4, p. 408, tom. iv. Curs. Compl. Patrol.: Paris, 1844.

seems that the argument in favour of the unity of the Church from the primacy of Peter implies and supposes the primacy of his successor in the see of Rome.

If, then, there are some circumstances in the conduct and expressions of Cyprian which appear to militate against the authority of the Roman pontiff, the weight of his testimony, as a dogmatic writer, is decidedly in favour of the Pope. He remonstrated against the decision of Stephen in the controversy about the rebaptism of heretics; but he did not deny his authority to decide. He considered it inexpedient for Stephen to say "I am primate, sic volo, sic jubeo," seeing that even Peter listened to the argument of Paul, when a dispute arose as to the continuation of circumcision. He would have discussion, and he would expect the Pope to take into account the reasons and suggestions of the other bishops of the Church, before deciding a question of faith and discipline. The warmth of Cyprian, his apparent obstinacy, his language amounting to disrespect, are attributable to the fact that he misunderstood the opinion of his adversaries, and especially of the Pope. Little, then, can be adduced from his writings against the primacy of the Roman pontiff, while his often-repeated argument of the unity of the Church from the primacy of Peter,—an argument which would have no logical sequence if the primacy did not continue in Peter's successors, is the clearest evidence of his deeply-seated conviction that the Pope is the centre of spiritual authority, the source of jurisdiction, the governor of the Church, whom all must ultimately obey.

Elsewhere I had occasion to mention the appeal of Basilides to the Pope, after he had been deposed by a council of bishops in Africa, his own country. The appeal was itself significant; and the allusion to it by Cyprian, without a word of comment on the act of the Pope in restoring him, save that it was brought about by misrepresentation, is sufficient proof that such acts of primatial authority were of ordinary occurrence, and that the jurisdiction of bishops was derived through the successor of Peter.

Then if we look to the conduct of the Roman clergy during the vacancies of the Roman see, the letters they wrote, the advice they tendered, the respect with which they were addressed, we must conclude at once that they looked upon themselves, and were regarded by others, as the temporary representatives of a great power in the Church.

And so the primacy of the Roman pontiffs is evinced by the writers of the second and third centuries, like the other articles of the Catholic faith. The witnesses of it are numerous, and as they are from various parts of the Church, their words represent a traditional belief, and are the echo of a universal conviction. And it was in the spirit of such a belief that Tertullian, in his "Book of Prescriptions," after speaking of the Churches of Asia and Greece, thus respectfully turns to the Roman Church, and points to its superior claims on the respect and veneration of the faithful. "If you are near Italy, you have Rome, whose authority is also for us—that so happy Church, to which the Apostles with their blood delivered all their doctrine, where Peter rivalled the sufferings of the Lord, where Paul was crowned with the same manner of death as John, where John the Apostle, after suffering in nowise from being cast into boiling oil, was banished to the island. Let us see what it has learned, what it has taught."[1]

---

[1] Tertul. Lib. de Præscr. c. 36, p. 49, tom. ii. Curs. Compl. Patrol.: Paris, 1844.

DIVISION IV.

PRAYER AND SACRIFICE.

§ 1. *Oblations and prayers for the dead.*—The usage of praying for the deceased members of the Church is frequently spoken of as an established fact by the fathers and writers of the third century. Tertullian (now a Montanist), speaking of the religious rites of Christians, in his book "De Corona Militis," enumerates among others the anniversary oblation for the dead. "On the anniversary day we make oblations for the dead."[1] Again, in his book "De Monogamia," written also after he had become a heretic, he advises his wife "to pray for his [her deceased husband's] soul, and to demand for him relief and participation in the first resurrection, and to offer on the anniversary of his 'demise.'"[2] It is admitted that Tertullian had ceased to be a Catholic when both these sentences were written; but his authority as an expounder of doctrine was not impaired, except as regards the points that were debated between the Church he had quitted, and the heretical body he had joined. He still claimed to belong to the true Church; and he refers to prayers and oblations for the dead, as practices that were universally customary in his day, and which were not only lawful, but in a certain sense compulsory on the surviving friends of the deceased.

The rhetorician Arnobius, that great convert to Christianity of the third century, has the following expostula-

---

[1] Tertul. de Coron. Mil. p. 79 B. Curs. Compl. Patrol.: Paris, 1844.

[2] *Ibid.* p. 942 c.

tion against the injustice of Pagan tyranny, in his treatise
"Adversus Gentes:"—"Why should our conventicles be
cruelly levelled with the ground,—in which the Almighty
God is invoked; in which peace and mercy are demanded
for all—magistrates, armies, kings, friends, enemies,—those
who are still in life and those who are freed from the
prison of the body?"[1] It is unnecessary to add that this
most learned man and fervent Christian must have been
intimately acquainted with the doctrine and ritual of the
Church; and consequently, when he affirms that peace and
mercy were demanded in prayer from God for those who
had "fallen asleep in Christ," demanded in the Church as
a matter of ordinary observance—demanded in prayer for
them in the same way as for the living—no reasonable
mind can hesitate to admit that the Church of the third
century believed in the existence of a place of temporal
punishment beyond the grave.

From Arnobius we turn to a writer of still higher repute, and from his testimony, striking and suggestive, to
words which convey the same doctrine enveloped with a
flood of light. The writer is St. Cyprian. The words
alluded to—the following passage extracted from his 64th
epistle:—"What the bishops, our predecessors, religiously
considering the matter, and making salutary provisions,
enjoined,—that no dying brother should nominate a cleric
to guardianship or charge, and, if any one do so, there
should be no oblation for him, nor should sacrifice be celebrated for his repose; for who strove to avert the priests
and ministers from the altar, deserves not to be named at
the altar of God in the prayers of the priests; and therefore as Victor, in opposition to the rule lately given in
council by the priests, has dared to appoint the priest
Geminius Faustinus a guardian, there must be no oblation
with you for his repose, nor any prayers repeated in the
church in his name."[2] There is not simply an allusion to

[1] Arnob. advers. Gen. lib. iv. c. 36, p. 1076, tom. v. Curs. Com.
Patrol.: Paris, 1844.

[2] Cypr. Ep. lxvi. s. 2, tom. iv. p. 309, *ibid.*

the practice of praying for the dead in this passage, but an outspoken declaration that the highest order of prayer —sacrifice—was offered for their repose as a matter of course, unless, by the violation of some grave ordinance, they rendered themselves amenable to the rigours of ecclesiastical law.

Cyprian does not limit his elucidation of this subject to a simple affirmation of the practice of prayers for the dead: he states, in a letter to Antonianus, that there is a prison in the next world—a purification by fire; and he contrasts the state of those who are immediately admitted to glory with that of others who undergo banishment and previous suffering for their misdeeds. He in fact interprets the texts of Holy Scripture cited in the first part of this work as probative of the existence of purgatory. His words are: "It is one thing to wait for pardon, another to attain to glory; it is one thing, consigned to prison, not to go out from it until one pays the last farthing, another to receive at once the reward of faith and virtue; it is one thing to be cleansed and purified from sin by long pain and torture, another by suffering martyrdom to purge away all sin; one thing to wait for the sentence of the Lord unto the day of judgment, another to be immediately crowned by the Lord."[1] It would be superfluous to dilate upon the character and orthodoxy of Cyprian, who was looked to in his day as a great authority in matters of faith and practice, almost as St. Augustine was regarded a century afterwards, when letters of consultation flowed in to him from the remotest Churches of the West.

By a coincidence it happens that the three ecclesiastical writers who have been here adduced as witnesses of the practice of praying for the dead in the third century were Africans, living and writing, two of them, Tertullian and Cyprian, in Carthage, and Arnobius in the diocess of Sicca. It would therefore appear, at first sight, that they ought

[1] Cypr. ad Anton. Ep. x. No. 20, p. 786, tom. iv. Curs. Compl. Patrol.: Paris, 1844.

o be received as vouchers for the faith of two diocesses
only. But an impartial consideration of their words and
trivial acquaintance with their characters and the objects for which they wrote, must lead us to a different
conclusion. They were Africans, it is true, but they were
also Christians, though one of them was unfortunately unorthodox. They were all men who were well known at
Rome, and in the East and West. Not only this, but one
of them—Cyprian—was in frequent communication with
Rome, witness his epistle xxx. to the clergy of that city,
and his many letters to Pope Cornelius. Another—Tertullian—had taught a celebrated public school of letters
and Christian doctrine for many years, with the knowledge
and approval of most Christian bishops. The third—
Arnobius—wrote as an apologist for persecuted Christians
of all countries.

Cyprian was a model of orthodoxy; so had been Tertullian; and Arnobius was necessarily a most cautious
writer: for the treatises of his which remain, were compiled
at the command of his bishop, as a test of his sincerity
and sound views previous to his being admitted to the
priesthood. Under these circumstances, it is clear that
they could not conjointly give utterance to a dogma which
was not approved by the belief of the universal Church.
And when we find three such men affirming that prayers
and sacrifices for the repose of the dead were offered
habitually in the churches of Christians, we are forced to
conclude that the doctrine of purgatory, put forward by
the Redeemer, referred to by St. Paul, plainly announced
in the second book of Machabees, was held by the entire
body of the disciples of Christ during the third century
of the Christian era.

§ 2. *Sacrifice.*— For reasons previously assigned, I
believe we will be fully justified in taking St. Cyprian as
the exponent of the belief of the Church in his age on the
subject of sacrifice. The life of this great bishop was cast
at an early period in Christian chronology. He was martyred about the year 253; so that we may take it that the

bulk of his writings saw the light before the middle of the third century. This latter circumstance we must keep in view, for it is of much significance, that when he came upon the stage to expound the doctrines of the Christian Church, not much more than a century had elapsed since the last great writer of the apostolic body had given to the disciples of Christ those sublime and mystical instructions which completed the codex of written revelation.

Cyprian speaks out on the subject of sacrifice. His words are not few,—his teachings are not obscure; but through his writings, whether cautiously composed treatises or hurriedly compiled epistles, he refers often and plainly to a sacrifice instituted by Christ, and perpetuated in his Church by his priests; and, as if to remove all ambiguity from the subject, he touches upon the nature of the victim, and lays down distinct rules, founded upon primitive usage, for the correction of certain abuses, which tended to destroy the bond of identity between the offering at the last supper, and the daily oblation which it was his privilege to make in common with his brethren in the ministry.

1. There is a sacrifice in the Church, and Christ is the institutor of it. "Cyprian to his brother Cæcelius, health. Though I know, beloved brother, very many bishops, by the Divine condescension, placed over the Churches of the Lord through the world to make account of the Gospel truth and the Lord's tradition; nor, by human and modern innovation, to depart from what the Master Christ enjoined and did; yet, as some, through ignorance or simplicity in sanctifying [*sanctificando*] the chalice of the Lord and ministering it to the people, do not what Jesus Christ, our Lord and God, the author and expounder of this sacrifice, did and taught, I have deemed it pious and necessary to direct this letter to you, that if there be one still involved in this error, having seen the light of truth, he may return to the root and origin, the tradition that has come from the Lord." [1]

---

[1] Cyp. Ep. lxiii. p. 373A, Curs. Compl. Patrol.: Paris, 1844.

2. This sacrifice is the Eucharist. But what is the sacrifice of which Cyprian here declares Christ to be the author, while he speaks in the supposition that it is perpetuated, and that the bishops of the Church are its ministers? From the words "sanctifying the chalice of the Lord and ministering it to the people," we would be forced to conclude—the Eucharist. And to confirm this conclusion and illustrate it, we need only consult the sequel of this text. "You should consider that we have been warned to observe the tradition of the Lord in offering the chalice, and not to do other than what the Lord first did for us, so that the chalice, which in commemoration of him is offered, be offered tempered with wine. For, as Christ says, 'I am the true vine' (John xv. 1), verily the blood of Christ is not water but wine."[1] Having here clearly identified the chalice referred to at the beginning of the epistle, with the chalice offered by our Lord at his last supper, and by implication identified the sacrifices, he proceeds to speak out more plainly. "Likewise, in the priest Melchisedech, we see prefigured the mystery of the sacrifice of the Lord, according as Divine Scripture attests and says: 'And Melchisedech, king of Salem, brought forth bread and wine.' (Gen. xiv. 18.) Now Melchisedech was a priest of the Most High God, and blessed Abraham. And that Melchisedech bore the type of Christ, the Holy Ghost declares in the Psalms, in saying to the Son in the person of the Father, 'Before the day star I begot thee. Thou art a priest for ever according to the order of Melchisedech' (Ps. cix. 4, 5), which order verily this is—arising out of that sacrifice, and derived from the facts that Melchisedech was priest of the Most High God, that he offered bread and wine, that he blessed Abraham. For who is more a priest of the Most High God than our Lord Jesus Christ, who offered a sacrifice to God the Father, and the same sacrifice as Melchisedech offered, that is, bread and wine, his own body and

---

[1] Cypr. Ep. No. 11, p. 374, Curs. Compl. Patrol.: Paris, 1844.

blood."[1] Here is the introduction of another element of the sacrifice of Christ, that is, bread—his body, which by implication he supposes to appertain to the sacrifices then offered. And having thus unmistakably laid down the doctrine that the Eucharist is a true sacrifice instituted by the Redeemer, he winds up in the following admonitory query: "But how of the creature of wine, shall we drink new wine with Christ in the kingdom of His Father, if we do not offer wine in the sacrifice of God the Father and Christ, nor according to Divine tradition, temper the chalice of the Lord?"[2]

It will be very difficult to take exception to the probative efficacy of these passages. Lest, however, the slightest grounds for misapprehension of his meaning should remain, St. Cyprian gives us further on a summary of the sentiments hitherto quoted, which contain the point now under discussion in the form of a clear and distinct affirmation. "Wherefore, beloved brethren, there is no reason why any one should think that the custom should be imitated of those who heretofore have decided that water alone should be offered in the chalice of the Lord. For they should be asked, whom they have followed. For, if in the sacrifice that Christ offered, Christ alone ought to be followed, surely we ought to attend and do what Christ did and commanded to be done, when he said in the Gospel, 'If you do what I command you, I will no longer call you servants, but friends.' (John xv. 14, 15). But if it be unlawful to break the smallest of the Divine commandments, how much more unlawful to violate (one) so great, so important, so pertinent to the Sacrament of the Lord's passion and our redemption, and by human tradition to change it to other than the divinely-instituted. For if Jesus Christ, our Lord and God, be the high-priest of God the Father, and first offered himself a sacrifice to the Father, and enjoined that this should be done in remembrance of Him; assuredly that priest truly performs the

---

[1] Cypr. Ep. No. 4, p. 375, Curs. Compl. Patrol.: Paris, 1844.
[2] Ibid. No. 9, p. 381.

office of Christ, who imitates what Christ did, and then he offers in the Church to God the Father a true and full sacrifice, if he beginneth to offer according as he sees Christ himself to have offered."[1]

3. The bishop Cyprian offered sacrifice. Writing to Pope Cornelius in the name of a synod held at Carthage, and justifying himself in having granted peace to certain classes of penitents, he has the following passage:—" We regret not to have given peace to such brave ones; rather it is the honour and glory of our episcopacy, to have given peace to martyrs; so that, priests as we are, who daily celebrate the sacrifices of God, we have prepared for Him hosts and victims."[2] Speaking, in another letter, of the ordination of Celerinus, a lector, he makes a passing allusion to his uncle and other relatives, who had died for the faith in these times: " You remember that we offer sacrifice for them as often as we celebrate the sufferings and anniversary days of the martyrs."[3] Rebuking Florentius Pupianus for his calumnious charges against himself, and his uncharitable criticisms of priests generally, he gives him the following severe lecture :—" Wherefore, brother, if you reflect on the Majesty of God who ordaineth priests, if you look to Christ, who by his will and authority, and by his presence, governeth the rulers and the Church with its rulers; if you form your estimate of the innocence of priests, not by human hatred, but by Divine discrimination; if you begin even at an advanced hour to do penance for your rashness, pride, and insolence; if you make full satisfaction to God and His Christ whom I serve, and to whom with pure and spotless mouth I unceasingly offer sacrifice, both in persecution and in peace, I may take account of your communication, still retaining respect and fear of the Divine indignation, so as first to consult my Lord, if by sign and warning he

---

[1] Cypr. Ep. No. 14, p. 384 B, 385 C, 386 A, Curs. Compl. Patrol.: Paris, 1844.

[2] Cypr. ad Cornelium Epistola Synodica, p. 857 A, tom. iii. *ibid.*

[3] Cypr. Ep. xxxiv. ad Clerum et Plebem, p. 323 A, tom. iv. *ibid.*

allow peace to be given you and admission to the communion of his Church."[1]

4. Sacrifice was offered for the martyrs in prison. Cyprian admonishes his priests and deacons to be cautious in their visits to those who are detained in prison for the faith. "Take counsel, and see that with moderation you may this more safely, so that the priests also who 'offer' at the confessors' abode [apud confessores] may each alternate with a deacon; for the change of persons and alternation of visitors diminishes suspicion."[2] He consoles Nemesian and other persons under the special privations they were forced to endure. "But not even in this, beloved brother, can you experience any loss of religion or faith; 'that liberty of offering and celebrating Divine sacrifices is given to the priests: you celebrate, yes, and you offer God a sacrifice, precious, glorious, and conducive to earn you heavenly rewards, as the Divine Scripture announces and says, 'A sacrifice to God is an afflicted spirit, a contrite and humbled heart, the Lord does not despise.'"[3]

5. To this sacrifice the greatest respect is due. "As when with the brethren we assemble together, and with the priest of God we celebrate Divine sacrifices, we ought to be observant of reverence and order."[4] Cyprian gives instances of visible judgments inflicted upon persons who with unworthy dispositions, presumed to approach and partake of the sacrifice. "But she who, grown up and of mature age, stole in secretly while we were sacrificing, receiving not food but a sword, and admitting as it were, a deadly poison between her mouth and breast, began to be tortured and oppressed with mental agony.... And another, because he too dared, when defiled, to receive a part secretly with the rest, when sacrifice had been cele-

---

[1] Cypr. Ep. lxix. ad Flor. Pup. de Oblectatione, p. 406 B, 407A, Curs. Compl. Patrol.: Paris, 1844.

[2] Cypr. Ep. iv. ad Presb. et Diacon. p. 231A, *ibid.*

[3] Ep. lxxvii. ad Nemes. et Cæter. in Metallo. Constitut. p. 417A, *ibid.*

[4] Liber de Orat. Dominic. p. 522 A, *ibid.*

rated by the priest, was not able to eat and carry in his
and the Holy of the Lord."¹

Such is St. Cyprian's teaching: such are his views of the
sacrifice of the last supper, and of the sacrifice of the
Church of Africa in the third century. His doctrine is
precisely that of the Catholic Church to-day. We are
content with his testimony, though we might corroborate
it by citing the words and sentiments of at least one other
writer of great repute, who was almost a contemporary of
his. But on a question of faith and discipline we need
not go beyond the consistent and often-expressed 'dicta'
of a great and good bishop, who, having lived a model of
Christian zeal and orthodoxy, laid down his life in testimony of the sincerity with which he adhered to the tradition of the universal Church. Such was Thascius Cyprian;
and whoever will call in question his authority as a witness
of the practice and belief of his age, will find it difficult to discover among the great and learned ones of the
ancient Church a name that he may follow, or a teacher
to whom he may commit his case, in the great controversy as to the apostolicity of Catholic doctrine.

¹ Liber de Lapsis, p. 486 A B. Curs. Compl. Patrol.: Paris,
1844.

DIVISION V.

SACRED RITES.

§ 1. *Baptism.*—Various controversies touching the sacrament of Baptism arose in the third age, and were maintained with spirit and even passion, as well between Catholic bishops as between the heretical leaders and the champions of orthodoxy. One point, however, appeared to be generally agreed upon, namely, that Baptism is necessary for salvation. Heretics admitted it—Catholics maintained it. If there was a voice of opposition raised from time to time, its murmurings were greeted with a storm of fierce and angry invective. " Though," says Tertullian, " it be laid down eminently in the words of the Lord, who said, ' Unless one be born of water, he hath not life' (Joan. iii.), that without Baptism no one obtains salvation; there arise scrupulous, I should rather say, rash cavillings of individuals; how, according to that rule, did the Apostles attain salvation, whom, with the exception of Paul, we find not to have been baptized [tinctos] in the Lord."[1] This objection, or, as he designates it, cavilling, excites the ire of Tertullian. The general doctrine of the absolute necessity of baptism is so clearly taught by the Redeemer, that he cannot hear a difficulty against it with patience. He therefore designates such difficulty a cavil, and those who raised it inconsiderate and rash. After all, it was only a difficulty, and not a positive objection to the doctrine. If his language in speaking of its movers is strong, it becomes positively abusive, when he comes to argue with outspoken and positive opponents. " Wherefore here," he says, " these most infamous men call forth questions. So,

---

[1] Tertul. Lib. de Bap., cap. xii. F. p. 1213, Curs. Compl. Patrol., series 1ma, tom. i.: Paris, 1844.

say they, for whom faith is sufficient baptism is not necessary, for, by no sacrament of water, but of faith, Abraham pleased God (Gen. xv.)."[1] Having thus stamped them with a character of insincerity and profanity, he proceeds to reply to their objection: "In times past salvation may have been attainable by faith merely, before the passion and resurrection of the Lord. But when faith received an augmentation by (the necessity of) believing in the nativity, passion, and resurrection of Him, there was adjoined to the symbol [sacramento] an amplification, the sealing of baptism, the garb, as it were, of faith, which before was nude and powerless without its law. For the law of baptizing [tingendi] was imposed, and the form prescribed. Go, said he, teach nations, baptizing [tingentes] them in the name of the Father and Son and Holy Ghost (Matt. xxviii. 19). The decree appended to this law, unless one be born again of water and the spirit, he shall not enter the kingdom of heaven (Joan. iii. 5), united faith to the necessity of baptism. Wherefore, henceforth all believers were baptized."[2] It is worth while to observe that Tertullian here uses the same passages of Scripture to evince the necessity of baptism which have been employed in the first part of this work, and which are commonly cited at the present day in the schools of Catholic divinity.

So far his teaching has been speculative. In theory baptism was essential; in practice it was administered as a matter of course to all who were aggregated to the body of the faithful. There are several passages in his writings in which he refers to the baptismal rite as one he had received in common with all who professed the Christian faith. Thus, in his "Liber de Spectaculis," he argues against Christians frequenting the public games, as follows:—We are baptized. In baptism we renounced the works of the devil. These games are the works of the

---

[1] Tertul. Lib. de Bap., cap. xiii. p. 1214, Curs. Compl. Patrol., series 1ma, tom. i.: Paris, 1844.

[2] *Ibid.*

evil one. We must not frequent them. His words are: "Lest any one may think I am merely arguing, I will turn to the principal authority—that of our signing. When entering the water, we profess the Christian faith unto the words of its law; we protest vocally that we have renounced the devil and his pomps and his angels."[1] Here we may notice an adjunct of the baptismal rite, which is in use at the present day. The Christians of Africa in the third century, when about to be baptized, made a formal renunciation of the devil. The little child in our own time, to the thrice-repeated question of the officiating minister, "Dost thou renounce the devil, and all his works, and all his pomps?" replies through the mouth of his sponsors, "I renounce him; I renounce them." Again, in his "Liber de Corona," Tertullian adverts to baptism, as a universally-received rite; where, too, he gives us another characteristic of it; *scil.* the triple immersion of its recipients. "Finally, that I may begin with baptism, about to go to the water,—in the same place, and also a little previously in the church, under the bishop's hand we affirm that we renounce the devil and his pomps and his angels; then we are thrice immersed, answering somewhat more than the Lord determined in the Gospel."[2] The triple application of water is still enjoined in the Catholic ritual. So another point of similarity occurs in the non-essential parts of the rite, as administered in modern and primitive times.

If baptism was so necessary in the judgment of the early Church, we would naturally expect that every precaution was taken that no one within the sphere of her influence should leave this world without receiving it. We are therefore prepared to hear from St. Cyprian, that it was in certain circumstances administered to infants and to the sick. In the third council of Carthage, held under the presidency of Cyprian, the subject of infant baptism was

[1] Liber de Spectac., cap. iv. p. 635 B. tom. i. Curs. Compl. Patrol.: Paris, 1844.

[2] Liber de Corona, cap. iii. p. 79 A. tom. ii. *ibid.*

discussed, and a strong letter of remonstrance addressed to one Fidus, who was opposed to the practice of baptizing within eight days after birth. The fathers of the council say, "As to the case of infants, whom you said it is not meet to baptize within the second or third day after their birth, and that the law of ancient circumcision is to be taken into account in such way that you are of opinion that the recently-born ought not to be baptized and sanctified within eight days, all in our council totally disagree with you. For no one agreed in your opinion, but we all judged that to no man born are the mercy and grace of God to be denied."[1] It would appear from the tenor of these words, and from other passages that occur in the same epistle, that infant baptism was generally practised in the days of Cyprian. It is at least apparent from them that the necessity of the sacrament involved its application to infants in many cases, and that there was no case occurring in which it might not be applied without fault on the part of its minister, or censure on the part of the Church.

The subject of clinical baptism, as it is called, is still more interesting, as it illustrates the administration of that sacrament by infusion. Cyprian alludes to clinical baptism, or the baptism of the sick in their beds, where immersion could not take place. The allusion—it is more than an allusion—it is a brief treatise on this subject, occurs in his epistle to Magnus. "You have also asked me," he says, "my dear son, what I think of those who in infirmity and sickness acquire the grace of God; are they to be had as genuine Christians who have not been washed, but on whom water has been poured [perfusi]."[2] Such is the question raised by Magnus, and it is evidently founded on a general practice. Cyprian answers it as follows: "I believe, as far as my weak ability allows me to judge, that the benefits of God cannot be impaired in any case, or enfeebled, and that no less happens in these cir-

---

[1] Concil. Carthag. 3ium, No. 11, p. 1015, tom. iii. Curs. Compl. Patrol.: Paris, 1844.
[2] Ep. ad Mag. No. 12, p. 1147, *ibid.*

cumstances, when with a full and firm faith of the giver and the receiver, that is received which is drawn from the Divine bounty."[1] Cyprian gives little more than his opinion here of the validity of baptism by infusion. Further on in the same epistle, he gives a positive decision on the subject, which, in a vital matter of the kind, must be regarded as a safe and practical rule: "Let it not disturb any of you, whether in receiving the grace of the Lord, the sick appear to undergo aspersion or perfusion, when the sacred Scripture says by the prophet Ezekiel—'And I will pour upon you clear water, and you shall be cleansed from all your uncleanness, and of all your idols I will purge you, and I will give you a new heart, and I will place a new spirit in you.'"[2] (Ezech. xxxvi. 25, 26.)

Here, then, is the sacrament of Baptism as it was administered in the third century. Regarded as essential, it was administered to all—to the sound, to the dying, to infants, to adult converts. It was administered, as it is now, with various accompanying ceremonies. By immersion, infusion, or aspersion, it was administered validly. It was operative of grace and salvation of its own nature. Tertullian told us that it produced the same effect under the new law that faith did under the old. Therefore, in his mind, it was an instrument of justification. And, as the Lord himself commanded, the three persons of the Holy Trinity were invoked in its administration, as of imperative and indispensable ordinance. "For," said Tertullian, "he having enjoined in the end that they should baptize in the Father, and the Son, and the Holy Spirit—not in one. Not once, but thrice—at each name we are baptized in three persons."[3] Manifestly this baptism is, in theory and practice, in its general features and in detail,

---

[1] Ep. ad Mag. No. 12, p. 1147, Curs. Compl. Patrol.: Paris, 1844.

[2] *Ibid.* p. 1148 A.

[3] Tertul. Liber adversus Praxeam, cap. 24, p. 190, tom. ii. *ibid.*

identical with that which the Catholic Church so scrupulously administers to all her children to-day.

§ 2. *Confirmation.*—As it is unquestionable that the Holy Ghost was given to Christians in the third century by a religious ceremony which was administered after baptism, the only difficulty to be encountered in treating of the sacrament of confirmation here is that which has been met and surmounted before; namely, How and in what manner was the Holy Ghost given—how did he descend upon the faithful—was it in respect to his external gifts, such as prophecy, miracles, tongues, or in respect to the internal and invisible gift, which is peculiarly his by attribution, viz., sanctifying and sacramental grace? There was but one way to escape from the Scriptural and patristic evidences of the existence of the sacrament of confirmation. This way was difficult and unsafe. The reformers entered upon it boldly; but they were beset with contradictions and dangers at every step. The Holy Ghost was given, they said; admitted. Hands were imposed and he fell upon the disciples; affirmed in terms in the sacred Scriptures, and therefore cannot be denied. But what follows? What is the consequence of this admission? Simply this, that the power of working miracles and the gifts of prophesying and speaking in unknown tongues were conferred upon the primitive disciples of the Lord. The Holy Ghost came upon them through the instrumentality of an external ceremony, but came only in respect to his visible and outward gifts. As the Scripture says, "He fell upon them and they began to speak in tongues and prophesy." The rite by which he came was temporary, as the effect which his coming produced. Both were ordained for a time, with a view to the propagation of the faith and religion of Christ. But when Christianity became once fully established, the rite and effect were destined to disappear.

So spoke the reformers, but unwisely. So speculated Zuingle, Melancthon, Bucer, Calvin, and a host of others. This was the by-path they entered upon to escape the necessity of admitting the sacramental efficacy of "the imposition of hands" which took place in the early Church. To this thorny way they were driven by their doctrine of two sacraments. If they admitted that the descent of the Holy Ghost (sine addito), in Scriptural language, meant the collation of abiding and inward grace, it would not be competent for them to deny the sacramental nature of "the imposition of hands" in that Church. For an external ceremony that was administered uniformly, that was administered unceasingly, that was administered to all, that was administered by the bishops of the Church, that was administered by apostolic institution, that, by the very fact of its administration, conferred inward sanctity on the recipient, had all the characteristics of a sacrament. But they could not allow the existence of any sacrament but baptism and the Lord's supper, consequently they entered upon the aforesaid explanation, which we have affirmed to be unsafe and untenable. This explanation of the expression "descent of the Holy Ghost," "receiving the Holy Ghost," in scriptural and patristic language is positively false. We have shown it to be false for the Scriptures in another place; we now come to prove that in the writings of Tertullian the meaning of "receiving the Holy Ghost" by the imposition of hands is receiving grace—not the outward grace which enables the outward man to do something extraordinary and disappears, but the inward grace which sanctifies, purifies, strengthens, enlightens, and abides in the soul, until forfeited by mortal sin. In his exhortation to chastity, Tertullian has a passage in which he makes the following affirmation :—1st. That the Holy Ghost abides in the faithful. 2nd. That, as compared to his abiding in the Apostles, his dwelling in the hearts of the faithful is partial as to its effects. 3rd. That the excess of divine operation arising therefrom in favour of the Apostles consisted in external works of power, such as tongues, prophecy, miracles. The whole passage is as follows :—" The faithful, too, have the spirit of God, but all the faithful are not Apostles. When, therefore, he who called himself faithful, subjoined that he possessed the spirit of God (which of the faithful no one doubts), he said so with a view to assume the rank of an Apostle. For the Apostles have the Holy Ghost peculiarly [proprie] in the works of prophecy and the working of miracles, and the gifts of tongues, not in part as the others."[1] There is a direct opposition between the words "peculiarly" and "in part." The Apostles have the Holy Spirit "properly," or "peculiarly." The faithful "partially." The peculiarity "of his dwelling in the Apostles" arises from the fact that he works in them prophecy, miracles, the knowledge of tongues. And they alone have him in this way; from which it is reasonably inferred that the miraculous gifts were not conferred upon the faithful at the time Tertullian wrote. Nevertheless they, the faithful, had the Holy Ghost; he abode in them. It is manifest, then, that he abode in them by sanctifying grace only. So far, then, it is clear that the Holy Ghost, as in the souls of the faithful of the Church of Carthage in Tertullian's time, was there as the principle of sanctity, not of miraculous operation, or, to use a theological term, he conferred upon them the " gratia gratum faciens " and not the " gratia gratis data."

This is further evinced by different facts laid down in the writings of Tertullian. Thus the Holy Ghost is the source and giver of patience under the trials and sufferings of this life. "Nor will any one deny that we, too, cannot suffer for God unless the spirit of God be in us, to make the confession on our behalf [de nobis]; still he suffereth not, but granteth us the power to suffer."[2] "His very nature is sanctity."[3] He is the "teacher of truth."[4] He is the regulator of Christian discipline."[5] With expressions and statements such as these before us, we can have no reasonable doubt as to Tertullian's meaning when he says that the faithful received the Holy Ghost by the "imposition

---

[1] Liber de Exhort. Cast., cap. iv. A. tom. ii. Curs. Compl. Patrol. : Paris, 1844.
[2] Liber adversus Hermog., cap. xxix. p. 195 A. *ibid.*
[3] *Ibid.* 933 c. [4] *Ibid.* 34 c. [5] *Ibid.* 1001 B.

of hands." They exhibit to us the spirit of God abiding in the souls of the faithful, as the principle of faith, constancy, and Christian piety. He remained with them as such; as such they received him. It makes little for the reformers whether by the imposition of hands miraculous gifts were conferred in the third century. Tertullian appears to say they were not conferred. But conferred or not by the descent of the Holy Ghost upon the faithful, the term or expression "descent of the Holy Ghost" does not mean their collation. It is not identical with their collation, nor does it imply their collation. If they were given, the principle of them, that is the spirit of sanctification, was given first, according to Tertullian, just as in the Acts of the Apostles, where it is said "the Holy Ghost came upon them" first, and then "they began to speak in tongues and prophesy." Then it will be absolutely necessary to admit that the rite which followed baptism in the Church of Carthage—the imposition of hands by which the Holy Ghost was given—was of sacramental efficacy, as it conferred sanctifying grace; and it will be further necessary to admit that it was a sacrament in the double supposition, that it was administered as a matter of course to all Christians, and that it was the perpetuation of the rite which the Apostles administered to the Samaritans, referred to in the eighth chapter of the Acts of the Apostles.

1st. Confirmation, or "imposition of hands," after baptism, was invariably administered to the Christians of Africa in the third century, in order that through it they might receive the Holy Ghost. This is evinced by various passages in the writings of Tertullian and St. Cyprian. The former, in his "Treatise on Baptism," having spoken of the rite of administering that sacrament, subjoins— "After that [*i.e.* after baptism] the hand is imposed, summoning by a benediction and inviting the Holy Ghost . . . . then that most Holy Spirit willingly descends from the Father upon bodies blessed and purified."[1] Here was

[1] Liber de Baptismo, cap. viii. tom. i. p. 1207 A. Curs. Compl. Patrol.: Paris, 1844.

the order of the ceremonial: baptism first, "imposition of hands," as a matter of course, some time subsequent to baptism. The same order is alluded to in his book "On the Resurrection of the Flesh," where he points to the prerogative with which the bodies of Christians in common are favoured in these words:—"That is, the flesh is washed, that the soul may be cleansed; the flesh is anointed, that the soul may be consecrated; the flesh is signed, that the soul may be fortified; the flesh by the imposition of hands is overshadowed, that the soul may be enlightened by the spirit." [1] Here, again, is baptism for all; "imposition of hands" for all equally with baptism. Not that the Church of the third century held that baptism and "imposition of hands" were equally necessary for salvation, for, while we find them affirming again and again the indispensable necessity of the former, they teach the possibility of salvation without the latter, in case that its administration was precluded by a sudden death. The author of an "Anonymous Book on Rebaptization," ascribed to the time of St. Cyprian, raises this question, and discusses it at some length. "If a person," he asks, "not baptized by a bishop in such a way that the hand is forthwith imposed upon him, die before he receive the Holy Ghost, think you has he attained salvation?" [2] With a view to answer this question, he states that the Apostles did not receive the Holy Ghost until long after their baptism, neither did the Samaritans whom Peter baptized. Then he adds—"In that interval of time, any of them might have been taken away without receiving the Holy Ghost, and deprived of the grace of the Holy Ghost." [3] But they, the Apostles and Samaritans, are admitted during that interval to have been the friends of God. Hence he concludes that "in cases that may and do occur in our time, when many die after baptism without the imposition

---

[1] Liber de Resurrectione Carnis, cap. viii. A. tom. ii. Curs. Compl. Patrol.: Paris, 1844.
[2] Anonymi Liber de Rebaptismo, s. iv. p. 1187 A, c. tom. iii. *ibid.*
[3] *Ibid.*

of the bishop's hands, they are to be esteemed as faithful in the full sense [pro perfectis fidelibus ;"][1] consequently they can be saved.

Yet, notwithstanding this conclusion, how clearly is this writer for the thesis that "imposition of hands" was administered as a matter of course in the Church of the third century. The case he makes is entirely exceptional; *scil.*, a person may accidentally die without imposition of hands. The objection which he answers—*scil.*, can any one be saved without imposition of hands?—is founded on a presumption manifestly arising from the invariable administration of that rite. Imposition of hands was, according to him, the universal rule in the case of every individual admitted to baptism, unless by an unexpected calamity he was suddenly called out of life.

By the sole light of Tertullian's writings, we are enabled to outstep the limits of the African Church, and to study the discipline of Rome in respect to the subject we now discuss. In the thirty-sixth chapter of his "Treatise on Prescriptions," he takes occasion to refer to the orthodoxy of the Church of Rome, as follows: "She knows one God, the Creator of the Universe, and Jesus Christ the Son of God the Creator, of the Virgin Mary, and the resurrection of the flesh. She blends the law and prophets with the evangelical and apostolic letters, and thence imbibes faith: it (faith) she signs with water, clothes with the Holy Ghost, nourishes with the Eucharist."[2] Here is the same order of sacred ministrations, which, he told us before, the African Church observed with regard to her children; baptism first — "signs with water;" then, imposition of hands—"clothes with the Holy Ghost," finally the Eucharist.

2. The "imposition of hands," as administered in the third century, was the continuation of the rite conferred upon the Samaritans by Peter and John, referred to in

---

[1] Anonymi Liber de Rebaptismo, s. iv. p. 1847 A, c. tom. iii. Curs. Compl. Patrol.: Paris, 1844.

[2] Tertul. Lib. de Præscr. cap. xxxvi. tom. ii. pp. 49, 50, *ibid.*

the eighth chapter of the Acts of the Apostles. This is plainly taught by St. Cyprian, in his "Epistle to Jubaianus:"—" They who believed in Samaria, believed with a genuine faith, and within the Church, which is one, and to whom alone is given the power of conferring the grace of baptism, and remitting sin, were they baptized by Philip the deacon, whom the same Apostles had sent. And, therefore, having received legitimate and ecclesiastical baptism, they could not be baptized again: but that alone which was wanting was supplied by Peter and John: that prayer being made for them, and the hand imposed, the Holy Ghost was invoked and poured upon them. Which now, too, is done with us in such way that they who are baptized in the Church, are presented to the prelates [*præpositis*] of the Church, and by our prayer and the imposition of the hand they receive the Holy Spirit, and are consummated by the seal of the Lord."[1] This passage is so clear that it requires no comment. In the treatise of an Anonymous Writer on Rebaptization, which was quoted a while ago, a passage occurs in which the same fact is affirmed, and in somewhat similar terms. It is as follows: " For as by the imposition of the bishop's hand, the Holy Ghost is given to every believer, as the Apostles did in the case of the Samaritan after Philip's baptism, by imposing the hand upon them, and in this way conferred upon them the Holy Ghost (to accomplish which, they prayed for them: for the Spirit had not yet descended upon any of them, but they were only baptized in the name of the Lord Jesus), so our Lord, after his resurrection, when he had breathed upon his Apostles and said to them, 'Receive the Holy Ghost' (1 John xx. 22), bestowed the Holy Ghost upon them."[2] Thus the rite of imposing hands, which originated with the Apostles, was perpetuated in the Church of the third century. We have seen that it was administered universally, that every Christian

---

[1] S. Cypr. ad Jubaian. section ix. p. 1115, tom. iii. Curs. Compl. Patrol.: Paris, 1844.
[2] Anonymi Liber de Rebaptismo, No. 3, p. 1187, tom. iii. *ibid.*

believer received it as a matter of course; we have likewise seen that it conferred the Holy Ghost; and from various incidental observations in the writings of Tertullian, we have discovered, that the meaning of " receiving the Holy Ghost " in his day, was receiving the principle of sanctification, or, in other words, receiving sanctifying and vivifying grace. We are, therefore, entitled to ask the question—What did this ceremony want of being in the most strict sense a sacramental rite? It was visible and significative of benediction and strength. It was operative and productive of its effect, irrespective of the positive acts of the receiver. It was proclaimed by the Apostles, and no doubt instituted by Almighty power. It was so far perpetual. It conferred sanctifying grace. It consequently wanted nothing to realize the definition commonly given of a sacrament of the new law; *scil.*, " an external, visible ceremony, instituted by Christ, signifying grace and conferring it—perpetual, and producing its effect by virtue of its due performance."

The sacrament of confirmation, as administered at the present day, is the imposition of hands of the Churches of Rome and Africa, in the third century. The resemblance is not in the general features of both ceremonies: but if we look into the matter, we shall find them alike in the minutest details. Thus: 1st. Confirmation is now conferred by a bishop only: we are told, by the writers of the third century, that " by the imposition of the bishop's hands, the Holy Ghost is given to every believer."[1] 2nd. In the ceremony of confirmation there is an imposition of hands, invoking the Holy Spirit to come, just as in the age when Tertullian said, " The hand is imposed, summoning by a benediction and inviting the Holy Ghost."[2] 3rd. The form of words used in the administration of confirmation is, " I sign thee with the sign of the cross and confirm thee with the chrism of salva-

---

[1] See previous quotation.   [2] *Ibid.*

tion, in the name of the Father and of the Son and of the Holy Ghost." Tertullian joins the signing of the flesh with the ceremony of the imposition of hands, when he says, "The flesh is signed, that the soul may be fortified; the flesh by the imposition of hands is overshadowed, that the soul may be enlightened by the Spirit." [1]
4th. The signing in confirmation is, anointing the forehead with a chrism composed of oil of olives and balsam, and blessed by the bishop. In the Church of the third century, Tertullian associated the anointing of the flesh with its being signed and overshadowed by the imposition of hands. "The flesh is anointed, that the soul may be consecrated; the flesh is signed, that the soul may be fortified; the flesh by the imposition of hands is overshadowed, that the soul may be enlightened by the Spirit;" [2] while the council of Carthage, held under St. Cyprian in the year 255, not only reiterates the sentiments of Tertullian, but gives unmistakable evidence of the custom of solemnly blessing oil at the time that it was held. Here are its words:—" It is likewise necessary that he who has been baptized be anointed, that having received the chrism, that is the unction, he may be the anointed of God and have in him the grace of Christ. Now, it is a ceremony of thanksgiving [eucharistia] by which the baptized are anointed with oil sanctified on the altar." [3]

There can be no reasonable doubt that the " imposition of hands " of the Churches of Rome and Africa, in the third century, was identical in all its essential circumstances with the sacrament of confirmation as now administered in the Church; it was likewise identical with a rite administered by the Apostles. It was always administered to every Christian believer, in the apostolic times, in the third century, at the present day. Call it what you will — " confirmation" or "imposition of hands" — it

---

[1] See previous quotation. [2] *Ibid.*

[3] Reliquiæ Sacræ, No. 11, p. 1040, tom. iii. Curs. Compl. Patrol.: Paris, 1844.

makes no difference. But one thing is perfectly clear, that, if all these facts be put together and considered impartially, an unprejudiced mind must come to the conclusion that the "rite" by which the Holy Ghost has been given to the faithful from the time of the Redeemer to the present day, is and always has been a sacrament. Nor can it be objected that Tertullian, on this subject, exhibits to us the faith and practice of a portion of the Church only; for in his book on "Prescriptions," he tells us that the "doctrine" of all the particular orthodox Churches of his time coincided in all respects with the teaching of the Apostles. "Forthwith then," he says, "the Apostles (whom this appellation is understood to designate 'the sent') having assumed by lot Matthias as the twelfth in the place of Judas, by the authority of prophecy, which is in the Psalms of David, having obtained the promised power of the Holy Ghost unto miracles and language, having proclaimed faith in Jesus Christ, and having established Churches, thence going out into the world, promulgated the same doctrine of the same faith to the nations, and in due course founded churches in every city; from which the other Churches in succession borrowed, and that they may be Churches, daily borrow, the branch of faith and the seed of doctrine; and by this they are reputed apostolic, as being the offshoots of apostolic Churches. Every species is to be necessarily assigned to its original. Wherefore, of so many and so great Churches, one is the first, the apostolic, from which all have come. So all are first and apostolic, whilst all by one evince (their) unity; whilst they have the communion of peace, and the appellation of brothers, and the connecting bond of hospitality, which observances are swayed by no other consideration than one tradition of the same symbol [sacramenti]."[1] If, therefore, the doctrine of these Churches was in all respects identical, as Tertullian seems to affirm, it is not too much to say, that they could not

---

[1] Tertul. Liber de Præscrip., cap. xx. p. 32, tom. ii. Curs. Compl. Patrol.: Paris, 1844.

differ as to the nature and form of a rite so public, so essential, so pre-eminently apostolic as was that of the imposition of hands.

§ 3. *Eucharist.*—We must travel back half a century, to take up the thread of tradition as it regards the sacrament of the Eucharist, for, where testimonies, clear and significant, occur, evidences, in the form of allusions to the dogma, which put the belief of the Church regarding it in a clear light, it is worth while to retrace our steps a little in order to gather them, and place them side by side with the teachings of the old African Church of the third century.

The real difficulties of the Eucharist in the Protestant view are—1st. The real presence, and 2nd. Transubstantiation. The two difficulties in reality are so far identified that one supposes the other. They lean upon each other. They depend upon each other. If one be solved the other is solved. If one be insurmountable, the other is a barrier that cannot be passed—a stumbling-block that prostrates its assailants. This is evidently the case as regards arguments from authority, whether this authority be the inspired words of sacred Scripture or the sayings of ancient historians and fathers, or others who may be said to have weight as chroniclers of the Church's belief. Authority is against both the Protestant positions, and it carries them both, and by the very assault through which it demolishes the obstacles to the real presence it is put in possession of transubstantiation as an accomplished and admitted fact.

As regards the authorities which we are about to adduce, then, it must be admitted that they are taken up with affirming and repeating the dogma of the real presence of the body and blood of Christ in the Eucharist, while they rarely refer to the mode or manner in which this presence is effected. Of course, the word transubstantiation is not in their vocabulary. Christ is present in the Eucharist, they say; his body and blood are there. The same body and blood that he had on earth are there present. Not having been there before, he came to be present, after the bread and wine had received the blessing of the consecrating priest. Then the bread and wine are not bread and wine after the consecration, but the body and blood of Christ. So far the fathers; so speak Justin, Irenæus, Tertullian, Cyprian. So far the fathers; and here they stop. But we go a little farther, and surely our argument is legitimate; *scil.*, if one substance, that of bread or wine, has ceased to be present; if another substance, that of the body of the Lord, occupies its place, and assumes its form; if the change has taken place in consequence of the use of a form of words—"this is my body," "this is my blood"—which signify it and operate it—it is evident that one substance has been converted into the other, which is all that Catholic doctrine means, when it designates this change by the word transubstantiation.

The fathers of the second and third centuries affirm the doctrine of the real presence. St. Justin (Anno Domini 150) thus refers to the Eucharist in his first apology. He has been speaking of the meetings of Christians for religious worship. He goes on: "Then bread and the cup of water and wine are brought to him who presides over the brethren, which having taken, he pours forth praise and glory to the Father of all, through the name of his Son and of the Holy Spirit, and performs at length the Eucharist, or giving of thanks for the gifts received from him. When he has finished prayers and the Eucharist, all the people cry out, Amen. Now, amen in the Hebrew tongue is the same as, be it so. Thus when he who presides has finished the prayers and all the people have cried out, they who are called with us deacons distribute the bread and wine and water, in which thanks have been given, to each of those present to partake of them, and they [the deacons] carry them to the absent."[1] The passage thus far does not touch upon the real presence. So far from supporting this doctrine, it would appear

[1] Just. Apol. I. No. 65, p. 219, tom. i. Sanctorum Patrum. Opp. Polemic. Wirceburgi, 1777.

to be opposed to it, as it denominates the consecrated species, bread, water, and wine. We must look for the mind of St. Justin in the next paragraph, which is professedly explanatory, where he again returns to the subject of the Eucharist and designates these elements "the flesh and blood of Jesus." " Now this aliment is called with us the Eucharist, of which no one is allowed to partake unless he who believes to be true what we teach, and has been washed in that laver for the remission of his sins, and lives as Christ has enjoined. Nor do we take these things as common bread and common drink, but as by the word of God, Jesus Christ made flesh, took flesh and blood for our salvation, so likewise have we been taught that this aliment in which thanks have been given by a prayer containing his words, by which our flesh and blood by a change are nourished, is the flesh and blood of that incarnate Jesus."[1] Justin had previously (No. 65) designated the sacred elements bread, water, and wine. Here he corrects himself. They are not bread and wine, "nor," he says, "do we take these things as common bread and common drink." If they were such, *i. e.*, common bread and drink, they would be taken as such obviously. From the fact, therefore, of their not being taken as common food and drink, it is concluded that they have assumed a new form or passed into a new substance. But what is this form? What is this substance? "We have been taught," Justin says, "that it is the flesh and blood of the incarnate Jesus." Lest there should be any doubt as to the real nature of this substance; lest it might be called figurative flesh, he illustrates this point fully and clearly. "Just as Jesus took flesh and blood, so this aliment (changed by the commemorative and consecrating word) is flesh and blood."[2] The meaning obviously is that it is the same flesh and blood that Jesus assumed at his incarnation. No figurative presence, then, according to St. Justin; no

[1] Just. Apol. I. No. 66, p. 219, tom. i. Sanctorum Patrum. Op. Polemic. Wirceburgi, 1777.
[2] *Ibid.*

spiritual presence, but the presence of the humanity of Christ, and this presence is such that what had been the bread and wine is correctly designated by the words "flesh and blood of Jesus." Now this is clearly the real presence; and as according to Justin this presence has been brought about by consecration, "by a prayer containing his words," there is a conversion of substances which may be fairly designated transubstantiation.

The subject of the Blessed Eucharist is discussed at length by Irenæus (Anno 170) in his treatises against heretics. He teaches the presence of the body and blood of Christ in that sacrament with singular clearness and strength. He introduces the doctrine of the real presence in his third book, where he is arguing against those who denied the divinity of the Son of God. "How," he asks, "can they be sure that the Eucharistic bread is the body of their Lord and the chalice his blood, if they do not acknowledge him as the Son of the Creator?"[1] Again, he introduces it in arguing against the Marcionites: "How, then, if he be the Son of another father, has the Lord, taking bread, which is the work of the Creator, declared that it is his body, and given his assurance that what is mixed in the chalice is his blood?"[2] Again he glances at it, in answering the objections of those who question the possibility of the future incorruptibility of the flesh. "It would follow from this that the Lord has not purchased us by his blood, and that the chalice of the Eucharist is not the communion of his blood, nor the bread that we break the communion of his body."[3]

These are plain expressions, and they are rendered doubly significant from the circumstances in which they are introduced. Heretics denied the divinity of the Son of God. Irenæus reproaches them with believing in the presence of their Saviour in the Eucharist. His argument

---

[1] Cited by Fleury, Histoire Ecclesiastique, tom. i. lib. 4, p. 169. Paris, 1840.

[2] *Ibid.*

[3] *Ibid.*

manifestly is—" A divine person alone could promise and give his body and blood as the food and drink of the faithful. If Christ be not admitted to be a divine person, there is no guarantee that his body and blood are in the Eucharist. Consequently, these heretics are inconsistent in admitting the real presence while they deny the Divinity of Christ." Except in the supposition of the real presence there would be obviously no argument. Other heretics denied the possibility of the flesh becoming incorruptible. How does Irenæus answer them? If this be the case, he says, Christ is not present in the Eucharist. Why so? Because to be present in the Eucharist, his body and blood should be incorruptible; but in the view of these heretics incorruptibility is impossible. Therefore, there would be a repugnance in supposing his human nature to be incorruptible. Here again his argument would fall to the ground, unless the real presence be assumed as its foundation and as a fact admitted by his adversaries.

Cyprian, like Irenæus, designates the Eucharist by the name " the body of the Lord." They who receive the Eucharist unworthily, " profane the holy body of the Lord," according to this learned Father. Complaining of the conduct of certain priests, who precipitately admitted those who had fallen in persecution to the participation of the sacred rites of the Church, he says, " They presumed against the law of the Gospel . . . . . to offer for them and give the Eucharist; that is, to profane the holy body of the Lord, when it is written, ' whosoever eateth the bread and drinketh the chalice of the Lord unworthily shall be guilty of the body and blood of the Lord '— (1 Cor. xi. 27)." [1] Cyprian does little more here than repeat the sentiment of the Apostle of the Gentiles. His words, however, are, in one sense, a little more explanatory than those of St. Paul. To profane the body of the Lord must mean, to treat it irreverently; to convert it from sacred to secular uses; to slight it. The profanation arises

---

[1] Cypr. ep. x. No. 1, p. 254 A, tom. iv. Curs. Compl. Patrol. Paris, 1844.

from the unworthiness of the communicant. He therefore must be said to have a share in the profanation of Christ's body, with the priest, who administers the Eucharist to him; consequently, he must receive the body of the Lord, though unworthily. The words of Cyprian demonstrate the real presence of Christ in the Holy Eucharist, in another passage that occurs in his "Liber de Lapsis," where referring to a certain class, *i. e.* those who were too soon admitted to the table of the Lord after their fall, he says, "They did violence to his body and blood," and they "sinned against him with their mouth and with their hands." These expressions are more explanatory, because they convey to our minds more clearly the idea of a physical injury, which implies a real reception. His words are: "Spurning and despising all these rules . . . before the offended (majesty) of God, indignant and threatening, has been appeased, violence is done to his body and blood, and in a manner they offend more against the Lord by their hands and mouth, than when they denied him."[1] Expressions such as these, which imply physical contact with the body and blood of the Lord, when the Eucharist is received, are of very frequent occurrence in the writings of St. Cyprian. Thus, 1st. He who bears with him the Eucharist, carries the body of the Lord: "Who, after leaving the Lord's assembly [dimissus e Dominico], and still carrying the Eucharist with him, as is the custom—hurrying away to the show—this infidel introduced the holy body of Christ among the obscene bodies of strumpets, deserving a worse damnation for his journey than for the pleasure of the show."[2] 2nd. He who receives the Eucharist drinks the blood of Christ and touches his body with his hands. Speaking of him who has fallen in persecution and is unwilling to do penance for his sin, he asks: "What good opinion can you have of him? what fear—what faith can you suppose him to have, whom fear could not correct—

---

[1] Liber de Lapsis, No. 16 A, p. 479. Curs. Compl. Patrol. Paris, 1844.

[2] Liber de Spectaculis, No. 5, p. 184 B. *Ibid.*

whom persecution has not reformed. The high and lofty neck, which, though fallen, is not bent. The proud and swelling mind, which, though conquered, is not broken. Wounded—fallen—he looks with curiosity at the erect and unblemished; and, sacrilegious, he is enraged with the priests, because he does not at once receive the body of the Lord in his unclean hands, or with polluted mouth drink the blood of the Lord."[1] 3rd. He who has received the Eucharist is exhorted to embrace the Lord, with that hand which, in receiving it, had taken his body. "Let us arm our right hand with the spiritual sword, that it may bravely refuse the abominable sacrifice—that, mindful of the Eucharist, having taken the body of the Lord, it may embrace him, about to receive from him hereafter the reward of a heavenly crown."[2] It is impossible to reconcile such expressions as these with the idea of a figurative or spiritual presence of Christ in the blessed Eucharist. If language is to have a fixed meaning, their signification cannot be doubted. We cannot be said to touch— to carry—to embrace a mere spirit, or to eat and drink a figure. Physical acts require a physical substance to act upon. If there was anything in the context of these passages which could give us ever so little reason to doubt as to Cyprian's meaning, we might say that his words would be realized and verified in the supposition of spiritual touching and embracing, and eating and drinking by faith. But, no; his words admit of no such interpretations. He compares physical with physical—corporal with corporal—material with material. A physical hand takes a thing physically, and what it takes must be a physical substance. A human body takes a thing among other corporal things by a physical exertion, and what it so takes must be a physical substance. The words of St. Cyprian are unmistakable, and necessarily, supposing the corporal and physical presence of the Lord, they

[1] Liber de Lapsis, c. iv. No. 22, p. 485. Curs. Compl. Patrol. Paris, 1844.
[2] Ep. lviii. No. 9, p. 357 A. *Ibid.*

suppose him substantially and really present in the most holy sacrament of the Eucharist.

In his "Liber de Lapsis" Cyprian relates some anecdotes illustrative of the Divine judgments on those who received the Eucharist unworthily, which are suggestive of his belief as to the awful sanctity of that sacrament. So striking are these instances that we cannot understand them except in the hypothesis of the real presence of the Saviour. " Listen to an event that happened in my presence and under my observation. It happened that certain parents taking flight, left a little infant girl under the care of a nurse, being too much frightened to complete their arrangements; the nurse took the abandoned child to the magistrate. Near an idol, to which the people flocked, they gave her bread steeped in wine, which remained of the immolation of the passers-by, because she could not from her age eat flesh meat. Subsequently, the mother recovered the child; but the girl could neither tell nor indicate the crime committed, no more than she could previously understand or prevent it. Wherefore, through ignorance it came to pass, that the mother introduced her with herself when I was offering sacrifice: But the girl, associated with the sanctified, impatient of our ceremonial and prayer, began to be convulsed with sobs at one time, then lamenting,—to be torn with mental agony, and as if the tormentor drove her to it, that simple mind, still of infant years, made manifest a consciousness of the fact by every sign that she could employ. Now when, at the conclusion of the solemnity the deacon began to offer the chalice to the bystanders, and the others having received, her turn came, the little child, through an instinct of the Divine Majesty, turned away her face, firmly closed her lips, refused the chalice. The deacon, however, insisted, and though she struggled against it, he infused the sacrament of the chalice. Then follows retching and vomit. In that body and defiled mouth the Eucharist could not remain. The drink sanctified in the blood of the Lord came forth from the polluted entrails. Such is the power of the Lord, such

His Majesty."[1] To speak moderately, it would be difficult to reconcile the events here recorded with modern theories regarding the Eucharist, such as that which says that it is simply a commemoration of the suffering of the Lord; or that other, which does not blush to say, that the Eucharist is common food unless it be received with faith. St. Cyprian continues his examples of the Divine judgments inflicted in this life. " So far the case of the infant, who was not of an age to tell the crime of another perpetrated in her regard. But she who, advanced and grown up, came in secretly while I was offering sacrifice—taking to herself not food, but a sword, and giving admittance to a deadly poison, as it were, between her mouth and stomach, began to be tortured and racked with mental excitement, and suffering no longer the pressure of persecution, but of her crime, fell to the ground palpitating and trembling. She who deceived man, experienced God as an avenger."[2] If in Cyprian's mind the Eucharist was not the "holy of holies," he would attach but little significance to the event he here records. The punishment in his view was suitable to the offence. Consequently, the latter must have been levelled at a substance which was intrinsically and essentially Divine. Another instance he gives in the following words: " And when a certain woman attempted with unworthy hands to open her chest in which was the Holy of the Lord, she was deterred from attempting to touch it by fire bursting out from thence."[3] And another as follows. " And a certain man, because, defiled by sacrifice, he dared secretly to receive a part with the others from a priest who had celebrated, was not able to eat and handle the Holy of the Lord, found that he carried ashes in his open hands."[4] It is the belief of Cyprian that we are to look for in these stories. The question comes to this, Is the Eucharist holy in itself, or is it not? Is it intrinsically holy? It is so

---

[1] Liber de Lapsis, No. 25, p. 484 c. 485 A, D. Curs. Compl. Patrol. Paris, 1844.
[2] *Ibid.* p. 486 A.   [3] *Ibid.* 486 B.   [4] *Ibid.*

holy in itself, according to St. Cyprian, that it cannot abide contact with soul or body that is defiled. God punishes those who touch it, even approach it unduly; the inference is, that it is essentially, intrinsically holy. Such is the faith of the great St. Cyprian. Is it too much to conclude that he believed in the real presence?

Tertullian refers to the Eucharist frequently, both in the treatises he composed before and after his fall into Montanism. In one of the latter, his fourth book against Marcion, he has a long passage, which is not only suggestive but demonstrative of his belief of the real presence of the Saviour in the sacrament. We will give the passage at length. "Wherefore, having proclaimed that with desire he desired to eat the Pasch as his own (for it would be unseemly that God desire anything foreign to him), having taken bread and distributed to his disciples, he made it his body [*corpus illum suum fecit*[1]], saying, 'this is my body,' that is, the figure of my body. But it would not have been a figure unless the body would be a reality [*figura autem non fuisset nisi veritatis esset corpus*]. Now, a void thing such as a phantom could not admit of a figure. Or if he, therefore, made bread his body, because he wanted the reality of a body, he should by consequence deliver up bread for us. He acted through condescension to Marcion, in such a way that bread was crucified! But why does he call bread his body, and not rather [*peponem*], which Marcion has in place of a heart? Not understanding that it was an ancient figure of the body of Christ, saying through Jeremias (Jeremias xi. 19), 'Against me they took counsel, saying, come let us put wood on his bread, that is, a cross on his body.' Wherefore, the interpreter of antiquity declared with sufficient clearness what he then wished bread to have signified, calling bread his body. So too in the mention of the chalice, making a testament sealed with his blood, he confirmed the substantial nature of the body. Now there can be blood of no body but of flesh. For if any property

---

[1] "Suum illum." Rhen. Sicul. Oberth.

not carnal of the body be opposed to us, assuredly not carnal it will not have blood. Consequently, the proof of the body consists of the evidence of flesh; the proof of the flesh of the evidence of blood."[1]

This passage is worthy of the deep, dark-flowing African rhetorician who penned it, yet, as I said above, it contains some very positive affirmations touching the real presence. Let us glance at the argument of it. The Marcionites held that what appeared to be the body of the Redeemer was not a body of flesh and blood, but a phantom. Tertullian is here occupied in refuting them. How does he do so? He refers to the Last Supper; and he says that the Redeemer then made his body that which had been in ancient times the figure of his body—*scil.*, bread. Now, he argues bread could not have been the figure of his body, unless that body was a reality, for there is no figure of a phantom. Therefore he concludes the body of Christ delivered to the disciples at the Last Supper was no phantom, but a reality. Consequently, the body of the Redeemer was one of flesh and blood. His second argument is taken from the chalice given to the Apostles at his Last Supper. It contained his blood—the behest of it was "the new testament of his blood." But a phantom has no blood. Therefore his body to which this blood appertained was no phantom. What was it then? Clearly a body of flesh. That this is the argument of Tertullian appears from the affirmations of the text. 1st. "He made bread his body." 2nd. "It would not have been a figure of his body unless the body should be a reality." 3rd. "So too in the mention of the chalice, making a testament sealed with his blood, he confirmed the substantial nature of his body. Now there can be blood of no body but of flesh." These three affirmations prove that his argument to evince the substantial nature of the body of Christ is not drawn from the fact of the Eucharist being a figure of it, but from the fact of the Eucharist being it in reality, and veri-

---

[1] Tertul. lib. iv. adversus Marcion, c. xl. p. 460 D. C. 461 A. B. Curs. Compl. Patrol. Paris, 1844.

fying ancient figures of it. For if in this passage he [re]garded the Eucharist as a figure only of the body [of] Christ, how could he say "he made it his body?" [If] somebody will say, look to the whole passage; it runs th[us] "He made it his body, that is, the figure of his bod[y]." True the text runs thus, but the meaning is, he made (that is, the figure of his body, *scil.*, bread) his body. [I] admit that this meaning appears strained and unnatur[al], but it is rendered necessary by the tense used in the co[n]secutive sentence—"It would not have been," &c. If t[he] reading was, he made it the figure of his body, the ne[xt] sentence should commence, "it would not be," instead [of] being as it is, "it would not have been." The Latin wo[rd] used should be "esset" instead of "fuisset." From t[he] fact, therefore, of his saying it would not have been t[he] figure of his body, it is clear that the figure of his bod[y] mentioned in the previous sentence was a past and ancien[t] and not a present and modern one. Hence we must con[clude that, not speaking of the Eucharist as a figure but [of] the reality of his body, the argument can be no other tha[n] the above. So from this passage, as evincing the mind o[f] Tertullian, we have a demonstrative proof of his belief in the real presence.

Here we must pause; and, for once in the course of this work, we must say a hard word plainly. The real presence was affirmed distinctly by men of great name in the second and third centuries. They all affirmed it in the same terms, as if they studied out of the same catechism. They came as witnesses to adore. From the east and west they came—from Gaul, from Egypt, from Pisidia—and their voices blended into one solemn concord, and they spoke out together the awful words, which they had heard from their predecessors, "the body of Jesus," "the blood of Christ," "the Eucharist," "profanation," "sacrifice," "life everlasting." For our instruction they said these things, and for the guidance of all true believers to the end. The blasphemy of modern mechanics!—mechanics? I should say machines—and the much more awful blas-

FIRST THREE CENTURIES. 317

...y of those who set them in motion. In some of our
...s, men who ought to be working at the loom or the
...gh undertake to rave about the Eucharist. Flippant
..., with ready fingers, are put forth to utter blasphemies,
...e they ought to be employed in mending shoes.
...erty leads to crime sometimes; but it has been re-
...ed for our day to witness poverty jibing the sayings of
... most high God. The poverty that drives to theft—the
...erty that drives to prostitution—the poverty, the last
...all, that drives to " Scripture reading to Roman Catho-
...s," which too often in this country is only another name
... the daily and systematic mockery of the sacred things
...th, Most High. For heaven's sake, if the men that set
...ese things, not persons, agoing, are ignorant of Church
...story and tradition and the Scriptures let them not
...eak through their contemptible organs, but let them eat
... contentment the crust which the law-Church gives them;
...t if they will speak on the Eucharist, let them remem-
...er that they are expected from their profession to be
...arned and from their rank to be gentle; and let them
...y nothing, above all, on so holy a subject as the Eucha-
...ist which may compromise them with good men as out
...t sea as regards ancient belief and practice and modern
courtesy and refinement.

§ 4. *Penance.*—We should look in vain in the writings
of the third century for a picture of the sacrament of penance similar in all respects to that we are accustomed to
contemplate. In the Catholic Church confession is auricular, that is, secretly whispered into the ear of the priest.
Such is the system. The priest sits in a chair, which
from its location is invested with an air of mystery and
solemnity; it is a confessional chair, deputed to the purpose, with the adjuncts of a kneeling-place for the penitents, "crates," sometimes crucifixes and other religious
emblems. Here the priest sits as a judge of consciences,
to hear the case, to weigh the evidences of guilt, to acquit
or condemn, " to bind " or " to loose," the sinner. Such
is the system according to which the sacrament of penance

is administered at the present day, and this system or mode of administration is traceable through the historical documents of many centuries.

Such is, according to the common routine, the system; we might suppose it different in certain cases without impairing the efficacy of the rite. Confession is not essentially auricular, inasmuch as it is an integral portion of the sacrament of penance, for it is universally held that a public confession would suffice when it could not be secretly made; it is not essentially integral, for in certain special cases the suppression of some sins is allowed; it is not essentially associated with external solemnity, for it is expressly provided and enjoined that in cases of haste, arising from extreme danger or the approach of death, confession and absolution may take place in a street, upon the sea, in bed—in a word, in any secular or profane place, and without soutane, stole, or surplice.

Then it appears that all the essential ingredients of the sacrament of penance are a confession, public or private, simple or solemn, a confession accompanied with sorrow for past sin, and an efficacious resolution to avoid relapse —a legitimate sacerdotal absolution, and, if possible, some external works of satisfaction commensurate with the sinner's guilt. Wherever such ingredients are discovered in the Church, there is the sacrament of penance. Now, as I said a while ago, we will find it difficult to discover in the third century a picture of auricular confession complete in all its details. We will find it, to be sure, affirmed that private and hidden sins were confessed, from which we will perhaps be forced to conclude that they were confessed privately; but with the "crates," the confessional, the stole, we must dispense; and we must content ourselves with discovering in the old Church of Africa the essential parts of the sacramental rite; that is, confession, absolution, contrition, and satisfaction. With these few preliminary remarks, let us raise the veil, and look at the penitential usages of the Church of Carthage in the days of Tertullian and St. Cyprian. 1st. According to Tertullian, there is a second penitential rite for those who have fallen after baptism, through which, as through the latter, the pardon of sin may be obtained. Having treated of the nature and effects of baptism, and the disposition it requires, he refers to this rite in the following terms: " I am grieved to make mention of the second and last hope, lest, treating of the remaining help of penance, I seem to point out another road to sin."[1] But what is this second penitential rite? He describes it in the following terms: " Wherefore, of this second and only penance, the proof is laborious in proportion to its difficulty, to such a degree that it is not only manifested by the conscience, but also regulated by some act. This act, which is expressed and usually designated by a Greek word, is the ' exomolo gesis' [confession] by which we confess our sin to God, not as ignorant of it, but inasmuch as satisfaction is regulated by confession, penance is born of confession; by penance, God is appeased. So the ' exomolo gesis' is a rite of prostrating and humbling man, prescribing to him a mode of life which attracts mercy. It lays down rules as to the dress and mode of life—to lie on sack-cloth and ashes—to deform the body by squalidness—to depress the mind by grief—to reform that which sinned by severe treatment—to know but food and drink of the simplest kind, and not for the indulgence of the appetite, but for the preservation of life; generally, too, by fasts to supply nutriment to prayer—to sigh—to shed tears—to groan to the Lord your God both day and night—to prostrate to the priests [advolvi præsbyteris]—to kneel to the friends of God—to impose on all the brethren the obligation of prayer in your behalf. All these the ' exomolo gesis' prescribes, with a view to recommend the penance to favour, by the apprehension of danger to honour God, by pronouncing sentence on the sinner to perform the office of the Divine wrath, and by temporal punishment not to frustrate but to expunge eternal torments. When, therefore, it prostrates a man it raises him the more; when it

---

[1] Tertul. de Pœniten. c. vii. p. 1240, tom. i. Curs. Comple. Patrol. Paris, 1844.

makes him squalid, it cleanses him the more; when it accuses, condemns, it absolves."[1] The penitential rite here alluded to by Tertullian consisted in "confession of sins" to God, and a variety of overt acts of humiliation and contrition, among which is mentioned, "prostration to the priests" of the Church; and the result of this rite was absolution from the guilt of sin. So far he has not determined for us whether this confession exceeded a simple acknowledgment of guilt in presence of the brethren, or whether the absolution was an invisible act on the part of God, or a sensible act on the part of his minister. But if we follow him into the next chapter of this treatise on penance, we will find both these doubts cleared up in a manner perfectly satisfactory to any reasonable mind. He proceeds to argue against those who put off the confession of their sins. They do so through shame:—"I presume," he says, "that there are many who avoid, or defer from day to day, this work of making the publication of their doings [publicationem sui], thinking more of shamefacedness than of salvation."[2] Now, if the confession in question here were only a general acknowledgment of guilt to God in presence of the brethren, there would be no such great shame attending it, and, consequently, from the difficulty of making it, we are justified in concluding that it must have been detailed and particular in the enumeration of sins. Then, according to Tertullian, a detailed confession was made. But this is not all. It was made to some man or men, who had a right to hear it all, for he subjoins:—"In sooth, if from the knowledge of men we hold back anything, shall we also conceal it from God? Are the knowledge of man and the apprehension of God to be compared?"[3] Then the confession was made to man; but what man? Some man who had the authority to absolve in open court; for he adds: "Is it better to be concealed unto damnation, or to be openly absolved?"[4] Now, if we

---

[1] Tertul. de Pœniten. c. ix. p. 1248 B. tom. i. Curs. Compl. Patrol. Paris, 1844.

[2] *Ibid.* c. vii. p. 1244.   [3] *Ibid.* p. 1245 B.   [4] *Ibid.*

compare this fact with the circumstance, that the penitent was " to prostrate himself to the priests," as a part of his penitential observance, we must come to the conclusion, that absolution was imparted by the ordained ministers of the Church. So here are the various points involved in these passages from Tertullian's treatise on penance:—
1. In the Church of Carthage, in his day, Christians who had fallen after baptism were reconciled to God, by a second rite, called penance. 2. This second rite consisted partially in works of self-denial and confession. 3. The confession was detailed to a certain extent; and in its details, it came to the ears of man. 4. Absolution was the result; it completed the formula, by which forgiveness before God was obtained. 5. This absolution must have been imparted by some one of the priests, to whom, as a matter of obligation, the penitent " prostrated himself," in an humble acknowledgment of sin. Such is Tertullian's doctrine: and it proves beyond dispute, that sacramental administration for the remission of sin was a usage of the Church of Carthage in the third century. It is worthy of remark, that there is not one sentence in the passages cited here which would enable us to decide the question as to whether the confession was a public one or auricular. The confession was shame-bringing; but it would be so if it were made to a single priest in private. It was a " publication of sinful doings;" but the expression is verified by the acknowledgment of them to a priest in private. The absolution following it was a public act: but even though the confession were auricular it ought to be so, for it was not only remissive of sin before God, but the termination of a course of public penance; it was the final act that released the sinner from the obligation of afflicting and punishing his body. But whether auricular or public, it matters not for the present; for we only undertake to show, that all that is essential to the sacrament of penance — that is, confession, satisfaction, contrition, and absolution—are affirmed by Tertullian to have been involved in the "exomologesis" of the Church of Carthage, when he lived and wrote.

The writings and letters of St. Cyprian throw still greater light on the subject of sacramental confession and absolution in the Church of the third century than even the treatises of Tertullian. Both writers are equally strong in insisting on the necessity of confession for the pardon of sins; but in addition the former distinctly affirms that sacerdotal absolution is indispensable. 1st. Confession is necessary according to St. Cyprian :—" Let each of you, beloved brethren, confess his sin, while he is yet in this world, while his confession can be received." [1] Again: " How many, for not doing penance and confessing the consciousness of their sin, are filled with unclean spirits; how many by the rage of folly are driven witless to insanity." [2] 2nd. So necessary, according to this writer, is confession, and the imposition of the hands of the clergy for penitents, that, without either or both, it was positively wrong to admit them to the communion of the faithful or the peace of the Church." " Yet I am informed that some priests, unmindful of the Gospel, and thoughtless of what the martyrs have written to us, nor allowing to the bishop the honour of his priesthood and see, have begun to hold communion with the fallen, and to offer for them and to give them the Eucharist, while it was meet that they should come to these (privileges) according to a certain order. For how much more expedient is it to proceed according to the discipline of the Lord in the case of crimes, most grievous and extreme, such as these, when even in the lesser sins which are not committed against God, penance is done for a reasonable time, and the " exomologesis " takes place with the inspection of the life of the penitent, nor does any such come to the communion (of the Church) unless the hand has been first imposed upon him by the bishop and clergy." [3] The necessity of confession and imposition of hands is further evinced by

[1] Cyprian, Liber de Lapsis, No. 29, p. 489, tom. iv. Curs. Compl. Patrol. Paris, 1844.
[2] *Ibid.* No. 26, p. 487.
[3] *Ibid.* Ep. xi. p. 257.

the fact, that penitents were not to be allowed to die without them, even though they might not have them without the violation of an important disciplinary regulation. " Since, however, I perceive that there is no possibility of going to you yet, and that the summer has commenced—a season beset with frequent and grievous diseases—I am of opinion that we must come to the aid of our brethren, in such way that they who have received tickets from the martyrs, and who by their privilege may be aided with God, can, if seized with any illness, or danger of infirmity, make the confession of their sin to any priest who may happen to be present, without waiting for my arrival, or, if a priest cannot be found, and death approaches, to a deacon, that the hand being imposed on them unto penance, they may go to the Lord in peace, to give them which the martyrs have besought us by letter."[1] A new feature of the right of penance turns up in this passage,—*scil.*, 3rd. Confession was to be made in secret to a priest, when the hour of death drew nigh. I will not go so far as to say that this was auricular confession; but most assuredly it was something different from the public acknowledgment of sin, which took place in the church, and in presence of all the brethren. Confession was to be made on the death-bed, in order that the dying sinner " might go in peace to the Lord." Here was a preparation for death, similar in every respect to that which would be made by a dying Catholic at the present day, consisting of confession, absolution, forgiveness. 4th. But is there any distinct mention of auricular confession in the letters or treatises of St. Cyprian? There appears to be an unmistakable reference to it in one passage, which occurs in his " Liber de Lapsis." The passage is as follows:—" In fine, of how much faith and more salutary fear are they, who, though not contaminated by the crime of sacrilege or ticket-presenting [aut libelli], yet as they have thought of doing so, confessing the same to the

---

[1] Cyprian, Liber de Lapsis, Ep. xii. p. 259, tom. iv. Curs. Compl. Patrol. Paris, 1844.

priests of God with grief and simplicity, make the 'exomologesis' of their conscience, expose the burden of their mind, seek a salutary cure for faults, though small and few, knowing that it hath been written; God is not mocked—(Gal. vi. 7)."[1] The confession of hidden sins is here commended by St. Cyprian. He praises those who make it. He does not say that such confession was of obligation, or generally made; but such as made it did well. Now, in what way must we suppose this confession was made? Privately, I think, from the nature of the case, first; and secondly, from the words of the context, "seek a salutary cure for faults though small and few." These words would appear to imply that a secret conference went on between the penitent and the priest, in which not only absolution was imparted, but advice was tendered on the hidden maladies of the soul. Now, if this be the case, we would have an example of auricular confession; a most perfect example, too, consisting in a secret confession of secret faults to a minister with a view to obtain their pardon.

Confession, then, and the absolution that followed it in the Church of Carthage, where Cyprian wrote, were not simply external observances; and the "pax" which resulted from them was not merely a restoration to the external communion of the Church. There was an invisible spirituality pervading the whole, which acted on the soul of the sinner, removed the stains of his sins, and restored him to the friendship of God. By absolution he became just, having been unjust before; by the words of the priest his bonds were burst; and having been previously a child of wrath and heir to perdition, he was rendered by the sacramental rite a child of God and heir to the Kingdom of Heaven. All these facts are sufficiently evidenced by the words we have hitherto cited. If a further confirmation of them be wanting, we will find it in another passage, the last we shall quote here, taken

---

[1] Cyprian, Liber de Lapsis, No. 28, p. 488, tom. iv. Curs. Compl. Patrol. Paris, 1844.

from a rather celebrated epistle of a synod of African bishops, presided over by St. Cyprian, and addressed to the Pope Cornelius:—" We had ordained before, beloved brother, after consulting among ourselves, that they who in the heat of persecution had been supplanted by the adversary and fallen, and by forbidden sacrifices defiled themselves, should do full penance for a length of time, and if the danger of sickness were urgent, should receive peace on the approach of death. Nor was it right, nor did paternal goodness and Divine clemency allow, that the Church should be closed to those who knock at its gate; and that the aid of saving hope should be denied to those who weep and pray, in such way that, leaving this world, they should be sent to the Lord without communion and peace, while He allows and hath ordained, that 'whatsoever is bound on earth may be bound in heaven also, and what is first loosed in the church may be likewise loosed there.'"[1] And so, according to Cyprian, the priest's absolution removed the guilt of sin before God, and rendered the Christian just before heaven. We want nothing more. This is the doctrine of the Catholic Church at the present day.

Without entering fully into the question of auricular confession, and without for the moment discussing the question as to forms, ceremonial, &c., we discover a naked fact in the writings of the two great lights of Africa in the third century—Tertullian the priest, and Cyprian the bishop of Carthage. The fact is this; confession was made by the faithful, publicly or privately, it matters not, and a grace-giving absolution was imparted by the priests. The evidence of this is so clear, from being often brought out, it becomes so burning, so brilliant, that to attempt to hide one's self from its influence is simply absurd. Confession was made, absolution was imparted, and sin was forgiven. The machinery of a sacrament is here. There is

[1] Cyprian, Epistola Synodica, p. 854A, 855A, tom. iv. Curs. Compl. Patrol. Paris, 1844.

the visible cause: the invisible effect: Divine institution, certainly, because the power of God alone could attach the infusion of justification to a human and physical ceremony; permanence likewise; because, if we revert to the Sacred Scripture, we shall find that a rite is introduced there in the words of the Redeemer, a power is given there of binding and loosing sin, of which the penitential ministration of the African Church is obviously the continuation and perpetuation. Now it only remains for us to demand of St. Cyprian, if we are to regard his testimony on this subject as limited, locally, as restricted to the boundaries of his see, or, in other terms, ought his words to be taken as conveying to us the general discipline of the Church in his age, or the local discipline of Carthage? To hear his response we need only glance at the titles of his letters, on the subject of admitting penitents to the peace of God and his Church. I select them indiscriminately: "Cyprian to Caldonius, bishop" (De Lapsis, ep. xix.); "Cyprian to the Clergy at Rome, about several confessors, and about the impudence of Lucian, and the modesty of the confessors Celerinus" (ep. xxii.); "Cyprian to the priests and deacons, being at Rome" (ep. xxix.); Cyprian to Antonianus, bishop" (ep. x.); "Cyprian to Cornelius, pope, on giving peace to the fallen" (ep. liv.); "Cyprian to Epictetus and the people of Assuntarium about Fortunatianus, their former bishop" (ep. lxiv.); "Cyprian to Stephen, pope, about Marcian, bishop of Arles, who joined the Novatians" (ep. lxviii.). "Cyprian to the clergy and people of Spain about Basilides and Martial" (ep. lxviii.). From these titles it is clear that the correspondence of Cyprian was very extensive. All the letters here referred to are taken up in a great measure with the discipline of penance. Rome, Italy, France, and Spain were within the limits of his experience and knowledge; and we ought to reasonably presume that their penitential order was not different from his. If it was, Thascius Cyprian was not the man to dissemble it. He would have told them so, and insisted upon explanation and uniformity. But, quite the contrary, he writes in the supposition that the penitential canons were everywhere the same, that the mode of reconciliation with God and his Church was uniform through all these countries. Therefore, the usage of Africa in the third century, in reference to penance, may be taken as fairly representing at that time the discipline and belief of the Catholic Church, and Thascius Cyprian is a voucher for us, that through the orthodox countries of Europe and Africa, the sacrament of penance was administered in the third century in substantially the same form in which it is administered at the present day.

§ 5. *Extreme unction.*—Without leaving the African Church, we have to migrate from Carthage to Alexandria, with a view to discover the traces of the sacramental rite mentioned by St. James, in the fifth chapter of his epistle—the last which Christians received when about to pass from time into eternity. Not that the Church of Carthage was without its sacrament of extreme unction; but there is no allusion to it by the two witnesses to the faith of that Church, whom we have hitherto brought forward; and in search of a solitary dogma it appeared desirable not to pass the limits of a nation whose national faith and practice had been taken as a fair illustration of those of the universal Church.

Origen, the writer whom we are about to cite here, was not only a very learned man, but he was about as travelled a Christian as any of the illustrious ones of his age. Let us just glance at his career. He was born in Alexandria, where he studied under St. Clement, who was then rector of the illustrious catechetical school of that city. At a suitable age he succeeded to the mastership of this school—so distinguished under him for deep learning and orthodoxy, that it was frequented by the greatest scholars of the day—so happy in the results of its training, that " innumerable doctors, priests, confessors, and martyrs came forth from its walls." The experience of Origen was not confined to his native city, nor was his acquaintance with Christian usages limited to his native Church. He went out into the world while yet a young man; and during a large portion of his eventful career, he conversed on terms of intimacy with the most orthodox bishops, and disputed with the impugners of Christian truth in various cities of the East and West. It will be sufficient to indicate here a few of the more remarkable places which history tells us he visited. He journeyed to Rome in the pontificate of Zepherinus, where he remained some time inspecting with delight that ancient Church, and illustrious capital of the universe. We find him at Antioch in the year 218; in Cæsarea in Palestine, in 230. About this time he undertook various journeys between Asia Minor, Palestine, and Egypt. In 238 he was sent on a mission into Arabia, for the purpose of remonstrating with Beryllus, bishop of Bosra, who had fallen into various errors relating to the Divinity of Christ. Afterwards he turns up in Cappadocia; subsequently, in Tyre, where he died in 253, in the sixty-ninth year of his age.

It must be admitted, that the experiences of Origen were rather extensive, and he cannot be regarded as other than a valuable exponent of Christian practice in his day. In his second homily on Leviticus, he alludes to the ceremony of anointing the sick with oil, as one of the sacred usages through which remission of sin is obtained in the new dispensation. His words are as follows:—" There is still a seventh remission of sin, difficult and laborious though it be—by penance, wherein the sinner watereth his bed with his tears, and his tears become unto him bread day and night, and wherein he blusheth not to tell his sin to the priest of God and to seek a remedy, after the manner of him who says—' I have said I will declare against myself my injustice to the Lord, and thou hast forgiven the impiety of my heart.' In which, too, the saying of the Apostle is fulfilled: ' Is any one sick among you, let him call the priests of the Church, and let them impose hands on him, anointing him with oil in the name of the Lord,' " &c.[1]

It is necessary to throw some light on this passage, in

---

[1] Origen in Levit., Homil. ii. No. 4, op. tom. ii. p. 191.

order that we may understand the precise significance of the concluding words, as employed by its distinguished author. The words in question are in substance taken from the epistle of St. James. They are used by Origen to illustrate the rite of penance, by which under the new law the pardon of sins is obtained. He had been speaking of the old law and enumerating its sacrifices for sin. It was natural that he should pass to the new law, and mention the means of justification furnished by it to its followers. Among these means, he says, is penance, which consists in penitential works and a declaration of sin to the priest of the Lord. Here we might suppose that Origen would stop, as the mention of the sacrament of penance was amply sufficient for his purpose. He chooses, however, to add, that the imposition of the priest's hands and anointing, which take place in the case of the sick, are also a penitential usage by which the guilt of sin is expunged. Observe, he does not say whether the sick of his day were anointed when death approached, neither does he say they were not. He does not speak of a practice, but of a principle. He does not speak of a usage general or local, but of a precept laid down by an Apostle. His words convince us that the injunction of St. James was not ignored in the Church of the third century. Then we naturally argue thus :—A rite, remissive of sin, consequently Divinely instituted, spoken of plainly by one of the Apostolic writers, was known and appreciated by Origen. Consequently, it was performed in its due circumstances through the Christian Churches, with which he was acquainted. If not, it was no practical illustration of the penitential order of the new law, nor a part of Christianity as distinguished from local religious customs.

§ 6. *Holy Orders.*—It was clearly shown in a previous section of this work, that the orders of a bishop are different from those of a priest. The candidate for the episcopacy of a given Church was generally from among those who had been some time before admitted to sacerdotal orders. Hands were imposed on him a second time, when he was about to be raised to the episcopal grade. In the history of the election of Sabinus, related in the synodical letter of the fourth council of Carthage, we are told that the episcopacy was given him first, and " that hands were then imposed on him ;" [1] by both of which acts he was substituted in the place of Basilides, deposed. Had he been first a priest? We are not told; but it is clear, that if he were taken from an inferior order of the clergy, the circumstance would not be passed over in silence. In the narrative of the election of Cornelius, episcopal ordination is still more distinctly illustrated. We are told that he had gone through all ecclesiastical offices before he was raised to the dignity of the priesthood. " Promoted through all ecclesiastical offices and in Divine ministrations, having often pleased God much, he ascended to the sublime height of the priesthood through all the grades of religion." [2] Here we have him certainly a priest, and we want to know after what manner he was elevated to the episcopal charge. The writer of the narrative, who is no other than St. Cyprian, tells us that " he was made a bishop " by many other bishops then at Rome, who subsequently sent abroad letters, in which they announced and attested his ordination. Cyprian's words are :—" He was made bishop by many of our colleagues, who were at that time in the city of Rome, who sent us letters of his ordination, honourable and praiseworthy, and distinguished by the evidence afforded of the fact announced." [3] Cornelius was ordained when he was made priest. He received a second application of the sacrament of orders when he was placed on the episcopal throne.

These two instances will be sufficient to prove to us that sacerdotal and episcopal orders were conferred at different times, and by ceremonies perfectly distinct. In what respect these ceremonies differed it is not easy to ascer-

---

[1] Reliq. Sacræ. No. 5, p. 1028, tom. iii. Curs. Compl. Patrol., series 1ma. Paris, 1844.

[2] Cypr. Ep. x. No. 8, p. 768, *ibid.*

[3] *Ibid.* p. 770.

tain from the documents of the time, as no specific picture of either of them is therein delineated. That priestly ordination was the work of one bishop, while episcopal ordination was conferred in the presence of more than one, we are justified in concluding from the letters of St. Cyprian, for whenever the election of a bishop is introduced, we are given to understand that several bishops attended. Indeed, this point is cleared up by a fact related of the priest Novatianus, in the sixth book of the ecclesiastical history of Eusebius. Novatian was a schismatic priest, who, to further his ambitious views, attempted to creep surreptitiously into the episcopacy. We may be perfectly convinced that, in the mode of ordination he concocted, he, for appearance sake, endeavoured to imitate the rite as administered by authority in the Church. What then did he do? Who did he get to ordain him bishop? Eusebius tells us, that " he decoyed three bishops, from the vilest part of the Church, shut them up to the tenth hour, and when they were feasted and full of wine, he forcibly compelled them, by a futile imposition of hands, to confer the episcopacy on himself."[1] Here we have an example of the episcopacy conferred by three—conferred by the imposition of hands—so conferred upon him who was already in sacerdotal orders.

Distinct as were the ceremonies by which the two grades of the priesthood were attained, they both agreed in one particular—they conferred grace. Like the imposition of hands of the apostolic Church, they poured a copious and permanent grace into the souls of their recipients. And it was in the virtue of this grace that priests and bishops alike consecrated the Eucharist, conferred the sacraments, absolved from sin, and preserved in the Church the succession of the ministry. Without this grace there would be neither priest nor bishop; but the rulers of the Church would be laymen, or perhaps assimilated to the unordained and powerless pastors whom heresy set over itself—to whom Cyprian refers in his treatise on "The Unity of

[1] Euseb. Hist., lib. vi. c. 43.

the Church." "These are they who of their own accord, without divine appointment, preside at foolhardy assemblies; who appoint themselves rulers without any law of ordination, who take to themselves the name of bishop where no one has given the episcopacy, whom, in the Book of Psalms, the Holy Spirit describes as sitting in the chair of scandal."[1] (Ps. i. 1.)

§ 7. *Matrimony.*—In speaking of matrimony in a previous part of this work, we admitted freely the obscurity of the Scripture references to this sacrament. Candour again compels us to admit that the allusions to marriage in the patristic writings of the third century are ineffectual to prove the sacramental nature of the ceremony by which it was contracted in the Christian Church of that period. Nevertheless there is much significance in what Tertullian says of marriage, especially if placed side by side with the Scripture testimonies referred to and quoted at length before. We saw that Christian marriage is indissoluble—that there is a sacredness in it which justifies the Apostle in comparing it to the spiritual union of Christ with his Church—that from the difficulties it involves and the duties it imposes, and from the economy of the Redeemer in granting sacramental help at the most critical periods of human life, it is only reasonable to suppose that a grace was communicated by it as a transitory contract, to abide between the married couple permanently and enable them to fulfil their obligations. This much we saw plainly; but we were at a loss to discover in the revealed and written Word a tangible reference to the ecclesiastical rite by which, according to divine institution, Christians entered upon that state. Tertullian, on this point, is more explicit than the Scriptures. He has three different passages that bear upon it, and he makes three different affirmations touching it, which prove to us beyond dispute that the contract of marriage took place in the Church, that a

[1] Cypr. de Unit. Eccles. No. x., p. 507, tom. iv. Curs. Compl. Patrol., series 1ma. Paris, 1844.

sacerdotal blessing accompanied it, and that for the further ratification of it, it was associated with the pomp of a most solemn religious observance. 1st. The private marriages of Christians are, according to him, profane and all but invalid. "Wherefore, with us, hidden alliances, that is, such as are not first professed at the Church [*non prius professæ apud ecclesiam*] run the risk of being judged the same as adultery or fornication."[1] Tertullian was a Montanist when this sentence was written. Nevertheless the usage to which he refers is reasonably presumed to be the discipline of the Catholic Church in reference to marriage, both from his mode of expression and from the fact that Montanism in this matter had no occasion to depart from the Catholic rite. He speaks still more clearly in his "Second Book to his Wife," a work which was certainly written while he was still among the rank of the orthodox. 2nd. Marriage was an ecclesiastical ceremony, and was blessed by some person in the Church. "How shall I describe the happiness of that marriage which the Church unites [*conciliat*], and the oblation confirms, and the benediction seals; the angels report it and the Father ratifies it."[2] This is plain enough. Marriage among Christians to be licit must be accompanied by sacrifice and a benediction. But what was this benediction? Who gave it? Tertullian, in his "Book of Prescriptions," gives us an obvious reason for concluding that it was administered by a priest or bishop of the Church. He is after affirming that "by the devil, whose office it is to subvert the truth, the very objects of the divine sacraments are rivalled by the mysterious rites of idols."[3] He goes on to say, "If I mistake not, Mithra [the devil] then signs his own soldiers in the forehead; also he celebrates the oblation of bread, and introduces a picture of the resurrection, and under the sword wins the crown [of martyrdom].

---

[1] Tertul. Lib. de Pudicitia, c. iv. p. 987, tom. ii. Curs. Compl. Patrol., series 1ma. Paris, 1844.
[2] Liber ii. ad Uxorem, c. xi. p. 1302, *ibid.*
[3] Liber de Præscr., c. xl. p. 544, *ibid.*

What do I say? He likewise appoints a supreme pontiff to marriages [*unius nuptus*]; he has his virgins, also his chaste ones."[1] The meaning of the passage is—Satan in all these observances imitates Christian rites. He has a high-priest to preside at the marriages of his children. Hence, as in this, he is imitative of Catholic usage—the Christian Church had a high-priest to preside at the marriage of Christians. And if the marriages of Christians were blessed, as he said before, the blessing was no doubt imparted by the presiding priest.

The Christian marriage of the third century was, then, undoubtedly a sacred ceremony. As, however, every sacred ceremony and public function of the Church is not a sacrament, it must be admitted that Tertullian does not give us "data" enough to decide the important question as to the immediate, the invisible, and the spiritual effect of this most important contract. The difficulty, then, still remains, so far as he is concerned—did the marriage contract infuse the grace of God into the souls of those who received it worthily? For the more satisfactory answer to this question we are thrown back upon the sacred Scripture in the first instance; and then we are naturally led to look into the period when traditionary writings become more abundant and more clear. There is light on both sides, which enables us to read the meaning of Tertullian. According to Scripture, marriage imposes the obligation of unchanging love and eternal fidelity. According to the belief of the eastern and western Churches from their separation, marriage is one of the sacraments. Tertullian is thrown in between both, and he tells us that marriage is a religious rite. We do not go beyond the limits of rational inference when we conclude that Tertullian and his contemporaries, in overtly proclaiming the religious nature of the ceremony, tacitly admitted its efficacy in maintaining religious practice and promoting it, which it did, by enabling the contracting parties to fulfil their most

---

[1] Tertul. Liber de Præscr., c. xl. p. 55a. Curs. Compl. Patrol. Paris, 1844.

onerous obligations, and which, again, is most effectually done by helping and enlightening them and sanctifying their souls by the infusion of sacramental grace.

DIVISION VI.

THE MARTYRS.

We are not without occasional references to the various branches of secondary worship, or the " cultus duliæ," as it is called, in the documents of the third age. We must not expect to find a complete picture; but hints and passing allusions will have much significance for us, if we keep in mind what we have gathered from the Scripture in the first part of this work, as illustrative of the primitive practice of venerating the saints and praying to them and reverencing their mementos and remains.

§ 1. *Respect rendered to their bodies.*—The martyrs, they who had died for the faith, were the saints of the third age. The reverence given to what remained of them upon earth, after their souls had passed to a blessed immortality, was respect to the relics of the saints. If they were venerated, the saints were venerated. Prayers addressed to them were prayers addressed to the saints. That the martyrs were regarded as crowned immediately after their demise is clear from many passages in the writings of Tertullian and St. Cyprian. 1st. All sins were remitted and all grace obtained by martyrdom. "For who when he has inquired does not draw near; who when he has approached does not wish to suffer, that he may acquire the full grace of God [*ut totam Dei gratiam redimat*], that from him he may obtain all pardon in exchange for blood [*compensatione sanguinis*] ? For to this work [martyrdom] all sins are remitted."[1] 2nd. Through martyrdom the society of angels was attained. "Wherefore from your letters have we seen those glorious triumphs of the martyrs, and with our eyes have in a manner beheld them arriving in heaven, and looked at them arrayed among the angels and heavenly powers and dominations."[2] 3rd. Martyrdom is the gate to eternal happiness. "But when one comes to the test of felicity, to the occurrence of the second baptism [martyrdom], to the very ascent of the divine abode, nothing is [more necessary] than patience."[3] 4th. Martyrdom leads at once to the vision of God. "Who will not labour with all his powers to attain to such glory, that he become the friend of God and immediately rejoice with Christ, and after the torments and punishments of this earth be put in possession of the rewards of heaven?"[4] These and innumerable passages which might be culled from the writings of this age, leave room for no doubt as to the effects attributed to the martyr's confession. Justification, perfect sanctification, and the rewards of eternal life, were all conferred on him together. He became at once a saint in the sense in which that term is now commonly used. It is consequently within the limits of strict truth to say that the respect shown to his body was illustrative of the devotion of the Church of the third century to the relics of the saints, while the honour rendered to his glorified soul may be taken as an evident proof that the faithful of these early times, as those of the present day, believed in the communion of the Churches triumphant and militant.

Any one acquainted with Catholic countries must be aware of the great respect and devotion of the faithful to

[1] Tertul. Apologet., p. 536A, tom. i. Curs. Compl. Patrol. Paris, 1844.
[2] S. Cypr., ep. xxvi. No. 11, p. 291B, tom. iv. *ibid*.
[3] Tertul. Liber de Patien., p. 1270A, tom. i. *ibid*.
[4] Cypr. Ep. ad Fortuna., p. 675, tom. iv. *ibid*.

dry bones and mutilated limbs and fragments of various sorts, which have fallen off the temples in which the now glorified soul dwelled while it was in this life. The old house is in ruins, but every joint and joining are preserved with religious care. The materials have crumbled into rubbish; and they would probably be allowed to remain in a state of utter confusion and neglect, but that Catholic faith remembers the saying of the Apostle, that they shall be built into a new and shining and imperishable edifice on the last day, to which the soul shall again return, never again to go forth. The relics of the saints are preserved and reverenced now. Those of the martyrs were reverenced and preserved in the Church of the third century. To allow the bodies of the martyrs to remain unburied was a crime in the opinion of St. Cyprian; to bury them religiously and carefully was an act of virtue that will be entitled to a supernatural reward. "And what is of the greatest importance, if the bodies of the martyrs and others be not buried, great danger threatens those on whom this work is incumbent. Wherefore, I am certain, that whichever of you shall have performed this work, on any occasion that may occur, will be regarded as a faithful servant, in such way, that having 'been faithful in small things, he shall be placed over ten cities.' "[1] If these words of St. Cyprian were written at the present day, would they be understood to inculcate more than decent and ordinary care for the obsequies of the Christian dead? Possibly, not much more; though the threat of Divine punishment and the hope of supernatural reward, might be justly regarded as rather strong inducements to hold out to the performance of such a duty; but spoken, as they were, during the reign of Roman paganism, when the practice of burning the bodies of the dead was in full force, they had a peculiar meaning. They were equivalent to this:—The bodies of the martyrs are not to remain in the hands of the executioners, lest they be profaned, left

[1] Cypr. ep. ii. p. 228, tom. iv. Curs. Compl. Patrol.: Paris, 1844.

unburied, or burned. But if they be valueless, why not allow the pagans to dispose of them as they wish? Cyprian does not answer this question explicitly; but, impliedly, he affirms, that they must be of much value in the Divine estimation, when he says, that they who bury them shall be rewarded by God, and they who, charged with their burial, neglect that duty, shall be exposed to the danger of being punished. But the expression of St. Cyprian's devotion to the bodies of the martyrs is not limited to this sentence. There is an epistle of his addressed to certain confessors detained in prison, which is full of the most feeling expressions of love and reverence towards their members, which, for Christ's sake, had suffered, or been the instruments through which their constant souls had affirmed their self-sacrificing fidelity. "What could happen to me more desirable or agreeable than to be with you, that you might embrace me with those hands which, pure, innocent, and adhering to the faith of the Lord, refused sacrilegious obsequiousness? What more pleasant and sublime than to kiss your mouth, which with glorious voice confessed the Lord; and present, to be looked upon by those eyes, which, despising the world, have been worthy to behold God. . . . . . Oh! happy prison, which your presence renders illustrious! Oh! happy prison, which sendeth men unto heaven! Oh! darkness brighter than the sun, and clearer than the light of this world, in which now are located your members—the temples of God, and to be sanctified by a Divine confession." [1] These are truly the words of a man that venerated the relics of the saints. The men to whom they are addressed had not yet suffered, it is true. They were confessors, and not yet martyrs; but if Cyprian entertained such tender and respectful sentiments towards their members, which had confessed Christ, what would be his reverence for these same members, when they had sealed this confession by their blood? He desired to look upon them, to touch them, to kiss them

---

[1] Div. Cypr. ep. lxxxi. No. 1, p. 424c, 425a, b, Curs. Compl. Patrol.: Paris, 1844.

when living; surely he would not refuse to place them in a rich shrine, or, as a pious author [1] says, "to wrap them up in silk and gold" when dead.

Cyprian, who had so warmly maintained the respect due to the bodies of the martyrs, experienced at the hands of the faithful the highest degree of honour they were capable of conferring, after he had laid down his life for the truth. His body, like those whose cause he pleaded so eloquently, was rescued from the pagan persecutors, and carried, amidst jubilation and pomp, to a Christian burying-ground, where it was deposited with the brethren who had departed this life in peace. His funeral is thus described in the proconsular acts of his martyrdom: "Thus suffered blessed Cyprian; and, to gratify the curiosity of the gentiles, his body was left in an adjoining place. Thence it was removed during the night, with wax-lights and torches, and carried with great joy and triumph to the fields of Macrobius Candidianus, the procurator, on the Mappalian way, near the fish-pond." [2]

With instances such as these before our eyes, we must, I think, acknowledge that the relics of the saints were valued, esteemed, and respected in the Christian Church of the third century. The various outward acts of affection and reverence rendered them, arose from one motive; viz., the sanctity and beatitude of the souls to which they had been attached, and with which they had operated. The respect then given them was spiritual, and the honour paid them was religious. Is this the "cultus reliquiarum," the veneration of relics, which the Church upholds at the present day? Unquestionably, it was very like it. But does it differ in intensity, if I may so speak? Not much, if at all; for there is scarcely any devotional practice of this kind now in vogue more profoundly expressive of veneration, than the triumphal solemnity with which the body of St. Cyprian was carried to the grave; nor do the usages

---

[1] Thomas à Kempis.

[2] Acta Proconsularia S. Cypr. s. v. p. 1505, tom. iii. Curs. Compl. Patrol.: Paris, 1844.

of reliquaries, shrines, ornaments of gold and precious stones, present us with more than a trifling development of the primitive custom of rescuing the bodies of the martyrs from the hands of the persecutors at great personal danger, and placing them in tombs distinct from the "columbaria," to which the ashes of the pagans were consigned.

§ 2. *Anniversaries of their Martyrdom.*—The reverence paid to the sainted dead of the primitive Church did not terminate with their obsequies. If their bodies were consigned with honour to the tomb, such portions of their relics as remained above the earth were preserved as holy deposits, to which the greatest value was attached. In the acts of the martyrdom of SS. Perpetua and Felicitas, we have a remarkable illustration of this truth. We read, there, that Saturus, when wounded and dying for the faith, gave to the soldier, Pudens, a trinket steeped in his blood, to be preserved as an heirloom and a memorial of his martyrdom. If we ask ourselves, why he did so, we cannot fail to discover in him a due appreciation of the value of a martyr's blood; and if we inquire whether he was singular or erroneous in so acting, we shall find a negative response in the matter-of-course way in which the circumstance is narrated, without comment, by the orthodox compiler of these very ancient acts. The event referred to is related as follows: "Then to Pudens, the soldier, 'Farewell,' he said, 'be mindful of my faith, and let not these things disturb but confirm you.' And at the same moment, he took a ring[1] from his finger, and dipping it in his wound, gave it back to him, leaving him both a heritage of his affection [hæreditatem pignoris] and a memorial of blood."[2]

Whatever may be said of such facts as the above, which

[1] The word in text is "ansulam;" it is "annulum" in the Cod. Salisbury.

[2] Passio. SS. MM. Perpet. et Felic. s. iv. p. 56A, tom. iii. Curs. Compl. Patrol.: Paris, 1844.

are simply suggestive of the disposition and feelings of the faithful of these ages, there is one practice, often referred to in contemporary ecclesiastical writers, which leaves us no room to doubt of the devotion of the Church to her saints. Their bodies were not forgotten, as far as we can judge; but certain it is, that their glorified souls were honoured by festivals and commemoration in the most solemn mysteries of religion. Their anniversaries were solemnly kept. The day on which they had fallen for the faith, which corresponded to the period of their new birth among the elect of God, was noted down, remembered, and celebrated annually. It was regarded as a matter of great importance to note the precise day on which they fell. Cyprian, who in various letters had affirmed that confessors who die during their imprisonment are to be regarded as martyrs, thus impresses upon his clergy the duty of keeping account of the day of their demise. "In fine, note down also the days of those who have departed;" and immediately he assigns the reason of this injunction,—" that we may be able to celebrate their commemoration among the memories of the martyrs."[1] Then he goes on to praise one of the brethren, who was punctual and diligent in keeping these accounts. "Though Tertullus, our most faithful and devoted brother, in accordance with the solicitude and care he imparts to the brethren in every obliging office, Tertullus (our most faithful and devoted brother), who in this respect is not wanting in the care of their bodies, has written, and writes and signifies to me the days on which our blessed brothers in prison depart by death to a glorious immortality;" the result of which was, that he, Cyprian, was able to celebrate their festivals in due order; "and by us here are celebrated oblations and sacrifices in their commemoration, which, with the Divine protection, we will celebrate soon with you." So spoke the illustrious Cyprian. Tertullian's doctrine on this subject is precisely similar, though con-

[1] Cypr. ep. xxxvii. No. 2, p. 328b, 329a, tom. iv. Curs. Compl. Patrol.: Paris, 1844.

veyed in fewer words. He makes distinct mention of the
annual commemoration, and of the oblation on the anniversary day. "We make," he says, "oblations for the
dead, for the birthdays on the anniversary."[1] From
these and similar passages it is quite evident that the
Church of Africa, in the third age, brought before the
minds of the faithful from time to time the virtues of the
martyrs and their rewards. We might conceive the object of the Church in so doing, to be either doctrinal or
devotional, or both. In other words, the Church might
propose to herself to instruct the faithful simply on such
occasions, by holding up for their contemplation the faith
and constancy of the martyrs; or her object might be to
honour the martyrs, by proclaiming their praises among
the faithful on earth; or both objects equally might have
given rise to these commemorations in the public offices
of religion. Any of these objects we might well conceive
to afford a reasonable foundation for such practices. But
before making up our minds as to which is the correct
one, we ought to weigh attentively the bearing of the
words, and the sense and meaning of the sentences in
which the commemorations in question are referred to
in the passages already cited. The martyrs were commemorated in the most solemn act of religion—sacrifice: "We
celebrate oblations and sacrifices in their commemoration,"
says Cyprian. If the object of the Church was simply to
propose their virtues to the imitation of the faithful, why
identify them with the most solemn act of religion? why
not rather preach their panegyric on the recurrence of
their festivals? Then, the mention of their names in the
liturgy of the Mass was not suited to represent their lives
and actions, unless in a very general way; and as the
liturgy is recited in a tone scarcely audible to the entire
congregation, the picture conveyed by it cannot be very
vivid; yet the martyrs' names were mentioned in the
liturgy, and sacrifice was offered in commemoration of

---

[1] Tertul. Liber de Corona, c. iii. p. 79B, tom. iii. Curs. Compl. Patrol.: Paris, 1844.

them; and not only this, but it would appear from the words of Tertullian, the faithful were thereby put in communication with them in the same way as with the ordinary dead, for whose repose the sacrifice was offered. Here, then, are circumstances in the commemoration of the martyrs, which would lead us to think that their virtues were honoured, and that they were honoured by the mention of their names and virtues; and that if the faithful, no doubt, were instructed in recalling their heroic deeds, they were moved in so doing to praise them, to venerate them, and perhaps to recommend themselves to their prayers. It will be scarcely deemed unreasonable, if we conclude, from such premises as these, that secondary worship, or the veneration of God's glorified servants, was an understood usage when scholars came from Numidia and Egypt to drink in knowledge in the schools of Carthage.

§ 3.—*Prayers to the Martyrs.*—The scope of this work will not allow us to allude to the more clear and interesting series of testimonies in favour of the practice of prayers to the saints in the primitive days of Christianity, as they do not fall within the period we have selected for the elucidation of Christian antiquity. I refer to the inscriptions which occur on the tombstones which mark the resting-places of the martyrs and other dead in the early Christian cemeteries. The wording of some of these is so clear, the sense is so unmistakable, that they leave no room for doubt or controversy. Many of these are the simple addresses of the surviving faithful to dear friends now deceased, requesting their prayers and influence in the kingdom of God. From these we are compelled to abstract, and from other interesting documents of a later period; and, as before, we must confine our view to the Church of Africa, and content ourselves with searching among fragments of letters and treatises for evidence of what Cyprian and his contemporaries believed and practised on this subject of prayers to the saints.

In this life, and before they had consumated the sacrifice, the prayers and merits of the martyrs were regarded

as of the greatest efficacy. "We believe," said Cyprian, "that the merits of the martyrs and the works of the just may have much influence with the Judge, when the day of judgment shall come, when, after the end of this life and world, his people shall stand before the tribunal of Christ."[1] And referring to the efficacy of their prayers for others in his book on "the Unity of the Church" he says—"He (God) can grant forgiveness; he can turn his sentence aside; he can mercifully pardon him who repenteth, worketh, asketh. He can accept of whatsoever the martyrs have demanded, or the priests have done for such."[2] No wonder if Cyprian, professing such principles as these, should warmly recommend himself to the prayers of the martyrs; and accordingly we find his epistles to the confessors in prison full of the most moving postulations for their intervention with that Master whom they served so heroically. In one of these, his fifty-seventh letter, he appears to recommend himself to the confessors even after their demise. He begs of them to remember him "always and everywhere." The passage is as follows:—
"Clearly as now your words in prayer are more efficacious, and your petition better suited to attain the object sought in the midst of trials, petition earnestly and ask that the Divine clemency may consummate the confession of us all, to the end that God may deliver us too in integrity and glory from this darkness and the snares of the world, in such way that, having been joined by the bond of charity and peace, and having stood together against the assaults of heretics and the persecution of the Gentiles, we may rejoice alike in the kingdom of heaven. I wish you, most blessed and beloved brethren, farewell in the Lord, and to remember me always and everywhere."[3] It would be scarcely fair to insist too much upon the concluding words; they may be fairly employed without any reference

---

[1] Cypr. Liber de Lapsis, No. 17, p. 480B, tom. iv. Curs. Compl. Patrol.: Paris, 1844.

[2] *Id.* Liber de Unitate Ecclesiæ, No. 36, p. 494, *ibid.*

[3] *Id.* ep. lxxvii. No. 7, p. 419, *ibid.*

to the next life. All that can be said of them is, that, if they be taken literally, they will apply to the whole period during which the soul of man exists. They will consequently include the period beyond the grave, and in this sense the words of Cyprian would involve a petition to the confessors, that they should remember him and pray for him, when crowned with the martyr's crown and standing before the throne of God.

Cyprian, if he be the author of the book "De Laude Martyrum," which appears among his writings, again approaches the subject of prayers to the martyrs, in a strain which sounds very like an address to the sainted dead. He begs of them to pray for him, "when God begins to honour martyrdom in their persons," which, with some probability, may be said to be when, in recompense for their sufferings, they are first admitted to the company of the blessed. His words are as follows:—"Wherefore, beloved brethren, though that be entirely (the work) of the Lord's promise and bounty, and though it be given from on high, nor be attained but by His power, and cannot be conceived by the mind, or expressed in words, or be revolved in prayer, or accomplished by any powers of eloquence; still this may be the work of your benevolence, as it will be of your charity and love, if you deign to be mindful of us when the Lord begins to honour martyrdom in you."¹ Again, we are forced to hesitate before we accept of Cyprian as an expounder of the doctrine of prayers to the saints, as it may perhaps be said that the Lord begins to honour martyrdom in His servants, not only when he confers its reward upon them in the next world, but when in this life He enables them by His grace to accept of the stroke of death for the faith.

The same form of expression occurs in his book "on the Dress of Virgins," where it appears to be susceptible of only one meaning. "Only remember me, when your virginity begins to be honoured."² Whatever may be said

¹ Liber de Laude Martyr. No. 30, p. 802, Curs. Compl. Patrol.: Paris, 1844.
² Liber de Habitu Virgin. No. 24, p. 464B, tom. iv. *ibid*.

of martyrdom, it cannot be believed that virginity "begins to be honoured" until it receives its reward in heaven. Therefore Cyprian here recommends himself to the prayers of the "spouses of Christ," not in their present but in their future state; not as in exile upon earth, but as crowned among the saints in heaven. He prays to them by anticipation, and he evidently implies that by their prayers before the throne of God, they may aid him in his difficulties and conflicts in this world. Here, then, is an overt address to the saints. Clearer still and more significant are the words with which he concludes his thirteenth epistle to Pope Cornelius. "Let us be mutually mindful of each other, in concord and unity. Let us everywhere and always pray for each other; let us by mutual charity lighten the pressures and difficulties (to which we are subjected); and if either of us by the celerity of the Divine mercy shall go before the other, let our love persevere before the Lord, and let not prayer for the brethren and sisters cease unto the mercy of the Father."[1] Some of the Protestant editors of the works of Cyprian, have raised a difficulty as to the interpretation of this passage, which it would be a loss of time to discuss. The sense is obvious. The doctrine of prayers to the saints is clearly floating on the surface.

Thus, being fully satisfied from the writings of St. Cyprian as to the prevalence of prayers to the saints in the African Church of the third century, we can afford to dispense with such facts as the annual commemoration of the martyrs, the inscriptions on the slabs which enclosed the bodies of the dead in the Christian cemeteries, the tradition on this subject expressed clearly enough in the apostolic time, and without the slightest ambiguity in the fourth and fifth centuries, all of which demonstrate beyond all controversy that prayers to God's glorified servants were a usage in all Christian times. Lest, however, it may be supposed that we are confined to one witness as

---

[1] Cypr. ep. xiii. ad Cor. No. 5, p. 887A, Curs. Compl. Patrol.; Paris, 1844.

to the practice of the African Church in this particular, where we seldom fail to find abundant materials for filling in the picture of the belief and practice of the people of God in these ages, we will conclude this subject with a few extracts from a letter of Celerinus, which is found among the letters of St. Cyprian. In this letter he beseeches Lucianus, to whom it is addressed, to pray for his sisters to the martyrs already crowned; he also demands of the martyrs that shall be first crowned, to obtain for them the remission of their sins, and Lucianus in his reply to this letter, where he grants the request of Celerinus, states that a distinguished martyr already deceased had given him authority to grant peace in his name to the first that should demand it after he should be called to immortality. The passage, or rather series of passages, will be best understood by quoting them at length. "Still you must know that I am in great tribulation, and as if you were present with me, I recall your former charity both day and night, God alone knows; and therefore I ask you that you yield to my desire and grieve with me on the death of my sister, who in this persecution has fallen from Christ. For she offered sacrifice, and excited the wrath of the Lord, which to me appears quite clear, for whose conduct I in this joyful time of Easter, weeping day and night, have spent my time, and spend it to the present, groaning in sack-cloth and ashes, until aid shall come from our Lord Jesus Christ and pity through you, or through those my lords who will have been crowned, or who have been crowned (coronati fuerint), whom you will ask to pardon the miserable transgression."[1] "Wherefore, I ask you, my lord, and beg of you through our Lord Jesus Christ, that you refer to the rest of your colleagues, your brethren, my masters, and demand of them, that which soever of you be crowned first, should remit this sin to those sisters of mine Numetria and Candida."[2] In his reply to this letter of

---

[1] Celerin, ad Lucian. ep. xx. inter Cyprian, No. 2, p. 276, tom. iv. Curs. Compl. Patrol.: Paris, 1844. [2] *Ibid.* No. 3, p. 277.

Celerinus, Lucianus has these remarkable words. "When the blessed martyr Paul was still in the body, he called me and said to me, 'Lucianus in the presence of Christ I say to you, if any one after my departure ask peace of you, give it in my name."[1] It cannot be denied that these passages have much significance, as regards the influence of the saints in the next world, while it must be admitted that they are not so outspoken on the subject of praying to them, as we would desire. However, as I said before, abundant light is shed on this subject by Cyprian, and by the voluminous writers of the fourth century.

DIVISION VII.

VENERATION OF THE CROSS, ETC.

If the Christians of the third century admitted and recognized a degree of blessedness in some material objects, they must have given them a certain amount of rational care and respect. It must be obvious to any one that both things must coexist. If, for instance, the Church of these remote times undertook, as it does now, to pour its benediction upon a statue, a rosary, or to sanctify a communion-cup or chalice for the use of the altar, it would be folly to suppose that she afterwards devoted them to profane or secular purposes. There are numberless modes of religious veneration, each differing in degree, that may be rendered to things which are regarded as holy, such as sovereign and supreme worship of mind and body to the Deity, then corporal prostration, genuflection, salutation in its various forms, reverent osculation ; and even contrectation, collocation in a certain place, separation from other objects, are all forms of respect, and may be made

---

[1] Lucian. ad Celer. inter Cyprian, No. 2, p. 280, tom. iv. Curs. Compl. Patrol.: Paris, 1844.

to embody the religious feelings of the mind in their tendency towards the sacred object. Suppose an object to be once sacred, and it must be venerated in some of the ways here assigned; if not, it may be at the same time appreciable and valueless, and while regarded as desirable, it may be treated with contempt.

Now, the Church of the third century, as she sanctified oil and water for certain purposes, must have given to them so sanctified a certain sort of religious respect. The Church, by her priests, did bless the water which was used in the administration of the sacrament of baptism. In a synodical letter, addressed by the fifth council of Carthage to Januarius and others, the following sentence occurs:—" Wherefore, it is meet that the water be first cleansed and sanctified by the priest, that it may, by its baptism, wash away the sins of the man that is baptized, &c."[1] And in reference to the blessing of oil, a more lengthy and clear exposition of the views of the synod occurs in the same epistle. " Who has been baptized must be anointed, to the end, that having received the chrism (that is, the unction), he may be the anointed of God, and have in him the grace of Christ. Now, it is a thanksgiving (eucharistia—a ceremony of thanksgiving) by which the baptized are anointed with oil sanctified on the altar. But they who have neither altar or Church, cannot sanctify the creature of oil. Consequently, there can be no spiritual unction among heretics, as it is clear that they cannot sanctify the oil and perform the ceremony of thanksgiving."[2] This council, the fifth of Carthage, was held in the year two hundred and fifty-five, and was presided over by St. Cyprian. The letter from which extracts have been given, is the genuine work of him, and of the other Fathers whose names are inscribed upon it. So we have it, that the African Church in the third century blessed, and thereby imparted blessedness to oil and

[1] Concil. Carthag. sub Cyprian. Quintum de Bap. Prim. No. 1, p. 1039A, tom. iii. Curs. Compl. Patrol.: Paris, 1844.
[2] *Ibid.* No. 2, p. 1040A.

water. This fact, surely, is significant as regards the doctrine of the veneration of holy things. For why is it that the "illuminati" of modern times do not venerate holy things? Simply because that they do not admit in them any blessedness "in se." According to their teaching, sanctifying grace is an imputation, something external, separated from the soul; how much more that inferior degree of holiness which the benediction of a consecrated minister can impart. All is external in the Protestant view; but such was not the doctrine of the council of Carthage. According to that council an aptitude to a certain end was imparted to oil and water by the sacerdotal benediction. Consequently, they were internally affected by such benediction. Therefore they were rendered holy "in se." If holy "in se," they were entitled to be regarded and treated as such. And as we must suppose that the faithful people and the enlightened prelates of the old African Church gave to all things their due, it is not too much to conclude that they gave to blessed water, and other similar things, about the same degree of respect that is rendered them to-day through the wide extent of the Catholic world.

The faithful of these days venerated the cross. The cross—a sign made in commemoration of the passion, contains no blessedness in itself. It is a simple representation of God's love, and of the wonderful events of the passion. Through the sensible cross the unseen sufferings of the God-man were reverenced; and by the use of it as a mark, a stamp upon material objects, or the human body, the strengthening and enlightening grace of the passion was invoked against the wiles and machinations of the devil. There was, consequently, a relative worship rendered to the cross in the third century of the Christian era. In Tertullian's second book to the Wife he alludes to the practice of signing with the cross the body and the bed of the Christian as a matter of course and indispensable usage. "Will you escape his (the pagan husband's) observation, when you sign your bed, your body .... when you rise at night to pray, and will you not rather seem to perform some magical operation?"[1]   And in his book on "the crown," he tells us plainly that the faithful used this sign at the commencement of all their principal actions. "At every walk and movement, at every ingress and egress, in putting on our shoes, at the bath, at table, at the light, in going to bed, in sitting down, whatever employment engages us, we mark our forehead with the sign of the cross."[2]

And so it appears that whole classes of religious practices which involved secondary religious worship and relative religious veneration, may have been as much in vogue in Tertullian's age as at the present day. The principle of them all, the very germ of them, is contained in the two cases here adduced from his writings. According to him, water and oil were blessed, and sanctified by the benediction. Then, on the same principle, salt and wax, houses, beads, cemeteries, medals, cords, vestments; in a word, all material objects destined to a sacred purpose, may have been then blessed and sanctified as they are now. And being so affected by the consecrating prayer of the Church, they would be entitled to respectful treatment at the hands of Christian believers. The cross was venerated, according to Tertullian. Then all the emblems of the passion of Christ, all the mementos of the sufferings of his martyrs, statues, pictures, and such objects which represented and brought to mind the sainted dead, may have been religiously preserved and respectfully venerated. So it must have been. On principle so it ought to be. So it is at the present day.

Conclusion.—We have traversed over the course that we proposed to ourselves at the beginning of this work, through smiling meadows sometimes on which the sun shone clearly, and anon through dark and rugged defiles. We have come to the end of our journey and surmounted

[1] Tertul. lib. ii. ad Uxor. c. v. p. 1296, tom. i. Curs. Compl. Patrol.: Paris, 1844.
[2] *Ibid.* tom. ii. Liber de Corona, c. iii. p. 80A.

the difficulties we have encountered, to our own satisfaction certainly, if not to the satisfaction of those who are outside the Catholic Church. In the investigation of history, all is not clear as day, nor could it be so, from the nature of the case; and if this be true of profane history, in its universal and detailed form, there is no reason why sacred history, grasping the operations of the mind of Europe and other continents for so many years, should be devoid of all difficulty. The period of sacred history which we have been reviewing ought to be about the least intelligible to the general reader, as the documents from which its events are supplied are less numerous than at other periods and more casual in their notices of discipline and faith. Through the three first centuries of the Christian era, we have, however, travelled without meeting any serious difficulty to us as Christian believers.

The difficulties of ecclesiastical history must depend, in degree, on the stand that is taken by the observer, and the point from which they are viewed. If a man is anxious to be a doubter, he will find there some points, be they the theories of individuals or the acts of communities, to which he may cling. If a man is involved in a system of religion which tutors him into scepticism, the common sense conclusions and the large facts which are fairly shown in every century since the age of Christ, will be for him involved in a mist. We know well that for those who stand within the Catholic Church all history is but a demonstration of what they have believed from their childhood.

I have been a young child, in whom all the faculties were asleep. Whim and fancy were to me what reason ought to be for those whose intellects have been fully developed. Young I was, and a child in taste and feelings —a Catholic child it is true, into whose soul faith had been infused by baptism—an infant Catholic believer without a demonstration of my religion, or a knowledge of what I believed. I was, in fact, a Catholic without knowing it. I grew up and went out to school, and was taken to the Sunday mass; and finding that there were other schools, where boys of a different religious denomination were sent, and other edifices than mine in which they assembled to worship God, I began to know and feel that I was a Catholic. "What is a Catholic?" I asked in the eagerness of boyish curiosity. "Oh," answered the others, as young as myself, "it is something that makes one better than these others, who are black, black Protestants." But the old ones shook their heads and said: "Boy! to be a Catholic in this country is to be a descendant of the robbed, the injured, the oppressed, the despoiled, the martyred." I went on to school and I was a prejudiced Catholic, ready to fight a hard battle for my religion, because I had heard that it was treated unfairly, and I saw with my eyes that it was sneered at by boys that I looked on as not one whit better than myself.

The conviction that I had hitherto of the truth of my religion was, in its essence, the work of God, and the fruit of the "habit" of faith that had been infused into my soul by baptism. So, at least, I will suppose for the present; but in its externation, so far as I was able to manifest it, it was little better than a prejudice, though involving a profound demonstration. If any one then asked me, why was I a Catholic, I would answer, perhaps, that my parents were so, and that I hated Protestants because they had invaded the country and robbed the people; so I might have said, little knowing the grace that God had given me, and that the people need not have been robbed and murdered, if they only renounced their faith, and that martyrdom, to a large extent, is not to be found outside the true Church.

A light streamed in upon my young intellect some time after, in which I saw many things connected with my religion, which substituted the reasons of the youth for the cuffs and abuse of the boy. First, I began to learn the catechism of my religion, then to read history from a better source, but one which could not dissemble its great facts; finally, to hear sermons and lectures in which Catholicity was explained and defended. The catechism said that the Church was perpetual and visible, and one, and holy, and catholic, and apostolical. Though I tired of learning the catechism, I respected its authority, and I believe that the Church must be as it said. On the one hand, I had a great everlasting Church from the catechism; on the other hand, history gave me Henry VIII. and Elizabeth, Luther and John Knox, the plantation of Ireland, and the expulsion of the Huguenots from France. I would not have been able to connect them to make an argument, and I was not. But my teachers in the Church were; and they compared for me the church of my catechism, and the church of the Protestant historian. Here was an argument truly calculated to win the heart of an Irish boy, sharp-witted and logical without knowing it. Christ and his Apostles first; then Martin Luther and his co-ordinate teachers: the old Church of my country and of England before the Reformation; then the Church of the Reformation, stiff and new, and unheard of hitherto: England changing her faith; Ireland adhering to the tradition: meanwhile the majority, the great body of Christian believers forming one great Church from the beginning—the catholic, the perpetual, the visible, the holy, the apostolical. I was a Catholic from deep conviction before leaving school; and since then how many events have contributed to enliven and strengthen my faith?

Books, and travelling, and experience must be for the matured intellect the sources of knowledge; and for the Catholic now grown to man's estate and capable of forming a solid judgment of things, it would appear that books, and travel, and experience coalesce into an irresistible argument in favour of his religion. So, at least, has it been with me. I have discovered in the religious political transactions outside Catholicity—expediency unmasked on the one hand, and on the other a determination to hold its own at any cost; and both have been for me an argument of the simple secularity of Christian religions that are not Catholic. England is an example of the first —Sweden, of the latter. Who can pretend that the Protestant religion in England is not, at least in principle, a creation of the state, after events that have occurred in our own time; and if the creation of the state, undoubtedly the creature of the state, to carry out her secular views? And in Sweden, or such a country, which is the other form of Protestantism as a state religion, I think it cannot be denied, that the laws which prohibit, under penalties, the aggregation of Protestants to another religion, evince its entire secularity, seeing that the programme of Protestantism is free discussion and free choice. Still more, the arguments which we commonly read as in favour of Protestantism, not so much among divines as secular writers, who undertake to defend the "great principle of the Reformation," have given me at least a strong suspicion, that in the minds of the profound thinkers of its schools it is a grand scheme of secularism. What are the arguments of these men? What does the *Times*—what do so many illustrious writers say? Progress—Protestantism is the foundation of progress. Progress, no doubt, is well enough. There is nothing to prevent a Catholic from progressing. He can wash himself, and put his house in order, and gird his loins. He can spin if he wish; and, if his taste so incline him, he can dig drains and erect fences. He can be the elegant man of the world, and the high courteous man of breeding. What is in his religion to prevent him from being a good member of a borough corporation, or a sound legislator? With all this, progress is the argument of Protestantism, and, as such, it squeezes the religious element out of it entirely. It is all absorbing. Progress, they say, is unlimited. Riches can be increased, comforts can be multiplied. All classes are to be educated thoroughly, in order that they may progress to riches and independence. The loom by day—speculation on its improvement in the evening. The desk and the counting-house in winter, all through without cessation—travelling in summer, with a knapsack full of books and a note-book. What about God? He comes in after: progress first: instead of having God first, and all progress, as everything else, directed to Him, with a view to the furtherance of His greatest precept—His love and the love of His rational creatures. But, some one will say, we advocate

progress as a means of alleviating the evils of humanity
and of rendering men better Christians, by removing the
vices to which poverty gives rise? In this advocacy of
progress I must unhesitatingly concur; but it is only an
individual advocacy, it is not the Protestant view. In the
general view, religion and progress are the measure of each
other. Progress is the standard of the truth of religion. So
they argue: The inhabitants of the Vallais (Switzerland) are
dirty, poor, and afflicted with the goitre: therefore they
are superstitious, morally degraded, and in error. Again,
Dutch men and women are thrifty, frugal, scrupulously
clean and orderly, industrious and rich. See the effects of
the truth which shone upon them at the Reformation.
Disguise it as you will, this is the argument. It secu-
larizes religion. God says, " mourning" the portion of
his disciples,—" Blessed are the poor of spirit,"—" You
shall lament and weep,"—" Love not the world,"—"Take
up your cross,"—" Renounce all that you possess,"—" Use
this world as if you used it not." Protestantism says true
faith is to be found in the houses of those who fair dain-
tily. There can be no true faith among those who, from
their condition, are necessitated to practice such doctrines
as these. Yet, in the eyes of God, what, for instance, do
the goitred peasants of the Drantz, or the idiotic-looking
pigmies of Sion (Vallais) want, to render them the realization of the Gospel picture of abnegation, but the internal
spirit (which they have), to sanctify their tribulations and
trials, and to render their sufferings meritorious. God is no
lover of good houses and fine clothes—He is a lover of virtue.
Progress in the arts and sciences is not His criterion of the
merit of the Christian soul, but progress in humility,
patience, self-denial, meekness, mortification. The argument in favour of Protestantism from progress is, in
theory, the secularization of religion, while, in fact and
deed, this same theory, applied to daily life, has removed
the masses of the Protestant population from the service
of God, and transferred them to " Mammon," the prince
of this world.

There are other experiences that are in my mind still

stronger in argument against the possible truth of Protestantism. Here, in Ireland, I find Protestantism consistent and orderly; for instance, in a given country town, where there is only one form of Protestantism, all appears to go on smoothly, the clergymen visiting their flocks from morning to night, and making superhuman efforts—efforts stamped with profound prudence and great talents—to make converts, the flocks united and happy, irreproachable in domestic matters, honourable in business transactions—no scandals, as far as I can see. But fortunately, or unfortunately, my experience of Protestantism is not limited to its aspect in the country town referred to. I have seen it in the city, and out on the highway of the world divided against itself. " No house divided against itself can stand." But how divided? On indifferent and unimportant points? No; but on the nature of the Son of God, on the necessity of baptism for salvation, on the ordination of its clergy, on the mission of its clergy. I find some great lights holding that salvation is attainable in the "Church of Rome;" others say that its promises are confined to all, who, from the "common protest against Rome," are classed under the general name Protestants. Must there not be sects of Protestants, and numberless individuals within sects, who, from the nature of the case, confine the promises of salvation to themselves? Then there is Protestantism divided in worship, divided in government, divided into as many specific "beliefs" as there are sects if not rather as many as there are individuals. Now, did I want to become a Protestant, where should I go? I am quite at home in Catholicity wherever I go. While opinions on undefined points may differ among Catholics, faith and practice are everywhere the same; the same churches, with the rites administered in them—namely, seven sacraments and a sacrifice; the same form of government—viz., the episcopal; the same devotion everywhere. If I leave this fold of unity, where I am free from personal responsibility, whither shall I go? To Irish Protestantism? Very well. But who agrees with me and vouches for the prudence of my choice? Do the high churchmen of England? Undoubtedly no; they are Puseyites, half Catholics, or at least they differ from Irish Protestants in their respect for Church authority. Oh! then shall I select the French Calvinists? If I do, I am deprived of episcopal government. Shall I go to the Kirk of Scotland? Lower in the scale—not even the pretence of ordination. But it is useless to follow the matter farther. The experience of the broad view of Protestantism is, man doubting of everything, until at length he doubts of the Scriptures, and sinks into the immoral cesspool of Mormonism, where he corrupts and rots away like everything around him, and falls asunder, a putrid mass of incredulity and sensuality combined.

Experiences of Protestantism and Catholicity are strong arguments for the Catholic, but none of them stronger than the absolute knowledge the Catholic has of the perfect spirituality of his religion and the matured sanctity it is capable of imparting. There are two sanctities,—*scil.*, sanctity of manners before the world, and sanctity of the soul before God. They may co-exist. They ought to co-exist. There cannot be perfect internal sanctity without external sanctity of manners. External sanctity includes the avoidance of such faults as cursing, lying, which give a bad name to the Christian. It is, in fact, external Christian propriety. Internal sanctity is the perfect purifying the affections, the absolute subjection of the rebellious passions, the possession of charity in both its branches. Though sanctity internal and external ought to be found together in the true Christian's life, yet the former is the more spiritual. Education and training may form a habit of external sanctity before the world, where there is not a particle of the internal spirit. Bad manners and bad training may leave behind them traces of external habits of vice, even when the soul has gone far in the attainment of internal sanctity. The experience of the internal sanctity of Catholics is striking, and to those who have seen it better than any proof. Are not Protestants sanctified as far as your experience goes, some one will say. There is much external propriety of manners among them;

first, among the respectable and rich, because they are the hereditary possessors of refinement and elegance; secondly, among the poor; they will not tell lies, nor will many of their women curse, because they have been watched over at school by the refined ladies of their church, and they have been taught from their childhood to be respectable. Of their internal sanctity I say nothing. I admit that I could say something comparatively, but I forbear. But of the internal and external sanctity of many Catholics, of the internal holiness of some, accompanied with some external faults, which they know do not exceed venial sin, of the perfect realization of all that is most difficult in the Gospel precepts and advices in the lives of numberless members of the Catholic faith, every one that has lived among them is aware from experience. The unspotted heart is there, on which the hot breath of sensuality has never blown—pure as it came from the hand of God, almost as if it had been nurtured among angelic choirs. The suffering and the afflicted soul is there, that has never tasted earthly comfort; there it is, rejoicing right through life from beginning to end, "at being accounted worthy to suffer for the name of Jesus." The poor labouring body is there "lifting up pure hands" every day to the Father of lights, and living on in patience, sustained by a filial confidence in Providence, which is positively incomprehensible in the natural view.

The experience of Catholicity is of chastity unspotted, of abnegation, of patience, of charity inflamed and burning, of earth undervalued, and of heaven esteemed; in a word, of all that is superhuman in the Gospel realized daily, and hourly, and naturally. What are the little portraits of holiness afforded by other sects to the Catholic? They are mere resemblances to his view; if they have blood, and life, and a soul, he sees it not; but he sees among his own co-religionists the genuine portraits and the original. Original in what?—in sanctity, gospel sanctity, sublime sanctity, unearthly sanctity, sanctity which could be born in true faith only, and which could not live and grow but by the constant operation of Divine grace.

But, on this subject of truth and error, history says still more than experience, and speaks out more clearly. History, for the last eighteen hundred years, has been the narrative of the struggles of the "one" with the many. This is undeniable. I find at the present day within the domain of Christianity one institution, that is the butt for the sarcasm and ridicule of all others, whose name is a war-cry, and a rallying word for sects that are otherwise in hostility to each other. The one and the many exist at the present day; singular! they existed always. In the early ages of the Church, certain Christians went out and combined revealed principles with the philosophical "dicta," and formed a new religion." Not one, but many did so. "Their name was legion." No matter what they called themselves—Montanists, Marcionites, Valentinians, Sabellians, Manachees, Gnostics. There were besides, in these days, congregations of religionists that were half Jews and half Christians, numerous like the others—Ebionites, Necolaites, Cerinthians. Differing in a thousand things from each other, they individually protested that they were the depositaries of truth. All the time there was one institution which stood aloof from them all, which they alternately feared and warred against, which condemned them all and which they all condemned. They all died out one by one from pure inanition; but the age which succeeded their demise, presented the phenomenon of the one and the many in an equally defined picture. No one will now say: even at the time no one of intelligence would have said, that there was not in the fourth and fifth centuries one institution distinguishable from Arians, Semiarians, Donatists, Macedonians, Pelagians, Nestorians, Eutychians, Semipelagians. What was the history of all these sects? Was it not their struggles with the one? Their bishops, such as they had them, were different from the bishops of the institution they all opposed: they worshipped in their respective conventicles. It is most remarkable—the authority assumed by the one over them all at this time, though they were numerically most formidable opponents. The general councils of these centuries were their official reprobation by the solitary institution that stood out from them all in its imposing independence. As it was in these early ages, so it was all through. There was a beacon always shining, to which right-thinking minds and pure hearts could always turn from the decoying tempters that abounded.

The fall of the Roman empire left the one in possession of the field. What remained of the old opponents were pushed away into obscure localities, where they lingered on for a few years, and at length died out, like everything purely human. The oneness of Christianity was, however, equally manifested in the days of her triumph, as in the centuries of her tears and persecutions. Gothic and Vandal nations, too unintellectual to give many opponents to Christianity, simple, without pride, believing what the world believed, rallied around the one institution of their choice with all the affection of children. But though Christianity might be said to be in peace, there was through the ages between the fall of Rome and the rise of modern Europe always enough of opposition to try her stability, and to prove her thorough independence. First came the controversy of the "three chapters;" then the Monothelites; then the Iconoclasts. And all this time there was brewing in the East, a rebellious spirit, which burst out into formal heresy and schism in the ninth century. Nothing, perhaps, in all history showed forth the oneness of Christianity in a clearer form than this same Greek schism. It did not want to have anything to do with the dreams of the early pagan heretics or the Judaizers, nor was it rebellious on such points as predestination—free will—the Divinity, and nature of the Son of God, like the heretics of the fifth and sixth centuries—it listened with child-like docility to all the doctrines of the Church, with a few exceptions. It did so then. It does so still. One sacrifice, seven sacraments, devotion to the saints, prayers for the dead, ordination, consecrations, "the sacramentalia," were and are as much Greek as Roman doctrine. Yet the utter oneness of the old Christianity! it stood out from the Greeks, agreeing with it in everything almost. No compromise here—one point of difference is foundation for eternal separation.

Read the history of the middle ages attentively, and peer into the old books that are falling to decay on the shelves of your library, and you will conclude with me that strong and clear intellects maintained the oneness of Christianity during these times, though perhaps their ideas found their way to life in language by no means Attic. The one at peace in the middle age showed herself in contrast to possible heresy, by being the censor of theological opinions, by criticising the teachings of the schools, by teaching herself decretorially, definitively, and by being always looked up to as the guardian and preserver of truth.

It could not, then, be reasonably expected that the Catholic would look upon the controversies of modern times as between two or more parties possessing equal claims to identification with the doctrines of primitive Christianity. The old times of a general intellectual movement had given many opponents to Christianity. It was but the old story revived, when the intellectual progress, incipient in the twelfth century and mature after the invention of printing and the diffusion of books in the sixteenth century, gave the Hussites and Wickliffites, Albigenses, Lutherans; Calvinists, and a host of others, as the enemies of his creed and Church. Here were "the one" and the many arrayed against each other in as imposing a manner as when Irenæus wrote in Lyons or the council sat at Ephesus. So it reads to me. Some one says—if by "the one" you mean Catholicity, "the one" had changed? it was not the institution that existed in primitive times. Where—when had it changed? I can't discover in history. It has not changed since the Reformation. An objector says, it has, by introducing the doctrine of the Immaculate Conception. Any one, however, who wishes to see and who has eyes to see, cannot deny that the definition of the immaculate conception is but an application in a particular case, of a doctrine firmly maintained at the Reformation, namely, the power and infallibility of the Church in explaining and evolving revelation. Catholicity has not substantially changed since the Reformation. Oh! the opponent says, the change was before the Reformation. Again, I ask,—where—when? Surely not since the Greek schism, in 869? Though some of the Greeks came to terms with the Occidentals in the council of Florence, it is historically true that the Orientals, as a body, adhered to the religious principles, with a few exceptions, in which they found themselves at the time of their separation. They did not borrow any article of faith from the Latins. They hated the Latins all through; yet, after a period of ten centuries since their separation from the Latins, their faith, with one or two exceptions, is the same as that of the Latins. Let us suppose the Latins changed their faith on various important articles—purgatory, sacrifice, ordination—within the period referred to, then the Greeks must have done the same. But would the Greeks during this time have followed the example of the Latins? On the contrary, is it not natural to suppose, that being in a position of hostility to the Latin Church, they would have been delighted to cry up, through Europe and Asia, the apostasy of the Latins in the hypothesis that the Latins had erred? It is simply absurd, then, to suppose that the Catholicity of the sixteenth century was not substantially the same as the Catholicity of the ninth century. My opponent will say again, even though I was to grant that the Catholic Church has not substantially changed since the ninth century, a period may be assigned between this and the primitive days, in which errors were introduced, and the faith of the Apostles lost. So say Protestant writers; but, so far as I am concerned, I must say, I can discover no foundation for the assertion in the ecclesiastical history of the times. I can fancy how a Protestant, seeing that all things human are changing, and believing Catholity to be a humanly-supported institution, may take it for granted that Catholicity must have substantially changed during so long a period as ten centuries. But such a Protestant must be reasonable and logical. If there was a change in Catholicity, there would be some evidence of it in the historical documents of these times. There is no such evidence, but the contrary. The position of the papacy was consolidated since the age of Constantine, and from this time until the age of the Greek schism the popes were jealously watching the faith and discipline of the Church. A change could not have taken place in either; and, *de facto*, no change was attempted without exciting the most angry disputes, and the most protracted controversies. This is not all. There were writers in the fourth and fifth and sixth centuries, learned and voluminous writers, that touched upon every point of morals and discipline, and elucidated every point of faith. They were orthodox writers—the fathers—believed to be such, admitted to be the defenders of the "one" against the many. Their works remain. You can open and read for yourself. The doctrine of the fathers of the fifth and sixth centuries you will find to be the same as the doctrine of the Church at the time of the Greek schism; that is to say, if you read them without prejudice. You will find some difficulties in the mode of expression now and then. But take them all together, and form your judgment of the doctrine of the Church in these centuries on the broad basis of the patristic writers as a body. Take a large, many-sided view of their works, and you cannot fail to come to the conclusion, that the faith and discipline of the ninth century were the faith and discipline of the third.

Now the faith of the third century was the faith of the first, if we have fairly represented both periods in the extracts we have made in the course of this work. The faith of Paul was the faith of Cyprian. The faith of the old Church of Africa was identical with that of the primitive Church, founded in Judea by the Redeemer. So we are led back by a line of witnesses, posted up through time to the source of truth; and there we discover our predecessors in the faith, grouped about the same altars as ourselves, and imbibing from the same spiritual fountains similar vivifying draughts to those which are vouchsafed the faithful through the sacramental symbols, in our own day.

Wonderful identity of the Church of God! Wonderful vitality! Sublime and admirable continuity! Every one thought in primitive times that the empire would bury the Church. The Church was in the bloom of youth, when the empire was convulsed, tottered, and collapsed, and she stood over the ruins soliloquizing on the fall of human greatness and the decadence of all that is earthly. Nor can the second civilization effect what the first civilization attempted in vain; for the Church which saw beauty arise out of chaos, and return to chaos again—and learning, in every variety of hostile theory, refute itself and die—and statesmen as proud in ancient times as in modern, and intellects as recusant and tongues as flippant in blasphemy—the Church which saw everything, and encountered everything, and which, because she preserves her traditions, remembers everything, is prepared for every crisis—nothing can be new to her—the honeyed accents of the seducer, and the ribald tongue of the reviler, and the uplifted arm of the persecutor; if she went into the catacombs again, it would be to come out in triumphant possession, for the yearnings of the world are towards her; and the human race—accustomed for so many centuries to see faith unbending and uncompromising — could not live in the religious anarchy which—sad and extended as it now is—must deluge the whole earth, if the Catholic Church—the mainstay of spiritual consistency—were removed for one year from the scene.

APPENDICES.

A.

In various passages of the Epistles of St. Paul and the "Acts" we are enabled to obtain a glance at the religious meetings of the early Christians. The faithful, we are told (Acts xx. 7), asembled together on the first day of the week in the upper chamber of the house of one of the most independent members of the congregation. The Christians were for the most part poor. They had not erected edifices for divine worship; in fact, to build churches then, would be a source of additional danger, probably a signal for persecution to a jealous Pagan world. In Jewish edifices the upper chamber was the most honourable (1 Kings ix. 25); it was the most secure; and there are grounds for believing that the room in which the faithful assembled was reserved for their meetings exclusively, for in it there was an altar (Heb. xiii. 10). Here let us view the congregation assembled: there is much piety in its aspect, the women modestly covering their heads "because of the angels" (1 Cor. ix), the rich and poor seated together without any distinction of rank (James i. 11). The body of the Lord and the chalice of his blood are distributed from the altar to the members of the congregation, by the Apostle or presbyter who presides (1 Cor. xi. 20 and following, 1 Cor. x. 21). They who have received miraculous gifts use them for the edification of the faithful (1 Cor. xiv. 34). An instruction is given (Epistles to Tim. and Tit.); and all is associated with the sweet singing of hymns and the light of many tapers (Acts xx. 8).

B.

Many other questions regarding the "episcopi" and "presbyteri" of the primitive Church would form useful subjects for discussion in a history such as this; and among them a first place ought to be given to the question of celibacy.

Not a few Protestant writers imagine that they can clearly prove from the Scriptures that the bishops and priests of the apostolic Church were married men, and that they did not observe celibacy even after their election to the priesthood. We cannot undertake to decide peremptorily the controversy on this head, as there does not appear to be sufficient "data" for so doing in the books of the New Testament. St. Paul, in his Epistle to Timothy (1 Tim. iii.), pointing to the characteristics necessary in the candidate for the priesthood, says that he must be a man "of one wife;" and he recommends his disciples to examine if such candidate "has brought up his children well and governed well his own household." On a cursory glance at these directions, we might be disposed to conclude that celibacy was not practised by the clergy of the first century. On a close and sober examination of them, however, it must appear that St. Paul could not be expected to speak otherwise, even though sacerdotal celibacy was a divine institution. He could not prudently recommend the selection of priests from among the young and unmarried converts, whose virtue could not have been yet proved; nor would it be wise to set up as the lights of the Christian flocks old unmarried men, who, in that wicked Pagan world, had abstained from matrimonial engagements possibly to give looser reins to their passions; men who, in most instances, had been steeped the more deeply in iniquity in proportion as they advanced in years. St. Paul's advice to Timothy is merely a prudential counsel to select grave, settled, serious men for the office of the priesthood, men whose virtue had been proved by their works, men whose aptitude to preside over the faithful had been evinced by their discretion in governing their own families and managing the affairs of their households. Besides, the Apostle obviously refers to the qualities to be looked for in the candidates before their ordination, and he makes no allusion to the course to be pursued by them in regard to marriage or celibacy subsequent to that event.

If the Apostles were married men, or if the bishops appointed by them were married, it must appear curious that there is no mention of their wives in the sacred Scripture. I am aware that there is a passage in the First Epistle to the Corinthians which is believed by some to decide the question. The passage is as follows :—" Have we not power to carry about a woman [γυναικα], a sister, as well as therest of the Apostles, and the brethren of the Lord, and Cephas?" (1 Cor. ix. 5). These words of St. Paul would prove that the Apostles were, after their ordination, in the married state, if the word γυναικα necessarily meant in scriptural language " a wife." The literal meaning of the word, however, is " a woman;" and in this sense it is often used in the writings of the New Testament. A candid critic, therefore, who cannot deny that such *may* be the meaning of the word here, and who, in fact, must admit that there is in the context a reason for limiting it to this sense, as the word " sister " is used to qualify it, is forced to the conclusion that no decretorial argument in favour of the marriage of priests can be founded on the passage, especially with the fact before him, of which no scriptural critic can be ignorant, namely, that " women " were accustomed to follow our Lord and the twelve Apostles in their journeys (Luke viii. 3), pious and generally married women, to supply their wants, and " to minister unto Him of their substance."

There are no reasons of moment in favour of the marriage of priests to be found in the Gospels, or the Epistles of St. Paul. We may plausibly infer that they were not married, or, at least, that they observed celibacy after their ordination, from the doctrine of the Apostle of the Gentiles in the 8th chapter of his First Epistle to the Corinthians. Virginity is there counselled, and by an inspired writer, who, as he himself says, has "obtained mercy of the Lord, that he may be faithful"—*scil.*, in giving this counsel,—it is recommended as a more perfect state than that of marriage. Who are to be believed to have embraced it if not they who, from their position as pastors and teachers of the flock, as well by example as by word of mouth, were expected to exhibit in their lives pictures of religious perfection? However this may be, the doctrine of the Apostle is well worth considering here. "It is good for a man," says St. Paul, "not to touch a woman" (1 Cor. vii. 1); and a little further on, "But I say to the unmarried and to the widows: it is good for them if they so continue, even as I" (verse 8). Explaining himself somewhat more plainly, he adds, "Now, concerning virgins, I have no commandment of the Lord; but I give counsel as having obtained mercy of the Lord to be faithful. I think, therefore, that it is good for the present necessity, that it is good for a man so to be" (verses 25 and 26). As the groundwork of the foregoing advice, he subjoins: "He that is without a wife is solicitous for the things that belong to the Lord, how he may please God. But he that is with a wife is solicitous for the things of the world, how he may please his wife, and he is divided. And the unmarried woman and the virgin thinketh on the things of the Lord, that she may be holy in body and spirit" (verses 32, 33, 34). He concludes in the following terms:—"He that giveth his virgin in marriage doeth well, and he that giveth her not doeth better" (verse 38).

It must not be supposed for a moment that St. Paul penned down the sentences quoted above without authority from his Divine Master. Every word of them was written advisedly and under the influence of divine inspiration. The Apostle admits that he has received no *precept* regarding virgins from the Lord; but he has received from Him the grace to be faithful in giving them a *counsel*. In reality the advice or counsel here given by St. Paul is but a repetition of that which is involved in the words of the Redeemer, quoted in the 19th chapter of the Gospel according to St. Matthew (Matt. xix. 12).

Supposing such a sublime counsel to be Gospel law, I repeat that it is difficult to bring oneself to believe that it was not observed by the austere, mortified, and heavenly-guided men to whom the ministry of preaching the Gospel was first committed.

C.

We ought not, perhaps, to leave the apostolic Church without bringing before our readers a few more of its customs and usages. We will, therefore, briefly indicate some further points of similarity between the "Church of Rome" and the Church of SS. Peter and Paul.

Fasting.—Fasting was practised in the Church after the ascension of our divine Redeemer. Whether it was an occasional or a periodical usage we cannot say on scriptural authority; but that it was soon to come into use among His disciples we are assured on the word of our Saviour. " But the Pharisees and scribes murmured, saying to his disciples: Why do you eat and drink with publicans and sinners? . . . . And they said to Him: Why do the disciples of John fast often and make prayers, and the disciples of the Pharisees in like manner; but thine eat and drink? To whom he said: *Can you make the children of the bridegroom fast whilst the bridegroom is with them?* But the days will come when the bridegroom shall be taken away from them, *then shall they fast in those days*" (Luke v. 30, 33, 34, 35).

Perpetual vows of chastity.—There is in the First Epistle to Timothy a short sentence, the meaning of which, it appears, can be culled only from comparing it with the context. It is as follows:—" But the younger widows avoid. For when they have grown wanton in Christ, they will marry; having damnation, because they have made void their first faith" (1 Tim. v. 11, 12). If we may transform this sentence, its latter clause would be fairly represented thus:— These young widows, in getting married, will violate " their first faith;" in violating their first faith they will incur damnation. What is their "first faith," the violation of which is visited with such an awful penalty? Evidently, it is their faith or fidelity to Christ. It is not her faith or fidelity to her first husband, for in her state of widowhood she is released from all obligations to him. If it be her faith to Christ, she must be espoused to Him in a special manner, for, in ordinary circumstances, a widow is free to get married a second time without incurring the guilt of sin. Now, what can be this special espousal to Christ? I think, after reflecting ever so long and deeply on the question, we must come to the conclusion that it can be no other than devoting herself to his service by a vow of perpetual chastity.

Religious poverty.—The "religious state," as it is called, which is at present so widely propagated through the Christian world, appears to have been foreshadowed in the discipline observed by the primitive disciples in Jerusalem. These latter were occupied in the offices of prayer and charity, and were maintained by the goods of each put into a common stock. The Scripture says of them, "And all they that believed were together, and had all things common. Their possessions and goods they sold, and divided them to all according as every one had need. And continuing daily with one accord in the temple, and breaking bread from house to house, they took their meat with gladness and simplicity of heart: praising God, and having favour with all the people" (Acts ii. 44, 45, 46, 47).

The "religious state," as it now exists, accords to a certain extent with this picture; and if we adjoin to the practice of individual poverty therein delineated the vow of chastity elsewhere alluded to by St. Paul, we may see in the primitive Church a state or condition of life analogous to that which is followed by the inmates of our monasteries and convents.

Excommunication.—The judicial sentence of excommunication, fulminated by the proper authority in the Catholic Church, deprives the erring and obstinate [contumax] Christian of the use of the sacraments, of the benefit of the prayers of the Church, and of various other spiritual favours and privileges; it almost hands him over to the dominion of the evil one. Not unlike this, was the sentence pronounced by St. Paul on the incestuous Corinthians "I, indeed" (the words are of the Apostle), "absent in body, but present in spirit, have already judged, as though I were present, him that hath so done, in the name of our Lord Jesus Christ, you being gathered together, and my spirit, with the power of our Lord Jesus Christ, to deliver such a one to Satan, for the destruction of the flesh, that the spirit may be saved in the day of our Lord Jesus Christ" (1 Cor. v. 3, 4, 5).

Many other doctrines and practices of the Catholic Church are illustrated in the sacred Scriptures. Justification, the necessity of good works, the merit of good works, the insufficiency of faith alone unto justification, and other equally interesting points of divinity, are as clearly spoken of in the Epistles of St. Paul as in the dissertations of the great Jesuit theologians or in the decrees of the Council of Trent.

INDEX.

	Page
Aaron, rod of	158
Africa receives the faith	236
———, faith and discipline of: Part iii. *per totum*.	
Altar	123, 125, 129, 303
Angels, worship of	141
——— conscious of events in the Church	142
——— reprobate, their power	38
Apollo, priests of	39
Apollonius, worker of miracles	56
Ark of the covenant venerated	159
Arnobius	280
Athens	10
Athenagoras on idol-worship	270
——— on Paganism	221
——— on resurrection of dead	227
Baptism necessary for salvation	90, 290
——— of precept	90, 290
——— of infants	293
——— clinical	293
——— by immersion	90
——— by infusion	293
Bardasanus on number of early Christians	50
Bishops, jurisdiction of, 63 *et seq.* 264 *et seq.*	
——— ordination of	78
——— superior (by orders) to priests	268 *et seq.*
———, decrees of, revised by Roman pontiff	261
———, succession of	253
———, election of	255
———, their mode of election in Africa	256
Bucer, his errors	295
Calvin	295
Carthage, council of	256
Christians, numerous in early age, 48 *et seq.*	
——— primitive, adhere to sound doctrine	179
——— adhere to their bishops	179
——— avoid heretics	182
——— put to death	179, 180
Church, victories of	47 *et seq.* 235 *et seq.*
——— one	236
——— infallible	190, 240
——— perpetual	191

	Page
Church catholic	191
——— suffering	134
——— triumphant	136
Clement, St., of Rome	62
——— of Alexandria	173, 182
Confirmation, a sacrament	91, 295
——— invariably administered	296, 300
——— the same (sub omni respectu) in ancient and modern times	302
Corinth, immorality of	11
Cyprian, St., on characteristics of Church	237 *et seq.*
——— on primacy of St. Peter	276
——— on sacrifice	284 *et seq.*
Deacons	76
———, ordination of	78
———, office of, as regards B. Eucharist	305
Dead, prayers for	156, 280
———, sacrifice for repose of	281
———, respect for Christian	149
Deposit of faith	165 *et seq.*
Diana, worship of	12
Διοίκησις	254
Direct proofs of Christianity	224
Easter, celebration of	185
Empedocles	282
Epicureans, opinions of	18
Eucharist	95 *et seq.* 305 *et seq.*
Exclusive salvation	241
Extreme unction	107 *et seq.* 327
Faith, the work of God	31
——— not a persuasion or opinion	32
——— preservation of, in second century	176 *et seq.*
——— identity of	165 *et seq.*
——— of Church unchanged	169 *et seq.*
First cause, philosophic ideas of	231
Gaul receives the faith	236
Geminius Faustinus	281
Gibbon	46, 49
Grecian society	10
——— philosophy	13
Hands, imposition of	78, 81, 296

	Page
Head of the Church	96
Hermias, philosopher, assails philosophy of the Gentiles	230 et seq.
Hierarchy, orders of	245
History (biographical) of philosophy	13
Human soul, philosophic views of its nature	230
IDOLATRY	219 et seq.
Immersion, triple, in baptism	392
Irenæus, St.	273
Irish converts to Protestantism	26
JEWISH prejudices	20 et seq.
Judaism refuted	211 et seq.
Jurisdiction	55, 63, 69, 264, 267, 270
Justin, St., refutes the Jews	212 et seq.
——— traces the origin of pagan deities	219
——— teaches the "real presence"	306
LAUSANNE	46
Lima, St., Rose of	138
MAHOMMEDANISM propagated, how?	29
Malachy, prophecy of	130
Marcion, heretic	272
Martyrdom of St. Cyprian	339
Martyrs, immediately crowned	335
———, respect to bodies of	337 et seq.
———, devotion to	340
———, prayers to	343
Matrimony, a sacrament	108, 332
Melancthon	295
Melchisedech, sacrifice of	129
Metropolitan	264
Miracles	33 et seq. 209
——— improperly called	38
Montanists	272
NATURE of God, philosophers err regarding	232
OIL blessed on altar	301
Orders, a sacrament	108, 329
Ordination, manner of	78
——— in Africa, circumstances accompanying	258
——— of bishops	329 et seq.
——— of Sabinus	258
Origen	327
PAGANISM	7, 218 et seq.
Pantheism	7, 223
Parishes	55 et seq. 268
Patricians	3
Penance, sacrament of	101, 317
Peter, primacy of	70, 252, 276
Philosophy	13
———, conflict of Christianity with	226
Plato, theories of	17
Plebeians	4
Pliny the younger	50, 55

	Page
Presbyterian system not system of early Church	116
Πρεσβυτερος justly translated priest	77
"Priests," English Catholic translation of πρεσβυτεροι	75
———, ordination of	78
———, inferior (in orders) to bishops	248 et seq.
———, further ordination of on ascending to episcopacy	329
———, jurisdiction of	55, 267
——— ordained in presence of people	256
——— not allowed to be guardians or executors	281
——— sacrificing ministers	117, 118, 286, 288
Prophecy	42
Protestantism propagated, how?	29
Purgatory	135, 280
Pythagoras, theories of	15
RANK of early converts	52 et seq.
Real presence	97, 100
———, taught by St. Irenæus	308
——— St. Cyprian	309
——— Tertullian	314
Receiving the Holy Ghost, meaning of in Scriptures	92 et seq.
———, in language of early fathers	296 et seq.
Relative worship	150
Relics of saints	148, 338 et seq. 340
Roman society	3, 4, 5
Roman pontiff successor to St. Peter	270
——— writes to Church of Corinth	271
——— consulted by St. Polycarp	272
——— referred to by Montanists	272
——— appealed to, to cancel the acts of bishops	261
——— appoints bishops of Church	263
Roman Church, all must conform to	273
——— praised by St. Ignatius	271
——— praised by Tertullian	300, 279
Roman clergy govern Church during interregnum	279
Rome	3
SACRAMENT, nature of	113, 302
Sacraments, number of, 89 to 115, 290 to 335	
Sacrifice of Christian Church	117, 280
Saints, veneration of	138
———, prayers addressed to	145
———, relics of	148
Savoy, piety of	154
Sceptics, doctrine of	18
Sibylline verses	225
Sicca, diocese of	265
Simon Magus	37
Slaves, Roman	5

INDEX.

	Page
Socrates, theories of	17
Spain evangelised	236
Stephen's burial	149
TERTULLIAN distinguishes episcopacy from priesthood	251
—— on prayers for the dead	280
—— teaches necessity of baptism	290
—— on Christian marriage	333
Theophilus	224, 172
Towns first receive the faith	54
Tryphon, St. Justin's dialogue with	212 et seq.

	Page
VENUS, temple of, at Corinth	11
Veneration of cross	157, 350
—— Blessed Virgin	144
Victor	281
Villages, Christian	55
WATER of baptism	90, 292
Worship, objects of pagan	221 et seq.
XAVIER, St. Francis	138
Xenophon	87
ZUINGLE	295

WORKS PUBLISHED BY THE
Catholic Publishing & Bookselling Company,
LIMITED.

A New English Grammar, calculated to perfect Students in the knowledge of Grammar, Parsing, Derivation, and the Principles of Composition. By M. D. KAVANAGH, of University College, London. 16mo. bound, 1s.

Just published, price 1s. 6d.,

A New Latin Grammar, calculated to perfect Students in Etymology, Syntax (including Subjunctive Mood), Principles of Prose Composition, and Prosody. By M. D. KAVANAGH, Author of "New English Grammar," &c.

Arithmetic, its Principles and Practice. By James W. KAVANAGH, late Head Inspector of National Schools, Ireland. Fifth edition, revised and enlarged. Price 2s., free by post 2s. 2d. On list of Books approved by Committee of Privy Council on Education in England; adopted in the Catholic University, and in the leading Catholic Colleges and Schools.

Price 4s. 6d.

Public Lectures on some Subjects of Ancient and Modern History, delivered before the Catholic University of Ireland. By JAMES BURTON ROBERTSON, Esq., Professor of Modern History, Translator of F. Schlegel's "Philosophy of History," and of Moehler's "Symbolism."

Recently published,

The Physical and Historical Geography of the British Empire. In Four Parts. A new and greatly-improved edition. By D. C. MACCARTHY, Certificated Teacher. The Colonial Geography occupies forty-four pages, and with other improvements, a new and copious Alphabetical Index has been added. 336 pp. 8vo. Price 2s. 6d.

"Your excellent geography."—*The Cardinal Archbishop of Westminster.*

Ancient History, from the Dispersion of the Sons of Noe to the Battle of Actium and Change of the Roman Republic into an Empire. By PETER FREDET, D.D., Professor of History in St. Mary's College, Baltimore. Fifth edition, carefully revised and enlarged, half-bound, leather back, 12mo. 4s.

Modern History, from the Coming of Christ, and the Change of the Roman Republic into an Empire, to the year of our Lord 1850. By PETER FREDET, D.D., Professor of History in St. Mary's College, Baltimore. Twelfth edition, enlarged and improved, half-bound, leather back, 12mo. 4s.

Catholic Publishing and Bookselling Company, Limited.

A Compendium of Ancient and Modern History, with Questions, adapted to the use of Schools and Academies; also, an Appendix, containing the Declaration of Independence, the Constitution of the United States, a Biographical Sketch of Eminent Personages, with a Chronological Table of Remarkable Events, Discoveries, Improvements, &c., from the Creation to the year 1850. By M. I. KERNEY. Tenth edition, large 12mo. half-bound, 4s. 6d.

Dolman's Catechisms.

Catechism of the History of England. 6d.

Catechism of the History of France. 6d.

Catechism of the History of Germany. By A. M. 18mo. 6d.

"It is Catholic, extremely well-condensed, lucid, and full enough for the purpose of an introductory outline."—*Tablet.*

Catechism of Spain and Portugal. 6d.

Catechism of Mythology. By R. O. 18mo. 6d.

N.B.—These Catechisms, being all written by Catholics, can be safely recommended for the use of Schools.

Gaume (Abbe). Paganism in Education. From the French of "Le Ver Rongeur des Sociétés Modernes." Translated by ROBERT HILL, Esq. 1s.

Juvenile Companion to the Atlas, with some Historical Notes. 18mo. cloth, 1s. 6d.

Reading Lessons for the Use of Schools: a New Series, from Words of Two Syllables upwards; in tablet form. By a Catholic Clergyman. Fifty-six Lessons, 2s. 6d. the set.

Catechisms. — Abridgment of Christian Doctrine. 1d.

Douay, or Second Catechism, 1½d.; Catechism for Confirmation, 1d.; First Communicants', 2d.; Fleury's Short Historical Catechism.

Catechism (The), or Christian Doctrine; by way of Question and Answer. Illustrated by the Sacred Text and Tradition. Composed by the Rev. A. CLINTON. 24mo. bound, 1s.

Irish made Easy; or, a Practical Irish Grammar. By the Author of "O'Brennan's Ireland." 12mo. 2s.

Catholic Publishing and Bookselling Company, Limited.

NEW WORKS AND EDITIONS.

Tyborne, and who went thither in the Days of Queen Elizabeth: a Sketch. By the Authoress of "Eastern Hospitals and English Nurses." 3s.

Just published, price 4s. 6d.,

Memories of Rome. By Denis O'Donovan, Esq.

Just published, price 1s.,

The Catholic in the Workhouse. Popular Statement of the Law as it affects him; the Grievances it occasions: with Practical Suggestions for Redress. By CHARLES A. RUSSELL, Esq., Barrister-at-Law.

Just published, price 6d.,

An Unlooked-for Conversion. By H. P. S., late Brother of the Little Oratory.

Just published, price 7s.,

Ceremonial according to the Roman Rite; translated from the Italian of Joseph Baldeschi, Master of Ceremonies of the Basilica of St. Peter at Rome, with the Pontifical Offices of a Bishop in his own diocese, compiled from the "Ceremoniale Episcoporum;" to which are added various other Functions and copious Explanatory Notes; the whole harmonized with the latest Decrees of the Sacred Congregation of Rites. By the Rev. J. D. HILARIUS DALE. New edition, revised, 8vo.

Just published, neatly bound in cloth, price 1s.,

Gems from Catholic Poets, with several Portraits and a Biographical and Literary Introduction. By JAMES BURKE, Esq., Barrister-at-Law.

Just published, price 4s. 6d.,

The Roman Catacombs; or, some Account of the Burial-places of the Early Christians in Rome. By the Rev. J. SPENCER NORTHCOTE, M.A. Second edition, with considerable additions both in matter and illustrations, and the whole re-arranged.

Price 10s. 6d.

The Life of Cardinal Ximenes, translated from the German of Hefele. By the Rev. JOHN DALTON.

Price 5s.

May Templeton: a Tale of Faith and Love. By the Authoress of "Eastern Hospitals and English Nurses."

Price 3s. 6d.

The Queens and Princesses of France. By G. WHITE, Esq.

Preparing for publication,

Celtic Legends in Ireland, Wales and Brittany; being those relating to SS. Patrick, Kadok, and Hervé. From the French of the Vicomte Hersart de la Villemarqué.

Catholic Publishing and Bookselling Company, Limited.

Works by the Rev. Dr. Lingard.

The History of England. By John Lingard, D.D.
The People's Edition. Handsomely printed in small octavo, uniform in size and type with the popular edition of "Alison's History of Europe." Completed in Sixty Parts, price 6d. each. Embellished with many Illustrations, from designs by HARVEY, J. DOYLE, HOWARD DUDLEY, and other artists, including a PORTRAIT and BIOGRAPHICAL MEMOIR of the HISTORIAN. Forming Ten Volumes, crown 8vo., 3s. 6d. each, cloth lettered.

This edition is reprinted from the fifth and last one, diligently revised by the author two years before his death, which was published in 1849, in ten octavo volumes. That edition embodies the substance of all the recent discoveries connected with English history, and contains a large quantity of new and important matter.

N.B.—For the convenience of persons who were prevented from subscribing to this edition during publication, it will continue to be supplied in weekly numbers, or single volumes, and may be obtained through the medium of any bookseller, or by order direct from the Publishers, who will supply it, post free, on receipt of the price of the volume or number.

An Abridgment of the History of England, with Continuation from 1688 to the Reign of Queen Victoria; adapted for the Use of Schools. By JAMES BURKE, Esq., B.A., Barrister-at-Law. 648 pages, 12mo. bound, 5s.

"Mr. Burke's 'Abridgment' is completely successful. We do not hesitate to pronounce the work, as a whole, one of the most valuable additions to our scanty school literature which we have met with for many years."—*Dublin Review.*

"Mr. Burke has done his work well, and the result is very satisfactory."—*Rambler.*

The History and Antiquities of the Anglo-Saxon Church, containing an Account of its Origin, Government, Doctrines, Worship, Revenues, and Clerical and Monastic Institutions. New edition, in 2 vols. crown 8vo. cloth, 10s.

Observations on the Laws and Ordinances which exist in Foreign States relative to the Religious Concerns of their Roman Catholic Subjects. 8vo. 1s.

A New Version of the Four Gospels; with Notes Critical and Explanatory. 8vo. boards, 5s.

Catechetical Instructions on the Doctrines and Worship of the Catholic Church. New edition, 18mo.; 9d. cloth, 6d. wrapper.

This work contains a short exposition of Catholic doctrine and Catholic practice, with the chief authorities on which that doctrine and practice are founded.

"A beautiful little volume, written with all that sobriety of style, power of language, and force of logic, for which the venerable author is remarkable."—*Tablet.*

Catholic Publishing and Bookselling Company, Limited.

A True Account of the Gunpowder Plot; extracted from Lingard's "History of England" and Dodd's "Church History of England," including the Notes and Documents appended to the latter. By the Rev. M. A. TIERNEY, F.R.S., F.S.A.; with Notes and Introduction, by VINDICATOR. 8vo. 2s. 6d.

Works by His Eminence Cardinal Wiseman,
Archbishop of Westminster.

Twelve Lectures on the Connection between Science and Revealed Religion; with Map and Plates. Third edition, in 2 vols. small 8vo. cloth lettered, 8s.

Lectures on the Principal Doctrines and Practices of the Catholic Church, delivered at St. Mary's, Moorfields, during the Lent of 1836. Second edition, entirely revised and corrected by the Author. Two vols. in one. 12mo. cloth, 3s. 6d.

The Real Presence of the Body and Blood of Our Lord Jesus Christ in the Blessed Eucharist, proved from Scripture. In eight Lectures, delivered in the English College, Rome. Second edition, 12mo. cloth, 3s. 6d.

Four Lectures on the Offices and Ceremonies of Holy Week, as performed in the Papal Chapels, delivered in Rome in the Lent of 1837. Illustrated with nine Engravings, and a Plan of the Papal Chapels. 8vo. cloth, 4s.

A Reply to Dr. Turton, the British Critic, and others, on the Catholic Doctrine of the Eucharist. 8vo. 3s. 6d.

Essays on Various Subjects. 3 vols. 8vo. cloth lettered. Published at £2. 2s., reduced to £1. 16s.
"These admirable volumes will entertain, instruct, and edify Catholics wherever the English language is spoken."—*Tablet.*

The Lives of St. Alphonsus Liguori, St. Francis de Girolamo, St. John Joseph of the Cross, St. Pacificus of San Severino, and St. Veronica Giuliana, whose canonization took place on Trinity Sunday, May 26, 1839. Edited by CARDINAL WISEMAN. Second edition, 18mo. cloth lettered, 2s.

Lives of the Fathers, Martyrs, and other principal Saints; compiled from Original Monuments and other Authentic Records; illustrated with the Remarks of judicious modern Critics and Historians. By the Rev. ALBAN BUTLER. Including the account of the Life and Writings of the Rev. Alban Butler, by CHARLES BUTLER, Esq.; and an Appendix containing General Indexes, Chronological Tables, &c. The original stereotype edition, well printed, in large type, in 12 vols. demy 8vo. cloth lettered, only £2. 2s.
The same, illustrated with above 40 plates, fine early impressions, only £2. 12s. 6d.
*** This edition will be re-issued in weekly and monthly parts at equally low prices, to render this esteemed edition of more easy access to the Catholic public.

Catholic Publishing and Bookselling Company, Limited.

The Holy Bible, translated from the Latin Vulgate, diligently compared with the Hebrew, Greek, and other Editions, in divers languages: the Old Testament, first published by the English College at Douay, A.D. 1609; and the New Testament, first published by the English College at Rheims, A.D. 1582. With Annotations, References, and an Historical and Chronological Index. Published with the approbation of the Right Rev. Dr. DENVIR, Bishop of Down and Connor. Beautifully printed in super royal 32mo. embossed roan, sprinkled edges, 2s. 6d.; or 3s. gilt edges.

The same edition, illustrated with Eight beautiful Engravings from the best Masters, bound in French morocco, 4s. 6d.; or extra gilt, 5s. 6d. The same in Turkey morocco, 6s.; or extra gilt, 7s.; also kept in various styles of elegant binding, suitable for presents.

The Holy Bible, translated from the Latin Vulgate, with Annotations, References, and an Historical and Chronological Index. Stereotype edition, with Episcopal Approbation. On fine paper, royal 8vo. morocco, 15s.

Another edition, handsomely printed on fine paper, imperial 8vo. with plates. Handsomely bound in calf extra, £1. 1s.

Reeve's History of the Bible. Best edition, illustrated with 233 Wood-engravings. 12mo. 2s. 8d.

The New Testament, with Episcopal Approbation. Stereotype edition, 12mo. bound, 1s. 6d.

Another edition, 18mo. bound, 1s.; Cape morocco, gilt, 2s. 6d.

The New Testament, with Annotations from Drs. WITHAM and CHALLONER. 4to. large type, with Illustrations, printed at Manchester, 1816, cloth gilt, only 5s.

The Pictorial New Testament, illuminated after Original Drawings, by W. H. HEWETT. Royal 8vo. cloth gilt, 12s. 6d.

A New Version of the Four Gospels; with Notes, Critical and Explanatory. By the Rev. Dr. LINGARD. 8vo. boards, 5s.

The Bible: its Use and Abuse; or, an Inquiry into the Results of Respective Doctrines of the Catholic and Protestant Churches, relative to the interpretation of the Word of God. By the Rev. PAUL MACLACHLAN. Fcap. 8vo. cloth, 2s. 6d.

The Holy Scriptures; their Origin, Progress, Transmission, Corruptions, and True Character. 18mo. cloth, 1s. 6d.

"Thinkest thou that thou understandest what thou readest? Who said: how can I, unless some man show me?"—*Acts* viii. 30, 31.

www.ingramcontent.com/pod-product-compliance
Lightning Source LLC
Chambersburg PA
CBHW030429300426
44112CB00009B/911